Mastering Sui

The Comprehensive Guide to Understanding and

Utilizing the Sui Blockchain

Mastering Sui

The Comprehensive Guide to Understanding and Utilizing the Sui Blockchain

WRITTEN BY KENNETH SCHICK

++++ **AAG** PUBLISHING

New York

Printed in the United States of America

First Edition: February 2025

Published by ++++ AAG Publishing

The Publisher is not responsible for websites or their content that are not owned by the publisher.

LSC-C

10 9 8 7 6 5 4 3 2 1

For the pioneers and visionaries of the Sui ecosystem,
whose relentless pursuit of innovation has laid the
groundwork for a transformative blockchain technology.

To the developers, coders, and dreamers who are tirelessly
working to expand the boundaries of what's possible with
Sui, turning complex ideas into tangible solutions that
empower users around the globe.

To the educators and enthusiasts who tirelessly share
knowledge, fostering a community where learning and
growth are paramount, ensuring that the future of Sui is
bright and accessible to all.

And to the believers in decentralized technology, whose
faith in the principles of transparency, security, and
freedom drives the continuous evolution of blockchain for
the betterment of society.

This book is for you, with the hope it serves as both a
compass and a catalyst in your journey with Sui

Contents:

1. The Genesis of Sui: From Meta to Mysten Labs
2. Philosophy of Sui: Speed, Security, and Scalability
3. Sui Architecture: An Overview
4. Understanding Move: The Programming Language of Sui
5. Objects in Sui: A New Data Paradigm
6. Sui's Consensus Mechanism: Delegated Proof-of-Stake Explained
7. Transaction Processing in Sui: Parallel Execution and Finality
8. The Sui Token (SUI): Utility, Economics, and Governance
9. Building on Sui: Developer's Guide to Smart Contracts
10. Sui's Developer Tools and Ecosystem
11. Sui for Gaming: Creating the Next Generation of Blockchain Games
12. Decentralized Finance (DeFi) on Sui
13. Sui and Non-Fungible Tokens (NFTs)
14. Interoperability: Sui's Role in the Multichain Future
15. Privacy and Security on Sui
16. Sui's Network Performance: Benchmarks and Real-World Scenarios
17. The Economic Model of Sui: Tokenomics and Incentive Structures
18. Case Studies: Real-World Applications of Sui
19. Future of Sui: Roadmap and Vision
20. Community and Culture: The Human Element of Sui
21. Sui's Contribution to Blockchain Governance and Community Building

"Blockchain is not merely a technology; it is a cosmic shift in trust, weaving a tapestry of transparency across the universe. By decentralizing power and immortalizing truth on an unyielding ledger, it challenges the very fabric of centralized control, inviting humanity to reimagine a reality where every transaction, every interaction, is a star in an infinite constellation of accountability and possibility."

- Kenneth Schick, Visionary

PREFACE

Welcome to "Mastering Sui: The Comprehensive Guide to Understanding and Utilizing the Sui Blockchain". This book is your gateway to exploring one of the most innovative blockchain platforms designed for speed, security, and scalability. Within these pages, you'll embark on a journey from the foundational principles of Sui to its cutting-edge applications.

You'll delve into the unique architecture of Sui, understanding how its object-centric model and consensus mechanism differentiate it from other blockchains. We'll explore Move, the programming language that powers Sui's smart contracts, offering you the tools to build on this platform.

This book covers everything from the technical intricacies like transaction processing and network performance to the broader implications of Sui in areas like gaming, DeFi, and NFTs. You'll gain insights into the economics of the Sui token, the community that drives it, and the future roadmap that promises to shape the blockchain universe.

Whether you're a developer looking to harness Sui's potential, an investor seeking to understand its value, or simply a blockchain enthusiast fascinated by new technologies, this book provides a thorough, engaging, and practical exploration of Sui. Get ready to unlock the secrets of Sui and envision how it can transform not just industries, but potentially, the very way we interact with digital assets and each other.

Chapter 1: The Genesis of Sui: From Meta to Mysten Labs

Part 1: From Diem to Sui

In the rapidly evolving landscape of blockchain technology, few stories are as intriguing as that of Sui. Its inception, rooted in the ambitious yet tumultuous journey of Meta (formerly known as Facebook) into the blockchain arena, is a tale of innovation, challenge, and redemption. Here, we explore how the lessons learned from Meta's Diem project laid the groundwork for what would become the Sui blockchain.

The Diem Project: A Bold Beginning

The story begins with Meta's venture into blockchain technology under the name Libra, later rebranded to Diem. Announced in June 2019, Diem was envisioned as a global currency and financial infrastructure backed by a basket of fiat currencies, aiming to facilitate cheaper and faster transactions across borders. However, the project was met with immediate regulatory scrutiny, political backlash, and concerns over privacy and financial stability.

Diem's architecture was revolutionary for its time. It introduced the Move programming language, designed to prevent common blockchain vulnerabilities like reentrancy attacks, while also offering high scalability through a unique consensus mechanism. The ambition was clear: to provide a stablecoin that could operate with the efficiency and ubiquity of traditional payment systems but with the transparency and security of blockchain technology.

Despite the regulatory hurdles, the tech developed for Diem was groundbreaking. It was this technology, particularly the Move language, that would later find a new life in the Sui project.

The Exodus to Mysten Labs

The saga of Diem took a pivotal turn when, amid increasing regulatory pressure, Meta decided to scale back its ambitions, eventually selling the assets and intellectual property of Diem to Silvergate Capital in January 2022. This was not the end but rather a catalyst for a new beginning for some of Diem's key architects.

A group of former Diem engineers, led by Evan Cheng, decided to take their accumulated knowledge and experience to forge a path independent from the corporate constraints they faced at Meta. This group included luminaries like Adeniyi Abiodun, Sam Blackshear, George Danezis, and Kostas Chalkias, each bringing unique skills and insights to the table:

- **Evan Cheng**, former director of engineering at Meta and Apple, was the driving force behind the blockchain efforts at both companies. His leadership was crucial in navigating the transition from Meta to a startup environment.

- **Adeniyi Abiodun**, with his deep product development experience, would focus on shaping Sui into a user-friendly blockchain platform.
- **Sam Blackshear**, the creator of Move, brought with him the vision and technical prowess to adapt and evolve this language for new applications.
- **George Danezis**, an academic turned practitioner, specialized in privacy and security, ensuring Sui would not repeat the privacy missteps seen in other blockchain projects.
- **Kostas Chalkias**, a cryptographer, whose expertise would be pivotal in ensuring the security of Sui's cryptographic underpinnings.

Together, they founded Mysten Labs in 2022, named after a mythical figure symbolizing wisdom and foresight, aligning with their mission to bring clarity and innovation to blockchain technology.

The Vision for Sui

Mysten Labs set out with a clear vision: to build a blockchain that could scale to billions of users, maintain high transaction throughput, and ensure user control over their digital assets, all while keeping the system decentralized. The experience with Diem taught them valuable lessons about regulatory landscapes, the importance of community trust, and the need for robust technological foundations.

Sui was conceptualized not just as another blockchain but as a "coordination layer" for the internet. This layer would allow for the seamless management and interaction of digital assets, from simple tokens to complex NFTs, in a way that was previously unattainable due to scalability issues in existing blockchain platforms. Here are the core tenets of Sui's vision:

- **Scalability:** Drawing from Diem's lessons, Sui aimed for a system where transactions could be processed in parallel, significantly increasing throughput.
- **Security:** Learning from both successes and failures, Sui would incorporate advanced cryptographic methods to ensure the safety of transactions and data.
- **User Experience:** With Abiodun's product vision, Sui was to be intuitive, making blockchain technology accessible to those beyond the tech-savvy.
- **Decentralization:** A commitment to true decentralization where no single entity would control the network, contrasting with the perceived centralization of Diem due to its corporate origins.

Funding and Early Support

Mysten Labs didn't have to look far for support. The credibility of its founders and the potential of their vision attracted significant investment. In late 2022, Mysten Labs announced a $300 million Series B funding round led by Andreessen Horowitz (a16z), with participation from other notable investors like FTX Ventures, Coinbase Ventures, and Binance Labs among others. This investment was not just financial backing but also a vote of confidence in Sui's potential to redefine blockchain technology.

Move: The Heart of Sui

Central to Sui's technical foundation is the Move programming language. Initially developed for Diem, Move was designed to address issues like reentrancy attacks, offering a resource-based model where each asset or piece of data is treated as a unique, immutable "object". This approach was revolutionary and perfectly suited for the needs of Sui:

- **Safety and Security:** Move's design inherently prevents many of the security flaws seen in other smart contract languages.
- **Scalability:** By allowing for parallel transaction processing, Move could leverage Sui's architecture for unprecedented scalability.
- **Simplicity:** For developers, Move promised a steep but rewarding learning curve, offering powerful features with a focus on safety.

Setting the Stage for Sui

The transition from Diem to Sui was not just about technology transfer but also about redefining the blockchain's role in the digital economy. Mysten Labs started with tech demos, showcasing Sui's capabilities, and began building a community of developers interested in this new paradigm. Early partnerships were formed with other blockchain projects and tech companies eager to explore what

Sui could offer in terms of interoperability and new application development.

The first public announcements from Mysten Labs about Sui painted a picture of a blockchain designed for the future, one where digital assets could be managed with the same ease as traditional assets but with the added benefits of blockchain technology.

The journey from Diem to Sui is a testament to resilience, innovation, and the relentless pursuit of a vision for a better blockchain ecosystem. By bringing together some of the brightest minds in the field under the banner of Mysten Labs, Sui was born out of the ashes of Diem, not as a mere continuation but as a bold new chapter in blockchain technology. This part of our story sets the stage for understanding how Sui's unique architecture, its focus on scalability, and its commitment to a decentralized future were conceived, leading into the deeper exploration of its technical and philosophical underpinnings in the subsequent sections of this book.

Part 2: The Birth of Mysten Labs

Following the disbandment of Meta's Diem project, a new era in blockchain technology was on the horizon. The formation of Mysten Labs was not merely the creation of another tech startup; it was the genesis of an ambitious vision to transform how blockchain could operate on a global scale. Here, we delve into the establishment of Mysten Labs, the individuals behind it, and their collective vision for the Sui blockchain.

Founders and Their Vision

Mysten Labs was founded by a group of ex-Diem engineers, each bringing a wealth of experience and a shared vision for what blockchain could achieve:

- **Evan Cheng**, the CEO, had a storied career in tech, notably at Apple where he was involved with LLVM, a compiler infrastructure project, and later at Meta where he spearheaded blockchain initiatives. His leadership was pivotal in steering the team towards creating a blockchain that could scale to meet global demands.
- **Adeniyi Abiodun**, the Chief Product Officer, had worked closely with Cheng at Meta, focusing on product strategy. His role at Mysten Labs was to ensure that Sui would not only be technically superior but also user-friendly, bridging the gap between complex blockchain technology and everyday users.
- **Sam Blackshear**, the Chief Technology Officer, was the architect behind Move. His continued involvement was crucial as Move would be central to Sui's programming environment, ensuring safety, scalability, and ease of use for developers.
- **George Danezis**, appointed as Chief Scientist, brought academic rigor to the project. His expertise in privacy and security was indispensable, aiming to address one of the biggest critiques of blockchain technology: privacy.

- **Kostas Chalkias**, with his background in cryptography, was instrumental in laying down the security foundations for Sui, ensuring that the blockchain would be resistant to attacks and maintain integrity under all conditions.

This team was not just united by their past at Meta but by a common goal to build a blockchain that could serve billions, offering speed and security that current technologies lacked.

Launching Mysten Labs

The decision to leave Meta was driven by the desire to explore blockchain's potential without the constraints of a large corporation. Mysten Labs was officially launched in 2022, with the name "Mysten" drawing from mythology, symbolizing wisdom and enlightenment, which resonated with the founders' aspirations for blockchain technology.

The initial steps included:

- **Tech Development:** Leveraging the Move language and the learnings from Diem, the team began developing Sui, focusing on creating an object-centric model where each asset or piece of data could be uniquely managed and transacted.
- **Securing Funding:** Even before Sui was fully conceptualized, the founders' reputation and the project's potential attracted significant investment. The Series B round, which was notably large at $300 million, was a testament

to the confidence in Mysten Labs' vision, led by Andreessen Horowitz and including other heavyweights like Coinbase Ventures and Binance Labs.
- **Community Building:** Recognizing that blockchain projects thrive on community support, Mysten Labs initiated early engagement with developers, setting up forums, hackathons, and educational content to foster a growing ecosystem around Sui.

The Vision for Sui

The vision for Sui was nothing short of revolutionary:

- **Scalability:** Sui was designed to handle transactions at a scale that could support the internet's future growth, using parallel processing to achieve high throughput.
- **Security:** Drawing from the cryptographic and security expertise within the team, Sui aimed to offer unparalleled security for digital assets.
- **User Empowerment:** Unlike many blockchain platforms where complexity often alienates users, Sui was intended to be intuitive, giving users direct control over their assets without needing to understand the underlying tech deeply.
- **Decentralization:** The architecture of Sui was specifically crafted to ensure that control remains distributed, avoiding the pitfalls of centralized governance encountered by other projects.

Setting the Stage for Innovation

Mysten Labs quickly moved from inception to showcasing Sui's capabilities through tech demos and technical white papers. They outlined a blockchain where:

- **Assets are Objects:** Each digital asset would be an object with its own state, making it possible to manage assets in a more granular and secure manner.
- **Move Powers Smart Contracts:** The Move language would be adapted and expanded for Sui, offering developers a secure environment to build decentralized applications.
- **A New Consensus Mechanism:** Sui would introduce a variation of Proof-of-Stake (PoS) tailored for speed and efficiency, aiming for near-instant transaction finality.

Early Challenges and Triumphs

The early days at Mysten Labs were marked by the challenge of proving that blockchain could be scaled without compromising on decentralization or security. They faced:

- **Technical Hurdles:** Adapting Move for a new blockchain was no small feat, requiring significant innovation to ensure it met the ambitious goals set for Sui.
- **Market Perception:** Coming from a high-profile project like Diem, there was both skepticism and high expectations. Mysten

Labs had to navigate this by focusing on tangible advancements rather than promises.

- **Community Engagement:** Building a community from scratch in the crowded blockchain space required careful strategy, transparency, and offering real value to developers and users.

Despite these challenges, the triumphs were evident. Sui's early demonstrations of speed and security turned heads, and the community began to grow, drawn by the potential to do more with blockchain than ever before.

The birth of Mysten Labs marked the beginning of a significant chapter in blockchain technology. With a team of seasoned innovators and a vision that pushed the boundaries of what blockchain could achieve, Sui was set on a path to redefine digital asset management, transaction processing, and user interaction with blockchain technology. This part of our narrative highlights the foundational steps, the visionaries involved, and the early groundwork that would soon lead to Sui's emergence as a formidable player in the blockchain space.

Part 3: Vision and Mission

The story of Sui cannot be fully appreciated without understanding the profound vision and mission articulated by Mysten Labs. This part delves into the philosophical and practical underpinnings that shaped Sui's development, highlighting how these ideals translate into tangible blockchain solutions aimed at transforming digital interactions.

Crafting the Vision

The vision for Sui was born out of a collective desire to transcend the limitations observed in existing blockchain technologies, particularly those encountered during the Diem project. Here are the key components of this vision:

- **Scalability at Scale:** The ambition was to create a blockchain that could handle the transaction volume of the internet itself, allowing for billions of users and assets to interact seamlessly. Sui was designed to scale horizontally, ensuring that as more users join, the network doesn't just maintain but enhances its performance.
- **Security as a Priority:** With the increasing threats to digital assets and privacy in the blockchain domain, Sui's founders aimed for a security model that was not just reactive but proactive. This involved leveraging advanced cryptographic techniques and a consensus mechanism that could guarantee transaction integrity and asset safety.
- **Empowerment through Simplicity:** Recognizing that blockchain's complexity often deters mass adoption, the vision included making the technology more accessible. This meant simplifying the user interface, improving developer tools, and ensuring that interacting

with blockchain assets felt as intuitive as using traditional internet services.

- **Decentralization as a Core Principle:** In the wake of criticisms against centralized blockchain projects, Sui was intended to embody true decentralization, where no single entity controls the network's fate. This principle was to be reflected in both the governance of the blockchain and how transactions are validated.

The Mission of Mysten Labs

The mission of Mysten Labs was to realize this vision by:

- **Building a Superior Blockchain Infrastructure:** This meant not just creating another blockchain but an infrastructure that could serve as the backbone for future digital economies. Sui was to be the layer where assets from any sector could be tokenized, managed, and exchanged securely and efficiently.
- **Fostering an Ecosystem:** Mysten Labs committed to developing not just the blockchain but an ecosystem around it. This involved nurturing developers, supporting dApps (decentralized applications), and providing the necessary tools and resources for innovation to flourish.
- **Advancing Blockchain Technology:** By pushing the boundaries of what blockchain can do, Mysten Labs aimed to contribute to the

broader field. This included research in consensus mechanisms, smart contract safety, and new paradigms for digital asset management.

- **Educating and Engaging Communities:** Understanding that blockchain's growth depends on widespread understanding, part of their mission was educational outreach. This ranged from developer education to public awareness campaigns about the benefits and realities of blockchain technology.

Philosophical Underpinnings

The philosophical approach of Mysten Labs to blockchain development can be broken down into several core beliefs:

- **Innovation with Responsibility:** The team believed in pushing technological boundaries while being mindful of the implications, especially in terms of security, privacy, and economic impact.
- **User-Centric Design:** Blockchain was to be reimagined from the ground up, with the end-user in mind. This meant focusing on usability, reducing friction in digital transactions, and ensuring that users have sovereignty over their digital lives.
- **Openness and Transparency:** In line with blockchain's ethos, Mysten Labs committed to an open-source approach where possible, ensuring that the development of Sui would be transparent and collaborative.

- **Sustainability:** There was a clear acknowledgment that for blockchain to be viable long-term, it had to be sustainable, both environmentally and economically. This influenced decisions around consensus mechanisms and network design.

Translating Vision into Reality

- **Move as the Foundation:** The adoption and evolution of Move were central to achieving this vision. It was seen as not just a programming language but a tool for creating a safe, scalable, and developer-friendly environment.
- **Object-Centric Model:** Sui introduced the concept of every asset being an object, fundamentally changing how digital assets could be interacted with, managed, and secured.
- **Parallel Transaction Execution:** To meet scalability demands, Sui was designed to process transactions in parallel, a significant departure from the sequential processing common in other blockchains.
- **Community-Driven Governance:** While the initial governance was more centralized due to the developmental phase, there was a clear roadmap towards more community-driven decision-making processes as the network matured.

Early Challenges and Strategic Directions

The journey from vision to reality was fraught with challenges:

- **Balancing Innovation with Stability:** The team had to innovate while ensuring the blockchain was stable enough for real-world applications.
- **Community Building:** Fostering a community that could contribute to and benefit from Sui's growth was a strategic priority, involving significant effort in education and engagement.
- **Regulatory Navigation:** Learning from Diem's regulatory woes, Mysten Labs aimed to be proactive in engaging with regulators and shaping a compliant but innovative blockchain space.
- **Ecosystem Development:** Beyond the blockchain, there was the task of encouraging an ecosystem of applications, services, and partnerships that could leverage Sui's capabilities.

Part 4: Setting the Stage for Sui

With the vision and mission of Mysten Labs clearly articulated, the stage was set for the practical realization of the Sui blockchain. This part examines the initial steps taken by Mysten Labs to bring Sui from concept to reality, the strategic decisions made, and the early activities that laid the groundwork for what would become a significant player in the blockchain space.

Announcements and Roadmaps

The first public mentions of Sui came through announcements and whitepapers:

- **Sui's Whitepaper:** Detailed the technical architecture, including the object-centric model, the use of Move, and the unique consensus mechanism. It was a foundational document that outlined how Sui intended to achieve its ambitious goals.
- **Roadmap Publication:** Mysten Labs shared a roadmap that included milestones like mainnet launch, developer tool releases, and ecosystem partnerships. This roadmap was not just about technical development but also about community engagement and education.

Tech Demos and Proofs of Concept

To build credibility and attract both developers and investors, Mysten Labs:

- **Showcased Technical Capabilities:** Early tech demos illustrated Sui's promise of high throughput and low latency, allowing for real-time transactions at scale. These demonstrations were crucial in distinguishing Sui from competitors.
- **Developer Previews:** Before the official launch, developers were given access to testnets where they could begin experimenting with Sui's infrastructure, providing feedback that would shape the platform further.

Building an Ecosystem

- **Developer Grants and Hackathons:** To foster innovation, Mysten Labs initiated developer grant programs and hosted hackathons. These events were designed to encourage developers to build applications on Sui, ranging from DeFi to gaming and beyond.
- **Partnerships:** Early on, partnerships were formed with existing blockchain projects, tech companies, and educational institutions to expand Sui's reach and integrate it into broader technology ecosystems.
- **Education and Documentation:** Comprehensive documentation was released alongside tutorials, workshops, and online courses to educate developers about Move and Sui's unique features.

Community Engagement

- **Community Forums and Social Media:** Mysten Labs actively engaged with potential users and developers through platforms like Discord, Twitter, and dedicated forums, fostering a community around Sui.
- **Transparency in Development:** Regular updates, AMAs (Ask Me Anything sessions), and open discussions about the development process were part of the strategy to keep the community involved and informed.
- **Incentive Programs:** To encourage participation and use, various incentive programs were launched, including token

airdrops for early adopters and rewards for community contributions.

Strategic Funding and Investments

- **Fundraising:** Beyond the initial Series B round, Mysten Labs continued to attract investment, focusing on strategic investors who could also contribute to the ecosystem's growth.
- **Investor Relations:** Maintaining strong relationships with investors was seen as key to not only financial backing but also for strategic guidance and network expansion.

Regulatory Strategy

- **Proactive Compliance:** Learning from the regulatory challenges faced by Diem, Mysten Labs adopted a proactive stance towards compliance, engaging with regulators and policymakers to ensure Sui could operate globally without legal hurdles.
- **Global Expansion:** Plans were laid for Sui's operation in various jurisdictions, adapting to local regulations while advocating for blockchain-friendly policies.

Technical Development

- **Move Language Evolution:** The team worked on enhancing Move, making it more suitable for Sui's specific needs while keeping its core principles of safety and scalability intact.

- **Consensus and Security:** Extensive work was put into refining the consensus mechanism to balance between decentralization, security, and speed. Security audits were conducted regularly to ensure robustness.
- **User Interface and Experience:** Even in early stages, there was a focus on making the interaction with Sui as straightforward as possible, aiming to attract users who were not necessarily blockchain experts.

Challenges Faced

- **Scalability vs. Security:** Balancing the need for high transaction speeds with maintaining security was a significant challenge, requiring innovative solutions in network architecture.
- **Community Expectations:** Managing the hype around Sui while setting realistic expectations for development and launch timelines was crucial for maintaining trust.
- **Market Conditions:** Navigating the volatile crypto market, especially with the backdrop of previous high-profile blockchain projects, demanded strategic planning to ensure long-term viability.

By taking these steps, Mysten Labs not only set the stage for Sui but also began to weave it into the fabric of the broader blockchain and tech ecosystem, preparing for its eventual launch and adoption.

Part 5: Philosophical Underpinnings

The creation of Sui was not just a technical endeavor but a deeply philosophical one, rooted in a set of beliefs about what blockchain technology should achieve and how it should function in society. This part explores the philosophical foundations that guided Mysten Labs in developing Sui, highlighting the principles that shaped its design, governance, and community engagement.

Innovation with Responsibility

At the heart of Mysten Labs' approach was a commitment to innovate responsibly:

- **Ethical Innovation:** The team recognized the potential of blockchain to disrupt industries, economies, and societies. However, they also understood the risks, such as enabling illicit activities or exacerbating economic inequalities. Thus, they aimed to design Sui in a way that maximized societal benefit while minimizing harm, incorporating features like robust security to prevent misuse.
- **Long-Term Thinking:** Unlike many blockchain projects driven by short-term market hype, Mysten Labs adopted a long-term view. They sought to build a platform that would remain relevant and effective decades into the future, focusing on sustainability in both technological and economic terms.
- **Impact Awareness:** The founders were acutely aware of the broader implications of their work. For instance, they considered how

Sui could empower individuals in underbanked regions, but also how it might challenge existing financial systems, necessitating careful thought about regulatory and social impacts.

User-Centric Design

A cornerstone of Sui's philosophy was placing the user at the center of the blockchain experience:

- **Accessibility:** Blockchain technology is often criticized for its complexity, deterring mainstream adoption. Mysten Labs aimed to change this by designing Sui to be as intuitive as traditional internet services. This involved simplifying user interfaces, reducing the technical knowledge required to interact with the blockchain, and ensuring that users could manage their digital assets with ease.
- **Sovereignty:** The team believed strongly in user sovereignty—the idea that individuals should have full control over their digital assets without intermediaries. This principle influenced Sui's design, particularly in how assets are managed as unique objects, ensuring users have direct, unencumbered access to their data and transactions.
- **Inclusivity:** Sui was envisioned as a platform that could serve a global audience, including those in regions with limited access to technology. This meant prioritizing low transaction costs, high speed, and compatibility with a wide range of devices,

from high-end computers to basic
smartphones.

Openness and Transparency

Mysten Labs embraced the ethos of blockchain by
committing to openness and transparency:

- **Open-Source Philosophy:** Where feasible,
  Sui's codebase was intended to be
  open-source, allowing developers worldwide to
  inspect, contribute to, and build upon the
  platform. This openness was seen as essential
  for fostering trust and encouraging innovation
  within the ecosystem.
- **Transparent Development:** The development
  process was designed to be as transparent as
  possible, with regular updates, public
  roadmaps, and community discussions. This
  transparency helped build trust and allowed
  the community to hold Mysten Labs
  accountable to its promises.
- **Collaborative Ecosystem:** Beyond just
  sharing code, Mysten Labs aimed to create a
  collaborative ecosystem where developers,
  businesses, and users could co-create value.
  This involved not just providing tools but also
  fostering a culture of shared learning and
  improvement.

Sustainability

Sustainability was a critical philosophical pillar, addressing both environmental and economic concerns:

- **Environmental Sustainability:** Recognizing the criticism faced by energy-intensive blockchains like Bitcoin, Mysten Labs designed Sui to be energy-efficient. This was achieved through its consensus mechanism, which avoided the computational waste of Proof-of-Work systems, and by optimizing transaction processing to minimize resource use.
- **Economic Sustainability:** The team also focused on creating an economic model that would ensure Sui's longevity. This involved careful design of tokenomics, ensuring that incentives for validators, developers, and users were balanced to maintain network health over time. The goal was to avoid the boom-and-bust cycles that plague many blockchain projects.
- **Social Sustainability:** Beyond technology and economics, Mysten Labs considered the social sustainability of Sui, aiming to create a platform that could benefit society broadly. This included ensuring that Sui could support applications in education, healthcare, and governance, thereby contributing to societal good rather than just financial speculation.

Decentralization as a Moral Imperative

Decentralization was not just a technical feature but a moral stance:

- **Power Distribution:** The founders believed that centralized control over digital systems often leads to power imbalances, where a few entities can dictate terms to many. Sui was designed to distribute power, ensuring that no single entity—be it Mysten Labs, a government, or a corporation—could control the network.
- **Resistance to Censorship:** By decentralizing control, Sui aimed to be resistant to censorship, allowing for free expression and economic activity even in regions with oppressive regimes. This was seen as a fundamental right in the digital age.
- **Community Governance:** While initial governance was necessarily more centralized due to the developmental phase, the philosophical commitment was to move towards community-driven governance. This meant creating mechanisms for users and stakeholders to have a say in the network's future, aligning with the democratic ideals of blockchain.

Balancing Ideals with Pragmatism

While these philosophical underpinnings were idealistic, Mysten Labs was pragmatic in their implementation:

- **Regulatory Engagement:** Rather than viewing regulation as an enemy, the team saw it as a necessary part of scaling blockchain technology. They engaged proactively with regulators to ensure Sui could operate legally while still pushing the boundaries of innovation.
- **Market Realities:** The team was aware of the speculative nature of the crypto market and designed Sui to offer real utility, not just speculative value. This involved focusing on use cases that could provide tangible benefits, such as in gaming, DeFi, and supply chain management.
- **Technical Trade-Offs:** Philosophically, absolute decentralization and security were ideals, but in practice, trade-offs were necessary. For instance, Sui's design prioritized speed and scalability, which required some compromises in how decentralization was initially implemented, with plans to enhance it over time.

Part 6: The Move Programming Language

At the core of Sui's innovative framework lies the Move programming language, a critical piece of technology that has shaped the blockchain's capabilities, security, and developer experience. This part discusses the origins of Move, its unique attributes, and how it serves as the foundation for Sui's smart contract environment.

Origins of Move

Move was initially developed for the Libra (later Diem) project by Meta, with Sam Blackshear leading its creation. It was designed to address several key issues in blockchain programming:

- **Security:** Move was built from the ground up to prevent common vulnerabilities found in other smart contract languages, like reentrancy attacks.
- **Resource Management:** It introduced a novel approach where each piece of data is treated as a resource, which must be explicitly managed, ensuring that assets can't be duplicated or lost.
- **Scalability:** The language was designed to support high transaction throughput, a necessity for any blockchain aiming for global adoption.

When the Diem project was discontinued, Move's potential was not lost. Instead, it found new life with Sui, where its core principles were further refined and adapted to meet the specific needs of this new blockchain.

Key Features of Move

Move's design philosophy is centered around safety, scalability, and developer-friendliness:

- **Resource Model:** In Move, everything is an object or resource. This paradigm shift from traditional data handling allows for precise control over digital assets, ensuring they are unique, owner-controlled, and managed with explicit permissions.

- **Linear Types:** Move uses linear types for resources, meaning once a resource is used, it's no longer available elsewhere, preventing double-spending and ensuring resource conservation.
- **Safety by Design:** The language's syntax and type system are designed to catch many programming errors at compile time, significantly reducing the risk of runtime errors in smart contracts.
- **Modular and Extensible:** Move was crafted to be modular, allowing developers to write reusable, safe code. This modularity supports the creation of complex applications from simple, secure building blocks.
- **Gas Model:** Move introduces a gas model that's more intuitive than many found in other blockchains, where the cost of operations is more predictable and aligned with the actual computational work done.

Move in the Context of Sui

For Sui, Move was not just adopted but adapted to maximize the blockchain's potential:

- **Object-Centric Model:** Sui's architecture treats everything as an object, a principle directly borrowed from Move. This allows for parallel execution of transactions since each object can be manipulated independently without conflicting with others.

- **Smart Contract Safety:** With Sui's focus on security, Move's inherent safety features were a natural fit. Sui smart contracts benefit from Move's design to prevent common security pitfalls.
- **Scalability:** By leveraging Move, Sui could achieve high throughput. The language supports parallel processing by design, aligning with Sui's goal to handle millions of transactions per second.
- **Developer Experience:** Move's simplicity compared to other smart contract languages was seen as a way to lower the barrier to entry for developers, encouraging broader participation in the Sui ecosystem.

Challenges and Adaptations

Adapting Move for Sui came with its challenges:

- **Performance Optimizations:** While Move was designed for scalability, further optimizations were necessary for Sui's specific transaction model and consensus mechanism.
- **Integration with Sui's Architecture:** Ensuring Move could fully leverage Sui's unique features like object-centric data management required significant work in how contracts interact with the blockchain's state.
- **Developer Education:** Move, while safer, was still a new language for many developers. Mysten Labs invested in educational

resources, documentation, and community support to foster a growing developer base.

- **Ecosystem Compatibility:** Making sure that Move could interoperate with existing blockchain ecosystems or be adapted for use in various applications was key, leading to ongoing developments in how Move interfaces with other technologies.

Future of Move with Sui

The commitment to Move is ongoing:

- **Continuous Improvement:** The language is expected to evolve, with new features being added to address emerging needs in the blockchain space, particularly around privacy, governance, and new asset types.
- **Community Contributions:** As Sui grows, so does the community's role in shaping Move. Open-source contributions, feedback loops, and collaborative development are anticipated to drive Move's evolution.
- **Cross-Blockchain Potential:** There's interest in seeing how Move can be used beyond Sui, potentially becoming a standard for secure, scalable smart contract programming across different blockchain ecosystems.

Move is not just a programming language; it's a pivotal element of Sui's identity, enabling its ambitious goals for security, scalability, and user empowerment. By adopting and enhancing Move, Mysten Labs has set a new standard for what blockchain programming can look like, aiming to make Sui a platform where developers can create with confidence, knowing their code is inherently safer and more performant. This part of the chapter underscores the technical innovation at the heart of Sui, providing a foundation for the subsequent exploration of how this language influences the development and operation of the Sui blockchain.

Part 7: Funding and Support

The journey to transform vision into reality requires not just innovation but also substantial financial backing and strategic support. This part explores how Mysten Labs attracted investment, the implications of this funding, and the broader support ecosystem that grew around Sui.

Initial Funding and Investors

From the outset, Mysten Labs knew that realizing Sui's potential would require significant resources:

- **Series B Funding:** In late 2022, Mysten Labs announced a monumental $300 million Series B funding round. This was led by Andreessen Horowitz (a16z), one of the most influential venture capital firms in the tech and crypto space, signaling strong market confidence in Sui's vision.
- **Notable Investors:** The round included participation from a diverse group of investors such as FTX Ventures, Coinbase Ventures, Binance Labs, Jump Crypto, and others. This

mix of strategic, industry-focused investors provided not just funds but also networks, expertise, and credibility.

The Significance of the Funding

This infusion of capital had several key implications:

- **Validation of Vision:** The investment validated the ambitious vision of Sui, particularly its focus on scalability, security, and user experience improvements over existing blockchain technologies.
- **Resource for R&D:** The funds allowed Mysten Labs to invest heavily in research and development, pushing the boundaries of what's possible with blockchain technology.
- **Talent Acquisition:** With financial backing, Mysten Labs could attract top-tier talent, both from within the blockchain industry and from other tech sectors, to bolster its team.
- **Marketing and Ecosystem Development:** Funding enabled extensive marketing efforts, ecosystem building, and developer support programs, which are crucial for adoption and growth.

Strategic Partnerships

Beyond financial investment, partnerships played a critical role:

- **Technology Collaborations:** Partnerships with other tech companies for integrations,

shared development goals, or mutual promotion helped expand Sui's reach and capabilities.
- **Academic Partnerships:** Collaborations with universities for research into blockchain applications, security, and economic models added an academic rigor to Sui's development.
- **Industry Alliances:** Aligning with industry bodies or other blockchain platforms for interoperability, standards setting, or joint ventures in areas like DeFi or gaming.

Community and Developer Support

The funding also facilitated:

- **Developer Grants:** Programs to incentivize developers to build on Sui, offering financial support, mentorship, and resources for projects that could enhance the platform's utility.
- **Hackathons and Competitions:** Events where developers could explore Sui's capabilities, win prizes, and gain visibility for their projects, fostering innovation within the ecosystem.
- **Educational Initiatives:** Training programs, workshops, and online courses to educate developers about Move, Sui's architecture, and blockchain technology in general.

Navigating the Market

The crypto market is notoriously volatile, and Mysten Labs had to navigate this landscape:

- **Market Timing:** Launching and fundraising at a time when crypto was regaining investor interest post a market slump showed strategic acumen in capitalizing on market recovery.
- **Long-Term Investment:** By attracting investors interested in long-term growth rather than quick gains, Mysten Labs positioned Sui for sustainable development, not just speculative bubbles.
- **Compliance and Regulation:** The expertise of some investors in navigating regulatory landscapes was invaluable in helping Sui prepare for global operations while complying with various legal frameworks.

Challenges of Funding

With great funding comes great responsibility:

- **Expectations Management:** Balancing the expectations of investors with the practicalities of blockchain development was a continuous challenge, especially given the high-profile nature of the investors involved.
- **Market Pressure:** High funding can lead to pressure for quick results, which could potentially rush development or lead to decisions that prioritize investor returns over platform integrity.
- **Sustainability:** Ensuring that the growth of Sui would be sustainable, not just driven by the

initial capital influx, required careful planning around tokenomics, community governance, and ecosystem health.

Broader Support Ecosystem

The support for Sui wasn't limited to financial backing:

- **Community Building:** An active community of users, developers, and enthusiasts who provided feedback, tested the platform, and evangelized Sui's potential.
- **Open Source Contributions:** Encouraging contributions from the open-source community to enhance Sui's codebase, tools, and documentation.
- **Media and Public Perception:** Managing PR to highlight Sui's innovations while addressing common blockchain criticisms like energy consumption or security concerns.

The funding and support garnered by Mysten Labs for Sui were not just financial lifelines but strategic partnerships, community engagements, and validations of the project's potential. This part of the chapter illustrates how financial backing, when strategically leveraged, can accelerate a blockchain project's journey from concept to reality, setting the foundation for Sui's future growth and influence in the blockchain space.

Chapter 2: Philosophy of Sui: Speed, Security, and Scalability

Part 1: Speed: The Imperative for Instant Transactions

Why Speed Matters:

In the digital age, speed is not just a convenience; it's an expectation. When it comes to blockchain technology, the time taken to process transactions can be the difference between a platform becoming a cornerstone of digital finance or remaining a niche curiosity. Traditional blockchains like Bitcoin or Ethereum have shown that while security and decentralization are achievable, speed often suffers. This lag can lead to user dissatisfaction, particularly in scenarios where transactions need to be nearly instantaneous, such as in:

- **Payments:** Whether it's buying coffee or settling international trade, the wait times of traditional blockchains are a bottleneck.
- **Gaming:** In blockchain-based games, slow transaction speeds can break immersion, affecting gameplay and user retention.
- **Decentralized Finance (DeFi):** High-speed transactions are crucial for arbitrage, yield farming, and other time-sensitive financial operations.

Sui's philosophy centers on addressing this bottleneck, understanding that for blockchain to truly disrupt and replace traditional systems, it must match or exceed the speed of those systems.

Sui's Approach to Speed:

Sui tackles the speed challenge through several innovative approaches:

- **Parallel Transaction Execution:** Unlike sequential processing in many blockchains, Sui's architecture allows for multiple transactions to be processed simultaneously. By treating assets as unique objects, transactions on different objects can occur in parallel, dramatically increasing throughput.
- **Instant Finality:** Sui's consensus mechanism is designed to confirm transactions almost instantly, eliminating the wait times associated with block confirmations in other systems. This is achieved through a variant of Delegated Proof-of-Stake (DPoS), where validators can reach consensus quickly.
- **Optimized Consensus Protocol:** Sui's consensus algorithm is tailored for speed, focusing on reducing the time to consensus without compromising on security, ensuring that transactions are not only fast but also final once confirmed.
- **Low Latency:** By minimizing the data that needs to be communicated across the network and optimizing how this data is handled, Sui reduces latency, which is critical for applications requiring real-time interactions.

Use Cases Where Speed is Critical:

- **Everyday Transactions:** For Sui to become a daily-use platform, it must handle small, frequent transactions with the same speed as credit card payments, making it viable for microtransactions or peer-to-peer payments.
- **Supply Chain:** In logistics, every second can translate into cost savings or losses. Sui's speed can facilitate real-time tracking and management of goods, enhancing efficiency.
- **High-Frequency Trading:** In DeFi, where speed can determine profit or loss in milliseconds, Sui's fast transaction processing is a game-changer, enabling more dynamic and responsive market interactions.
- **Gaming and NFTs:** The ability to transfer assets or execute game actions instantly without waiting for block confirmations can significantly enhance user experience, making blockchain gaming more competitive with centralized alternatives.

The Philosophical Commitment to Speed:

Sui's focus on speed isn't just about outpacing competitors; it's about redefining what's possible with blockchain technology. The philosophy here is rooted in the belief that for blockchain to achieve widespread adoption, it must blend into the fabric of internet services, becoming as seamless and real-time as the web itself. This commitment to speed also reflects a broader vision of democratizing access to financial services, where anyone can engage in transactions as effortlessly as they check their email or send a text message.

Challenges in Achieving Speed:

While the vision is clear, the execution comes with its own set of challenges:

- **Balancing with Security:** Speed must not come at the expense of security. Sui's developers are tasked with ensuring that fast transactions are also secure, using cryptography and consensus mechanisms that don't allow for shortcuts.
- **Scalability:** Speed is closely tied to scalability; as more users join, maintaining speed becomes harder. Sui's approach to scalability must evolve in tandem with its speed enhancements.
- **Network Congestion:** Even with parallel processing, there's a limit to how many transactions can be executed simultaneously. Managing network load to prevent congestion is a continuous challenge.
- **Regulatory Compliance:** Ensuring that fast transactions can also meet the standards of various regulatory bodies around the world without introducing bottlenecks is a nuanced task.

Sui's philosophy of prioritizing speed is not merely about technical prowess but about fulfilling the promise of blockchain to revolutionize how we interact with digital assets. By focusing on instant transaction finality, parallel execution, and optimized consensus, Sui aims to make blockchain technology as fast and intuitive as any service on the internet, setting a new standard for what users can expect from decentralized systems.

Part 2: Security: Building Trust in a Decentralized World

Security Philosophy:

At the heart of Sui's philosophy is the principle that security is not just a feature but the cornerstone of trust in a blockchain ecosystem. In a decentralized world where there's no central authority to fall back on, security becomes the bedrock upon which all other functionalities rest. Sui's approach to security is comprehensive, focusing on:

- **Asset Integrity:** Ensuring that digital assets are safe from theft, duplication, or loss.
- **Data Privacy:** Protecting user data and transaction details from unauthorized access.
- **Network Stability:** Safeguarding the network against attacks that could disrupt or halt operations.
- **User Sovereignty:** Enabling users to have control over their assets without the fear of external manipulation or censorship.

This philosophy is reflected in every layer of Sui's architecture, from its consensus mechanism to the programming language it employs.

Innovations in Security:

Sui introduces several innovations to bolster its security:

- **Move Programming Language:** Move was designed with security as a primary concern. Its resource model ensures that each asset is unique and can only be controlled by its owner. This prevents common smart contract vulnerabilities like reentrancy attacks. Move's type system catches many errors at compile-time, reducing the risk of runtime exploits.
- **Advanced Cryptography:** Sui leverages state-of-the-art cryptographic techniques for encryption, digital signatures, and secure multi-party computation to protect transactions and data. This includes zero-knowledge proofs for privacy-preserving transactions.
- **Consensus Mechanism:** Sui's consensus protocol is designed to be both fast and secure, using a Delegated Proof-of-Stake (DPoS) model where validators are incentivized to act honestly. The protocol includes mechanisms for rapid fault detection and response to mitigate risks like double-spending or 51% attacks.
- **Security Audits and Formal Verification:** Regular audits by independent security firms and the use of formal verification methods ensure that both the protocol and its smart contracts maintain the highest security standards.

Compliance and Privacy:

Navigating the balance between regulatory compliance and user privacy is a significant aspect of Sui's security philosophy:

- **Regulatory Adaptation:** While aiming for global adoption, Sui designs its systems to be adaptable to different regulatory environments, ensuring compliance without compromising on its decentralized nature. This includes features for KYC (Know Your Customer) and AML (Anti-Money Laundering) where necessary.
- **Privacy by Design:** Sui incorporates privacy features to protect user identity and transaction details. This includes optional privacy settings for transactions, ensuring users can choose how much of their activity is public or private.
- **Audit Trails:** While protecting privacy, Sui also ensures there's enough transparency for audits, enabling accountability without exposing personal data.

Challenges in Security:

Achieving this level of security comes with its own set of challenges:

- **Balancing Transparency with Privacy:** Ensuring the blockchain remains transparent enough for trust yet private enough for user protection is a delicate balance.

- **Scalability vs. Security:** As the network scales, maintaining security becomes more complex. Sui must innovate continuously to ensure that security doesn't degrade as transaction volume increases.
- **Regulatory Evolution:** As regulations evolve, especially around cryptocurrencies and data protection, Sui must be agile enough to adapt without sacrificing its security principles.
- **Human Factor:** No security system is foolproof against human error or malice. Training developers, educating users, and fostering a security-conscious community are ongoing tasks.

Philosophical Commitment to Security:

Sui's dedication to security is not just about protecting assets but about fostering an environment where users can trust the system with their digital lives. This philosophy extends beyond the technical:

- **Community Engagement:** Security is also about community, where users and developers collectively contribute to and benefit from a secure environment.
- **Education and Awareness:** By promoting understanding of security practices, Sui aims to empower its users to protect themselves.
- **Open-Source Contributions:** Encouraging transparent development and allowing the community to scrutinize, contribute to, and improve security measures.

The security philosophy of Sui is about building a blockchain where trust is inherent, where users can transact with confidence, and where the system is resilient against both current and future threats. This commitment to security is what sets Sui apart, making it not just a platform for transactions but a foundation for a secure digital future. By intertwining security with speed and scalability, Sui aims to redefine what it means to trust a blockchain.

Part 3: Scalability: Designing for Millions, Ready for Billions

The Scalability Challenge:

Scalability has been the Achilles' heel for many blockchain platforms, often leading to slow transaction times, high fees, and network congestion as user numbers grow. Traditional blockchains face a trilemma of balancing scalability with security and decentralization. Sui's approach to this challenge is grounded in the philosophy that for blockchain to truly achieve mass adoption, it must scale to handle the demands of millions of users with the potential to grow to billions without compromising on its core values.

Sui's Scalability Solution:

Sui tackles scalability through a combination of innovative design principles:

- **Object-Centric Model:** Instead of a global state like in many blockchains, Sui uses an object-centric model where each asset or piece of data is treated as a unique object. This allows for:

- **Parallel Processing:** Transactions involving different objects can be processed in parallel, dramatically increasing throughput.
- **Fine-Grained State Management:** Only the state of the affected objects needs to be updated, reducing the computational load and storage requirements for each transaction.

- **Move Programming Language:** The language's design supports Sui's scalability:

  - **Resource Management:** By treating assets as resources, Move ensures that each asset's lifecycle can be managed efficiently, avoiding duplication or loss.
  - **Safety and Performance:** Move's safety features mean fewer errors and less need for costly transaction rollbacks, improving overall system efficiency.

- **Consensus Mechanism:** Sui's consensus protocol is optimized for speed and scalability:

  - **Delegated Proof-of-Stake (DPoS):** By selecting validators to process transactions, Sui can achieve consensus quickly, reducing the bottleneck at the validation layer.

- Asynchronous Execution:
  Transactions can be validated in a
  non-blocking manner, allowing the
  network to handle a high volume of
  transactions without waiting for each
  one to be processed.
- **Network Sharding:** Although not fully
  implemented at launch, the architecture of Sui
  allows for future sharding, where the network
  can be split into smaller, more manageable
  pieces, each handling a portion of the
  transaction load.

Future-Proofing:

Sui's scalability solutions are designed with future
growth in mind:

- **Horizontal Scaling:** As more users join the
  network, Sui can scale horizontally by adding
  more validators or nodes, ensuring that
  performance doesn't degrade.
- **Modular Architecture:** The design allows for
  the integration of new features or
  improvements without overhauling the entire
  system, ensuring that Sui can adapt to
  technological advancements.
- **Ecosystem Expansion:** By supporting a wide
  array of decentralized applications (dApps),
  Sui encourages an ecosystem where each app
  can contribute to and benefit from the
  network's scalability.

Philosophical Commitments to Scalability:

- **Decentralization:** Even as it scales, Sui maintains a commitment to decentralization, ensuring that increased throughput does not lead to centralization of control.
- **User Experience:** Scalability directly impacts user experience; thus, Sui focuses on making interactions with the blockchain as seamless as possible, regardless of network load.
- **Economic Scalability:** The tokenomics of Sui are designed to work at scale, ensuring that fees remain reasonable and incentives for network participation are sustainable.

Challenges and Considerations:

- **Security at Scale:** As the network grows, maintaining security becomes more complex. Sui must ensure that its solutions for scalability do not introduce new vulnerabilities.
- **Resource Management:** With an object-centric model, managing the lifecycle of millions or billions of objects efficiently is a challenge, requiring sophisticated data structures and algorithms.
- **Network Effects:** While scalability can lead to network growth, it also means dealing with network effects like congestion if not managed properly.
- **Adoption Curve:** The speed of adoption can outpace the scalability solutions if not planned correctly, leading to growing pains.

Sui's philosophy on scalability is about creating a blockchain that can grow without bounds, supporting an ever-increasing user base and application ecosystem. By focusing on an object-centric model, leveraging the Move language, and optimizing its consensus mechanism, Sui aims to redefine what's possible in terms of blockchain scalability. This part of the chapter underscores that scalability isn't just about handling more transactions but ensuring that as the network grows, it remains true to its core principles of speed, security, and decentralization, offering a platform where billions can interact with digital assets as effortlessly as they do with the internet today.

Part 4: Interplay of Speed, Security, and Scalability

Synergy:

The philosophy of Sui is not just about excelling in speed, security, or scalability in isolation but about how these three aspects synergistically enhance each other to create a robust, user-friendly blockchain platform:

- **Speed Enhancing Security:** Fast transaction processing can reduce the window of opportunity for malicious actors to exploit vulnerabilities. By achieving near-instant finality, Sui minimizes risks associated with transaction reversals or double-spending.
- **Security Enabling Scalability:** A secure foundation is crucial for scaling. Without robust

security, increasing transaction throughput could lead to more vulnerabilities. Sui's approach to security ensures that as the network scales, the integrity of transactions and data remains uncompromised.

- **Scalability Supporting Speed:** The ability to process transactions in parallel due to scalability measures directly contributes to speed. As Sui scales up, its speed remains consistent, supporting more users and transactions without slowdowns.

Engineering Trade-offs:

In designing Sui, several trade-offs were considered to balance these core principles:

- **Decentralization vs. Speed:** While centralization can speed up processes, Sui maintains a decentralized model, ensuring that speed does not come at the cost of network control. The DPoS consensus mechanism is a compromise that allows for speed while still distributing power.
- **Security vs. Scalability:** To scale without security risks, Sui had to innovate in how state is managed and how consensus is reached. The object-centric model and Move's resource handling are solutions to this trade-off, allowing for scaling while keeping security intact.
- **User Experience vs. Technical Complexity:** To maintain simplicity for users, Sui had to manage the complexity behind the scenes, like ensuring that the benefits of parallel

processing are felt by users without them needing to understand the underlying mechanics.

Interconnected Design Principles:

- **Atomicity:** Each transaction in Sui is treated atomically, ensuring that operations are complete or not at all, which is vital for both security and speed in transaction processing.
- **Consistency:** Sui's architecture ensures data consistency across the network, crucial for security but also for allowing scalable parallel execution without conflicting states.
- **Isolation:** By ensuring transactions are isolated from each other when necessary, scalability is enhanced as different transactions can proceed without interference, yet this isolation must be balanced with the need for fast, secure consensus.
- **Durability:** Once a transaction is confirmed on Sui, its durability (persistence) is guaranteed, which is fundamental for user trust and the security of the system.

Philosophical Implications:

- **Empowerment Through Efficiency:** The interplay of these principles aims to empower users by providing a blockchain that feels as reliable and fast as traditional systems while offering the benefits of decentralization.
- **Trust as a Product:** By ensuring that speed, security, and scalability work in harmony, Sui

builds a layer of trust, making it a platform where users can confidently engage with digital assets.

- **Sustainable Growth:** This synergy is designed to support not just immediate needs but a sustainable growth model where the network can expand without degrading performance or security.

Challenges in Harmonizing These Principles:

- **Regulatory Adaptation:** Balancing speed, security, and scalability while navigating different regulatory environments globally can introduce complexities, especially in how transactions are validated or data is handled.
- **Resource Allocation:** As the network grows, allocating resources like computational power, storage, and bandwidth becomes more complex, requiring sophisticated management to maintain the balance.
- **User Education:** Users need to understand the benefits of this interplay without being overwhelmed by the technical details, which means continuous education and intuitive design are necessary.
- **Technological Evolution:** As new challenges arise or technologies evolve, Sui must adapt its approach to maintain the harmony between speed, security, and scalability, which includes ongoing R&D.

The interplay of speed, security, and scalability in Sui is not just about technical prowess but about creating a philosophy where these elements enhance each other to provide a superior blockchain experience. This part of the chapter emphasizes how Sui's design choices reflect a deep understanding that for blockchain to truly serve as a foundational layer for digital interactions, these three aspects must not only coexist but complement and amplify each other. This holistic approach is what sets Sui apart, aiming for a blockchain that can scale to global demands while maintaining the trust and efficiency users expect.

Part 5: Philosophical Commitments

Sui's development is guided by a set of philosophical commitments that go beyond mere technical specifications, aiming to shape the blockchain's role in society, economy, and technology. These commitments reflect the vision of Mysten Labs and the broader community surrounding Sui.

Decentralization:

- **Core Ethos:** Decentralization is at the heart of Sui's philosophy. It's not just about distributing network control but about ensuring that no single entity can monopolize the platform or dictate its evolution.
- **Mechanisms for Decentralization:** Sui implements this through its consensus mechanism, governance models, and the way validators and nodes are managed, ensuring that power is spread across a wide network of participants.

- **Implications:** This commitment to decentralization means that Sui aims to be resistant to censorship, foster innovation through community governance, and provide a platform where users truly own their digital assets.

User Empowerment:

- **Control Over Assets:** Sui's design ensures users have direct control over their digital assets, with mechanisms in place to prevent unauthorized access or manipulation.
- **Simplicity and Accessibility:** By focusing on speed and scalability, alongside security, Sui aims to make blockchain technology accessible to everyone, not just tech-savvy individuals. This includes user-friendly interfaces and tools that abstract the complexity of blockchain operations.
- **Economic Participation:** Sui's economic model is designed to allow broad participation in network governance and rewards, empowering users to contribute to and benefit from the ecosystem's growth.

Sustainability:

- **Environmental:** While blockchain is often criticized for its energy consumption, Sui's consensus mechanism is designed to be more energy-efficient than traditional Proof-of-Work systems, aligning with environmental sustainability goals.

- **Economic:** The tokenomics of Sui are structured to promote long-term health of the network, avoiding hyperinflation or deflation scenarios that could destabilize the economy.
- **Social:** Beyond tech and finance, Sui's philosophy includes a commitment to societal benefits, supporting applications that can bring positive change in areas like education, healthcare, and governance.

Openness and Transparency:

- **Open-Source Development:** Sui's codebase is intended to be open-source where possible, encouraging transparency, community contributions, and fostering trust.
- **Transparent Governance:** Even though the initial phases might see more centralized decision-making, there's a clear path towards more open, community-driven governance models.
- **Audit and Accountability:** Regular security audits, open discussions on platform changes, and clear communication about network performance and issues reflect this commitment to transparency.

Innovation with Responsibility:

- **Ethical Considerations:** Sui's development is guided by ethical considerations, ensuring that innovations are not just for profit but for the betterment of users and society.

- **Safety First:** The adoption of Move and other security-focused technologies underscores a commitment to innovation that prioritizes user safety over speed to market.
- **Impact Awareness:** Understanding the global impact of a blockchain, Sui aims to innovate in a way that considers regulatory landscapes, cultural differences, and the digital divide.

Community-Centric Approach:

- **Community as Stakeholders:** Sui views its community not just as users but as stakeholders in the platform's success, inviting input, feedback, and involvement in various aspects of development and governance.
- **Educational Initiatives:** By investing in education, Sui aims to grow its community's understanding and capability, ensuring that the platform's growth is accompanied by an informed user base.
- **Ecosystem Development:** Sui's philosophy includes fostering an ecosystem where developers, businesses, and individuals can thrive, creating a network effect that benefits all participants.

Challenges in Upholding These Commitments:

- **Balancing Speed and Security:** While speed is essential, ensuring it doesn't compromise security requires constant vigilance and innovation.

- **Scalability without Centralization:** As Sui grows, maintaining decentralization while scaling up is a significant challenge, requiring innovative governance and network design.
- **Sustainability in a Volatile Market:** Crypto markets can be unpredictable, making it hard to maintain long-term economic and environmental sustainability.
- **Regulatory Navigation:** The commitment to user empowerment and decentralization sometimes conflicts with regulatory requirements, necessitating a nuanced approach to compliance.

The philosophical commitments of Sui are what define its identity beyond code and algorithms. They represent a vision for a blockchain that not only works better but also aligns with broader societal values like trust, empowerment, and sustainability. These principles guide Sui's development, ensuring that as it grows, it does so in a way that benefits its users, the broader community, and the global digital ecosystem. This part of the chapter serves as a reminder that technology, especially in the blockchain space, is not just about what it can do but what it should do for the world.

Part 6: Comparative Analysis

To fully understand Sui's philosophy, it's helpful to compare it with existing blockchain platforms and traditional financial systems. This comparative analysis will highlight Sui's unique position, showcasing how its principles of speed, security, and scalability not only set it apart but also aim to redefine expectations within the blockchain industry.

Against Legacy Financial Systems:

- **Speed:** Traditional banking systems can take days for cross-border transactions or even local ones depending on the banks involved. Sui's near-instant transaction finality offers a stark contrast, aiming to make blockchain transactions as swift as or faster than existing digital payment systems like PayPal or Visa.
- **Security:** While banks invest heavily in security, they are centralized, making them potential targets for hacks. Sui's decentralized security model distributes risk and uses advanced cryptography, offering a different but potentially more resilient security paradigm.
- **Scalability:** Legacy systems scale through centralized infrastructure upgrades, which can be costly and slow. Sui's design allows it to scale horizontally with the network's growth, potentially offering a more sustainable model for handling an increasing number of transactions.

Against Other Blockchain Platforms:

- **Speed:** Compared to Bitcoin's 10-minute block times or Ethereum's variable block times, Sui's approach to immediate finality is revolutionary. Even newer blockchains like Solana or Avalanche, while fast, face challenges in consistency across their networks, which Sui aims to address through its object-centric model.

- **Security:** While many blockchains have had significant security breaches due to smart contract vulnerabilities, Sui's use of Move aims to prevent these from the ground up. This contrasts with platforms like Ethereum where security often depends on the quality of individual contract code.
- **Scalability:** Ethereum, facing scalability issues, has moved to Ethereum 2.0 with sharding, but Sui's approach from the start was to design for scalability, potentially offering a smoother path to handling billions of transactions without the need for such extensive upgrades.

Future of Blockchain:

- **Setting New Standards:** Sui's philosophy could set new standards for what blockchain platforms should strive for in terms of user experience, reliability, and efficiency, pushing other projects to rethink their approaches.
- **Interoperability:** While Sui initially focuses on its ecosystem, its principles could lead to a future where interoperability between blockchains is standard, driven by the need for speed and scalability across networks.
- **Regulatory Influence:** As Sui navigates global regulations with its commitments, it might influence how other blockchains approach compliance, potentially leading to a

more harmonious relationship between decentralized tech and regulatory bodies.

Philosophical Advantages:

- **User-Centric:** Unlike many blockchains that prioritize developers or miners, Sui's philosophy centers around the end-user, aiming for a blockchain that feels intuitive and secure for everyday use.
- **Sustainability:** With its approach to consensus, Sui might influence the industry towards more environmentally friendly blockchain designs, contrasting with energy-intensive Proof-of-Work systems.
- **Decentralization in Practice:** While many blockchains claim decentralization, Sui's architecture and governance models aim to make it a reality, potentially setting a benchmark for others.

Challenges in Comparison:

- **Market Perception:** New entrants like Sui must overcome the inertia and established user bases of older, well-known blockchains.
- **Technological Maturity:** Being relatively new, Sui's infrastructure might be scrutinized more harshly than more established platforms, despite its innovative approach.
- **Adoption Hurdles:** While Sui's philosophy might be superior on paper, real-world adoption depends on network effects,

developer tools, and practical use cases, which require time to develop.

This comparative analysis underscores that Sui isn't just another blockchain but a platform with a distinct philosophy aiming to push the boundaries of what's possible. By focusing on speed, security, and scalability in a way that's both user-centric and sustainable, Sui positions itself not just to compete but to potentially redefine the blockchain space. This part of the chapter serves as a lens through which we can appreciate the ambition and innovation of Sui, setting the stage for understanding its potential impact on the future of digital transactions, asset management, and decentralized systems.

Part 7: Challenges and Vision

Sui's ambitious philosophy of speed, security, and scalability presents both unique challenges and a compelling vision for the future of blockchain technology. Here, we delve into the obstacles that Sui must navigate and the long-term vision that drives its development.

Challenges:

- **Scalability vs. Decentralization:** One of the most persistent challenges in blockchain is balancing scalability with true decentralization. As Sui grows, ensuring that its network remains decentralized while scaling to meet global demand will require continuous innovation in consensus mechanisms, validator selection, and network architecture.

- **Security at Scale:** With increased speed and scalability comes the challenge of maintaining security. Protecting the network against new forms of attacks that might arise with higher transaction volumes or more complex smart contracts is an ongoing task.
- **User Adoption:** For all its technical prowess, Sui's success hinges on user adoption. Convincing users to switch from familiar platforms or traditional financial systems to a new blockchain requires demonstrating clear benefits in terms of speed, cost, and user experience.
- **Regulatory Compliance:** Operating globally means navigating a patchwork of regulations. Sui must adapt to regulatory demands without compromising its core principles, especially around decentralization and privacy.
- **Market Volatility:** The crypto market's volatility can affect funding, investor confidence, and the economic model of any blockchain. Sui needs to design its tokenomics to be resilient against market swings.
- **Competition:** The blockchain space is increasingly crowded. Sui must distinguish itself not just through its philosophy but by providing real-world applications that leverage its unique advantages.
- **Technological Evolution:** Blockchain technology evolves rapidly. Sui must keep pace with or lead in innovations in consensus

mechanisms, cryptography, and smart contract languages to remain at the forefront.

Vision:

- **A Universal Coordination Layer:** Sui envisions itself as more than just a blockchain; it aims to be a fundamental layer for coordinating digital assets across the internet, making transactions as seamless as data exchange is today.
- **Empowerment and Inclusion:** By focusing on speed and accessibility, Sui's vision includes empowering individuals worldwide, particularly those underserved by traditional financial systems, providing them with secure, fast, and scalable financial tools.
- **Interoperability:** Sui's long-term vision includes not just being a standalone blockchain but a part of a broader, interoperable blockchain ecosystem where assets and data can move freely between different networks.
- **Sustainability:** In line with its philosophical commitments, Sui aspires to lead in sustainable blockchain practices, both environmentally through efficient consensus mechanisms and economically through a balanced incentive structure.
- **Innovation in Applications:** Beyond finance, Sui sees itself as a platform for innovation in gaming, supply chain, identity management, and beyond, leveraging its capabilities to drive new forms of digital interaction.

- **Community Governance:** The vision includes evolving towards a model where the community has significant say in the network's direction, ensuring that Sui remains adaptable, fair, and aligned with user needs over time.
- **Global Adoption:** Ultimately, Sui aims for widespread adoption where blockchain technology becomes as integral to daily life as the internet is today, with Sui being at the heart of this digital transformation.

Strategic Roadmap:

- **Short-term Goals:** Launching and stabilizing the mainnet, growing the developer ecosystem, and demonstrating real-world use cases.
- **Mid-term Vision:** Expanding the network's capabilities, enhancing security features, and beginning to move towards more decentralized governance structures.
- **Long-term Ambitions:** Achieving global scale, becoming a standard for secure, fast blockchain transactions, and integrating with or influencing the broader tech infrastructure.

The challenges facing Sui are significant but are met with an equally grand vision. By addressing these challenges head-on, Sui not only aims to build a blockchain but to redefine the purpose and utility of blockchain technology in our digital lives. This part of the chapter encapsulates the journey from current obstacles to future aspirations, illustrating how Sui's philosophy of speed, security, and scalability is not just about technical excellence but about shaping a digital future where blockchain is ubiquitous, user-centric, and transformative.

Chapter 3: Sui Architecture: An Overview

Part 1: Foundational Concepts

The architecture of Sui is not just a technical blueprint but a realization of its foundational philosophy, aiming to deliver speed, security, and scalability in a way that's unprecedented in the blockchain space. This part introduces the key concepts that form the bedrock of Sui's design, providing readers with the context necessary to understand its technical intricacies.

Introduction to Sui's Design Philosophy:

- **Speed:** At its core, Sui is designed to make transactions as fast as possible. This isn't merely about reducing wait times but about enabling real-time applications, from payments to gaming, where every second counts.
- **Security:** Security in Sui isn't an afterthought but a fundamental aspect of its architecture. By leveraging innovative cryptographic and consensus mechanisms, Sui aims to provide a platform where assets are safe by design, not just by defense.
- **Scalability:** Sui's architecture is crafted to grow with demand, ensuring that as more users join, the network's performance does not degrade. This scalability is crucial for global adoption and for supporting a wide array of decentralized applications.

Key Components Overview:

- **Object-Centric Model:** Unlike traditional blockchains where the state is managed globally, Sui treats every piece of data or asset as an individual object. This approach fundamentally changes how transactions are processed, allowing for significant scalability and speed improvements.
- **Move Programming Language:** Central to Sui's architecture is the Move language, which ensures that smart contracts are safe and efficient, providing a foundation for secure asset management and transaction logic.
- **Consensus Mechanism:** Sui employs a Delegated Proof-of-Stake (DPoS) model, tailored for speed and efficiency, where validators are chosen by stake-holders to process and confirm transactions, ensuring quick consensus without the energy consumption of Proof-of-Work systems.
- **Transaction Processing:** With an emphasis on parallel execution, Sui's architecture allows for multiple transactions to be processed simultaneously, which is key to achieving high throughput.
- **Network Layer:** Comprising various node types like validators and full nodes, this layer ensures robust network operations, from transaction broadcasting to consensus formation.
- **Storage and State Management:** Sui's approach to storage is optimized for quick

access and updates, managing the state of objects in a way that supports both scalability and security.

- **Security Protocols:** Beyond the consensus mechanism, Sui's security is enhanced through advanced cryptographic techniques, ensuring the integrity and privacy of transactions and data.

Comparison with Traditional Blockchain Models:

- **State Management:** Traditional blockchains often manage state in a monolithic manner, which can lead to bottlenecks. Sui's object-centric model allows for more efficient state updates, reducing the computational load.
- **Transaction Processing:** While many blockchains process transactions sequentially within blocks, Sui's parallel processing model allows for a higher transaction throughput without compromising on security.
- **Smart Contract Execution:** The integration of Move provides Sui with a safer environment for smart contract execution, significantly reducing common vulnerabilities seen in other blockchain platforms.

Setting the Stage for Deeper Exploration:

This introduction sets the stage for a deeper exploration into each component of Sui's architecture. Understanding these foundational concepts is crucial for appreciating how Sui achieves its goals:

- **Scalability through Object Management:** By focusing on individual objects, Sui can scale operations without the need for entire network state updates.
- **Security by Design:** With Move at its core, security is embedded in every aspect of Sui's architecture, from transaction execution to data management.
- **Speed through Innovation:** The combination of parallel transaction processing and an optimized consensus mechanism aims to make Sui one of the fastest blockchains available.
- **Network and Consensus:** The way nodes interact and consensus is achieved is designed to support both the speed and security objectives without centralization.

The foundational concepts of Sui's architecture are where its philosophy meets practicality. This part has laid out the basic principles that guide Sui's development, offering a lens through which to view its technical choices. As we delve deeper into specific aspects in the following parts of this chapter, these foundational concepts will serve as a constant reference, illustrating how each piece of the architecture aligns with Sui's overarching goals.

Part 2: Object-Centric Model

At the heart of Sui's innovative approach to blockchain architecture is its object-centric model. This paradigm shift from traditional state management in blockchains offers significant advantages in terms of scalability, speed, and user interaction. This part explores the intricacies of this model, its implementation, and its impact on Sui's performance.

Definition and Comparison:

- **What is an Object-Centric Model?** In Sui, every piece of data or asset is treated as an "object" with its own state, lifecycle, and set of rules governing its interaction. Unlike traditional blockchains where the state is a single, global ledger, Sui's state is composed of numerous independent objects.
- **Comparison with Traditional Models:** In traditional blockchains like Bitcoin or Ethereum, state changes are recorded in blocks, affecting the entire state. This can lead to computational bottlenecks as the state grows. In contrast, Sui allows for operations on individual objects without necessarily affecting others, enabling parallel processing.

Benefits for Scalability and Speed:

- **Parallel Transaction Processing:** With each object being independent, transactions that modify different objects can be executed simultaneously. This parallelism drastically increases the network's throughput, allowing for a higher number of transactions per second.
- **Reduced Network Congestion:** Only the state of involved objects needs updating,

which means less data needs to be propagated across the network for each transaction, reducing congestion.

- **Efficient State Sharding:** Although not yet implemented, the object-centric model naturally lends itself to sharding, where different parts of the state can be managed by different segments of the network.
- **Quick State Updates:** Since operations are confined to specific objects, state updates can be quicker and more localized, enhancing the speed of transaction finality.

Implementation Details:

- **Object Lifecycle:** Each object in Sui has a lifecycle, from creation to destruction, managed by rules defined in smart contracts. This lifecycle includes ownership, permissions, and how objects can interact with each other.
- **Object Ownership:** Objects can be owned by addresses (accounts), providing a clear model for asset control and transfer, which is intuitive for users familiar with digital or physical property.
- **Smart Contracts:** Written in Move, smart contracts define the behavior of objects, including how they can be modified, transferred, or destroyed. This ensures that each operation on an object follows the rules set forth by its governing contract.
- **State Management:** Sui's database stores object states in a way that allows for quick retrieval and updates. This is crucial for

maintaining the speed of transaction processing and verification.

Challenges and Considerations:

- **Complexity in Object Management:** While offering benefits, managing a vast number of objects introduces complexity in terms of database design, indexing, and ensuring state consistency across the network.
- **Security Implications:** Each object must be secured independently, which can be both a strength (localized security) and a challenge (ensuring no vulnerabilities in how objects interact or are managed).
- **User Experience:** While developers can leverage the object model for fine-grained control, translating this into a user-friendly experience requires careful UI/UX design.
- **Interoperability:** As Sui grows, ensuring that its object-centric approach can interoperate with other blockchains or systems that might not understand this model is a significant consideration.

Impact on Sui's Ecosystem:

- **Developer Flexibility:** Developers can build applications with a more nuanced control over assets, leading to innovative use cases in gaming, digital art, or financial instruments where each asset can have unique characteristics.

- **User Empowerment:** Users have a clearer, more direct relationship with their assets, which aligns with Sui's philosophy of user empowerment and asset sovereignty.
- **Scalability of Applications:** The model supports applications that can scale independently, where different components or assets of an application can grow without affecting the performance of others.

The object-centric model is more than just an architectural choice for Sui; it's a fundamental shift in how blockchain can operate, offering a blueprint for scalability and speed that traditional models struggle with. This part has outlined how this model works, its benefits, and the challenges it presents, setting the stage for understanding how Sui leverages this concept to achieve its ambitious goals in the blockchain space.

Part 3: Move Programming Language Integration

Integral to Sui's architecture is the Move programming language, which not only shapes how smart contracts are written but also influences the overall security, efficiency, and functionality of the blockchain. This part delves into how Move is integrated into Sui, its impact on smart contract development, and its role in achieving Sui's core objectives.

Role of Move:

- **Safety by Design:** Move was created with security in mind, aiming to prevent common smart contract vulnerabilities like reentrancy attacks. Its resource model ensures that each asset is treated as a unique object, aligning perfectly with Sui's object-centric approach.

- **Resource-Oriented Programming:** In Move, every piece of data is a resource that must be explicitly managed, preventing duplication or loss of assets. This aligns with Sui's philosophy of clear asset ownership and control.
- **Modularity and Reusability:** Move encourages the development of modular code, allowing developers to build complex systems from simpler, safer components, which is essential for scaling and maintaining large decentralized applications.

Impact on Smart Contracts:

- **Smart Contract Safety:** By using Move, Sui ensures that smart contracts are inherently safer. The language's type system catches many errors at compile-time, reducing the risk of runtime errors that could lead to security breaches.
- **Efficient Execution:** Move's design supports the parallel execution of transactions, complementing Sui's architecture for speed and scalability. This is because operations on different resources can proceed without blocking each other.
- **State Management:** Move's approach to state where each resource has its own lifecycle directly supports Sui's object-centric model,

making state management more intuitive and less error-prone.

- **Gas Optimization:** Move introduces a gas model where costs are predictable and more aligned with the actual computational work done, which helps in managing transaction fees and network load.

Integration with Sui's Architecture:

- **Object-Centric Model:** Move's resource model is a natural fit for Sui's object-centric architecture, allowing developers to define how objects behave, interact, and evolve within the Sui ecosystem.
- **Consensus and Transaction Processing:** Since Move code defines how state changes occur, it's deeply integrated with Sui's consensus mechanism, ensuring that transactions are processed according to the rules set by the smart contracts.
- **Security Layer:** Move acts as an additional security layer for Sui, enforcing rules at the contract level that ensure data integrity and asset ownership, complementing the cryptographic security provided by the blockchain itself.
- **Developer Experience:** By providing a language that's both secure and geared towards the unique needs of blockchain applications, Move reduces the learning curve for developers, encouraging more innovation on the Sui platform.

Challenges and Adaptations:

- **Performance Tuning:** While Move is designed for efficiency, optimizing it for Sui's specific needs, especially in terms of transaction speed and gas costs, required ongoing work and adaptation.
- **Tooling and Ecosystem:** The integration of Move meant developing or adapting tools, IDEs, and libraries to support Move development within Sui's ecosystem, which is an ongoing effort to enhance developer productivity.
- **Community Adoption:** Encouraging developers to adopt Move, especially those accustomed to other smart contract languages, involves significant educational efforts and demonstrating Move's benefits over alternatives.
- **Interoperability:** As Sui aims for broader blockchain interoperability, ensuring Move can interact or be understood by other ecosystems presents both technical and conceptual challenges.

Future Enhancements:

- **Language Evolution:** Move is expected to evolve, potentially adding features for enhanced privacy, more sophisticated asset management, or improved cross-chain interactions.
- **Integration with New Technologies:** As blockchain technology advances, Move's

integration might expand to include new consensus mechanisms, off-chain compute, or zero-knowledge proofs for privacy.
- **Education and Community:** Continuous investment in developer education, hackathons, and community engagement will be key to leveraging Move's full potential within Sui.

The integration of the Move programming language into Sui's architecture is not just a technical choice but a strategic one that aligns with Sui's vision for security, scalability, and user empowerment. This part has explored how Move enhances Sui's capabilities, offering a safer, more efficient platform for smart contract development. By understanding Move's role in Sui, we gain insight into one of the key pillars supporting Sui's ambitious goals in the blockchain industry.

Part 4: Consensus Mechanism

The consensus mechanism is a pivotal element in any blockchain's architecture, determining how transactions are validated and added to the ledger. For Sui, the choice and implementation of its consensus mechanism are crucial in achieving its goals of speed, security, and scalability. This part examines Sui's Delegated Proof-of-Stake (DPoS) system, detailing how it functions, its benefits, and the specific adaptations made to suit Sui's unique architecture.

Delegated Proof-of-Stake (DPoS) Overview:

- **Basic Principles:** In DPoS, token holders vote for a select number of validators (also known as delegates or block producers) who are responsible for creating blocks and maintaining the network's integrity. This system aims to achieve consensus quickly while still maintaining a level of decentralization.
- **Validator Selection:** Sui's DPoS involves stakeholders delegating their stake to validators they trust. These validators then take turns proposing and validating blocks based on their stake and the votes they've received.
- **Transaction Validation:** Validators in Sui process transactions, propose them in blocks, and then these blocks are voted on by other validators to achieve consensus. Only when a supermajority agrees is a block considered finalized.

Achieving Speed and Security:

- **Speed Optimization:** Sui's DPoS is designed for speed. By limiting the number of validators actively producing blocks, consensus can be reached rapidly, leading to near-instant transaction finality. This is crucial for applications requiring real-time transaction processing.
- **Security Measures:** While the number of active validators is limited, Sui implements

additional security measures:

- ○ **Voting:** Validators must vote on each block, reducing the risk of a single validator manipulating the chain.
- ○ **Stake-Based Influence:** The influence of each validator is proportionate to their stake, incentivizing honest behavior since malicious actions could lead to significant financial losses.
- ○ **Slashing:** There are mechanisms in place to penalize ("slash") validators who fail to perform their duties correctly or attempt to act maliciously.
- **Finality:** Sui achieves transaction finality once consensus is reached among validators, which is far quicker than in systems like Proof-of-Work, where multiple confirmations might be needed.

Sui's Adaptations to DPoS:

- **Parallel Consensus:** Sui's architecture allows for parallel processing of transactions, but this also extends to consensus. Multiple validators can work on different sets of transactions simultaneously, speeding up the overall consensus process.
- **Object-Centric Consensus:** Given Sui's object-centric model, consensus isn't just about block validation but also ensuring the correct state of objects. This requires validators to agree not only on transactions but also on the state changes of objects involved.

- **Dynamic Validator Sets:** Sui might implement features where the set of validators can change more frequently than in traditional DPoS setups, allowing for more flexibility and potentially better performance as the network grows.

Challenges and Considerations:

- **Centralization Risks:** While DPoS can be more scalable than PoW, there's always the risk of centralization if only a few entities control the majority of the stake. Sui must balance this through governance and incentive structures.
- **Security Against Attacks:** Even with DPoS, Sui must guard against potential attack vectors like bribing or colluding validators. Continuous monitoring, incentive design, and possibly integrating additional security protocols are necessary.
- **Scalability of Consensus:** As the network scales, ensuring that consensus remains fast and secure with an increasing number of transactions and validators is a significant challenge.
- **User Trust:** Users need to trust the validators they delegate to. Transparency in validator operations, performance metrics, and perhaps even social scoring systems could be implemented to build this trust.

Impact on Sui's Ecosystem:

- **Decentralized Governance:** While not purely decentralized in the traditional sense, DPoS allows for a form of governance where token holders have a say in who validates transactions, potentially leading to a more dynamic and responsive ecosystem.
- **Scalability:** By reducing the computational load required for consensus, Sui can handle more transactions, supporting a broader range of applications without degrading performance.
- **Energy Efficiency:** Compared to PoW, DPoS is significantly more energy-efficient, aligning with Sui's commitment to sustainability.

Sui's consensus mechanism is a tailored version of DPoS, adapted to meet its specific architectural needs and philosophical goals. This part has explored how this consensus mechanism supports Sui's objectives of speed, security, and scalability, while also highlighting the challenges inherent in such a system. Understanding this mechanism is key to appreciating how Sui aims to provide a robust, fast, and secure blockchain platform.

Part 5: Transaction Processing

Transaction processing is where the rubber meets the road in blockchain technology, and Sui's approach to this aspect of its architecture is central to its promise of delivering unmatched speed and scalability. This part delves into how Sui processes transactions, the mechanisms that enable parallel execution, and how it achieves instant finality, setting it apart from many other blockchain platforms.

Parallel Execution:

- **Concept:** Sui's design allows for transactions to be processed in parallel. This is made possible by its object-centric model, where each asset is an independent object. Transactions involving different objects can thus be executed simultaneously without waiting for others to complete.
- **Implementation:** When a transaction is submitted, it's evaluated to determine which objects it affects. If these objects are not involved in other pending transactions, the transaction can proceed independently. This requires sophisticated transaction routing and scheduling algorithms to manage dependencies and ensure no conflicts occur.
- **Benefits:** This parallel processing significantly increases the network's throughput, enabling a high volume of transactions to be processed at once, which is crucial for applications like gaming, DeFi, or any high-frequency transaction environment.

Instant Finality:

- **Definition:** Instant finality means that once a transaction is confirmed by the consensus mechanism, it's considered finalized and immutable. In Sui, this happens almost immediately due to the efficiency of its DPoS consensus.

- **Mechanism:** After a transaction is validated by a group of validators, the consensus process ensures that a supermajority agrees on the transaction's outcome. Once this agreement is reached, the transaction is considered final, with no further confirmations needed.
- **Impact:** This rapid finality is vital for user experience, particularly in scenarios where users need immediate feedback on transactions, like in real-time gaming or urgent financial transfers.

Transaction Lifecycle in Sui:

- **Submission:** Users submit transactions to the network, specifying which objects are involved.
- **Validation:** Validators check the transaction for validity, ensuring the sender has the necessary permissions and that the transaction complies with the rules of the involved objects (as defined by Move smart contracts).
- **Execution:** If valid, the transaction is executed. If it involves multiple objects, they might be processed in parallel if possible.
- **Consensus:** Validators then reach consensus on the outcome of these transactions, ensuring all agree on the new state of affected objects.
- **Commitment:** The new state is committed to the blockchain, and the transaction is considered final.

Handling Complex Transactions:

- **Dependency Management:** For transactions that depend on the outcome of others, Sui's system manages these dependencies, ensuring they're processed in the correct order or are batched appropriately.
- **Batching:** In some cases, transactions might be batched together for efficiency, especially if they involve the same set of objects or are part of a larger operation like a complex DeFi transaction.

Security Considerations:

- **Atomicity:** Transactions are atomic; either they fully execute or not at all, ensuring no partial state changes that could compromise security.
- **Race Conditions:** With parallel execution, managing race conditions where transactions might try to access or modify the same object simultaneously is critical. Sui's architecture includes mechanisms to prevent such conflicts.

Scalability and Performance:

- **Scalability:** By focusing on individual objects, Sui can scale its transaction processing capabilities as the network grows, without a linear increase in computational requirements.
- **Performance Tuning:** The system is designed with performance in mind, from the consensus mechanism to how transactions are queued

and executed, aiming for minimal latency and
high throughput.

Challenges:

- **Consistency:** Ensuring global state
  consistency across the network with parallel
  execution can be complex, requiring robust
  algorithms for state reconciliation.
- **Resource Management:** Efficiently managing
  computational resources among many parallel
  processes is a continuous challenge to
  maintain speed without sacrificing security.
- **User Experience:** While backend processes
  are optimized, ensuring that these
  complexities don't affect user experience or
  complicate development is crucial.

Sui's transaction processing architecture is a
testament to its design philosophy, leveraging parallel
execution and instant finality to offer a blockchain
platform that can handle the demands of modern
digital interactions. This part has outlined how Sui's
approach to transactions not only supports its
scalability and speed objectives but also how it
navigates the inherent challenges of such a system,
providing a foundation for a wide array of
decentralized applications.

Part 6: Network

The network layer of Sui is essential for ensuring that
all components of the blockchain—from transactions
to consensus—are effectively communicated and

coordinated across a decentralized environment. This part explores how Sui's network architecture is designed to support its high-performance goals, maintain security, and facilitate scalability.

Node Structure

Sui's network consists of different types of nodes, each with specific roles:

- **Validators** are responsible for processing transactions, proposing blocks, and reaching consensus. They are selected through the DPoS mechanism, ensuring that only trusted, staked nodes can influence the chain.
- **Full Nodes** maintain a complete copy of the blockchain's state, allowing them to serve data to clients, verify transactions, and support light clients. They don't participate in consensus but are crucial for the network's integrity and accessibility.

Communication Protocols

Efficient communication is key to Sui's speed:

- The network employs optimized protocols for broadcasting transactions, consensus messages, and state updates. This includes using advanced networking techniques to reduce latency and ensure high throughput.
- Sui's design considers the geographical distribution of nodes, aiming for a topology that

minimizes latency in transaction propagation and consensus voting.

Security

Security at the network level involves:

- Ensuring network messages are authenticated and encrypted, protecting against man-in-the-middle attacks and ensuring only authorized nodes participate in network activities.
- Implementing mechanisms to detect and respond to network-level attacks like DDoS, securing the network's availability and integrity.

Scalability

Sui's network architecture is built with scalability in mind:

- The system is designed to handle an increasing number of nodes without proportional degradation in performance, leveraging the object-centric model where state updates can be localized.
- There's potential for future enhancements like network sharding, where different segments of the network could handle different portions of the transaction load, further enhancing scalability.

Interoperability

While focusing on its ecosystem, Sui's network design also considers:

- Future interoperability with other blockchains, potentially through sidechains or cross-chain communication protocols, ensuring Sui can integrate into a broader blockchain landscape.

Challenges

- Balancing decentralization with the need for high-speed, low-latency communication across a global network.
- Ensuring that as the network grows, it remains resilient against various attack vectors, from network congestion to sophisticated cyber threats.

The network architecture of Sui is a critical component that underpins its ability to deliver on its promise of speed, security, and scalability. By crafting a network that supports parallel processing, instant finality, and secure communication, Sui lays the groundwork for a blockchain platform that can scale to meet global demands while maintaining the integrity and performance expected from a next-generation blockchain. This part has shown how network design in Sui is not just about connecting nodes but about enabling the entire ecosystem to function at peak efficiency.

Part 7: Storage and State Management

Sui's approach to storage and state management is pivotal to its performance and scalability. By treating every piece of data as an object, Sui redefines how blockchain state is handled, allowing for operations that are both secure and efficient.

At the core of Sui's storage system is the object-centric model, where each asset or piece of data is an independent entity with its own lifecycle and state. This design means that instead of maintaining a single, monolithic state, Sui manages a vast array of objects, each with its own set of rules for interaction. This approach significantly reduces the computational load when processing transactions, as changes are localized to specific objects rather than affecting the entire state.

The storage layer in Sui is optimized for rapid access and updates. When a transaction modifies an object, only that object's state needs updating, which minimizes the data that must be propagated across the network. This is crucial for achieving high transaction throughput and low latency. Sui employs sophisticated indexing and caching strategies to ensure that accessing or updating an object's state is as fast as possible, supporting the blockchain's speed objectives.

State consistency is another critical aspect. Given the parallel execution of transactions, ensuring that all nodes agree on the current state of every object is vital. Sui addresses this through consensus mechanisms that not only validate transactions but also ensure that the final state of each object after a transaction is uniformly recognized across the network. This involves complex algorithms for conflict resolution and state reconciliation, where multiple transactions might try to modify or depend on the same object.

Security in state management is paramount. Each object's lifecycle is governed by smart contracts written in Move, which ensures that only valid state transitions are possible. This prevents unauthorized or erroneous changes to an object's state, adding a layer of security that's intrinsic to the blockchain's operation rather than an afterthought.

For scalability, Sui's storage design allows for growth without bottlenecks. As more objects are added, the increase in data doesn't necessarily lead to performance degradation because of how operations are isolated to individual objects. This model supports Sui's vision of being able to scale to billions of users and assets, with each object managed independently.

However, managing such a distributed, object-centric state brings its challenges. Ensuring that the state remains consistent, especially under high load or during network partitions, requires robust mechanisms. Additionally, as the number of objects grows, so does the complexity of managing them, necessitating advanced database technologies and algorithms.

In summary, Sui's storage and state management strategy is a testament to its innovative approach, aligning with its architectural philosophy of providing a blockchain that's fast, secure, and scalable. By focusing on object-centric state management, Sui not only enhances its performance metrics but also sets a new standard for how blockchain data can be handled, ensuring that its ecosystem can evolve and expand without compromising on its core values.

Part 8: Security

Security is the bedrock upon which trust in Sui's blockchain is built. From its inception, Sui has been designed with a security-first mindset, integrating advanced cryptographic techniques and consensus mechanisms to safeguard transactions, data, and the network itself.

Sui's security begins with its consensus mechanism, Delegated Proof-of-Stake (DPoS), which inherently protects against many of the vulnerabilities traditional Proof-of-Work systems face, like 51% attacks, by distributing trust among a set of validators. However, Sui goes beyond this with additional layers of security:

The Move programming language plays a crucial role in Sui's security architecture. By enforcing a resource model where all data is treated as unique, Move prevents common smart contract vulnerabilities such as reentrancy attacks or unintended duplication of assets. The language's type system catches many programming errors at compile-time, significantly reducing the risk of runtime vulnerabilities.

Cryptography is another pillar of Sui's security. Sui utilizes state-of-the-art cryptographic methods for transaction verification, ensuring that only the rightful owner can initiate changes to an asset's state. This includes the use of digital signatures for authentication, hash functions for data integrity, and potentially zero-knowledge proofs for privacy-preserving transactions. These cryptographic measures ensure that even if a transaction's details are public, the privacy of the parties involved can be maintained when desired.

The network's security is further enhanced by measures to protect against network-level attacks. This includes network partitioning strategies to maintain consensus in the face of network failures, DDoS mitigation techniques, and secure communication protocols to prevent man-in-the-middle attacks. Sui's architecture also considers the physical security of validator nodes, encouraging geographic distribution to prevent localized risks from affecting the network as a whole.

Sui's approach to security also involves proactive measures like regular security audits, both internal and by third-party experts, to identify and patch vulnerabilities. The blockchain's open-source nature allows for community scrutiny, which can be an additional layer of security through collective vigilance.

However, security in a blockchain like Sui comes with unique challenges. Balancing speed with security means constantly innovating to ensure that the rapid transaction processing doesn't open new vulnerabilities. As Sui scales, maintaining security without centralization is a significant concern, requiring ongoing adjustments to governance and validator selection processes.

Moreover, Sui must navigate the evolving landscape of regulatory compliance without compromising its security model. This includes implementing features for identity verification or transaction monitoring where necessary, ensuring the blockchain can operate globally while adhering to diverse legal frameworks.

In essence, Sui's security strategy is not just about protecting against known threats but about creating an ecosystem where security is woven into every aspect of the platform's operation. By prioritizing security in its architecture, Sui aims to provide a blockchain where users can trust the integrity of their transactions and the safety of their digital assets, setting a high bar for what blockchain security can achieve.

Part 9: Scalability Architecture

Scalability is not just an afterthought in Sui's architecture; it's a foundational principle that permeates every aspect of its design. Sui's approach to scalability is multi-faceted, aiming to support a blockchain that can grow with demand, handle billions of transactions, and serve a vast ecosystem of applications without compromising on speed or security.

Central to Sui's scalability is its object-centric model. By allowing transactions to operate on individual objects, Sui can process multiple transactions in parallel. This parallelism inherently increases the network's capacity to handle transactions, as changes to one object don't necessarily block or delay changes to another, assuming there's no direct dependency.

The consensus mechanism, Delegated Proof-of-Stake (DPoS), is tailored for scalability in Sui. By selecting validators based on stake and delegation, Sui ensures that consensus can be reached quickly among a manageable number of nodes, which is crucial for scaling. This approach avoids the energy and time costs associated with Proof-of-Work systems, allowing for a more scalable consensus process.

Sui's use of the Move programming language also contributes to its scalability. Move's resource model ensures that smart contracts are executed efficiently, minimizing computational overhead and storage requirements. This efficiency is key when scaling up, as it means that more complex contracts or applications can be run without significantly increasing the load on the network.

The network layer of Sui is designed with scalability in mind. The architecture allows for the addition of more nodes as the network grows, ensuring that performance scales horizontally. This is particularly important for maintaining low latency and high throughput as user numbers increase.

Looking forward, Sui's architecture lays the groundwork for future scalability enhancements like sharding. Although not implemented at launch, the design of Sui's state management and consensus could naturally support sharding, where different parts of the network manage different segments of the state, dramatically increasing the blockchain's capacity.

However, scalability brings its own set of challenges. Ensuring that the network remains decentralized as it grows is a continuous balancing act. Sui must innovate to keep the validator set diverse and prevent centralization of power. Additionally, as the number of objects increases, managing their lifecycle, ensuring consistency across the network, and providing quick access to them becomes more complex.

Another aspect is the scalability of applications built on Sui. While the blockchain itself might scale, applications need to be designed with scalability in mind, leveraging Sui's capabilities like parallel transaction processing. This requires developer education and the provision of tools and best practices to build scalable dApps.

In summary, Sui's scalability architecture is a testament to its forward-thinking design, aiming to create a blockchain that can evolve alongside technological and user demands. By focusing on parallel processing, efficient consensus, and an object-centric approach, Sui sets a new standard for what scalable blockchain infrastructure can look like, ensuring it can support the next generation of decentralized applications and services.

Part 10: Interoperability and Ecosystem Integration

Interoperability and ecosystem integration are crucial for Sui to not only thrive as a standalone blockchain but also to be part of a larger, interconnected web of blockchain technologies. This part explores how Sui facilitates interactions with other systems, supports a vibrant developer ecosystem, and integrates with external services to broaden its utility and adoption.

Interoperability:

Sui acknowledges that no single blockchain can exist in isolation if it aims to be part of the future of digital finance and data management. Here's how Sui approaches interoperability:

- **Cross-Chain Communication:** While not immediately implemented, Sui's architecture is designed with the potential for cross-chain interactions in mind. This could include mechanisms like bridge protocols or direct blockchain-to-blockchain communication, allowing assets or data to move between Sui and other blockchains.
- **Standardization:** Sui aims to align with emerging blockchain standards and protocols, ensuring that it can communicate with other networks using common frameworks, like those proposed by the Inter-Blockchain Communication (IBC) protocol or other interoperability standards.

- **Sidechains and Layer 2 Solutions:** The architecture of Sui supports the possibility of integrating or supporting sidechains for specific use cases or layer 2 solutions for scaling, which can interact with the main Sui chain, thereby enhancing interoperability.

Ecosystem Integration:

- **Developer Tools and APIs:** Sui provides a rich set of APIs and developer tools to facilitate building on its platform. These include SDKs, libraries, and frameworks that abstract the complexities of blockchain development, making it easier for developers to integrate their applications with Sui.
- **Wallet Support:** Ensuring that wallets can easily interact with Sui is crucial. This involves not just native wallets but also integrating with popular multi-chain wallets, enabling seamless asset management across different ecosystems.
- **Oracles and External Data Feeds:** For applications requiring real-world data, Sui's ecosystem supports integration with oracle services, providing smart contracts with off-chain data securely and reliably.
- **Decentralized Exchanges (DEXs) and DeFi Platforms:** By fostering an environment where DEXs and DeFi protocols can be built or integrated, Sui aims to become a hub for financial innovation, where assets from Sui can interact with those from other chains or traditional finance.

Community and Ecosystem Growth:

- **Incentive Programs:** Sui incentivizes developers through grants, hackathons, and other programs to build on its platform, fostering a rich ecosystem of applications.
- **Educational Initiatives:** To support growth, Sui invests in education, providing resources, workshops, and documentation to lower the entry barrier for developers and users alike.
- **Partnerships:** Strategic partnerships with other blockchain projects, tech companies, or traditional businesses can enhance Sui's utility, offering new use cases and integrations that extend its reach.

Challenges:

- **Technical Complexity:** Achieving seamless interoperability without compromising security or performance is technically challenging. Sui must continuously innovate to ensure that cross-chain operations are as secure and efficient as on-chain activities.
- **Regulatory Navigation:** As Sui interacts with other ecosystems, it must navigate an increasingly complex regulatory landscape, ensuring compliance across jurisdictions.
- **Market Adoption:** For interoperability to be meaningful, there must be market demand for assets or data moving between chains, which depends on both Sui's and its partners' adoption rates.

- **Standardization:** The blockchain space lacks universal standards for interoperability, so Sui must be proactive in contributing to or adapting to emerging standards.

Sui's approach to interoperability and ecosystem integration is about creating a blockchain that isn't just a standalone entity but part of a larger, synergistic network. By focusing on developer tools, cross-chain communication, and community engagement, Sui positions itself as a platform where innovation can flourish, assets can move freely, and the benefits of blockchain technology can be shared across different digital ecosystems. This part highlights how Sui's architecture is designed not just for its own success but for the success of the broader blockchain landscape.

Part 11: Performance Metrics and Benchmarks

Understanding the performance of Sui in real-world scenarios is critical to assessing its viability and potential impact in the blockchain industry. This part focuses on the performance metrics and benchmarks that define Sui's capabilities in terms of speed, scalability, and reliability, contrasting these with other blockchain platforms where possible.

Sui's architecture is engineered for high throughput and low latency, aiming to process transactions at a speed that rivals or exceeds traditional financial systems. The primary metric here is transactions per second (TPS), where Sui's design allows for significant parallelism in transaction processing, potentially outstripping many existing blockchains. This is due to its object-centric model, which permits multiple transactions to be executed simultaneously when they don't conflict.

Latency, or the time from transaction submission to confirmation, is another key performance indicator. Sui's consensus mechanism, coupled with its approach to instant finality, means transactions can be confirmed almost immediately, providing users with a near-real-time experience. This low latency is particularly important for applications like gaming, where delays can detract from user experience, or in financial trading where timing is crucial.

Scalability is measured not just by how many transactions Sui can process now but how well it can maintain or increase performance as the user base and transaction volume grow. Here, Sui's architecture shines by allowing for horizontal scaling; as more validators or nodes join the network, the capacity to process transactions can increase without a corresponding increase in latency or decrease in security.

Gas fees, which are the costs associated with transactions on Sui, are another performance aspect. Sui's design aims for predictable and low gas costs by optimizing how computational resources are used, particularly through Move's efficient execution model. This makes Sui more accessible for microtransactions or applications where high fees would be prohibitive.

Reliability, measured through network uptime, consensus consistency, and the robustness against attacks, is also a benchmark for Sui. The DPoS consensus mechanism, while potentially more centralized than others like PoW, is designed for high reliability and resilience, with mechanisms in place to penalize or remove dishonest validators.

Comparative benchmarks against other blockchains like Ethereum, Solana, or even traditional payment systems provide context for Sui's performance. While direct comparisons can be complex due to different architectures and use cases, Sui often aims to outperform in areas of speed and scalability, focusing on being a platform for mainstream adoption.

However, these metrics are not without their challenges. As with any blockchain, scaling to meet global demand while maintaining these performance benchmarks requires ongoing innovation and adaptation. Network congestion, for instance, could impact performance if not managed correctly, and real-world conditions might not always align with theoretical maximums.

Moreover, benchmarks are only as good as the scenarios they're tested under. Sui's performance in production, under stress from high transaction volumes or during network anomalies, will truly define its capabilities. Therefore, continuous monitoring, real-world testing, and community feedback are integral to ensuring that performance metrics translate into a reliable user experience.

In conclusion, Sui's performance metrics and benchmarks set ambitious goals for what blockchain can achieve in terms of speed, cost, and reliability. By focusing on these areas, Sui not only positions itself as a competitor to existing blockchains but also as a potential disruptor in how digital transactions and asset management are conducted globally.

Chapter 4: Understanding Move: The Programming Language of Sui

Part 1: Origin of Move

The story of Move begins in the halls of Meta, back when the company was exploring the vast, untapped potential of blockchain technology with its ambitious project, Libra, later rebranded as Diem. This was a time when the blockchain world was grappling with numerous challenges, from scalability bottlenecks to security vulnerabilities that plagued smart contracts. The creation of Move was a response to these challenges, aiming to craft a language that could serve as the backbone for a blockchain that was not only secure but also scalable and user-friendly.

Move was conceived by Sam Blackshear and his team at Meta, with the primary mission to address the fundamental issues that had become evident in existing blockchain and smart contract platforms. The most notorious of these were smart contract vulnerabilities, particularly reentrancy attacks, which had led to significant financial losses in the Ethereum ecosystem. But beyond security, there was a clear vision to design a language that could support high transaction throughput, necessary for any blockchain aiming to serve millions, if not billions, of users.

The philosophy behind Move was to treat data not as amorphous bytes in memory but as 'resources'—unique, identifiable, and managed entities within the blockchain. This was a paradigm shift from how most blockchain platforms handled state and data. In traditional blockchains, assets or data could be replicated or lost through programming errors, but Move's resource model would ensure each piece of data or asset was uniquely owned and controlled, preventing duplication or unintended loss.

The design of Move incorporated lessons from various programming paradigms, borrowing from Rust for its safety features, but it went further by introducing concepts like linear types for resources. This meant that once a resource was used in one place, it could not be referenced or used elsewhere until relinquished, ensuring a form of guaranteed ownership and control over assets. This was a groundbreaking approach to prevent common coding errors that could lead to security breaches.

As the Diem project progressed, Move was refined, becoming more than just a language; it was a manifestation of a philosophy about how blockchains should operate. It was designed with an inherent focus on safety, ensuring that many potential errors would be caught at compile time rather than runtime, a significant advantage when dealing with financial transactions where even a single error could have catastrophic consequences.

However, the journey of Move took an unexpected turn when Meta decided to pivot away from Diem due to regulatory and political pressures. This could have spelled the end for Move, but instead, it found a new home with the creation of Mysten Labs by former Diem engineers, including Sam Blackshear himself.

Mysten Labs aimed to realize the full potential of Move by integrating it into their new blockchain project, Sui.

The transition of Move from Diem to Sui was not just a transfer of code but a transformation of its purpose and application. Sui was conceived as a blockchain that could support the digital economy of the future, where every transaction, every digital asset, could be managed with unprecedented speed, security, and efficiency. Move was pivotal in this vision, offering a programming environment that could ensure these qualities.

In Sui, Move was adapted to fit into an object-centric architecture, where every asset or piece of data was an object with its own lifecycle, managed by rules defined in Move scripts. This alignment was perfect; Move's resource model was essentially an object model in disguise, where each resource was an object with defined behaviors and constraints.

The integration of Move into Sui also meant revisiting its design to optimize for Sui's unique requirements. This included enhancing Move's capabilities for parallel transaction processing, a feature crucial for Sui's scalability ambitions. Move's modularity was further exploited to allow for the creation of complex smart contracts from smaller, safer components, offering developers flexibility while maintaining high security standards.

Move's development wasn't without its challenges. The language had to balance being secure and performant while also being accessible to developers familiar with other programming languages. This meant creating a comprehensive ecosystem around Move—tools, documentation, and community support—to lower the entry barrier for new developers.

Moreover, Move's evolution within Sui was guided by a commitment to open-source development, inviting the broader community to contribute, review, and improve upon the language. This openness was not just about code but about fostering a community of practice around Move, ensuring it could adapt and grow with the blockchain industry's needs.

As Move became more entrenched in Sui's architecture, it began to influence not just how smart contracts were written but also how developers conceptualized blockchain interactions. It encouraged thinking in terms of resources, ownership, and safety by design, principles that would become central to the ethos of Sui and its community.

The journey of Move from its inception at Meta, through the trials of Diem, to its rebirth with Sui, illustrates a remarkable tale of innovation in the face of adversity. It's a testament to how a programming language can be more than just syntax and semantics; it can be a vehicle for a new way of thinking about digital assets, security, and scalability in the blockchain space.

Move's story is one of resilience, adaptation, and vision, setting the stage for what would become one of the most intriguing developments in blockchain technology. As we delve deeper into the intricacies of Move in the following sections, we'll explore how this language has not only shaped Sui but how it's poised to influence the future of blockchain programming at large.

Part 2: Fundamentals of Move

Move, as the programming language of Sui, introduces a unique set of principles and paradigms that drastically differ from traditional programming languages used in blockchain contexts. At its core, Move is designed to mitigate the complexities and vulnerabilities inherent in blockchain programming, offering a safer, more intuitive environment for developers to create smart contracts that govern digital assets.

The philosophy of Move revolves around the concept of resources. Unlike other languages where data might be treated as mutable values that can be copied or lost, Move conceptualizes data as resources—unique, immutable entities with a clear lifecycle from creation to destruction. This resource model is central to understanding how Move functions within Sui's ecosystem.

In Move, every piece of data that represents something valuable or critical to the state of the blockchain is treated as a resource. This includes digital assets like tokens, NFTs, or any data structure representing a state or function within a smart contract. Resources in Move are characterized by uniqueness, ensuring no duplication; ownership, where resources are owned by accounts; linear types, which control resource usage to prevent misuse; and explicit destruction, only under conditions set by the smart contract. This model fundamentally changes how developers think about and manage state within a blockchain, aligning perfectly with Sui's object-centric architecture where each asset is an object with its own lifecycle managed by Move scripts.

Move's type system is another cornerstone of its design, aimed at ensuring safety at compile time. It employs static typing where all variables must be explicitly typed, reducing runtime errors by catching type mismatches early. Resource types enforce rules on how resources can be managed, while generics allow for flexible and reusable code structures without compromising safety. This strong type system addresses many security vulnerabilities before the code even runs on the blockchain, preventing issues like reentrancy attacks by ensuring a resource cannot be used if it's already in use.

Move encourages modularity through its module system. This approach promotes code reuse, reduces redundancy, and enhances the maintainability and upgradability of smart contracts. Modules encapsulate functionalities, defining resources, functions, and structures with access control to ensure sensitive operations are only performed by authorized code.

Safety by design is at the heart of Move's philosophy. It eliminates common vulnerabilities by enforcing strict resource management rules, performs compile-time checks for many potential runtime errors, and ensures memory safety, drawing inspiration from languages like Rust. This focus on safety means that many of the programming pitfalls seen in other smart contract languages are significantly mitigated in Move.

Move's syntax might be familiar to those who know languages like Rust or C++, but it includes additional constructs tailored for blockchain, such as resource declaration, function and method definitions with special resource handling annotations, pattern matching for handling different resource states, and access modifiers for controlling visibility and access within modules.

The design of Move also contributes to Sui's scalability. By treating assets as resources with well-defined lifecycles, it enables parallel execution of transactions, allowing for increased throughput when transactions affect different resources. Efficient state management is achieved since resource manipulation is localized, and the gas model becomes more predictable, tying costs directly to resource actions rather than arbitrary computation.

Despite its benefits, Move does present a learning curve for developers. They must shift from thinking in terms of mutable state to managing resources, which can be a significant conceptual shift. Additionally, while Move's syntax might be familiar, its unique features require new learning. However, the Sui ecosystem has been proactive in supporting developers through comprehensive documentation, educational resources, improved tooling, and community support.

Move's integration with Sui is seamless because both are designed with similar principles in mind. Move's resource model aligns with Sui's object-centric state management, enhancing transaction safety, and supporting Sui's consensus mechanism by ensuring predictable and verifiable state changes. This integration isn't just about adopting a new language but about embracing a new way of thinking about digital assets, their lifecycle, and how they interact within a blockchain ecosystem.

Move represents a significant leap forward in blockchain programming languages. By focusing on resources as the core of its model, it not only enhances security but also paves the way for more scalable and efficient blockchain applications. This part of our journey into Move has laid out the foundational concepts, showing how these principles manifest in practical applications, developer experiences, and the future of blockchain development.

Part 3: Move in Action

The true power of Move lies not just in its theoretical underpinnings but in its practical application within the Sui ecosystem. This part explores how developers can use Move to write, compile, and deploy smart contracts that leverage Sui's unique architecture for secure, scalable blockchain applications. We'll walk through the process from a developer's perspective, showcasing how Move's principles of safety, resource management, and modularity come to life in real-world scenarios.

Getting Started with Move

To begin using Move, developers first need to set up their development environment. This involves installing the Sui toolkit, which includes the Move compiler, a testnet node, or access to Sui's mainnet. Once the environment is set up, developers can start writing Move code, which generally involves defining modules, resources, and functions.

A simple Move module might look like this:

```move
module example::my_module {
    use sui::object::{Self, UID};
    use sui::transfer;
    use sui::tx_context::{Self, TxContext};

    // Define a resource (like a token)
    struct MyResource has key, store {
        id: UID,
        value: u64
    }

    // Function to create a new MyResource
    public entry fun create(ctx: &mut TxContext) {
        let resource = MyResource {
            id: object::new(ctx),
            value: 0
        };
        transfer::transfer(resource, tx_context::sender(ctx));
    }
```

```
    // Function to increment the value of MyResource
    public entry fun increment(resource: &mut MyResource) {
        resource.value = resource.value + 1;
    }
}
```

This module defines a resource called `MyResource`, which could represent something like a token or any digital asset, with an ID and a value. It includes functions to create this resource and increment its value, demonstrating basic operations that can be performed on Move resources.

Writing Smart Contracts

Move smart contracts are written within modules. Each module can contain multiple resources, functions, and structs. Here's a deeper look into how Move supports smart contract development:

- **Resource Management:** When defining resources, developers must specify if the resource `has key` (meaning it can be stored on-chain with a unique ID) or `has store` (allowing it to be stored in another resource or passed between functions). This granularity in resource definition ensures clear ownership and control.
- **Functionality:** Functions in Move can be public (accessible from outside the module), private (only within the module), or entry (can be called directly by transactions). Entry functions are particularly important in Sui as

they act as the interface between user actions and blockchain state changes.
- **Safety Checks:** Move enforces safety through its type system. For example, trying to manipulate a resource in a way not defined by its type will fail at compile time, preventing many common errors.

Compiling Move Code

Compilation is where Move's safety features shine. The Move compiler not only translates the high-level code into bytecode that runs on the Sui VM but also performs exhaustive checks for:

- **Type Safety:** Ensuring that only allowed operations are performed on resources.
- **Resource Ownership:** Verifying that resources are handled according to the rules of their type.
- **Access Control:** Checking that functions are called with the proper permissions.

Errors caught during compilation are detailed, helping developers to understand exactly where and why their code might be unsafe or incorrect. This process significantly reduces the likelihood of deploying contracts with vulnerabilities.

Deploying Contracts

Deploying a Move module to Sui involves:

- **Packaging:** The compiled bytecode along with metadata is packaged into a module that can be deployed.
- **Publishing:** Using Sui's CLI or API, the module is published to the blockchain. This action is a transaction itself, requiring gas, and once published, the module's code is immutable, ensuring that the logic cannot be altered post-deployment.
- **Interaction:** Once deployed, users or other contracts can interact with the module's public or entry functions through transactions.

Here's a simple example of how a user might interact with the `my_module` we defined:

```bash
sui client call --package <PACKAGE_ID> --module my_module --function create --gas-budget 1000
```

This command would call the `create` function, deploying a new `MyResource` to the user's account.

Practical Example: A Simple Token

Let's extend our example to create a basic token system using Move:

```move
module example::token {
    use sui::object::{Self, UID};
    use sui::transfer;
    use sui::tx_context::{Self, TxContext};
```

```
// Define the token resource
struct Token has key, store {
    id: UID,
    amount: u64,
}

// Mint new tokens
public entry fun mint(amount: u64, ctx: &mut TxContext) {
    let token = Token {
        id: object::new(ctx),
        amount,
    };
    transfer::transfer(token, tx_context::sender(ctx));
}

// Transfer tokens
public entry fun transfer(token: Token, recipient: address,
ctx: &mut TxContext) {
    transfer::transfer(token, recipient);
}

// Burn tokens (destroy them)
public entry fun burn(token: Token) {
    let Token { id, amount: _ } = token;
    object::delete(id);
}
}
```

This module introduces a token system where tokens can be minted, transferred, and burned. Here, Move's resource model ensures:

- **Uniqueness:** Each token object is unique due to its UID.
- **Ownership:** Tokens are explicitly transferred between addresses, preventing unauthorized access.

- **Lifecycle Management:** Tokens can be created and destroyed (burned) under controlled conditions.

Handling Complex Scenarios

Move's design excels in handling complex scenarios where state changes must be atomic and safe. Consider a scenario where tokens are used in a game where players can stake tokens to gain rewards:

```move
module example::game {
    use sui::object::{Self, UID};
    use sui::transfer;
    use sui::tx_context::{Self, TxContext};
    use example::token::{Self, Token};

    struct StakedToken has key {
        id: UID,
        token: Token,
        reward: u64
    }

    // Stake a token
    public entry fun stake(token: Token, ctx: &mut TxContext) {
        let staked = StakedToken {
            id: object::new(ctx),
            token,
            reward: 0
        };
        transfer::transfer(staked, tx_context::sender(ctx));
    }

    // Unstake and claim reward
    public entry fun unstake(staked: StakedToken, ctx: &mut TxContext) {
```

```
    let StakedToken { id, token, reward } = staked;
    // Here you would calculate and distribute the reward
    // For simplicity, we'll just transfer the token back
    transfer::transfer(token, tx_context::sender(ctx));
    object::delete(id);
  }
}
```

This example demonstrates how Move manages state transitions safely, ensuring that the staked token cannot be used elsewhere while staked, and upon unstaking, the reward mechanism can be implemented securely.

Parallel Transaction Execution

One of Sui's strengths is its ability to execute transactions in parallel. Move supports this by ensuring that transactions are independent unless they explicitly depend on the same resource. For instance, if two users stake tokens, these operations can happen simultaneously without conflict, increasing the blockchain's throughput.

Debugging and Testing

Move provides tools for debugging and testing:

- **Unit Testing:** Move modules can include unit tests written in Move, allowing developers to ensure individual functions behave as expected.
- **Simulated Transactions:** Before deploying to the live network, developers can simulate

transactions to see how they would affect the state, catching potential issues in a safe environment.

Community and Ecosystem

The Move community around Sui is growing, contributing to:

- **Libraries:** Standard libraries for common functionalities, reducing the need to write everything from scratch.
- **Frameworks:** Higher-level abstractions that make building complex applications easier.
- **Tooling:** From IDE plugins to profilers, the ecosystem is expanding to support developer productivity.

Challenges and Considerations

While Move offers many advantages, developers must consider:

- **Learning Curve:** The paradigm shift to resource-based programming requires time to master.
- **Performance Optimization:** Understanding how to write Move code that minimizes gas usage is crucial for scalable applications.
- **Security:** Although Move is designed for safety, developers must still be vigilant, especially with complex logic that might not be caught by compile-time checks.

Future of Move Development

As Sui and Move evolve:

- **Language Enhancements:** New features might be added to Move to support emerging blockchain use cases, like privacy-preserving computations or more complex financial instruments.
- **Integration with Other Technologies:** Move might see integration with off-chain compute or other blockchain networks, broadening its application scope.
- **Education and Adoption:** Continuous efforts will be made to educate developers and encourage adoption, ensuring a vibrant community of Move developers.

Move in action within Sui showcases a new era of blockchain programming where safety, efficiency, and scalability are not afterthoughts but foundational elements of the language. By walking through the process of writing, compiling, and deploying smart contracts, we see how Move's design principles translate into practical benefits for developers and users alike. This exploration into 'Move in Action' not only demonstrates the language's capabilities but also invites developers to innovate within this secure and performant environment, pushing the boundaries of what blockchain applications can achieve.

Part 4: Safety and Security Features

Move was conceived with a primary focus on enhancing the security of smart contracts, addressing the vulnerabilities that have historically plagued blockchain ecosystems. This part delves into the myriad of safety and security features intrinsic to Move, explaining how they collectively contribute to a safer blockchain development environment within the Sui ecosystem.

The cornerstone of Move's security is its resource model. Unlike traditional programming where data can be mutable, copied, or lost, leading to potential security breaches, Move treats all significant data as resources. Each resource is unique, identified by a unique ID, ensuring no duplication or double-spending. Ownership is explicit, meaning only the owner of a resource can modify or transfer it, providing precision and security in asset management. Move utilizes linear types to ensure resources are explicitly handled throughout their lifecycle, significantly reducing the chance of accidental data loss or unauthorized access. Additionally, Move's type system enforces safety through static typing, where type mismatches are caught at compile time, drastically reducing runtime errors. Resource types dictate how resources can interact, ensuring operations are safe by design.

Move's design inherently prevents several common smart contract vulnerabilities. It mitigates reentrancy attacks by ensuring a resource cannot be accessed if it's already in use, preventing scenarios where a function is called multiple times before its first invocation completes. Move handles integer overflow and underflow conditions safely, either preventing them or managing them predictably. Unintended state changes are minimized with resources at the core of state management, making state alterations more deliberate. Access control is managed through function annotations, ensuring only authorized code can perform sensitive operations.

Compile-time safety checks in Move are rigorous. The compiler verifies type correctness for every operation, ensuring they match with the type constraints of the involved resources. It also checks for correct resource usage, ensuring no resource is left unhandled or used improperly. Move distinguishes between functions that alter state and those that do not, aiding developers in writing safer code by understanding the impact of their functions.

Memory safety in Move takes inspiration from languages like Rust. Move's ownership model prevents references to resources that have been destroyed or moved, and ensures no use-after-free errors since resources must be explicitly returned or transferred once used.

Move's modular approach enhances security by promoting encapsulation, organizing code into modules to keep sensitive logic within well-defined boundaries, reducing exposure to external manipulation. This modularity also supports reusability, allowing secure, well-tested code to be employed across different contracts without rewriting potentially error-prone logic.

The safety of Move extends to transaction execution, ensuring atomicity where each transaction is either fully executed or not at all, thus preventing partial state changes that could compromise security. Consistency is maintained through the resource model, ensuring all state changes align with the defined rules for each resource, keeping the blockchain state's integrity intact.

Move also encourages secure development practices. Its structure facilitates effective static analysis, which can verify the security properties of smart contracts before they're deployed. The language includes capabilities for writing unit tests directly within modules, fostering a culture of testing critical for security.

However, Move's security comes with challenges. The complexity of managing resources and state transitions can be demanding for developers. As new attack vectors emerge, Move must adapt, potentially through language updates or additional security libraries. Ensuring developers understand and leverage Move's safety features is an ongoing educational challenge.

Move benefits from being part of an open-source ecosystem, where community scrutiny can catch issues that might be missed by developers. Regular security audits by both the Sui team and the community help maintain and enhance Move's security. Collaboration within the community leads to shared knowledge, tools, and best practices, further bolstering security.

Move's approach to safety and security is transformative for blockchain development. By making these aspects foundational, Move reduces the risk of common vulnerabilities and encourages a culture where security is integral to every line of code. This exploration has shown how these features work in practice, offering developers a toolset that inherently promotes safer blockchain applications. As Move evolves, its commitment to security will likely shape the future of blockchain programming, setting a new standard for smart contract safety.

Part 5: Performance and Scalability

Move's design is not only about security but also about enabling Sui to be one of the most performant and scalable blockchain platforms. This part explores how Move contributes to Sui's goals of high throughput, low latency, and efficient resource usage, setting the stage for applications that can scale to serve millions or even billions of users.

A pivotal contribution of Move to scalability is its support for parallel transaction execution. Move's resource model allows transactions to be processed in parallel when they affect different resources. Since each resource in Move is an independent entity, transactions that don't interfere with each other's resources can be executed simultaneously, reducing the typical bottleneck where transactions are processed sequentially. This is achieved by ensuring transactions are only serialized when they depend on the same resource, enhancing overall system throughput.

Move's approach to state management is crucial for scalability. When a transaction modifies a resource, only that specific resource's state needs updating, not the entire state of the blockchain. This localized state change reduces the computational load and storage requirements for each transaction. The modular state approach further enhances efficiency by allowing changes to one part of the state without necessitating a global update, promoting a more streamlined state management system.

Regarding gas optimization, Move's resource model directly influences how gas is calculated. Operations on resources are clear and predictable, allowing for more accurate gas pricing. This contrasts with other platforms where gas might be less predictable due to complex state transitions. Gas is charged based on resource manipulation rather than just computational steps, aligning costs more closely with the actual impact on the blockchain's state.

The modularity of Move contributes to performance. Developers can build complex applications from smaller, already optimized modules, reducing redundant code and ensuring efficiency. Additionally, modules can be upgraded or replaced without affecting other parts of the system, allowing for performance improvements over time without necessitating large-scale rewrites.

Move's integration with Sui's architecture further boosts performance. Its deterministic behavior ensures that validators can quickly reach consensus on transaction outcomes, contributing to Sui's instant finality. The alignment of Move's resource model with Sui's object-centric architecture, where each asset is an object, facilitates direct performance benefits like parallel execution.

However, while Move offers significant scalability advantages, it also faces challenges. As the number of resources grows, managing them efficiently becomes more complex. Move addresses this through its type system and resource lifecycle management. The network layer must also scale alongside Move's optimizations, with Sui's broader architecture, including its consensus mechanism, playing a crucial role. Developer practices are vital; to fully leverage Move's scalability, developers must adopt practices that minimize unnecessary resource operations and understand their code's performance impact.

Looking to the future, Move's evolution might include advanced resource management for even more granular control, performance-oriented features tailored for specific use cases, and better integration with or delegation to off-chain computations, reducing on-chain complexity for certain operations.

Performance in Move and Sui is measured through metrics like transactions per second (TPS), where Move's design aims to enable high TPS through parallel execution; latency, where instant finality helps reduce the time from transaction submission to confirmation; and gas efficiency, ensuring transactions can be executed with minimal cost, promoting scalability for microtransactions.

The performance of Move within Sui is not just a result of its design but also a community effort. Developers contribute optimization libraries that reduce performance overhead, share best practices for writing efficient Move code, and provide feedback that leads to language and ecosystem improvements, directly impacting scalability and performance as the network grows.

Move's design principles are fundamentally aligned with the goals of performance and scalability in blockchain technology. By enabling parallel execution, optimizing gas costs, and providing a framework for efficient state management, Move not only supports but actively enhances Sui's scalability ambitions. This part has explored how Move's features contribute to these goals, highlighting the importance of developer practices, community involvement, and ongoing evolution of the language to maintain and improve performance as the network scales. As we continue to explore Move, we see it not just as a language but as a key enabler for the next generation of blockchain applications.

Part 6: Move's Integration with Sui's Architecture

The integration of Move into Sui's architecture is a testament to how both were designed with complementary philosophies, aiming to create a blockchain that's not only secure and scalable but also user-friendly and developer-centric. This part explores how Move's unique features are woven into Sui's fabric, enhancing its capabilities and defining its operational paradigm.

Move was specifically chosen for Sui due to its alignment with Sui's object-centric model. In Sui, every piece of data or asset is an object with its own state, lifecycle, and set of rules for interaction, which mirrors Move's resource model. This synergy allows for a seamless integration where Move's resources directly correspond to Sui's objects, providing a natural fit for managing state and performing transactions.

State Management and Object Lifecycle

In Sui, state management is not about a monolithic ledger but about managing a collection of objects. Move's resource model supports this by defining how these objects can be created, modified, and destroyed:

- When a smart contract written in Move interacts with an object in Sui, it does so by manipulating resources, ensuring that changes to an object's state are atomic and consistent with the rules defined by the contract.
- The lifecycle of an object in Sui, from creation to destruction or transfer, is governed by Move scripts, which provide a safe environment where each step is controlled and predictable,

reducing the risk of state corruption or
unauthorized changes.

Consensus and Transaction Processing

Move plays a critical role in how transactions are
processed and how consensus is achieved:

- Sui's consensus mechanism, Delegated
  Proof-of-Stake (DPoS), relies on the
  deterministic nature of Move to ensure that all
  validators agree on the outcome of
  transactions. Since Move's execution is
  predictable, it's easier for validators to reach
  consensus without needing to re-execute
  transactions, which speeds up the process.
- The parallel processing of transactions in Sui
  is enabled by Move's resource model.
  Transactions that affect different objects can
  be processed concurrently, significantly
  increasing throughput.

Smart Contract Safety and Execution

Move's safety features directly enhance the safety of
smart contract execution on Sui:

- By preventing common vulnerabilities like
  reentrancy attacks, Move ensures that smart
  contracts in Sui operate securely, reducing the
  risk of exploits.
- The compile-time checks in Move mean that
  many potential issues are caught before the

code even runs on the blockchain, ensuring that only safe, well-verified code is deployed.

Gas and Resource Efficiency

The integration of Move with Sui also affects how gas (transaction fees) is calculated and how resources are managed:

- Move's resource model allows for a more nuanced gas calculation where the cost is aligned with the actual manipulation of resources rather than just computational steps. This can lead to more predictable and potentially lower fees for users.
- Resource efficiency is improved as Move encourages developers to write code that uses resources judiciously, knowing that each operation has a direct impact on the blockchain's state and gas costs.

Developer Experience

Move's integration into Sui's architecture benefits developers in several ways:

- Developers can leverage Move's modularity and type safety to build complex systems from safe, reusable components. This aligns with Sui's aim to be developer-friendly, encouraging innovation by reducing the complexity of writing secure smart contracts.
- The tooling around Move, developed with Sui in mind, includes IDEs, debugging tools, and

testing frameworks that understand Sui's object model, making development more intuitive.

Challenges and Considerations

Despite the advantages, there are challenges to consider:

- Developers must learn to think in terms of Sui's objects and Move's resources, which can be a paradigm shift for those used to other blockchain models.
- Ensuring that Move can handle all the unique requirements of Sui's design, like parallel execution, requires ongoing refinement and possibly enhancements to the language itself.
- As Sui and Move evolve, maintaining compatibility while introducing new features or optimizations is a delicate balance that requires careful planning.

Future Enhancements

The future of Move's integration with Sui might include:

- More sophisticated ways to represent and manage objects, potentially allowing for more dynamic or conditional states not currently supported.
- Enhancements to Move that could make it even more performant or compatible with

emerging blockchain standards or technologies.
- New patterns or best practices that emerge from the unique combination of Move's resource management with Sui's object-centric approach, leading to novel application designs.

Community and Ecosystem Growth

The integration of Move with Sui is not static but grows with community involvement:

- As developers build on Sui with Move, they contribute to a growing ecosystem of libraries, frameworks, and best practices that enhance both the language and the platform's capabilities.
- Community feedback directly influences the evolution of Move within Sui, ensuring that it continues to meet the needs of developers and users alike.

Move's integration with Sui's architecture is a harmonious blend of philosophy and technology, where each component enhances the other. This part has elucidated how Move's features are not just an addition to Sui but are fundamental to how Sui operates, ensuring that the blockchain can achieve its goals of speed, security, and scalability. As both Move and Sui continue to develop, this integration will likely become even more profound, pushing the boundaries of what's possible in blockchain technology.

Part 7: Developer Experience with Move

The developer experience is a critical factor in the adoption and success of any programming language, especially one as specialized as Move within the blockchain ecosystem of Sui. This part explores how Move is designed to be accessible, productive, and supportive for developers, detailing the tools, resources, and community aspects that facilitate the development of secure, scalable applications on Sui.

Move was crafted with the developer in mind, aiming to reduce the complexity commonly associated with blockchain development. Its focus on safety, resource management, and modularity directly translates into a development environment where developers can concentrate more on logic and less on avoiding pitfalls. Move's syntax and semantics draw from well-known programming languages like Rust, providing a sense of familiarity that helps reduce the learning curve. This allows developers to quickly grasp Move's unique concepts like resource management and linear types.

Sui provides a robust set of tools tailored to Move, enhancing the developer experience. Integrated Development Environments (IDEs) have extensions offering syntax highlighting, code completion, and error detection specific to Move, making coding more intuitive. The Move compiler not only translates code into bytecode but also provides detailed error messages to help developers understand and fix issues. Debuggers allow for step-by-step execution of Move scripts, invaluable for troubleshooting. Testing frameworks within Move encourage developers to write tests alongside their code, promoting safer, more reliable smart contracts. The Sui CLI includes commands for compiling, deploying, and interacting with Move contracts, streamlining the development cycle from code to blockchain.

Documentation and learning resources for Move are comprehensive. The official documentation covers everything from basic syntax to advanced contract patterns, including examples and best practices. Tutorials and guides walk developers through setting up their environment, writing their first Move module, and deploying it to Sui, catering to both beginners and experienced developers. Community resources like blogs, YouTube tutorials, and forums further enrich the learning landscape, accommodating different learning styles and levels.

The Move community within Sui acts both as a resource and a support system. Forums, discussion groups, and platforms like Discord or Reddit allow developers to ask questions, share knowledge, and collaborate. Hackathons and challenges encourage innovation while providing learning opportunities through mentorship. Code reviews and pair programming offer avenues for developers to receive feedback or work together, enhancing learning through peer review.

While Move introduces new concepts, there's a strong focus on easing developers into them. Learning is approached modularly, starting with basic resource management and gradually moving to more complex contract designs. The emphasis on safety means developers can practice writing secure code from the start, learning best practices for blockchain development. Guides on gas optimization teach developers to consider performance and cost from the beginning.

For developers transitioning from other languages, workshops are available to help them understand Move's unique features. Comparative guides highlight similarities and differences between Move and other smart contract languages like Solidity, aiding in the transition.

Despite these supports, developers face challenges. The conceptual shift from traditional state management to resource-based programming requires a change in mindset, which can be demanding. The maturity of tooling might not yet match that of more established platforms, though this is rapidly evolving. As the Move ecosystem grows, it might not have all the libraries or frameworks developers are accustomed to from other platforms, but this is being addressed with time.

Looking to the future, the developer experience with Move on Sui is set to improve. Enhanced tooling, including better IDE support, more sophisticated debuggers, and performance profilers, is on the horizon. The ecosystem will expand as more developers adopt Move, offering more libraries, frameworks, and third-party tools. Educational expansion might include more formal paths like certifications, bootcamps, or academic courses focused on Move and Sui development.

In conclusion, the developer experience with Move on Sui is tailored towards enabling developers to create secure, efficient, and scalable blockchain applications with less friction than might be encountered with other platforms. Through intuitive design, comprehensive tooling, extensive documentation, and a supportive community, Move aims to lower the barriers to entry while pushing the quality and security of blockchain applications forward. As we continue to explore Move, it's clear that its developer experience is not just about writing code but about fostering an environment where innovation is nurtured and supported.

Part 8: Future Directions for Move

Move, being a relatively new language tailored for the unique requirements of blockchain technology, particularly within the Sui ecosystem, has a bright future ahead. This part discusses potential advancements, enhancements, and the broader impact Move might have on blockchain development and applications.

As Move evolves, one of the key areas of focus could be privacy enhancements. With privacy becoming increasingly significant in blockchain applications, future versions of Move might incorporate advanced privacy-preserving techniques. This could include zero-knowledge proofs for transactions, allowing for confidential operations where only the necessary information is revealed, thus maintaining privacy while ensuring blockchain's transparency.

Another direction for Move could involve cross-chain capabilities. As interoperability becomes crucial for blockchain ecosystems, Move might evolve to support cross-chain smart contracts or interactions. This could involve developing standards or protocols within Move to facilitate asset movement or state queries across different blockchains, broadening the scope of applications that can be built on Sui.

To cater to more sophisticated DeFi applications, Move might introduce new abstractions for complex financial instruments like options, futures, or even more intricate derivatives, all managed securely within the language's safe environment. This would enable developers to build more advanced financial products with the inherent security guarantees of Move.

In terms of performance and scalability, further optimization for parallel execution is anticipated. Move's current support for parallelism could be refined to handle even more complex transaction dependencies, ensuring that as Sui grows, it can maintain or increase transaction throughput. Enhancements in resource management might offer more granular control over resource lifecycle management, potentially allowing for dynamic resource allocation or more advanced state transitions. The gas model could also be refined to reflect real computational and storage costs more accurately, encouraging developers to write more efficient contracts by design.

The developer tools and ecosystem around Move are expected to expand significantly. Improved IDE support could see more sophisticated features like contract analysis, gas estimation, or automated testing suggestions, going beyond basic syntax highlighting. The ecosystem might see an expansion in specialized libraries and frameworks for different use cases, abstracting complex logic into simpler, reusable components. Educational platforms dedicated to Move could emerge, offering structured learning paths from beginner to advanced levels, potentially including certification programs.

Move's integration with emerging technologies could be transformative. It might evolve to better support off-chain computations, enabling smart contracts to leverage external compute resources for tasks that don't need to be on-chain, thus reducing costs and enhancing scalability. As layer 2 scaling solutions become more common, Move could adapt to work seamlessly with these technologies, offering new ways to scale while maintaining its security guarantees. Furthermore, there might be developments allowing Move smart contracts to interact with AI models, either for decision-making processes or for optimizing operations based on predictive analytics.

Community and standardization efforts are also likely to shape Move's future. Community governance could become more formal, allowing developers and users to have a say in its evolution, mirroring how other open-source projects manage their direction. There could be efforts to standardize certain aspects of Move, making it easier for developers to write cross-compatible smart contracts or for Move to be adopted by other blockchain platforms. Continuous security audits and the establishment of best practices will be crucial as the language grows, ensuring that Move remains secure and reliable.

However, these advancements come with challenges. Balancing innovation with stability is vital to avoid disrupting existing applications while pushing the boundaries of what's possible. Adoption and education will be key as Move evolves, ensuring the developer community can keep pace with new features. Ensuring interoperability or pathways for legacy systems to leverage these advancements will also be a challenge.

The future of Move is intrinsically linked to the future of blockchain technology itself. By focusing on privacy, scalability, and developer experience, Move aims to remain at the forefront of blockchain programming languages. Its evolution will not only enhance Sui but could set precedents for how blockchain applications are developed across the industry. This part has explored potential directions, acknowledging that the path forward will be shaped by community needs, technological advancements, and the ever-evolving landscape of blockchain applications. As Move continues to develop, it promises to be a key player in defining what's possible in blockchain technology.

Part 9: Challenges and Learning Curve

While Move presents numerous advantages for blockchain development, particularly within the Sui ecosystem, it also introduces unique challenges and a learning curve that developers must navigate. This part explores these challenges, offering insights into how developers can overcome them to leverage Move's full potential.

One of the primary challenges for developers transitioning to Move is adapting to its resource-oriented programming model. Traditional programming languages deal with mutable state, but Move treats everything as immutable resources, which requires a fundamental shift in thinking about data and state management. Similarly, the concept of linear types, where resources must be explicitly managed throughout their lifecycle, adds complexity. It ensures safety but can be initially counterintuitive for developers used to more flexible memory management.

Move's unique syntax, although influenced by familiar languages, has specific constructs like resource declarations, module structures, and the interaction of functions with resources that require learning. Developers need to understand how these elements work together to create secure, efficient smart contracts. The strong type system and compile-time checks, while beneficial, demand meticulousness in how types are defined and used, leading to a steeper learning curve for those accustomed to more lenient systems.

Performance optimization in Move involves understanding gas management, where developers must consider the economic impact of their code from the outset. This is less common in traditional software development. To leverage Sui's parallel transaction processing, designing contracts so that transactions are as independent as possible is challenging, especially when creating complex, interconnected systems.

The ecosystem and tooling around Move are still evolving. The relative novelty of Move means the ecosystem of tools, libraries, and support might not be as mature as that of more established blockchain platforms. Developers might find themselves needing to contribute to or even build parts of the ecosystem they require. Debugging and testing in Move, particularly in the blockchain context where state is immutable, can be challenging. Developers must learn to simulate blockchain conditions effectively to test their code.

Given Move's newness, there's less collective knowledge to draw upon compared to languages with a longer history. This can make it harder for developers to find solutions to obscure problems or learn from others' experiences. Although improving, the documentation and learning resources for Move might not cover all edge cases or advanced use scenarios that developers encounter.

To overcome the learning curve, educational initiatives by the Sui and Move communities are crucial. These include tutorials, workshops, and hackathons designed to help developers learn. Engaging with the community through forums, Discord channels, or GitHub can provide support, share best practices, and enable collective problem-solving. Developers are encouraged to approach learning incrementally, starting with simpler contracts and gradually tackling more complex ones. Code review and pair programming can accelerate understanding and adoption of best practices.

Looking forward, improvements in documentation will come as the community grows, making it easier for newcomers to learn Move. Enhancements in tooling, such as IDEs, debuggers, and testing frameworks, will make development more intuitive and less error-prone. As patterns and best practices emerge, they will standardize the way developers approach Move, reducing the variability in how one might solve problems.

The challenges and learning curve associated with Move are significant but not insurmountable. They stem from Move's innovative approach to blockchain programming, designed to yield safer, more scalable, and efficient applications. Developers who embrace these challenges will find themselves at the forefront of blockchain technology, capable of harnessing Move's capabilities for groundbreaking applications on Sui. This part has aimed to shed light on these hurdles, providing a roadmap for developers to navigate them successfully.

Part 10: Case Studies

To truly appreciate the capabilities, security, and innovative potential of Move within the Sui ecosystem, examining real-world or conceptual case studies is instrumental. This part presents various scenarios where Move's unique features have been or could be leveraged to solve complex problems or to innovate within the blockchain space, demonstrating the practical implications of Move's design in various industries and applications.

Case Study 1: Decentralized Finance (DeFi) Lending Platform

Imagine a DeFi lending platform where users can engage in lending or borrowing activities with a level of security and efficiency that traditional finance systems might envy. In this scenario, Move's resource model plays a crucial role by ensuring that each token or asset is uniquely identifiable and managed, preventing issues like double-spending or unauthorized duplication. This model is particularly beneficial in DeFi where asset integrity is paramount. Move's safety features come into play through smart contracts that define how assets can be lent, borrowed, or returned, with compile-time checks reducing the likelihood of vulnerabilities that have plagued other blockchain platforms. These contracts can automatically manage interest rates, collateral, and repayment schedules with precision, ensuring that all parties adhere to the agreed terms without the need for intermediaries.

Furthermore, the scalability of the platform is significantly enhanced by Move's support for parallel transaction processing. This means that as the number of loans and borrowers increases, the platform can handle the increased load without succumbing to network congestion or delays. The outcome here is a DeFi platform where users trust the security of their assets, transactions are processed swiftly, and the system scales well with user growth. This showcases Move's design as not just theoretically sound but practically effective in creating a seamless, secure financial ecosystem.

Case Study 2: NFT Marketplace

In the vibrant world of digital art and collectibles, an NFT marketplace stands as a testament to creativity and innovation. Here, Move's role is foundational in ensuring the uniqueness and security of each Non-Fungible Token (NFT). By treating each NFT as a unique resource, Move guarantees that no two NFTs are exactly alike, thus preserving the authenticity and preventing any form of replication or counterfeit. This is crucial for artists and collectors in maintaining the value and provenance of digital works.

Move also facilitates sophisticated smart contracts that can automatically enforce royalties for creators on every secondary sale of their works. This automatic royalty enforcement is a game-changer, allowing artists to benefit from the ongoing value of their creations even after the initial sale. The gas model in Move encourages developers to write efficient contracts, which is particularly important in an NFT marketplace where numerous small transactions occur frequently. This efficiency can lead to lower costs for buyers and sellers, enhancing the overall user experience.

The result is an NFT marketplace where creators can reliably monetize their work, collectors enjoy secure ownership and transfer of assets, and the platform itself operates with high performance and low costs, all thanks to Move's resource and gas management capabilities.

Case Study 3: Decentralized Gaming Platform

The gaming industry is ripe for disruption by blockchain technology, and a decentralized gaming platform leverages Move to achieve this. Here, in-game assets are not just digital items but true assets owned by players, tradable and with real-world value. Move ensures that each item, from weapons to skins, is a unique resource, granting players indisputable ownership. This ownership model fosters a deeper investment in the game, as players know they control their digital possessions.

Game logic execution becomes transparent and secure with Move's safety features, ensuring that rules are followed strictly, reducing cheating or manipulation. This transparency not only builds trust in the gaming community but also allows for verifiable gameplay outcomes. The scalability aspect of Move is particularly beneficial here; by supporting parallel transaction processing, the platform can handle real-time gameplay for thousands of users without lag, which is critical for maintaining an immersive gaming experience.

This leads to a gaming ecosystem where players enjoy secure, transparent gameplay, can trade assets freely, and the game developers benefit from a more engaged and invested community. Such a platform could revolutionize how games are played, monetized, and experienced, moving towards a future where players have significant control over their gaming environment.

Case Study 4: Decentralized Supply Chain Management

Supply chain management on the blockchain involves tracking goods from production to consumption with unprecedented transparency and security. Here, Move's design allows each step in the supply chain to be recorded as a resource, creating an immutable ledger of the product's journey. This ensures that every transition, from manufacturing to shipping, and finally to the consumer, is logged securely and transparently, providing all stakeholders with verifiable proof of authenticity, origin, and compliance.

Move's ability to manage complex resource states can reflect the various stages of a product's lifecycle with precision, from raw material to finished product. This granular tracking can be essential in industries where product integrity, like in pharmaceuticals or luxury goods, is crucial. Additionally, while maintaining this transparency when needed, Move can incorporate privacy features for sensitive data, ensuring that proprietary or personal information is protected.

The outcome is a supply chain where trust is built through transparency, counterfeit goods are easier to detect, and compliance with regulations can be efficiently verified, significantly improving efficiency, trust, and accountability in logistics.

Case Study 5: Identity Management

In the realm of identity management, a decentralized approach could empower individuals with control over their personal data in a way that's both secure and user-centric. Move's resource model allows for personal data to be treated as resources that individuals own and can control. This means users can grant or revoke access to their data at will, creating a permissioned access system through smart contracts that define complex rules about who can see or use what part of one's identity.

Move's safety features play a significant role in preventing unauthorized access or data breaches, ensuring that personal information is handled with the utmost security. This approach not only enhances privacy but also reduces the risk of identity theft or misuse of personal data, which is rampant in centralized systems.

The result is an identity management system where privacy is significantly enhanced, individuals have sovereignty over their data, and interactions with services or institutions become more transparent and secure. This could lead to a new era of digital identity, where users are not just data points but active participants in managing their digital selves.

These case studies illustrate the breadth and depth of Move's application in building innovative, secure, and scalable applications across various sectors. By leveraging Move's resource model, safety features, and scalability, developers can construct solutions that address some of the most pressing challenges in blockchain technology. As Move continues to evolve, its applications in these and new areas will likely expand, showcasing the language's versatility and power in real-world blockchain development, potentially redefining how we interact with digital assets, manage data, and engage with technology in our daily lives.

Chapter 5: Objects in Sui: A New Data Paradigm

Part 1: Introduction to Traditional Blockchain Data Models

In the vast, digital cosmos of blockchain technology, where decentralization reigns supreme and trust is algorithmically woven into the fabric of every system, the handling of data has always been a cornerstone of functionality and innovation. From the very inception of blockchain with Bitcoin's introduction in 2009, data management has evolved, yet it has remained tethered to a paradigm that fundamentally views data through the lens of transactions. This chapter embarks on a journey from these traditional data models to understand how they've shaped the blockchain landscape, setting the stage for the revolutionary object-centric model introduced by Sui.

Imagine, if you will, the blockchain as a ledger, an ancient but digital book where every page is a block, and each line within it represents a transaction. This is the essence of how the majority of blockchains have operated. Each transaction is an update to this ledger, a transfer of value from one address to another, recorded immutably in a chain of blocks. Here, data isn't stored in complex, relational structures but rather as a series of discrete entries, each one a financial or contractual event that has left its indelible mark on the blockchain.

Bitcoin, the progenitor of blockchain technology, exemplified this model. Its primary function was to facilitate secure, peer-to-peer transactions without the need for intermediaries, using a distributed ledger to record these transactions. The data model was straightforward: an address had a balance, and transactions either increased or decreased that balance. This simplicity was its strength, ensuring that the system was both secure and comprehensible in its operations. However, this simplicity also set limits on what could be done with data.

As blockchain technology matured, so did the ambitions of what it could achieve. Ethereum introduced the concept of smart contracts, which expanded the ledger's capabilities. Now, transactions could not only transfer value but also execute complex logic defined by the contract's code. This was a leap forward, allowing for decentralized applications (dApps) where data could be more than just numbers on a ledger; it could represent states of contracts, user identities, or even assets in games. However, even with smart contracts, the underlying data model remained transaction-centric. Every change in state, every update to an application's logic, was still fundamentally a transaction to be recorded on the blockchain.

This transaction-based model has its merits. It ensures that every change in the system is not only recorded but also verified by the network, providing a high degree of security and immutability. The simplicity of the model means that even with the complexity of smart contracts, the core of what's happening remains clear: one party is transferring something of value, or control, to another. However, this model also brings with it inherent limitations, particularly when it comes to the richness of data interaction and the complexity of state management.

For one, the transaction-centric model is inherently stateful in a very linear way. Each transaction results in a new state of the world, but managing this state across multiple transactions, especially in complex systems, can become cumbersome. Imagine trying to maintain the state of a digital asset that evolves over time, perhaps a character in a game that gains skills or a piece of digital art that can be modified or combined with others. In traditional blockchain models, each change would require its own transaction, leading to increased complexity, cost, and potential inefficiencies in terms of network load and scalability.

Moreover, this model often struggles with privacy. Since every transaction is public, managing sensitive data or ensuring that only the intended parties can view or interact with certain pieces of information becomes challenging. While solutions like zero-knowledge proofs have been developed to address privacy concerns, they add layers of complexity and computation to what should be simple data operations.

Then there's the question of asset representation. In traditional blockchain models, assets are often represented through tokens, which can be fungible or non-fungible. But these tokens are limited in how they can interact with each other or evolve. They're static in nature unless explicitly programmed otherwise through smart contracts, which again, are transaction-based operations.

This approach also impacts how applications can be built. Developers are constrained by what can be efficiently managed through transactions. Complex applications, particularly those requiring real-time interactions or those involving multiple, interdependent state changes, find these constraints limiting. The process of updating multiple related pieces of data often requires multiple transactions, each with its own cost and verification time, leading to an experience that can feel clunky or inefficient compared to centralized systems.

The traditional blockchain data model, while revolutionary for secure, decentralized value transfer, has thus been criticized for its rigidity. It's well-suited for straightforward financial transactions or simple contractual agreements but struggles when developers aim for more dynamic, interactive, or privacy-focused applications. The limitations in how data can be represented, managed, and interacted with have been a bottleneck for innovation, particularly as the digital world seeks to mirror the complexity and fluidity of the physical one.

As we've seen, the journey from Bitcoin's simple ledger to Ethereum's smart contract-enabled world was significant, yet it still operated within the bounds of this transaction-centric data model. This model has served blockchain well for certain applications, but as the demands on blockchain technology grew, so did the need for a new paradigm - one that could offer more than just the transfer of value or the execution of pre-defined logic. This is where Sui steps in, introducing a model where data isn't just entries in a ledger but objects with lives of their own, capable of far more nuanced interactions and state management.

Thus, understanding these traditional data models is crucial not just for appreciating the leap Sui makes but also for recognizing the constraints that have shaped blockchain development up to this point. It's a history of innovation, limitations, and the constant push towards more capable, efficient, and user-centric blockchain systems. As we delve deeper into Sui's object-centric model in the following sections, this backdrop will highlight just how transformative this new approach to data on blockchain can be.

Part 2: The Shift to an Object-Centric Model in Sui

As the blockchain landscape continued to evolve, the limitations of the traditional transaction-centric data model became increasingly apparent, akin to a canvas too small for the artist's vision. The digital world craved more dynamic, interactive, and complex systems than could be easily facilitated by merely recording transactions. Enter Sui, with its groundbreaking shift towards an object-centric model, a paradigm that redefines how data is perceived, managed, and interacted with on a blockchain. This part of our exploration will delve into this new model, illustrating its departure from the past and the vast potential it unlocks for future blockchain applications.

Imagine a world where data isn't just a static entry in a ledger but an entity with its own characteristics, behaviors, and lifecycle. This is the vision that Sui brings to life. Here, every piece of data, every asset, is conceptualized as an "object". This isn't merely a change in terminology; it's a fundamental shift in how we think about data on a blockchain. In traditional models, data was passive, acted upon by transactions. In Sui, objects are active participants in the ecosystem, capable of containing their own logic, state, and even the ability to evolve over time.

The transition from a transaction-centric to an object-centric model can be likened to moving from a world where books are judged only by their covers to one where each book has its own unique story, characters, and plot twists, all accessible and editable within its own confines. This model borrows from the principles of object-oriented programming (OOP), where objects have attributes (data) and methods (functions) that operate on that data. In Sui, each object can encapsulate not just simple values but complex states, relationships with other objects, and rules for how they can be interacted with or modified.

Consider a digital token in this new light. Instead of just being a number in an account, representing ownership or value, it becomes an object with properties like rarity, ownership history, or even interactive elements like skills if it's part of a game.

This object can have methods to change its state, perhaps allowing it to be upgraded, combined with other tokens, or even to participate in autonomous behaviors within an application. The implications of this are profound, offering a richness of interaction that was previously cumbersome or outright impossible within the confines of traditional blockchain models.

One of the first and most significant benefits of this model is the way it handles state changes. In traditional blockchains, every state change is a transaction, leading to a plethora of transactions for complex operations, each with its associated costs and network load. In Sui, because objects carry their state, changes can be managed more efficiently. An object can update its own state through internal methods, reducing the need for external transactions for every small change. This not only improves efficiency but also reduces costs for users and developers, making complex applications more feasible for blockchain environments.

Security and privacy are also transformed in this model. Each object can have its own access controls, determining who can see or modify its data. This granular level of control allows for applications where sensitive data can be managed with much higher precision than before. Imagine a medical record on the blockchain; with Sui's model, different healthcare providers could have access to different parts of the record based on their role, all managed by the object itself rather than through complex smart contract logic spread across transactions.

Moreover, the object-centric approach fosters a more intuitive development paradigm. Developers no longer need to think in terms of transactions for every interaction; instead, they can focus on the lifecycle of objects. This aligns more closely with how developers work in other software environments, potentially lowering the barrier to entry for those accustomed to object-oriented programming. It also opens up possibilities for more sophisticated dApps where objects can interact in ways that simulate real-world dynamics more closely, like in gaming where characters or items can have autonomous behaviors or evolve based on interactions.

The implications for asset management are particularly noteworthy. With objects, assets can be represented in ways that go beyond mere tokens. They can have attributes that change over time, interact with other objects in predefined ways, or even be part of larger, more complex systems like virtual worlds or supply chains. This model allows for digital assets to carry not just value but also functionality, history, and potential for future development, all managed within the object itself.

However, this shift is not without its challenges. Managing such a system requires a different approach to consensus and state management. Sui's architecture, with its focus on parallel execution and instant finality, is designed to handle this complexity. Transactions in Sui aren't just about moving value; they're about orchestrating changes across a network of objects, which requires a consensus mechanism that can manage this with efficiency and security.

The object-centric model also changes how developers think about scalability and performance. With traditional models, each transaction meant potentially updating many parts of the ledger, leading to bottlenecks as the system scaled. In Sui, because objects manage their own state, the system can scale by distributing the load across these objects, potentially achieving higher throughput and lower latency for complex operations.

In essence, Sui's shift to an object-centric model is a leap towards mirroring the complexity of the real world within the digital realm of blockchain. It acknowledges that the world isn't just about transactions but about the relationships, states, and evolutions of entities within it. By treating data as objects, Sui not only expands what's possible with blockchain technology but also aligns it closer to how we naturally think about and interact with the world around us.

This new paradigm doesn't just solve existing problems; it opens up a universe of possibilities for what blockchain can become. From more engaging digital content, complex financial instruments, to autonomous and interactive systems, the object-centric model in Sui is a beacon for innovation, inviting developers, users, and thinkers to reimagine what decentralized systems can offer. As we delve further into the specifics of how this model impacts smart contracts, asset management, and beyond, it becomes clear that we're standing at the threshold of a new era in blockchain technology.

Part 3: Smart Contracts and Object Management

In the evolving narrative of blockchain technology, smart contracts have long been celebrated as the scriptwriters of decentralized applications, orchestrating actions based on coded conditions. However, as we've explored the shift from traditional transaction-centric models to Sui's object-centric paradigm, we stand before a new chapter where smart contracts evolve from mere executors of transactions to maestros of object lifecycles. This segment will delve into how this transformation redefines smart contract development, offering developers a canvas broader than ever before for crafting decentralized solutions.

Traditionally, smart contracts in blockchain ecosystems like Ethereum operate by defining conditions under which transactions can occur. They manage states through transactions, updating the ledger based on these conditions. This approach, while revolutionary, confines the functionality of smart contracts to what can be managed through these transactions. Imagine a script that can only move pieces on a chessboard but can't alter the rules of the game or the nature of the pieces themselves without extensive, transaction-based logic.

In contrast, Sui introduces a model where smart contracts are not just about managing transactions but about managing the lives of objects. Here, smart contracts become more akin to object constructors, state managers, and interaction facilitators. They define not just how objects can change hands but how they can change in essence, behavior, and relationship with other objects. This paradigm shift redefines what a smart contract can be, turning them into dynamic systems capable of managing complex, evolving digital entities.

Let's visualize this transformation through an analogy. In the traditional blockchain model, a smart contract might be like a play where actors (data) move across the stage (ledger) following a script (contract conditions). With Sui's object-centric model, the smart contract becomes more like a director who not only decides who moves where but also how the stage can transform, how characters evolve, and how scenes can be dynamically rewritten based on the actors' interactions. Each object in this play has its own script, its own rules for evolution, and the smart contract orchestrates these individual stories within the larger narrative.

This new approach to smart contract development allows for:

- **Lifecycle Management:** Instead of merely executing transactions to alter states, smart contracts in Sui can manage the entire lifecycle of an object. This includes creation, where an object comes into existence with initial attributes; evolution, where its attributes or capabilities can change over time;

interaction, defining how this object can interact with others; and even destruction or transformation into new forms. This lifecycle management is crucial for applications where assets need to grow, combine, or change in response to user actions or system events.

- **State Complexity:** With objects carrying their own state, smart contracts can deal with more nuanced data structures. An object could represent anything from a simple token to a complex asset like a piece of land in a virtual world, with each having attributes, methods, and even relationships with other objects. This allows for applications where the state of an object is not just a balance or a flag but a complex system that can be managed autonomously or through specific interactions.

- **Efficient Resource Use:** By managing state changes within objects, rather than through numerous transactions, Sui's smart contracts can reduce the overhead typically associated with complex operations on traditional blockchains. This efficiency is not just in computational terms but also in how it impacts gas fees, making more sophisticated applications economically viable.

- **Enhanced Interactivity:** Smart contracts can now define how objects interact with each other in real-time or based on certain conditions without necessarily involving external transactions for each interaction. This opens up possibilities for games where characters can autonomously interact, or for financial instruments that can evolve based on market conditions or user interactions, all managed by the logic within the objects themselves.

- **Security and Access Control:** With each object potentially having its own access control mechanisms, smart contracts can define who can interact with what aspects of an object and under what conditions. This granularity can lead to more secure systems where privacy and access are managed at the object level, reducing the attack surface and enhancing user control over their digital assets.

For developers, this means a shift in thinking from writing contracts that merely react to transactions to crafting contracts that define and manage the behavior of digital entities. It requires a deeper understanding of how to encapsulate logic within objects, how to design these objects to interact in meaningful ways, and how to ensure that this complexity does not compromise the system's security or performance.

However, this new power comes with its challenges. The complexity of managing object states, ensuring that interactions are secure and efficient, and designing systems where objects can evolve without breaking the integrity of the blockchain are all non-trivial tasks. Developers must now think about the lifecycle of data, how changes propagate, and how to design for scenarios where objects might need to interact in ways not initially foreseen.

Moreover, the need for a consensus mechanism that can handle this object-centric world adds another layer of complexity. Sui's approach, with its emphasis on parallel execution and instant finality, is tailored to manage these intricacies, but developers must still navigate the nuances of ensuring that object states are consistently and correctly updated across the network.

Despite these challenges, the potential is immense. This model allows for applications that are more dynamic, responsive, and reflective of real-world complexities. From decentralized games where characters have lives of their own, to supply chains where goods evolve through their lifecycle, to financial systems where instruments can adapt to real-time market data, the possibilities are as varied as they are exciting.

In summary, Sui's object-centric model transforms smart contracts from simple transactional scripts into sophisticated management systems for digital entities. This evolution not only broadens the scope of what blockchain can achieve but also aligns it more closely with the complex, interactive nature of the real world, promising a future where the digital and physical realms can interact in ways previously unimaginable.

Part 4: Asset Management with Objects

The transition to an object-centric model in blockchain technology, as exemplified by Sui, heralds a new era in asset management where digital assets transcend their traditional representations. In this part, we explore how Sui's approach redefines asset management, offering a framework where assets are not merely tokens but dynamic, interactive objects within a digital ecosystem. This shift transforms how we conceptualize, interact with, and manage assets, opening avenues for innovation that mirror the complexities and fluidity of the physical world.

In traditional blockchain systems, assets are often represented as tokens, whether fungible like cryptocurrencies or non-fungible like NFTs. These tokens are essentially ledger entries, their value or uniqueness defined by their scarcity or the data associated with them. The interaction with these tokens is typically limited to transfers or simple state changes facilitated by smart contracts. However, this model struggles to encapsulate the richness of real-world assets where attributes, conditions, and interactions are far more nuanced.

Sui's object-centric model changes this narrative. Here, an asset is not just a token but an object with its own set of attributes, behaviors, and lifecycle. This paradigm shift enables a level of asset management that is both more intuitive and powerful. Imagine an asset like a digital car in a blockchain-based game. In a traditional model, this car might be a token with a few static attributes like speed or color. In Sui, this car becomes an object with:

- **Dynamic Attributes:** The car's speed, condition, or even paint color can change over

time, perhaps through wear and tear or upgrades, all managed within the object itself.
- **Interactive Behaviors:** This car can interact with other objects in the ecosystem in ways that mimic real-world interactions. It could race against other cars, be repaired by interacting with a mechanic object, or even be customized through interactions with accessory objects.
- **Lifecycle Management:** From being manufactured (created on the blockchain) to being sold, upgraded, or even recycled (transforming into new objects), the entire lifecycle of the car can be managed, providing a narrative and history to the asset.

Such complexity in asset representation and management has profound implications:

- **Enhanced User Experience:** By allowing assets to have a life of their own, the user experience in applications becomes richer. Players in games, investors in financial instruments, or collectors of digital art can engage with assets that evolve, interact, and respond to their actions in ways that feel more "alive" and engaging.
- **Complex Asset Composition:** Assets can now be composed of other objects, leading to complex digital items. A piece of digital art could be composed of multiple layers, each an object with its own properties or even independent histories. This composition allows for creative expressions and asset

management that was less feasible or efficient in traditional models.

- **Autonomy and Automation:** With objects carrying their own logic for interaction and evolution, assets can operate autonomously to an extent. In a business context, this could mean supply chain components that automatically update their status based on real-world events or digital contracts that self-execute upon meeting certain conditions defined within the objects.
- **Security and Provenance:** Each object's history, modifications, and interactions are inherently part of its state, making provenance tracking more straightforward and secure. This is particularly valuable for high-value or unique assets where authenticity and history are key.
- **Economic Models and Utility:** The way assets can now evolve or combine opens new economic models. For instance, in gaming, players could combine basic items to create rare ones, adding a layer of strategy and economic interaction not possible when assets are static tokens.

However, managing these complex assets in an object-centric environment also presents challenges:

- **Scalability and Performance:** The richness of object interactions and state changes could strain network resources if not managed efficiently. Sui's architecture aims to mitigate this through parallel execution, but developers must design with scalability in mind.

- **Interoperability:** While objects within Sui can interact richly, ensuring they can also function or be recognized in other ecosystems remains a challenge. This requires thoughtful design around standards and interfaces.
- **Complexity in Development:** The potential for more complex asset interactions means developers need to think not just about the initial state of an asset but its entire lifecycle, interactions, and potential evolutions. This requires a shift towards more holistic system design.
- **Security Considerations:** With more autonomous behaviors comes the need for robust security measures to prevent unauthorized state changes or interactions that could compromise an asset's integrity.

Despite these challenges, the opportunities are transformative. Consider a digital land parcel in a virtual world. In a Sui-like environment, this land could:

- **Grow or Change:** Over time, with user interactions or environmental changes within the game, the land could evolve, perhaps becoming more valuable or changing in characteristics.
- **Interact with Other Assets:** The land could be part of a larger ecosystem where it interacts with weather objects, neighboring properties, or even digital flora and fauna.
- **Have a History:** Every transaction, modification, or interaction is part of its history,

creating a narrative or value beyond its current state.

In essence, Sui's approach to asset management with objects allows for a digital economy that more closely mimics the physical one, where assets have histories, can change, degrade, improve, or combine in ways that reflect real-world dynamics. This not only enhances the functionality of blockchain applications but also enriches the narrative and user engagement with digital assets, making them true reflections of their physical counterparts in complexity and interaction.

As we delve deeper into these concepts, it becomes clear that Sui is not just advancing blockchain technology but redefining what digital ownership, interaction, and asset management can be in the digital age.

Part 5: Security, Privacy, and Control

In the realm of blockchain technology, where decentralization and transparency are often hailed as virtues, the triad of security, privacy, and control emerges as both a challenge and an opportunity. Sui's object-centric model presents a transformative approach to these critical aspects, offering nuanced solutions that traditional blockchain models have struggled with. This part explores how Sui's architecture reimagines these elements, providing a framework where users can enjoy the benefits of blockchain while safeguarding their digital lives.

Security in an Object-Centric World:

Security in blockchain has always been about safeguarding transactions and maintaining the integrity of the ledger. However, with Sui's model, security extends beyond transactions to encompass the state and behavior of objects themselves. Here, each object can have its own security protocols:

- **Object-Level Security:** Each object can define its own access controls, determining who can view or modify its state. This granular control means that security policies can be tailored to the specific nature of each asset, much like how different locks secure different doors in a building.
- **State Integrity:** Since objects manage their own state, ensuring this state is not tampered with becomes a primary security concern. Sui's consensus mechanism, designed to handle object interactions, ensures that state changes are both authorized and accurate, reducing the risk of unauthorized modifications.
- **Interaction Validation:** With objects having the capability to interact autonomously or through user-initiated actions, validating these interactions to prevent malicious activities or unintended consequences is crucial. This requires smart contracts that not only manage but also secure these interactions.
- **Defense Against Exploits:** The complexity of object behaviors could potentially introduce new vectors for exploits. However, Sui's

approach allows for defensive programming at the object level, where vulnerabilities can be mitigated by designing objects with security in mind from the ground up.

Privacy Reimagined:

Privacy on traditional blockchains is notoriously tricky due to their transparent nature. Sui introduces concepts that could make privacy more manageable:

- **Privacy at the Object Level:** Objects can encapsulate private data within their state, allowing for selective disclosure. This means a user could share certain aspects of an object's state while keeping others private, akin to revealing the title of a book but not its contents.
- **Zero-Knowledge Proofs and More:** While traditional blockchain systems have used zero-knowledge proofs to enhance privacy, Sui can integrate these and other cryptographic techniques directly into how objects handle and share data, offering privacy without sacrificing the benefits of decentralization.
- **Controlled Access:** By defining who can interact with what parts of an object, users gain control over their data's visibility. For example, a digital medical record object could allow a doctor to see test results but not family history unless explicitly permitted.
- **Pseudonymity and Anonymity:** Sui's model supports scenarios where users can interact with objects in ways that do not reveal their

identity, enhancing privacy in transactions or interactions.

Control Over Digital Assets:

The true power of the object-centric model lies in the control it returns to users over their digital assets:

- **Fine-Grained Permissions:** Users can set permissions for how their objects can be used, modified, or transferred. This extends the concept of ownership to include nuanced control over usage rights, much like copyrights in the physical world.
- **Lifecycle Management:** Users can dictate the lifecycle of their assets, deciding when they can be destroyed, how they can evolve, or even under what conditions they can be combined with other assets.
- **Autonomy:** Objects can act autonomously based on pre-defined rules, giving users control over how their assets behave in different scenarios without constant intervention.
- **Delegation of Control:** Users can delegate control over certain aspects of an object to others, enabling complex scenarios like shared ownership or custodianship, all managed through the object's logic.

However, with these advancements come new considerations:

- **Complexity in Management:** The more control and privacy options available, the more complex it becomes to manage these systems. Users need interfaces and tools designed to make these controls accessible without overwhelming them.
- **Scalability of Privacy:** Ensuring privacy while maintaining the scalability of the network is a delicate balance. Sui's approach must scale these privacy mechanisms as the number of objects and interactions grows.
- **Regulatory Compliance:** With enhanced privacy and control comes the challenge of ensuring that these capabilities comply with varying global regulations regarding data privacy and asset management.
- **Security of Security Measures:** Implementing security at the object level means that the security mechanisms themselves must be robust against attacks or exploits, requiring continuous updates and vigilance.

Sui's object-centric model doesn't just tackle these issues; it redefines them. By embedding security, privacy, and control into the very fabric of how data and assets are managed, Sui offers a vision where users can trust in the security of their digital possessions, maintain privacy over their data, and wield unprecedented control over their digital lives. This paradigm shift could lead to applications where users are not just participants but truly sovereign in the digital realm, a significant step towards aligning blockchain technology with the nuanced needs of its users in an increasingly digital world.

Part 6: Future Implications and Broader Impact

The narrative of blockchain technology has been one of constant evolution, from the rudimentary, yet groundbreaking, ledger of Bitcoin to the complex, smart contract-driven ecosystems of today. With Sui introducing an object-centric model, we stand at the precipice of yet another profound shift, one that could redefine not only how we interact with digital assets but also how we envision and build the digital world around us. This final part of our exploration contemplates the future implications and the broader impact of this new paradigm on blockchain technology, digital economies, and beyond.

Imagine a world where the digital isn't just a mirror of the physical but an extension of it, where the boundaries between the two blur to the point of irrelevance. In this future, the object-centric model of Sui could serve as the foundation for digital spaces where assets have lives as vibrant and complex as their real-world counterparts. Here, a digital painting isn't just a static image but a living piece of art that evolves, reacts to its environment, or even interacts with its viewers. A digital car in a virtual world could degrade with use, require maintenance, or be upgraded, mirroring the lifecycle of a physical vehicle.

This model's impact on smart contract development is transformative. Developers are no longer confined to writing scripts for transactions but are empowered to craft ecosystems where objects can autonomously evolve, interact, and adapt. This shift encourages a new breed of decentralized applications (dApps) where the focus is on the lifecycle of digital entities rather than mere transactional interactions. The implications are vast:

For gaming, this means games where characters or items have their own narratives, changing and growing with player interactions, creating a more immersive and engaging experience. In finance, we could see financial instruments that dynamically adjust to market conditions, or decentralized autonomous organizations (DAOs) where governance tokens could evolve in capabilities or privileges based on participation or performance, without needing constant human intervention.

The economic models that emerge from this could be revolutionary. Digital scarcity, traditionally a cornerstone of asset value in blockchain, could give way to or be complemented by concepts of digital longevity, utility, or evolution. Assets could gain or lose value not just based on supply and demand but on their history, interactions, or potential for future development. This could lead to economic systems where the value of an asset is as much about its story and potential as its immediate utility or rarity.

In terms of privacy and security, the object-centric model allows for a more nuanced approach. Privacy becomes less about hiding data and more about controlling its exposure and use. Security evolves from protecting transactions to safeguarding the entire lifecycle of an object, ensuring its integrity from creation to potential destruction. This could lead to digital identities where personal data is compartmentalized into objects, each with its own access controls, allowing for a level of privacy and security in identity management that's been elusive in previous blockchain models.

The implications for scalability are equally profound. Traditional blockchains often struggle with scalability due to the linear nature of transactions and the need to broadcast and verify each one across the network. In Sui's model, where objects manage their own state, changes can be localized, reducing the need for global consensus for every minor state alteration. This could lead to blockchain networks capable of handling complex, real-time interactions at a scale previously thought unattainable, opening up possibilities for applications in areas like real-time gaming, IoT networks, or even digital twins of physical systems.

However, this vision of the future doesn't come without its challenges. The complexity of managing objects with their own behaviors and states requires a new level of sophistication in both infrastructure and development. Consensus mechanisms must evolve to handle this complexity efficiently, ensuring that the autonomy of objects doesn't lead to network fragmentation or security vulnerabilities. Developers will need to adopt new patterns for thinking about and coding applications, focusing on lifecycle management, interaction protocols, and lifecycle security.

Moreover, the regulatory landscape will need to adapt. As digital assets gain complexity and autonomy, questions of ownership, rights, and responsibilities become more nuanced. How do we regulate an asset that self-modifies or interacts with others in unforeseen ways? How do we ensure that this new digital autonomy doesn't lead to ethical or legal quagmires, especially in areas like AI, where objects could start resembling entities with their own "will"?

The community and social aspects of blockchain will also transform. With Sui's model, the community could engage with the blockchain not just as users or developers but as co-creators of the digital ecosystem. The ability for objects to have a life of their own could lead to a new form of digital citizenship, where individuals contribute to the evolution of digital spaces, much like contributing to open-source projects but with immediate, tangible effects in the digital realm.

The educational impact is another facet to consider. As this model becomes more prevalent, education in blockchain development will need to include not just programming or economics but also concepts of object lifecycle management, digital rights management, and perhaps even digital ecology, where developers learn to manage the "digital environment" in which their objects live.

Looking further into the future, this model could influence how we think about digital permanence and impermanence. Digital objects might have lifecycles that reflect natural processes, with creation, growth, decay, and potentially rebirth or transformation. This could lead to digital ecosystems where the lifecycle of digital items contributes to a broader narrative or environmental system, perhaps even in virtual worlds that serve as experimental spaces for ecological or economic theories.

In essence, the object-centric model of Sui isn't just an advancement in blockchain technology; it's a paradigm shift that could ripple through how we conceptualize digital ownership, interaction, and creativity. It challenges us to think of the digital not as a static ledger but as a dynamic, living space where digital assets can have the complexity, autonomy, and narrative depth of physical ones. This could lead to a future where digital art, financial instruments, identities, and even entire virtual worlds operate with a level of autonomy and interaction that blurs the line between the digital and the real, offering new avenues for human expression, economic models, and social structures.

As we stand on this verge of transformation, the journey of blockchain technology continues to be one of expanding horizons, where each step forward in technology prompts us to reimagine not just what's possible but what it means to live in an increasingly digital world. The implications are as exciting as they are complex, promising a future where the digital and physical weave together in ways that enrich our lives, challenge our norms, and expand the very concept of what it means to be part of a digital society.

Chapter 6: Sui's Consensus Mechanism: Delegated Proof-of-Stake Explained

Part 1: Introduction to Consensus in Blockchain

In the sprawling digital landscape of blockchain technology, where trust is not a given but something that must be engineered into the very fabric of the system, the concept of consensus stands as a monumental pillar. It's the process that transforms a cacophony of individual actions into a symphony of collective agreement, ensuring that all participants in a decentralized network see the same version of reality. This chapter begins our journey into understanding Sui's innovative approach to consensus through the Delegated Proof-of-Stake (DPoS) mechanism, but before we can grasp the nuances of Sui's implementation, we must first explore the broader concept of consensus in blockchain.

Imagine, for a moment, a world without centralized authorities like banks or governments to arbitrate transactions or enforce rules. In such a world, how do you ensure that everyone agrees on who owns what, or what the current state of any digital asset is? This is the crux of the problem blockchain technology aims to solve. Consensus mechanisms are the ingenious solutions devised to achieve this agreement in a decentralized manner, where trust is distributed across participants rather than concentrated in one entity.

The story of consensus in blockchain begins with Bitcoin, which introduced Proof-of-Work (PoW). In PoW, participants (miners) compete to solve complex mathematical puzzles, and the first to solve it gets to add the next block of transactions to the blockchain, receiving newly minted bitcoins as a reward. This method, while revolutionary for establishing trust in a trustless system, has its drawbacks. It's energy-intensive, as the puzzles require significant computational power, leading to concerns about environmental impact and scalability issues as the network grows.

The quest for alternatives led to the development of Proof-of-Stake (PoS). Here, the probability of being chosen to validate transactions and create new blocks is proportional to the number of tokens one holds and stakes (locks up) as a form of security deposit. This shift from computational power to economic stake aims to reduce energy consumption and potentially increase transaction throughput. However, PoS systems still face challenges, particularly around how to prevent wealth concentration from leading to centralization of power or how to handle the "nothing at stake" problem, where validators might vote for multiple blockchain histories without significant risk.

Enter Delegated Proof-of-Stake (DPoS), a variation that seeks to address some of these issues by introducing a layer of democracy into the validation process. In DPoS, instead of all token holders participating in consensus, they elect a smaller number of delegates or validators to do the work on their behalf. These validators are responsible for maintaining the blockchain, adding new blocks, and ensuring the integrity of transactions. This system aims to combine the benefits of PoS with a governance model where the community can influence who gets to validate transactions, theoretically leading to better representation and accountability.

But why is consensus so crucial? At its core, consensus is what makes blockchain technology secure and trustworthy. Without a consensus mechanism, a blockchain would be susceptible to attacks where bad actors could rewrite history or double-spend coins. Consensus ensures that once something is recorded on the blockchain, it's nearly immutable, providing a single source of truth that all parties can rely upon. This is not just about financial transactions; it's about establishing a digital reality where agreements, contracts, identities, and even laws can exist independently of a central authority.

The beauty of consensus in blockchain is in its diversity. Different blockchains have experimented with various mechanisms, each with its philosophy on how best to balance speed, security, decentralization, and energy efficiency:

- **PoW** offers high security at the cost of energy and time.
- **PoS** tries to mitigate the energy issue but grapples with fairness and centralization risks.
- **DPoS**, as we'll explore with Sui, aims to streamline the process further by involving the

community in choosing validators, potentially offering faster transactions and lower energy use while trying to maintain a level of decentralization.

However, consensus mechanisms are not just technical solutions; they are deeply intertwined with economic, social, and governance structures. They define how wealth, power, and influence are distributed within the ecosystem. For instance, PoW can be seen as rewarding those who can afford to invest in mining hardware, potentially leading to centralization if only a few can compete at the highest level. PoS, on the other hand, rewards those who hold the most tokens, which might encourage wealth concentration unless balanced by other mechanisms.

The choice of consensus mechanism also influences the blockchain's usability. PoW's slow confirmation times can be a barrier for applications requiring instant transactions. PoS or DPoS, by contrast, could theoretically offer quicker confirmations, making them more suitable for a broader range of applications, from finance to gaming or supply chain management.

In the context of Sui, understanding consensus is critical because it underpins how the blockchain ensures the integrity and order of transactions in its object-centric model. The efficiency, security, and inclusivity of the consensus mechanism directly impact how well Sui can handle complex object interactions, manage asset states, and scale to support vast, interactive digital ecosystems.

But consensus is more than just a technical challenge; it's a philosophical one. It asks us to consider what it means to reach agreement in a world where trust is not assumed, where every participant could be an adversary, yet they all must cooperate to achieve a common goal. In this sense, consensus mechanisms are not just algorithms but social contracts written in code, defining how we will interact, govern, and evolve together in digital spaces.

As we delve into Sui's implementation of DPoS in the subsequent parts of this chapter, we'll see how it attempts to navigate these complex waters. We'll explore how Sui's approach aims to balance the scales between efficiency and security, between the power of the few and the voice of the many, and how it seeks to provide a foundation for a blockchain that's not just a ledger but a platform for dynamic, real-world applications.

This introduction to consensus in blockchain isn't just about laying the groundwork for understanding Sui's specific implementation; it's about appreciating the profound implications these mechanisms have on everything from environmental sustainability to economic equality, from governance models to the very nature of digital interaction. As we move forward, this foundation will help us comprehend why Sui's choice of DPoS is not merely a technical decision but a statement on how they envision the future of decentralized systems.

Part 2: The Basics of Delegated Proof-of-Stake (DPoS)

In the vast, intricate tapestry of blockchain technology, where the very notion of trust is reimagined through decentralized consensus, Delegated Proof-of-Stake (DPoS) emerges as a compelling thread. This mechanism, an evolution of the Proof-of-Stake (PoS) model, seeks to marry efficiency with democracy, aiming to create a blockchain environment that's not only secure and scalable but also inclusive in its governance. Here, we delve into the core principles of DPoS, exploring how it functions, its advantages, and the challenges it faces, setting the stage for understanding its application within the Sui ecosystem.

Delegated Proof-of-Stake, at its heart, is about empowerment through delegation. Unlike Proof-of-Work (PoW), where miners compete in a computational arms race to validate transactions, or traditional PoS, where validators are chosen based on the size of their stake, DPoS introduces a layer where the community directly influences who validates transactions. This is done by allowing token holders to vote for a select number of delegates, often called validators or block producers, who then take on the responsibility of maintaining the blockchain's integrity.

Imagine a digital world where every citizen has a say in electing their leaders, but instead of governing a country, these leaders govern the flow and security of digital transactions. In DPoS, token holders cast their votes based on the quantity of tokens they hold, reflecting a system where one's stake in the system correlates with their voting power. These votes determine who will serve as validators for a given period. The number of validators can vary from one blockchain to another, but the idea is to keep this number manageable to ensure efficiency while still allowing for enough decentralization to prevent monopolistic control.

The process begins with token holders staking their tokens, either to run as candidates for validator positions or to support others. Staking here serves dual purposes: it's an investment in the network's security and a vote of confidence in the chosen validators. Those who stake their tokens to become validators pledge to act in the network's best interest, knowing their stake could be at risk if they fail to perform their duties correctly or if they attempt malicious actions.

Once elected, validators have the critical task of creating blocks, which involves gathering transactions, verifying them, and adding them to the blockchain. In this system, the creation of a block is not just a technological act but a democratic one, as validators are the ones chosen by the community to uphold the ledger's sanctity. They work in a round-robin fashion or through a scheduling algorithm designed to ensure fair distribution of block creation opportunities among validators, thus preventing any single entity from gaining too much control over the network.

But what makes DPoS potentially superior to other consensus mechanisms?

Firstly, **efficiency**. By limiting the number of validators, DPoS can achieve consensus much faster than PoW or even traditional PoS systems, where every node might be involved in validation. This efficiency translates into quicker transaction confirmations, which is vital for applications requiring real-time processing, like financial transactions or interactive gaming.

Secondly, **energy efficiency**. DPoS significantly reduces the energy consumption associated with maintaining the network since it doesn't rely on the energy-intensive mining processes of PoW. Validators in DPoS do not need to compete with computational power; instead, they are chosen by vote, and the system's security is underpinned by economic stakes rather than electricity.

Thirdly, **democratic governance**. DPoS introduces a governance model where token holders can influence who runs the network. This democratic aspect can lead to a more responsive and accountable system, where validators are incentivized to perform well not just for financial rewards but to maintain community trust and support for future elections.

However, the beauty of DPoS is not without its complexities or criticisms. One of the primary concerns revolves around **centralization**. By reducing the number of validators, there's a risk that only a few powerful entities could dominate the network, either through wealth, influence, or collusion. This could undermine the decentralized ethos of blockchain technology if not carefully managed.

Another challenge is **vote buying**, where individuals or entities might offer incentives or rewards to token holders in exchange for votes. While this is not unique to DPoS, the system's structure might exacerbate such practices if there aren't robust measures in place to detect and deter them.

Then there's the matter of **security**. While staking provides a deterrent against malicious behavior through potential financial penalties, the system's security heavily relies on the integrity of the validators. If a majority of validators collude or if a significant portion of the stake is controlled by a few, the network could be compromised.

Despite these challenges, DPoS offers mechanisms to mitigate risks:

- **Rotation of Validators:** Many DPoS systems implement a system where validators serve only for a limited time before new elections or rotations occur, preventing long-term monopolies on validation power.
- **Slashing Conditions:** Validators can face penalties, including the loss of their staked tokens, for failing to perform their duties or for acting maliciously, providing a strong economic disincentive against bad behavior.

- **Delegation Limits:** Some systems impose limits on how much stake one can delegate to a single validator to prevent centralization.
- **Community Governance:** Beyond just electing validators, DPoS can incorporate broader governance models where community members can propose and vote on changes to the protocol, ensuring the system evolves with community input.

The philosophy behind DPoS is not just about achieving consensus; it's about creating a blockchain where the power dynamics are more reflective of a democratic society. It's an attempt to balance the need for efficiency and scalability with the core blockchain principles of decentralization and community involvement.

Looking deeper into the mechanics, the actual process of block production in DPoS is designed to be as transparent and fair as possible. Once validators are elected, they are often scheduled to produce blocks in a predictable sequence, which can be known in advance by the network's participants. This predictability adds a layer of trust and reduces the chance of block withholding or other forms of manipulation.

Moreover, the economic model of DPoS often includes rewards for validators, distributed in the form of newly minted tokens or transaction fees, incentivizing honest participation. However, this also introduces questions about inflation, token distribution, and the long-term economic health of the network.

As we move towards understanding Sui's specific implementation of DPoS, it's crucial to appreciate that DPoS isn't just a technical framework; it's a social one. It redefines how participants in a blockchain ecosystem can interact, govern, and evolve their digital environment. The success of DPoS in any blockchain, including Sui, hinges not only on the technical robustness of the implementation but also on how well it aligns with the values, needs, and expectations of its community.

In conclusion, Delegated Proof-of-Stake represents a significant evolution in consensus mechanisms, offering a pathway towards more efficient, less resource-intensive, and potentially more democratic blockchain networks. As we delve deeper into Sui's approach to DPoS, we'll explore how these theoretical benefits are realized in practice, the unique adaptations Sui makes, and how they address or navigate the inherent challenges of this consensus model.

Part 3: Sui's Implementation of DPoS

In the vibrant ecosystem of blockchain technology, where innovation is the currency of progress, Sui introduces a tailored version of Delegated Proof-of-Stake (DPoS) that seeks to harness the benefits of this consensus mechanism while addressing its challenges in a novel way. This part of our exploration dives deep into how Sui uniquely implements DPoS, weaving together the technological, economic, and social fabric of its network to create a blockchain that's not only secure and efficient but also reflective of a community-driven ethos.

At the core of Sui's philosophy is the idea that blockchain should be an accessible, inclusive, and highly functional platform for a wide range of applications. To achieve this vision, Sui's DPoS model is designed to balance the need for speed, security, and decentralization, with a keen eye on fostering a vibrant developer and user community.

Sui's journey with DPoS begins with the selection of validators. Unlike some implementations where the number of validators might be fixed, Sui opts for a dynamic approach. This means the number of validators can adjust based on network needs, potentially scaling up during times of high demand or scaling down for efficiency during quieter periods. This flexibility aims to optimize the network's performance while maintaining a level of decentralization that prevents any single entity from exerting undue influence.

The process of becoming a validator in Sui is both an opportunity and a responsibility. Potential validators must stake a significant amount of SUI tokens, demonstrating their commitment to the network's health. However, Sui introduces a nuanced system where not only the wealth but also the reputation and performance of candidates are considered. This multi-faceted approach to validator selection includes:

- **Stake Amount:** Like in traditional DPoS, the amount of SUI staked plays a role, but it's not the sole criterion.
- **Reputation Score:** Sui might employ mechanisms where validators are rated or scored based on their past performance, community feedback, or adherence to certain operational standards.
- **Community Endorsement:** A form of social proof where community members can endorse validators, adding a layer of democratic selection that goes beyond mere financial investment.

This selection process is underpinned by Sui's commitment to transparency and community involvement. Elections or selections for validators are not shrouded in mystery but are events where the community can actively participate, either by voting directly or influencing the selection through their interactions and endorsements within the ecosystem.

Once selected, validators in Sui are tasked with more than just adding blocks to the chain. They are custodians of the network's integrity, particularly in Sui's object-centric model where transactions involve not just value transfer but complex state changes of digital objects. Here, validators must ensure:

- **Accuracy of State Transitions:** Each transaction or interaction with an object must be verified to ensure that the state changes are correct and intended.

- **Consistency:** Across the network, all nodes must agree on the state of objects after each transaction.
- **Security:** Validators must guard against malicious attempts to alter object states or manipulate transactions.

To manage these responsibilities, Sui's DPoS system incorporates:

- **Efficient Block Production:** Validators are scheduled to produce blocks in a manner that maximizes throughput while minimizing conflict. This scheduling could be influenced by the validator's performance metrics, ensuring that those who contribute most effectively to the network's health are rewarded with more opportunities.
- **Parallel Execution:** Given Sui's focus on handling complex object interactions, the consensus mechanism is designed to support parallel processing of transactions, allowing for multiple validators to work on different transactions simultaneously, significantly increasing the network's capacity.
- **Instant Finality:** Unlike some blockchains where transactions might require several confirmations, Sui aims for transactions to be considered final as soon as they are included in a block, leveraging the trust in its validator set.

The economic model surrounding validators in Sui is another critical aspect. Staking SUI to become or support a validator is an investment with potential rewards, but it also comes with risks:

- **Rewards:** Validators earn through block rewards and transaction fees, incentivizing active participation and network maintenance.
- **Penalties:** Misbehavior, such as going offline without notice, attempting to alter transactions maliciously, or failing to uphold network standards, can lead to slashing of staked tokens or temporary exclusion from the validator set.
- **Inflation Control:** The issuance of new SUI tokens to reward validators is managed with an eye on long-term economic stability, balancing the need to incentivize participation with the risk of inflation.

Sui also introduces mechanisms to ensure that the validator set remains dynamic and reflective of the community's wishes over time:

- **Validator Rotation:** Similar to political elections, there's a process where validators can be voted out or new ones voted in, ensuring no permanent control by a few.
- **Delegation Flexibility:** Token holders can delegate their stake to validators they trust or believe in, but also have the freedom to shift their support, encouraging validators to perform well continuously.
- **Self-Healing Networks:** If a validator fails or is compromised, the system can quickly adapt,

reassigning roles or increasing the number of validators to maintain network integrity.

This implementation of DPoS by Sui isn't just about technical prowess; it's about creating a social contract where participants feel they have a stake in the network's future. It's an acknowledgment that the security, efficiency, and direction of Sui are co-authored by its community, not dictated by a handful of nodes.

However, this approach doesn't come without its challenges:

- **Scalability vs. Decentralization:** As the network grows, balancing the number of validators with network performance and security becomes more complex. Too few could lead to centralization; too many might slow down consensus.
- **Voter Apathy:** If the community doesn't actively participate in the selection or governance of validators, the system could drift towards centralization or inefficiency.
- **Complexity for Users:** The nuanced system of selecting validators based on more than just stake requires users to be more engaged or informed, which could be a barrier for mainstream adoption.
- **Security Risks:** While the system aims for robustness, any flaw in how validators are selected, rewarded, or penalized could be exploited.

Sui's response to these challenges includes continuous engagement with its community, transparent governance processes, and a commitment to evolving the DPoS model as the network learns and grows. Educational efforts, user-friendly interfaces for staking and delegation, and clear, enforceable rules for validator conduct are all part of this broader strategy.

In essence, Sui's implementation of DPoS is a testament to the belief that blockchain networks should not only be technically innovative but also socially dynamic. It's an attempt to craft a consensus mechanism that doesn't just secure transactions but nurtures a community where each member has the power to influence the network's future. As we delve into the specifics of staking and token economics in Sui, these foundational principles will become even more apparent, showcasing how Sui envisions a blockchain where technology serves the collective good.

Part 4: Staking and Token Economics in Sui

In the intricate dance of blockchain economics, where every token, transaction, and stake plays a role in the symphony of network health and community engagement, Sui's approach to staking and its token economics stands out as a meticulously designed choreography. This part of our exploration delves into the heart of Sui's economic model, focusing on how staking SUI tokens not only secures the network but also shapes its economic landscape, governance, and the incentives that drive participation.

Staking, in the context of Sui, is not merely a technical requirement for running nodes or becoming validators; it's a profound economic and social mechanism that empowers token holders to have a direct impact on the network's operation and future. By staking their SUI tokens, users commit their assets to the network's consensus process, effectively betting on the integrity and growth of Sui. This commitment serves multiple purposes:

First, it acts as a security deposit, ensuring that validators have skin in the game. If a validator acts maliciously or fails to perform their duties adequately, a portion or all of their staked tokens can be "slashed" or forfeited, providing a strong financial incentive against bad behavior.

Second, staking is the gateway to earning rewards. Validators who successfully add blocks to the chain or help maintain network stability are rewarded with new SUI tokens or transaction fees, distributing the benefits of network growth among those who contribute to its security and efficiency. This reward system not only incentivizes staking but also helps in distributing the newly minted tokens in a manner that supports network decentralization.

Third, staking in Sui is intertwined with governance. Holding and staking SUI tokens can come with voting rights, allowing token holders to influence decisions about the network's development, validator selection, or changes to protocol rules. This aspect of staking turns token holders into stakeholders with a say in the network's direction, fostering a sense of ownership and responsibility.

The mechanics of staking in Sui are designed to be accessible yet incentivize long-term commitment:

- **Staking Process:** To stake, users lock up their SUI tokens within the network for a period, which could be influenced by the need for network stability or to reward long-term commitment. This process can be done directly if one wishes to run a validator node or indirectly by delegating stake to existing validators.
- **Delegation:** Recognizing that not everyone has the resources or desire to operate a validator node, Sui allows for token holders to delegate their stake to validators they trust or believe in. This delegation is not a passive act; it's a vote of confidence and a way to earn rewards without the operational overhead of running a node.
- **Reward Distribution:** Validators earn from block rewards and transaction fees, but a portion of these rewards is often shared with those who have delegated their stake to them. This sharing mechanism ensures that even those who don't run nodes can benefit from the network's success, promoting broader participation.

The economics of the SUI token within this staking ecosystem are carefully calibrated:

- **Token Supply:** Sui might employ a strategy where the total supply of SUI tokens is either fixed or grows at a controlled rate to combat inflation while ensuring there's enough incentive for staking. The issuance rate of new tokens as rewards can be adjusted based on network needs or economic conditions.
- **Inflation and Deflation:** By managing the token supply and staking rewards, Sui aims to maintain a balance where inflation doesn't devalue the token significantly, yet there's enough incentive to keep tokens staked, thus securing the network. In scenarios of high staking, the rewards per staked token might decrease, naturally controlling inflation.
- **Economic Incentives:** Beyond rewards, the economic model might include mechanisms like fee discounts for stakers, priority in network operations, or special rights in governance, all of which serve to make staking an attractive proposition.
- **Liquidity Considerations:** While staking locks tokens away, Sui might introduce features like staking pools or liquid staking derivatives to allow staked tokens to be used in DeFi applications or traded without unstaking, thus maintaining liquidity.

The governance aspect of staking cannot be overstated. In Sui, governance might extend beyond validator elections to include:

- **Proposals and Voting:** Staked token holders could vote on proposals regarding network

upgrades, fee structures, or other governance issues. This process ensures that changes to the network reflect the community's collective will.
- **Dynamic Governance:** As the network evolves, so might the governance model, with staking potentially influencing how new governance proposals are made, how often elections occur, or how decisions are implemented.

However, the staking and token economics model in Sui comes with its set of challenges and considerations:

- **Centralization Risks:** If a few entities accumulate large stakes, they could dominate validator elections or governance decisions, which could lead to centralization. Sui must balance this by encouraging broad participation in staking.
- **Staking Commitment:** Long-term staking is beneficial for network stability but could deter participation if users prefer liquidity. Sui needs to make staking attractive without compromising on the commitment aspect.
- **Economic Fluctuations:** The value of SUI and thus the attractiveness of staking rewards can fluctuate, impacting staking participation. A robust economic model must account for these fluctuations to maintain network security.
- **Reward Distribution Fairness:** Ensuring that rewards are distributed in a way that incentivizes participation without favoring the

already wealthy or well-staked is crucial. Sui's model must strive for this balance to maintain decentralization.

- **Security of Staked Assets:** With significant amounts of SUI staked, the security of these assets becomes paramount. Sui needs to ensure that staking mechanisms are protected against hacks or exploits.

Sui's approach to staking and token economics is thus a delicate balance act. It's about creating an ecosystem where:

- **Security** is maintained through economic incentives.
- **Decentralization** is preserved through inclusive staking policies.
- **Growth** is fostered by rewarding participation.
- **Governance** is democratized by giving voice to staked token holders.

This economic model, when executed well, can lead to a virtuous cycle where more people stake, leading to a more secure and decentralized network, which in turn increases the value and utility of SUI, encouraging even more staking. However, it requires continuous monitoring, adjustments based on real-world performance, and perhaps most importantly, a community that's engaged and believes in the vision of Sui.

As we look at how this model plays out in practice, we see that Sui's staking isn't just about securing transactions but about building a community where each member feels they have a stake in the network's success. This part of Sui's design philosophy aims to make the blockchain not just a technological marvel but a living, breathing ecosystem where economics, governance, and community converge to create something greater than the sum of its parts.

Part 5: Security and Decentralization in Sui's DPoS

In the narrative of blockchain technology, where security and decentralization form the twin pillars upon which trust and innovation rest, Sui's implementation of Delegated Proof-of-Stake (DPoS) stands as a testament to the quest for a harmonious balance between these ideals. This chapter segment explores how Sui navigates the complex waters of ensuring network security while fostering an environment of true decentralization, where power is distributed rather than concentrated.

Security in blockchain isn't just about protecting data; it's about safeguarding the trust that users place in the system's integrity. In the context of Sui's DPoS, security is multifaceted, involving not only the technical aspects of consensus and state management but also the economic incentives and governance structures that underpin the network's operation.

At the heart of Sui's security model is the principle that the cost of attacking the network should far outweigh any possible gain. This is achieved through:

- **Economic Stake:** By requiring validators to stake significant amounts of SUI tokens, Sui ensures that those with the power to alter the blockchain's state have a substantial financial incentive to act honestly. The threat of slashing – losing a portion or all of their staked tokens – serves as a deterrent against malicious behavior.
- **Validator Performance:** Sui's approach to validator selection isn't solely based on the amount staked but also on performance metrics, which might include uptime, block production rates, or even community feedback. This performance-based selection encourages validators to maintain high standards of operation, contributing to network security.
- **Transparent Governance:** Security is also bolstered by open governance processes where changes to the protocol, including security upgrades or responses to vulnerabilities, can be proposed and voted upon by the community. This transparency ensures that security measures evolve with community consensus, reducing the risk of unilateral decisions that could compromise the network.

However, economic incentives alone aren't sufficient; the technical design of the consensus mechanism plays a crucial role:

- **Parallel Execution:** Sui's architecture supports the parallel processing of transactions, which not only increases throughput but also complicates potential attacks by requiring adversaries to compromise multiple validators simultaneously, significantly raising the attack's complexity and cost.

- **Consensus Algorithms:** Beyond just DPoS, Sui might employ additional consensus protocols or checks to ensure that no single validator or group can unilaterally dictate the state of the blockchain. This could involve cross-validation, where transactions are verified by multiple validators before being considered final.
- **State Management:** Given Sui's object-centric model, ensuring the integrity of object states across the network is a security challenge. Validators must coordinate to confirm that state changes are legitimate, requiring a robust mechanism for consensus on complex state transitions.

Decentralization, on the other hand, is where the ideal meets reality. Sui's DPoS model aims to distribute control and decision-making power across a broad base of participants:

- **Broad Validator Base:** While DPoS traditionally reduces the number of validators for efficiency, Sui seeks to maintain a balance where the validator set is large enough to prevent control by a few but small enough to ensure efficiency. This might involve dynamic adjustments to the number of validators based on network conditions or community decisions.

- **Delegation and Participation:** By making it easy for token holders to delegate their stake, Sui encourages widespread participation in governance and security. This delegation model ensures that even those without the resources to run a node can have a say in network operations, diluting potential power concentration.
- **Voting and Governance:** Decentralization is further supported by giving staked token holders voting rights in critical decisions, from validator elections to protocol upgrades. This participatory governance model aims to reflect the community's collective will, reducing the chances of centralization through unilateral control.
- **Economic Incentives for Diversity:** Sui's economic model might include incentives for new validators or those from underrepresented regions or communities, aiming to keep the network's power base diverse and reducing the risk of centralization.

Yet, achieving and maintaining this balance between security and decentralization presents several challenges:

- **Centralization Risks:** Despite the mechanisms in place, there's always the potential for wealth concentration leading to a few dominant validators. Sui must continuously monitor and adjust its policies to counteract this, perhaps through caps on stake concentration or additional incentives for smaller stakes.

- **Security of the Staking Mechanism:** The very system that makes staking attractive also makes it a target. Sui must ensure that staking pools, delegation mechanisms, and the staking process itself are secure against hacks, ensuring that staked assets remain safe.
- **Performance vs. Decentralization:** As the network scales, the temptation might be to optimize for performance by reducing the validator count. Sui needs to resist this, finding ways to scale that don't compromise on decentralization, possibly through technological innovations like sharding or layer-2 solutions.
- **Community Engagement:** Decentralization depends on active participation. Apathy or disengagement can lead to a small group making decisions for the many. Sui must foster a vibrant, engaged community, perhaps through educational programs, user-friendly interfaces for governance participation, or rewards for active involvement.
- **Adapting to Threats:** The blockchain space is dynamic, with new security threats emerging regularly. Sui's security must adapt, learning from incidents or vulnerabilities in other networks, and evolving its consensus and governance models to stay ahead.

Sui's strategy to mitigate these challenges involves:

- **Continuous Monitoring and Adaptation:** Regular audits of the network's health, validator performance, and economic balance to ensure that security and decentralization are not just ideals but realities.
- **Community Education and Involvement:** Efforts to keep the community informed, engaged, and capable of participating in governance, thus ensuring that decentralization is a living, breathing aspect of the network.
- **Technological Innovation:** Investing in research and development to find new ways to secure the network while maintaining or even enhancing its decentralized nature. This could mean exploring new consensus mechanisms or enhancing the current one with additional layers of security.
- **Economic Model Tweaks:** Fine-tuning the economics of staking, rewards, and penalties to encourage a healthy distribution of power and participation without inadvertently promoting centralization.
- **Transparent Incident Response:** When security issues arise, as they inevitably will, having clear, community-involved processes for response and resolution helps maintain trust and demonstrates commitment to both security and decentralization.

In essence, Sui's approach to security and decentralization within its DPoS framework is about crafting a system where the network's integrity is protected not just by code and algorithms but by the collective vigilance and participation of its community. It's an acknowledgment that in blockchain, security is as much a social construct as it is a technical one, where decentralization is not merely about distributing nodes but about empowering individuals with a stake in the system's success and governance.

As Sui continues to evolve, this delicate balance will be its ongoing challenge and opportunity, proving that in the blockchain world, security and decentralization are not just features but the very essence of the ecosystem's resilience and potential.

Part 6: Future Prospects and Challenges

As we cast our gaze towards the horizon of blockchain technology, with Sui's unique implementation of Delegated Proof-of-Stake (DPoS) as our focal point, we stand at the threshold of a future rich with possibilities yet fraught with challenges. This final chapter segment explores the potential trajectories of Sui's consensus mechanism, the hurdles it might face, and how these could shape the broader landscape of decentralized systems.

The future of Sui's DPoS model is a canvas painted with the strokes of innovation, community, and adaptation. One of the most promising prospects lies in scalability. As blockchain applications grow in complexity and demand, the ability of a network to handle an increasing number of transactions without compromising on speed, security, or decentralization becomes paramount. Sui's DPoS, with its focus on parallel execution, offers a fertile ground for scaling solutions:

- **Enhanced Parallelism:** Future iterations might see even more sophisticated use of parallel processing, allowing for an exponential increase in transaction throughput. This could transform Sui into a backbone for real-time applications, from financial transactions to interactive virtual worlds.
- **Dynamic Validator Sets:** Sui could refine its approach to adjust the number of validators in real-time based on network load, offering a balance between efficiency during peak times and security during quieter periods. This adaptability would ensure that the network scales with demand, maintaining performance without sacrificing decentralization.
- **Layer-2 Solutions:** Integrating or developing layer-2 scaling solutions could further amplify Sui's capacity. These could range from state channels for microtransactions to more complex sidechains or rollups that handle certain types of transactions off the main chain, reducing congestion and enhancing speed.

The evolution of Sui's consensus mechanism might also delve into security enhancements:

- **Advanced Cryptographic Techniques:** Incorporating cutting-edge cryptography, like zero-knowledge proofs for privacy or homomorphic encryption for secure computation, could make Sui a leader in secure, private transactions without compromising on the public nature of blockchain.

- **AI and Machine Learning:** Future developments could see AI used in anomaly detection for network security, predicting validator performance, or even optimizing the consensus process itself, making the network more resilient against attacks and more efficient.
- **Quantum-Resistant Algorithms:** As quantum computing looms on the horizon, ensuring that Sui's consensus mechanisms and cryptographic protocols are resistant to quantum attacks will be crucial, safeguarding the network's long-term security.

On the governance front, Sui's DPoS could evolve to become even more participatory:

- **Decentralized Autonomous Organizations (DAOs):** Sui might integrate more deeply with DAO frameworks, allowing for community-driven decision-making on a broader scale, from validator elections to protocol changes, making governance more fluid, transparent, and inclusive.
- **Token Holder Rights:** Further evolution might include expanding the rights of token holders, perhaps with mechanisms for proposing changes directly to the protocol or initiating community votes on operational aspects of the network.

- **Governance 2.0:** Looking further ahead, governance could become more dynamic, with smart contracts that adapt to community feedback or market conditions, ensuring that Sui's governance remains relevant and effective as the ecosystem grows.

However, these prospects come hand in hand with challenges:

- **Regulatory Adaptation:** As blockchain technology becomes more mainstream, the regulatory landscape will evolve. Sui will need to navigate these changes, ensuring compliance while advocating for regulations that support innovation and privacy. This might involve geo-specific adaptations or even influencing regulatory frameworks through community action.
- **Environmental Sustainability:** Despite being more energy-efficient than PoW, the environmental impact of any blockchain, including DPoS systems, will come under scrutiny. Sui might need to explore further optimizations or even offset mechanisms to maintain or improve its environmental footprint.
- **Interoperability:** The future of blockchain is likely to be multichain, where networks like Sui must interoperate with others for a seamless user experience. Developing standards or protocols for cross-chain communication without compromising security or decentralization will be a significant challenge.

- **Centralization Tendencies:** Even with DPoS's democratic ethos, the constant battle against centralization will persist. Sui must innovate in its economic models, perhaps introducing new ways to distribute power or incentivize participation from underrepresented groups.
- **User Experience:** For broader adoption, the complexities of staking, governance, and even using the blockchain must be abstracted into user-friendly interfaces. This challenge involves not just technological solutions but also educational efforts to demystify blockchain for the average user.
- **Security vs. Innovation:** As Sui pushes the boundaries of what's possible with blockchain, balancing this innovation with maintaining the network's security will be a tightrope walk. Each new feature or integration must be scrutinized for potential vulnerabilities.
- **Economic Models:** The sustainability of the token economy, including managing inflation, ensuring fair reward distribution, and preventing market manipulation, will require ongoing adjustments to Sui's economic policies.

Looking beyond these challenges, the broader impact of Sui's DPoS on the blockchain industry could be profound:

- **A Model for Decentralized Governance:** Sui could become a case study for how blockchain can facilitate true democratic governance, influencing other projects to adopt similar models.

- **Setting New Standards for Consensus:** As Sui refines its consensus mechanism, it might set new benchmarks for what's expected from blockchain networks in terms of speed, security, and decentralization, pushing the entire industry forward.
- **Ecosystem Growth:** By solving these challenges, Sui could attract a diverse array of applications, from finance to gaming, IoT to supply chain, each leveraging the robustness of its DPoS model for their unique needs.
- **Cultural Shift:** Perhaps most importantly, Sui's approach could contribute to a cultural shift in how we view digital assets, governance, and community involvement in technology, fostering a more inclusive, participatory digital future.

In conclusion, the journey of Sui's DPoS is emblematic of the broader journey of blockchain technology – one of continuous evolution, where each step forward is a negotiation between ideals and practicalities, between the vision of a decentralized future and the realities of achieving it. The future of Sui, and by extension, the future of blockchain, hinges on how well it can address these challenges, innovate within its consensus model, and engage its community in the co-creation of this digital ecosystem. As we continue to witness and participate in this saga, Sui's DPoS stands not just as a technical achievement but as a narrative of human collaboration, ambition, and the relentless pursuit of a more decentralized, secure, and inclusive world.

Chapter 7: Transaction Processing in Sui: Parallel Execution and Finality

Part 1: Introduction to Transaction Processing in Blockchain

In the vast, digital tapestry of blockchain technology, where every thread represents a transaction, a piece of information, or a moment of consensus, the process of transaction processing stands as one of the most critical components. This process defines how data moves through the network, how trust is maintained, and how the blockchain's promise of security, transparency, and efficiency is fulfilled. In this chapter, we delve into Sui's innovative approach to transaction processing, focusing on parallel execution and finality, but first, we must understand the context and evolution of transaction processing in blockchain systems at large.

Imagine the blockchain as a digital ledger, not just of financial transactions but of any kind of data that needs to be recorded in a tamper-proof manner. From the outset, with the inception of Bitcoin in 2009, blockchain technology introduced the world to a method of transaction processing that was revolutionary for its time. Bitcoin employed a system known as Proof of Work (PoW), where transactions are bundled into blocks, and miners compete to solve complex mathematical puzzles to add these blocks to the chain. This process, while secure due to its computational intensity, came with significant drawbacks, particularly in terms of speed and scalability.

The heart of the issue with traditional blockchain transaction processing lies in its sequential nature. Each transaction, or more accurately, each block of transactions, is processed one after the other. This sequential processing ensures that the state of the blockchain remains consistent across all nodes, but it also means that as more transactions are added, the time it takes for each transaction to be confirmed increases. This can lead to bottlenecks, especially during times of high network demand, where transactions might wait in a queue for confirmation, sometimes for hours or even days in extreme cases.

This limitation has profound implications:

Firstly, it impacts user experience. In a world where digital interactions demand instantaneity, waiting for a transaction to be confirmed can be frustrating, particularly for applications requiring immediate feedback, like online gaming, real-time bidding, or even simple payments.

Secondly, it affects scalability. As the number of users and transactions on a blockchain grows, the network's ability to process these transactions at a rate that keeps up with demand becomes a bottleneck. This scalability issue has been one of the most significant challenges for blockchain adoption in mainstream applications.

Thirdly, it influences security and consensus. In PoW systems, the security of the network is tied to the difficulty of solving these puzzles, which scales with the number of transactions. However, this also means more energy consumption and longer confirmation times, creating a trade-off between security, speed, and environmental impact.

Recognizing these limitations, the blockchain community has been on a quest for alternative mechanisms that could process transactions more efficiently. Ethereum introduced smart contracts, which added a layer of complexity to transactions by allowing conditional execution based on code, but still within a sequential processing framework. Other blockchains experimented with different consensus mechanisms like Proof of Stake (PoS), aiming to reduce energy consumption and speed up transaction times, yet these solutions still struggled with the fundamental problem of sequential processing.

Enter Sui, with its vision of a blockchain where transactions are not just processed with speed but with a level of parallelism that redefines what's possible in a decentralized environment. Sui's approach is built on the foundation of understanding that many transactions in the real world do not depend on each other; they can and should be processed concurrently. This parallelism is not just about doing things faster; it's about reimagining how a blockchain can function in a world where applications demand not just security and immutability but also real-time interaction.

The shift from sequential to parallel processing in Sui is underpinned by several key innovations:

- An object-centric model where transactions are not just transfers of value but interactions with digital objects that can exist independently on the blockchain. This model allows for a more nuanced understanding of transaction dependencies, enabling many to be processed in parallel.
- A consensus mechanism designed to support parallel execution, ensuring that the network can validate multiple transactions at once without compromising on the integrity of the ledger.
- An architecture that prioritizes finality - ensuring that once a transaction is processed, it's considered irreversible almost immediately, which is crucial for applications where timing is everything.

This shift towards parallelism in transaction processing is not merely technical; it's transformative for the potential applications of blockchain technology. It opens up possibilities for:

- Financial services where transactions need to be settled in real-time, without the delays that could frustrate users or cause market inefficiencies.
- Gaming ecosystems where player actions, asset movements, or game state changes need to reflect instantly across all participants to maintain immersion and fairness.

- Supply chain management where the real-time tracking of goods, certifications, or compliance status could revolutionize logistics and transparency.

However, this transformation also poses new challenges:

- Ensuring that parallel transactions do not lead to conflicts or inconsistencies in the blockchain state is crucial. Sui must employ sophisticated conflict detection and resolution mechanisms.
- Scalability in terms of handling an increasing number of parallel transactions while maintaining network performance and security.
- Educating developers and users on how to leverage this new model of transaction processing, as the traditional mindset of sequential operations needs to evolve.

Sui's journey in transaction processing is a narrative of pushing boundaries, not just in terms of what blockchain can do but in redefining what it means to interact with digital assets. It's about creating a blockchain environment where the latency between action and outcome is minimized, where the digital world can mimic the immediacy of physical interactions, and where the barriers to entry for complex, real-time applications are significantly lowered.

As we proceed through this chapter, we will explore how Sui achieves this parallelism, the mechanics of its transaction processing, and the implications for finality - all crucial aspects that not only define Sui's capabilities but also signal a potential paradigm shift for blockchain technology at large. This introduction sets the stage for understanding how Sui's innovative approach could be a harbinger of a new era in blockchain, where efficiency, speed, and user experience are not just improved but fundamentally redefined.

Part 2: The Concept of Parallel Execution

In the labyrinthine world of blockchain technology, where the promise of decentralization meets the practicalities of scalability and speed, the concept of parallel execution emerges as a beacon of innovation. Parallel execution in the context of blockchain transaction processing is not merely an upgrade; it's a paradigm shift that redefines how digital interactions can occur across a decentralized network. Here, we delve into the intricacies of parallel execution, exploring how this concept is applied in Sui to transform the landscape of blockchain operations.

At its core, parallel execution is about breaking away from the linear, one-at-a-time processing that has characterized traditional blockchain systems. In those systems, transactions are processed sequentially, much like cars on a highway with a single lane. If one car slows down, the entire line behind it must wait. This metaphor aptly describes how blockchain networks like Bitcoin or early Ethereum handled transactions, leading to congestion, high fees, and long confirmation times during peak usage periods.

Parallel execution, on the other hand, is akin to creating multiple lanes on that digital highway, allowing many cars (transactions) to move forward simultaneously, dramatically increasing the throughput of the network. This isn't just about speed; it's about reimagining how transactions can interact, or more importantly, how they often don't need to interact at all to proceed concurrently.

The fundamental principle behind parallel execution in blockchain is the recognition that not all transactions are interdependent. Many transactions can be processed independently because they don't affect the same state variables or digital objects. For instance, if Alice sends Bob some cryptocurrency and Charlie sends tokens to Denise, these two events can happen in parallel because they don't conflict; they are independent updates to the blockchain state.

Here's how this concept plays out in a more technical sense:

In traditional blockchains, each block contains a set of transactions, and these blocks are added to the chain sequentially. Each transaction within a block must be processed in order, checking for conflicts with previous transactions. This means if one transaction depends on the state change of another in the same block, it must wait until that state change is confirmed.

Sui, however, introduces a model where the dependency graph of transactions is analyzed to determine which can be processed in parallel:

- **Transaction Dependency Analysis:** Before transactions are executed, they are analyzed for dependencies. If two transactions do not share dependencies, they can be processed simultaneously. This analysis can be complex, as it involves understanding not just explicit dependencies (like a transaction that spends coins created by another) but also implicit ones that might arise from shared resources or states.
- **Dynamic Scheduling:** Once dependencies are understood, transactions are scheduled for execution. Sui's architecture allows for dynamic scheduling where the order of transaction execution can adapt based on current network conditions or the specific nature of the transactions. This means that even if the network experiences high load, transactions without conflicts can still proceed without delay.
- **Execution Environment:** Sui's execution environment is designed to handle multiple transactions at once, leveraging the computational power of the network in a distributed manner. This involves not just the hardware capabilities of the nodes but also sophisticated software that can manage and orchestrate this parallel execution.

The benefits of parallel execution in Sui are manifold:

- **Increased Throughput:** By allowing multiple transactions to be processed simultaneously, the network can handle a significantly higher volume of transactions per second, potentially reaching throughputs that are orders of magnitude higher than traditional blockchains.

- **Reduced Latency:** For users and applications, this means transactions can be confirmed much faster. In scenarios where time is of the essence, like in financial trading or real-time gaming, this reduction in latency can be transformative.
- **Scalability:** As the network grows or as demand for transactions increases, parallel execution allows for scaling without the need for a proportional increase in resources or a compromise on security. This scalability is crucial for blockchain to be viable for mainstream applications.
- **Efficient Resource Use:** Instead of every node in the network processing every transaction sequentially, parallel execution means that resources (like computational power, storage, and bandwidth) are used more efficiently, potentially leading to lower operational costs and environmental impact.

However, implementing parallel execution is not without its challenges:

- **Conflict Management:** Even with sophisticated dependency analysis, conflicts can arise. Managing these conflicts without stalling the entire network requires robust mechanisms to either resolve conflicts on-the-fly or to requeue conflicting transactions for later execution.

- **Consistency and Integrity:** Ensuring that the blockchain's state remains consistent across all nodes when multiple transactions are updating it simultaneously is complex. Sui must employ advanced consensus algorithms and state management techniques to guarantee that the final state of any transaction is the same across the network.
- **Security Implications:** Parallel execution can introduce new attack vectors or vulnerabilities if not implemented correctly. Ensuring that no malicious transactions can exploit the parallelism to compromise the integrity of the blockchain is paramount.
- **Complexity for Developers:** Moving from a sequential to a parallel processing model requires developers to think differently about how they write smart contracts or design applications. They must now consider how their transactions interact or don't interact with others, which can be a learning curve.
- **Network Load Balancing:** As transactions are processed in parallel, ensuring that no single part of the network is overloaded while others are underutilized becomes crucial. This involves load balancing strategies that might be more complex than in traditional systems.

The vision of parallel execution in Sui is to not just handle more transactions but to change the very nature of what a blockchain can do:

- **Real-Time Applications:** With transactions processed in parallel, real-time applications become feasible on a blockchain scale. This could revolutionize areas like gaming, where actions need to reflect instantly across thousands of users, or in financial markets where trading speeds can define success or failure.

- **Complex Digital Interactions:** Sui's object-centric approach combined with parallel execution allows for complex interactions between digital assets. Imagine a virtual world where objects can change, combine, or interact in real-time, all managed by the blockchain.
- **Enhanced User Experience:** By reducing wait times and increasing the responsiveness of the network, Sui can offer a user experience that rivals or even surpasses centralized systems, making blockchain technology more accessible and appealing to a broader audience.
- **Economic Efficiency:** With lower transaction times and potentially lower fees due to increased efficiency, the economic models around using blockchain for various services could become more viable, encouraging more widespread adoption.

As we look forward, the journey of parallel execution in Sui is one of continuous refinement and innovation. It will involve not just technological advancements but also a shift in how developers, users, and the blockchain community at large perceive and interact with digital transactions. The promise of parallel execution is to unlock a blockchain where speed, scalability, and security converge to create a platform not just for value transfer but for the dynamic, real-time operation of digital economies, societies, and games.

In essence, parallel execution in Sui isn't just about doing more; it's about doing differently, about reimagining the potential of blockchain as not just a database but as a living, breathing digital ecosystem where transactions are the lifeblood of interaction, creation, and evolution.

Part 3: Sui's Architecture for Parallelism

In the intricate dance of blockchain technology, where every step towards scalability, speed, and security must be meticulously choreographed, Sui introduces an architecture that redefines the possibilities of parallel transaction processing. This part explores how Sui's foundational design supports the concept of parallelism, making it possible to handle transactions in a manner that traditional blockchains could only dream of. The journey into Sui's architecture reveals a system where the digital world can operate with the fluidity and dynamism of the physical, where transactions are not just points of data but moments of interaction in a vast, decentralized ecosystem.

At the heart of Sui's architecture is its object-centric model. Unlike traditional blockchains where transactions are primarily about transferring value or updating simple states, Sui treats data as objects with their own lifecycle, behavior, and state. This paradigm shift is crucial for parallelism because it allows for a more granular understanding of transaction dependencies. In an object-centric world, transactions are not just about moving value from A to B; they're about how different objects interact or change state. This approach enables Sui to identify which transactions can truly run in parallel by examining which objects are involved, allowing for transactions that do not touch the same or related objects to be processed concurrently.

The next pillar of Sui's architecture supporting parallelism is its consensus mechanism, which is tailored to accommodate the asynchronous nature of parallel execution. While many blockchains use consensus to agree on a single, sequential chain of blocks, Sui's consensus is designed to handle a network where transactions can be agreed upon in parallel. This involves a sophisticated process where validators not only agree on the validity of transactions but also on the order of transactions when necessary, ensuring that even in a parallel environment, the blockchain maintains a consistent state. This consensus is achieved through a combination of Delegated Proof-of-Stake (DPoS) and additional protocols that manage the timing and coordination of these parallel operations.

Sui's architecture leverages an innovative transaction execution environment that is inherently parallel. This environment is where the magic happens; transactions are not just processed one after the other but are managed in a way where multiple can be executed simultaneously. This execution environment is built on the ability of the network to distribute computational tasks across validators efficiently. Each validator can work on different transactions or parts of the same transaction, depending on the dependencies, using a scheduling algorithm that dynamically allocates resources based on the current state of the network and the complexity of the transactions.

To ensure that parallel execution does not lead to inconsistencies or conflicts, Sui employs a complex but elegant dependency analysis system. Before execution, transactions are analyzed to map out their dependencies. This analysis is not just about seeing if two transactions touch the same account or asset but involves understanding the broader context of how objects relate within the system. If transactions are independent, they proceed in parallel; if they share dependencies, they are queued or executed with precautions to manage potential conflicts, ensuring that the blockchain's state remains consistent across all nodes.

The architecture also includes a robust conflict resolution mechanism. Even with sophisticated dependency analysis, conflicts can arise due to unforeseen interactions or changes in object states. When conflicts occur, Sui's system can either resolve them in real-time, rollback one of the conflicting transactions, or delay one until the conflict is resolved, all while ensuring that the integrity of the blockchain is maintained. This mechanism is crucial for maintaining the trust in the system, as it provides a way to handle the complexities introduced by parallel execution without compromising on the fundamental principles of blockchain technology.

Another critical aspect of Sui's architecture is its approach to state management. In a parallel execution environment, managing the state of the blockchain becomes exponentially more complex. Sui uses a state model where each object can have its state updated independently, but these updates must be coordinated to ensure global consistency. This involves not just the data but also how changes are propagated across the network, requiring sophisticated algorithms to ensure that the final state of the blockchain is the same for all participants, regardless of the parallel paths taken to reach it.

Scalability is inherent in Sui's design for parallelism. Traditional blockchains often face a trade-off between scalability and security; increasing the number of transactions processed often comes at the cost of network congestion or security risks. Sui's architecture aims to break this trade-off by allowing the network to scale by adding more validators or enhancing the parallel processing capabilities without a proportional increase in security risks. This scalability is not just about handling more transactions but doing so in a way that maintains or even improves upon the user experience, network performance, and security.

To support this complex architecture, Sui's network infrastructure is designed with high-performance networking in mind. This includes considerations for latency, bandwidth, and node efficiency. The network must be capable of broadcasting and receiving transaction results quickly and accurately across potentially thousands of nodes, each possibly executing different parts of the transaction set. This infrastructure supports not just the technical execution of parallel transactions but also ensures that these transactions are communicated and verified with minimal delay, crucial for applications requiring real-time interaction.

Finally, the architecture of Sui for parallelism is not static but designed with evolution in mind. As new use cases emerge or as the technology landscape changes, Sui's architecture is built to adapt, whether that's through updates to the consensus mechanism, enhancements in conflict resolution, or further optimizations in how transactions are scheduled and executed. This forward-thinking approach ensures that Sui's ability to process transactions in parallel can grow and evolve, supporting the ever-expanding horizon of blockchain applications.

In conclusion, Sui's architecture for parallelism is a testament to the innovative spirit of blockchain development. It's not just about doing more transactions faster; it's about reimagining how transactions can interact, how data can evolve, and how a blockchain can serve as the backbone for complex, real-time digital ecosystems. This architecture positions Sui as a potential leader in the next wave of blockchain technology, where the limits of what's possible are continually expanded by the ingenuity of parallel processing.

Part 4: Achieving Finality in Sui

In the realm of blockchain technology, where each transaction represents a commitment etched into the digital ledger, the concept of finality becomes paramount. Finality is the assurance that once a transaction is recorded, it is irreversible, providing the certainty needed for trustless systems. Sui's approach to achieving this finality in the context of its parallel execution model is not only innovative but crucial for its ambition to support high-throughput, real-time applications. This section explores how Sui redefines finality in blockchain, offering insights into the mechanisms and philosophies that underpin this cornerstone of its architecture.

Finality, in traditional blockchain systems, often comes with a caveat. Many blockchains operate on probabilistic finality, where a transaction's irrevocability is based on the number of subsequent blocks added to the chain. The more blocks, the higher the confidence that the transaction will not be undone. This model, while effective for security, introduces latency and uncertainty, particularly in scenarios demanding instant transaction confirmation. Sui challenges this paradigm by aiming for what can be described as "instant finality," where transactions are considered final almost immediately after processing.

The foundation of Sui's instant finality lies in its consensus mechanism, which is designed to support parallel transaction processing while ensuring that once a transaction is validated, it is irrevocably part of the blockchain's state. Unlike systems where consensus might be achieved over several blocks, in Sui, the consensus for a transaction can be reached in a single step, thanks to the efficiency of its DPoS (Delegated Proof-of-Stake) model. Validators in Sui work not just to agree on transactions but to ensure that these agreements are final from the outset, leveraging the trust and stake of the validator set.

Sui's approach to finality is deeply intertwined with its object-centric model. Each object in Sui has a unique identifier, and transactions affecting these objects are processed with the understanding that once an object's state is changed and agreed upon by the necessary validators, that change is final. This object-centric view simplifies the process of achieving finality since it focuses consensus efforts on the state of individual or groups of objects rather than on entire blocks of transactions. This granularity allows for a more precise and rapid confirmation of transaction outcomes.

To achieve this, Sui employs what can be thought of as a "finality gadget," a term for the combination of protocols and algorithms ensuring that once a transaction's state is determined, it's locked in for good. This involves:

- **Immediate Agreement:** Through its consensus protocol, validators quickly reach an agreement on the validity of a transaction, reducing the time from submission to finality.
- **State Finality:** Once a transaction's impact on an object's state is agreed upon, that state

change is considered final, with no rollback unless under specific, rare conditions (like network-wide agreement on a critical error).

- **Conflict Resolution:** Any conflicts or potential forks are resolved in real-time, ensuring that only one valid state path is taken, thus maintaining a single, consistent blockchain history.

The security of finality in Sui is bolstered by its economic model. The high stake required from validators not only incentivizes honest behavior but also makes the cost of attempting to reverse finality prohibitively expensive. If a validator or a group of validators were to attempt to alter a finalized transaction, they would risk losing significant portions of their stake, making such actions economically unfeasible.

However, achieving instant finality in a parallel execution environment introduces unique challenges:

- **Consistency Across Validators:** With transactions potentially being processed by different validators simultaneously, ensuring that all nodes agree on the final state of transactions requires sophisticated coordination. Sui uses a combination of pre-consensus checks and post-execution validations to maintain this consistency.
- **Handling Dependencies:** When transactions depend on each other, even if they're processed in parallel, finality for one can only be assured once all dependencies are

resolved. Sui's architecture includes mechanisms to track and manage these dependencies, ensuring finality is not compromised.

- **Network Latency:** Even with the best consensus mechanisms, network latency can pose a challenge to instant finality. Sui mitigates this through strategic node placement, optimized network infrastructure, and algorithms that account for latency in consensus processes.
- **Security Against Attacks:** While the economic model deters malicious activities, Sui also needs to guard against theoretical attacks where a significant portion of validators might collude. Here, the finality mechanism includes safeguards like multiple confirmation layers or additional checks before declaring finality.

The implications of Sui's approach to finality are profound for both developers and users:

- **User Experience:** For end-users, the promise of instant finality means transactions are confirmed in real-time, akin to using traditional financial systems but with the added benefits of decentralization and security.
- **Application Development:** Developers can craft applications that rely on immediate transaction outcomes, opening up possibilities for more dynamic, responsive dApps, particularly in areas like gaming, real-time bidding, or instant financial settlements.

- **Economic Models:** With finality achieved quickly, the economics around transaction fees, staking rewards, and network usage can be more finely tuned, potentially leading to lower costs for users and more effective reward systems for participants.

However, the pursuit of instant finality is not without its considerations:

- **Complexity in Implementation:** Ensuring that finality is both instant and secure requires complex algorithms and continuous monitoring by the network, demanding high technical competency from developers and maintainers.
- **Scalability Concerns:** As the network scales, maintaining instant finality might require more validators or more sophisticated consensus algorithms, which can complicate governance and network management.
- **Adaptation to New Use Cases:** While Sui's finality model serves current needs well, future applications might demand even more nuanced approaches to finality, pushing for further innovations in how transactions are confirmed.

In conclusion, Sui's approach to achieving finality in a parallel execution environment is a testament to the blockchain's evolution from a simple ledger to a sophisticated platform for real-time digital interactions. It redefines what's possible in decentralized systems, offering a level of certainty and speed traditionally associated with centralized systems but with all the benefits of blockchain technology. This innovation not only enhances the practical utility of blockchain for everyday transactions but also sets a new standard for what users and developers can expect from decentralized networks in terms of reliability, speed, and trust.

Part 5: Performance Metrics and Real-World Implications

In the dynamic and ever-evolving landscape of blockchain technology, performance metrics serve as the yardstick by which we measure the efficacy, scalability, and practicality of these digital ledgers. Sui, with its focus on parallel execution and instant finality, pushes the boundaries of what's possible, aiming to redefine these metrics for a new generation of blockchain applications. This part examines how Sui's unique approach to transaction processing manifests in performance metrics like throughput, latency, and scalability, and explores the real-world implications of these advancements across various sectors.

Throughput, or the number of transactions a blockchain can process per second, is one of the most critical metrics for any blockchain system. Sui's architecture, designed for parallel execution, significantly enhances this metric. By allowing multiple transactions to be executed simultaneously, Sui can potentially process thousands of transactions per second, far exceeding the capabilities of traditional blockchains like Bitcoin or even early iterations of Ethereum. This increase in throughput is not just about handling more transactions but doing so in a way that keeps step with the demand of modern, high-volume applications without compromising on security or decentralization.

Latency, the time it takes for a transaction to be processed and confirmed, is another area where Sui shines. Traditional blockchains often suffer from high latency due to their sequential processing nature and the time required to achieve consensus across a network. Sui's model of instant finality means that transactions can be considered confirmed almost immediately after they are processed, offering latencies that can be measured in seconds or less, rather than minutes or hours. This low latency is crucial for applications where timing is critical, transforming user experiences in sectors like finance, gaming, and real-time data handling.

Scalability is the ability of a blockchain to grow without a proportional increase in resources or a drop in performance. Sui's approach to scalability is inherently built into its design for parallel execution. As the network grows, Sui can add more validators or enhance its parallel processing capabilities, allowing for scaling in both transaction volume and the complexity of interactions without the typical trade-offs in security or decentralization seen in other systems. This scalability ensures that as Sui's ecosystem expands, it can continue to serve its community efficiently.

The implications of these performance metrics in real-world scenarios are vast and transformative:

- **Financial Services:** With high throughput and low latency, Sui can facilitate real-time settlements, high-frequency trading, and microtransactions with unprecedented efficiency. This could lead to new financial products or services where blockchain acts as the backbone for instant global transactions, potentially disrupting traditional banking and payment systems.
- **Gaming:** In gaming, where player actions need to reflect instantly across all participants, Sui's performance metrics allow for seamless, real-time interactions. This can enhance the gaming experience by supporting complex, interactive environments where assets can change hands or evolve in real-time, opening up new possibilities for GameFi (gaming finance) or NFT-based gaming economies.
- **Supply Chain Management:** The ability to process transactions quickly and securely can revolutionize supply chain management. With Sui, each step in a supply chain can be recorded almost instantly, from manufacturing to delivery, providing real-time transparency, reducing fraud, and enhancing trust among all parties involved.
- **Digital Identity and Rights Management:** Low latency and high throughput can support systems where digital identities or rights need to be verified or transferred quickly, such as in voting systems, intellectual property management, or access control to digital services.

- **Internet of Things (IoT):** As IoT devices grow in number, the need for a blockchain that can handle the volume of data they generate becomes apparent. Sui's scalability could enable secure, efficient data logging from IoT devices, facilitating smart contracts that automatically execute based on real-time data inputs.

However, these performance enhancements also bring with them new considerations:

- **Network Fees:** With increased throughput and reduced latency, the economics of transaction fees could shift. Sui might implement dynamic fee structures that adjust based on network load, ensuring that even during peak times, transactions remain economically viable.
- **User Experience:** The performance of Sui directly impacts user experience. Applications built on Sui can offer interfaces and interactions that feel as responsive as centralized systems, potentially driving wider blockchain adoption due to the familiar feel of instant feedback.
- **Security and Decentralization:** While performance improves, maintaining the delicate balance between security, decentralization, and speed remains a challenge. Sui's approach must continuously evolve to ensure that these core blockchain principles are not sacrificed for performance gains.

- **Regulatory Compliance:** As performance metrics allow for new applications, especially in finance, the regulatory landscape will need to adapt. Sui's ability to handle transactions at scale might necessitate new regulatory approaches to ensure compliance without stifling innovation.
- **Environmental Impact:** Although Sui's consensus mechanism is more energy-efficient than Proof of Work, the scaling of blockchain operations still requires careful consideration of environmental sustainability. As throughput increases, so does the computational demand, albeit in a less energy-intensive manner.

The real-world implications of Sui's performance metrics extend beyond these immediate applications:

- **Economic Models:** The efficiency of Sui could lead to new economic models within its ecosystem, where staking, governance, or even the creation and management of digital assets become more accessible and interactive due to the reduced cost of transactions and increased speed.
- **Interoperability:** With high-performance capabilities, Sui could become a hub for cross-chain interactions, where its speed and scalability facilitate the seamless transfer of assets or data between different blockchains, enhancing the overall blockchain ecosystem.
- **Innovation in Application Development:** Developers can explore new paradigms in application design, leveraging Sui's capabilities

for creating complex, stateful applications where the blockchain is not just a database but an active participant in the application's logic and user interaction.

In conclusion, the performance metrics of Sui's transaction processing system are not just numbers on a chart; they are a promise of what blockchain can achieve in real-world scenarios. They signify a shift towards blockchain technology that is not just viable but competitive with or even superior to centralized systems in terms of speed, efficiency, and user experience. As Sui continues to evolve, these metrics will serve as the benchmarks for its success, pushing the boundaries of what decentralized technologies can offer to our digital lives.

Part 6: Challenges and Future Directions

As we navigate through the innovative corridors of Sui's approach to transaction processing, parallel execution, and finality, we encounter not just the promise of a new blockchain era but also the inherent challenges that come with pushing the boundaries of technology. This concluding part of our exploration into Sui's transaction processing focuses on the challenges faced by this system and the potential directions for its future, reflecting on how these might shape not only Sui but the entire blockchain landscape.

Challenges in Parallel Execution and Finality:

One of the primary challenges in Sui's model of parallel execution is managing complex dependencies between transactions. Even with sophisticated dependency analysis, unexpected interactions can occur, especially as the system scales or when dealing with more intricate smart contracts. Ensuring that the network maintains consistency and avoids conflicts without stalling the parallel processing is a delicate balance that requires continuous refinement of algorithms and protocols.

Scalability vs. Security:

As Sui aims to increase its transaction throughput and manage more parallel processes, the balance between scalability and security becomes more nuanced. Adding more validators to handle increased load could potentially lead to centralization if not managed correctly, while ensuring each validator upholds the network's integrity adds layers of complexity to the consensus mechanism.

Network Latency and Global Consistency:

In a globally distributed network, latency can be a formidable adversary to the ideal of instant finality. Achieving a consensus that feels instantaneous across different parts of the world, with varying network conditions, requires innovative solutions in network topology, data propagation, and possibly even satellite or other low-latency communication methods.

Complexity for Developers:

The shift to parallel execution and an object-centric model means developers must adapt to think in new ways about how applications interact with the blockchain. This shift could initially deter developers accustomed to sequential processing, necessitating a significant educational push and perhaps new development tools or frameworks tailored to Sui's paradigm.

Economic and Governance Models:

With high performance comes the challenge of designing economic models that incentivize participation without leading to inflation or wealth concentration. Similarly, governance of such a complex system must evolve to handle rapid changes in technology, use cases, and community expectations, potentially requiring more dynamic or even AI-assisted governance models.

Security in a Parallel World:

Parallel execution opens up new attack vectors that traditional blockchain security models might not adequately address. Ensuring that parallel transactions do not introduce vulnerabilities where attackers could exploit timing or ordering to manipulate outcomes is critical. This might involve new cryptographic techniques or consensus adaptations.

Future Directions:

Looking forward, one of the most promising directions for Sui could be in **interoperability**. As blockchain ecosystems become more interconnected, Sui's performance could make it a prime candidate for serving as a bridge or hub for cross-chain transactions, potentially leading to a new standard for how blockchains communicate and share data.

Layer-2 Solutions and Beyond:

Sui might explore or develop layer-2 scaling solutions that leverage its parallel execution capabilities. Such solutions could include state channels for microtransactions, sidechains for specialized processing, or even more innovative approaches like zero-knowledge rollups, all designed to enhance Sui's capacity without compromising its core principles.

AI and Machine Learning Integration:

The future might see Sui integrating AI and machine learning to optimize various aspects of its operation. From predicting network load for better transaction scheduling to enhancing security through anomaly detection or even aiding in governance by analyzing community sentiment, AI could play a pivotal role in making Sui more adaptive and resilient.

Enhanced Privacy Features:

With the foundation of parallel execution and instant finality, Sui could further innovate in privacy. Implementing privacy-preserving technologies like homomorphic encryption or advanced zero-knowledge proofs could enable Sui to offer unparalleled security and privacy for transactions and data management, appealing to sectors where confidentiality is paramount.

Evolving Consensus Mechanisms:

As the network matures, Sui might refine or even overhaul its consensus mechanism to tackle new challenges or to benefit from emerging cryptographic or consensus technologies. This could mean integrating elements from other consensus models or developing entirely new approaches that maintain or enhance the speed, security, and decentralization triad.

Community and Ecosystem Growth:

The success of Sui's future will heavily rely on its community. Fostering a vibrant ecosystem where developers, users, and validators are active participants in the network's evolution will be crucial. This involves not just technical advancements but also community-building initiatives, educational programs, and perhaps even novel ways to engage with the community through decentralized governance or DAOs.

Environmental Sustainability:

As blockchain technology faces scrutiny over its environmental impact, Sui's future directions might include further optimizations to reduce its carbon footprint. This could involve more energy-efficient consensus protocols, better node distribution to leverage renewable energy sources, or even carbon offset programs integrated into the blockchain's operations.

Regulatory Adaptation:

The regulatory landscape for blockchain is ever-changing. Sui will need to navigate these waters, potentially influencing or adapting to new regulations. This might involve creating compliance tools within its platform, engaging with regulators, or even pioneering new regulatory frameworks that leverage blockchain's unique capabilities.

Cultural Shift in Blockchain Use:

Perhaps one of the most profound impacts of Sui's developments could be a cultural shift in how we view and use blockchain technology. By demonstrating that blockchain can operate with the speed and efficiency of centralized systems while retaining its core benefits, Sui could normalize blockchain use in everyday scenarios, from digital art to global trade, fundamentally altering our digital interactions.

In conclusion, the journey of Sui through the challenges of parallel execution and instant finality is emblematic of the broader journey of blockchain technology towards maturity and widespread adoption. The future directions not only point towards technical advancements but also towards a reimagining of how decentralized systems can integrate with and enhance our digital lives. As Sui evolves, it will continue to face these challenges head-on, potentially leading the charge in defining what the next generation of blockchain networks can achieve. This ongoing evolution will be watched closely, not just for the sake of Sui, but for the insights it provides into the future of decentralized technology at large.

Chapter 8: The Sui Token (SUI): Utility, Economics, and Governance

Part 1: Introduction to the SUI Token

In the grand tapestry of blockchain technology, where each thread represents a unique project or innovation, the SUI token stands as a pivotal element within the Sui ecosystem. This token is not merely a digital asset but an integral part of a vision that seeks to redefine how blockchain networks operate, interact, and evolve. The inception of the SUI token is deeply rooted in the philosophy and ambitions of Sui, a blockchain platform that aims to bring unprecedented levels of speed, security, and scalability to the decentralized world.

The story of SUI begins with the creation of Sui itself, emerging from the minds at Mysten Labs, a company founded by former Meta (previously known as Facebook) researchers. These individuals, with a deep understanding of both the potential and the pitfalls of blockchain technology, sought to craft a platform where the barriers to entry are lowered, and the capabilities are expanded. The SUI token was conceived as the economic and governance backbone of this platform, embodying the principles of accessibility, utility, and community governance.

From its very inception, SUI was designed to be more than just a cryptocurrency. It was intended to serve as the primary means of interaction within the Sui ecosystem, facilitating everything from basic transactions to complex governance operations. The vision behind SUI was to create a token that would not only drive the economic model of the blockchain but also empower its users, developers, and validators to shape the future of the network collaboratively.

The utility of SUI is multifaceted, akin to the diverse roles oxygen plays in our biological systems. Just as oxygen fuels life, SUI fuels the operations of the Sui blockchain. It is used for transaction fees, ensuring that those who benefit from the network's speed and efficiency also contribute to its maintenance. It serves as a staking token, where holders can lock up their SUI to participate in network security and governance, earning rewards in return. This staking mechanism isn't just about securing the network; it's about giving those who hold SUI a voice and stake in its development and direction.

The economic model of SUI was crafted with a long-term perspective, aiming for a balance between incentivizing participation and maintaining economic stability. Unlike many cryptocurrencies that start with a fixed supply or a rapid inflation model, SUI's initial distribution and ongoing issuance are thought out to foster growth while preventing hyperinflation or value dilution. The model includes mechanisms for rewarding early adopters, developers, and those who contribute to the network's health, all while ensuring that the token's value can appreciate over time due to increased demand and utility.

Governance is another realm where SUI plays a crucial role. The token is not just a passive asset but a means for its holders to influence the trajectory of Sui. By staking SUI, users gain the ability to vote on proposals, elect validators, or even propose changes to the protocol itself. This democratic approach to blockchain governance is designed to keep Sui responsive to its community's needs, fostering a decentralized environment where power is distributed rather than concentrated.

The creation of SUI was guided by the principle that a blockchain's token should reflect its ethos. For Sui, this means a token that supports speed, by enabling low-latency transactions; security, through economic incentives for honest participation; and scalability, by ensuring that the token's economics do not become a bottleneck as the network grows. Each aspect of SUI's design reflects these core values, aiming to make blockchain technology more practical and appealing for everyday use.

The initial distribution of SUI was approached with care to avoid the pitfalls of many early blockchain projects where tokens were concentrated in the hands of a few. A combination of public sales, allocations to the team, advisors, and early contributors, as well as strategic reserves for ecosystem development, was used to ensure a fair launch. This initial distribution plan was coupled with a vesting schedule to prevent sudden dumps that could undermine the token's value and the network's stability.

Beyond its role in transactions, staking, and governance, SUI was envisioned as a tool for developers. By providing economic incentives through the SUI token, Sui encourages the creation of decentralized applications (dApps) that leverage its unique features. This not only expands the utility of SUI but also enriches the entire Sui ecosystem, creating a virtuous cycle where more applications attract more users, which in turn increases the demand for SUI.

Security is another pillar where SUI contributes significantly. Through staking, validators are economically incentivized to act in the best interest of the network. The more SUI staked, the more secure the network becomes, as those with a stake have a vested interest in the network's integrity. This economic security model mitigates risks like 51% attacks, common in other blockchain systems, by aligning the financial incentives of participants with the health of the network.

However, with great utility comes great responsibility. The success of SUI hinges not only on the technological robustness of the Sui platform but also on how well it navigates the complex landscape of token economics. The token supply, inflation rate, reward distribution, and mechanisms for burning or locking tokens must all be managed with foresight to avoid economic pitfalls like inflation, deflation, or centralization of wealth.

Looking at the broader picture, SUI's introduction was a statement of intent from Sui to not just participate in the blockchain space but to lead in redefining what blockchain can achieve. It's a token that encapsulates the promise of a blockchain where speed, security, and scalability are not just buzzwords but lived realities. As we delve deeper into the specifics of SUI's utility, economics, and governance in the following sections, it's clear that this token is the heart of a blockchain designed to empower its users in unprecedented ways.

In conclusion, the SUI token is not merely an appendage to the Sui blockchain; it is its life force, driving interaction, security, governance, and development. Its introduction marks the beginning of a journey where the barriers that have historically limited blockchain adoption are systematically dismantled, paving the way for a future where decentralized technology is as integral to our digital lives as the internet is today. As we move forward, understanding the nuances of SUI will be crucial for anyone looking to engage with or build upon the Sui ecosystem.

Part 2: Utility of SUI

The SUI token, integral to the fabric of the Sui ecosystem, serves as a multifaceted utility token, embodying the essence of what makes blockchain technology revolutionary. Its utility extends far beyond the typical functions of a cryptocurrency, weaving through the economic, operational, and governance threads of the Sui network to create a vibrant, interactive blockchain environment. This part explores the extensive roles SUI plays, highlighting how it acts as the lifeblood of Sui's operations, enabling a wide array of functionalities that are central to the platform's vision and user experience.

Transaction Fees:

At its most fundamental level, SUI is used to pay for transaction fees on the Sui network. This utility ensures that those who utilize the network for transferring assets, interacting with smart contracts, or executing any form of transaction contribute to the network's upkeep. By setting transaction fees in SUI, the network not only generates revenue for validators but also optimizes transaction prioritization based on fee bids, ensuring that the network remains both accessible and efficient. This fee mechanism also helps in managing network congestion, providing a dynamic pricing model that adjusts to demand.

Staking for Network Security:

SUI's role in staking is pivotal for the security and decentralization of the Sui network. By allowing token holders to stake their SUI, they not only participate in securing the network but also earn rewards based on their stake. This staking mechanism is crucial for Sui's Delegated Proof-of-Stake (DPoS) consensus model, where staked tokens determine who can validate transactions and create new blocks. Staking SUI thus serves dual purposes: it incentivizes honest participation in network governance and provides an economic barrier against malicious activities, as validators risk losing their stake if they act against the network's interests.

Governance Participation:

Beyond security, staking SUI grants token holders governance rights. This utility aspect turns SUI into a democratic tool where holders can vote on proposals that affect the network's development, from protocol upgrades to changes in economic policies or validator elections. This governance model is designed to ensure that the evolution of Sui remains aligned with the community's vision, making SUI not just a token but a voice within the ecosystem. It empowers users, developers, and investors to have a say in the future of the platform, fostering a sense of ownership and responsibility among participants.

Access to Network Services:

SUI also opens the door to various services within the Sui ecosystem. For developers, this might mean access to specialized APIs, computational resources, or even funding through grants or incentives programs for building on Sui. For users, holding or using SUI could unlock premium features in decentralized applications (dApps), such as faster transaction processing, exclusive content, or participation in certain financial instruments or games. This utility aspect of SUI encourages the creation and adoption of diverse applications, enriching the ecosystem.

Liquidity and Decentralized Finance (DeFi):

Within the DeFi space, SUI serves as a base asset for financial instruments. It can be used in lending protocols, where users can borrow against their SUI or lend it out to earn interest. SUI can also be pooled in liquidity pools, providing the backbone for decentralized exchanges (DEXs) operating on Sui. This utility not only increases the liquidity of SUI but also integrates it into the broader DeFi ecosystem, where it can be used for yield farming, staking derivatives, and other financial operations, thus enhancing its value proposition.

NFT and Digital Asset Management:

In the context of NFTs and digital asset management, SUI plays a crucial role. Whether it's minting new NFTs, participating in auctions, or managing the lifecycle of digital assets on Sui, SUI is the currency that facilitates these interactions. Its use here extends to governance of digital asset standards, trading fees, and even as a means to reward creators or curators within NFT marketplaces or gaming platforms built on Sui.

Incentivizing Ecosystem Growth:

SUI is also used to incentivize growth within the ecosystem. This includes rewards for developers who create valuable dApps, grants for research and development, or even airdrops to users for participating in network activities like stress testing or community governance. These incentives not only drive the adoption of SUI but also ensure that the ecosystem remains vibrant, innovative, and user-centric.

Cross-Chain Interoperability:

Although not immediately apparent, the utility of SUI extends to potential cross-chain interactions. As blockchain ecosystems become more interconnected, SUI could serve as a bridge asset or be wrapped to be used on other chains, enhancing its utility by allowing seamless transfer of value and data across different blockchain environments. This would further solidify SUI's role in a multi-chain future, where interoperability is key to expanding the reach and functionality of blockchain technology.

Economic Stability Mechanisms:

SUI's utility also includes contributing to the economic stability of the Sui network. Through mechanisms like token burns or dynamic fee adjustments, SUI can influence the network's inflation rate, ensuring that the token's value does not erode over time due to oversupply. These mechanisms are vital for maintaining the token's utility and encouraging long-term holding and investment in the ecosystem.

User Adoption and Reward Systems:

For new users, SUI can act as an entry point into the blockchain world. Through referral programs, educational rewards, or even gamified learning experiences where users earn SUI by engaging with the platform or its applications, the token helps in onboarding new participants. This not only expands the user base but also fosters a community around Sui, where every member has a stake in its success.

Privacy and Security Features:

Lastly, SUI could be used to access privacy-enhancing features or security services within the Sui network. Whether it's for private transactions, securing digital identities, or accessing secure communication channels, the token could unlock capabilities that prioritize user privacy and security, aligning with Sui's commitment to creating a safe and efficient blockchain environment.

In essence, the utility of SUI is broad and integral to realizing the full potential of the Sui blockchain. It's not just about enabling transactions or securing the network; it's about creating a dynamic ecosystem where every participant can contribute, benefit, and have a say. As we move through the chapters, the multifaceted utility of SUI will become even clearer, showcasing how this token is not just a currency but a catalyst for innovation, participation, and growth within the Sui network.

Part 3: Economic Model of SUI

In the vibrant and often volatile world of blockchain economics, the SUI token stands out with an economic model designed to foster stability, growth, and widespread participation within the Sui ecosystem. This model is not just about the creation and distribution of a digital asset but about crafting a sustainable financial framework that supports the network's objectives while adapting to the dynamic nature of decentralized technologies. Here, we delve into the intricacies of SUI's economic model, exploring how its supply mechanics, incentives, and economic policies aim to balance between encouraging network activity and maintaining long-term value.

Initial Supply and Distribution:

The journey of SUI begins with its initial supply and how it was distributed. Unlike some cryptocurrencies that start with a massive pre-mine or a fixed, unchangeable supply, Sui's approach to SUI's initial supply was strategic, aiming for a balanced launch that would neither flood the market nor starve it for liquidity. The initial distribution was carefully planned to allocate tokens to different stakeholders:

- **Public Sale:** A portion of SUI was made available through a public sale, ensuring that a broad base of individuals could acquire the token, promoting decentralization from the outset.
- **Team and Advisors:** Tokens were allocated to the team and advisors to incentivize long-term commitment to the project. These tokens typically come with a vesting period, preventing immediate sell-offs that could destabilize the market.
- **Foundation or Reserve:** A reserve was set aside, often managed by the Sui Foundation or a similar entity, for ecosystem development, including grants, partnerships, and community

initiatives. This reserve acts as a catalyst for growth and innovation within the network.
- **Staking Rewards:** An allocation was made for staking rewards, ensuring that from the start, there was an incentive for participants to secure the network and participate in governance.
- **Airdrops and Incentives:** Some SUI might be set aside for airdrops, incentivizing early adopters, developers, or participants in community events, fostering engagement and ecosystem growth.

Tokenomics and Inflation Control:

The economic model of SUI places a significant emphasis on managing inflation to maintain the token's value over time. Inflation in this context refers to the increase in the total supply of SUI through mechanisms like staking rewards:

- **Annual Inflation Rate:** Sui might implement an annual inflation rate that is predictable yet adjustable based on network conditions. This rate could be set to decrease over time, ensuring that the supply growth does not outpace the demand for SUI.
- **Staking Rewards:** Rewards for staking SUI are a primary source of new token issuance. However, these rewards are structured to incentivize long-term staking, potentially by offering higher rewards for longer lock-up periods or by adjusting reward distribution

based on the total amount staked in the network.

- **Burn Mechanisms:** To counteract inflation, Sui could introduce burn mechanisms where a portion of transaction fees or other network activities results in the permanent removal of SUI from circulation, thus reducing the total supply over time. This could be tied to specific actions or network milestones, creating a dynamic supply model.

Economic Incentives for Network Participation:

The backbone of Sui's economic model is the incentives it provides for various forms of network participation:

- **Validator Rewards:** Validators, who secure the network and process transactions, are rewarded with SUI. This reward structure is designed to ensure a healthy number of validators while preventing centralization through high staking requirements or reward caps.
- **Developer Incentives:** Developers are crucial for ecosystem growth, and thus, Sui might offer economic incentives like grants, bounties, or revenue-sharing models where developers receive a portion of the fees generated by their applications.
- **User Engagement:** To encourage user participation, there might be mechanisms like referral rewards, participation in governance, or even token airdrops for users who interact

with the network or contribute to its health, like reporting bugs or participating in network stress tests.

Staking and Economic Redistribution:

Staking is not just about securing the network; it's also an economic tool for redistribution and maintaining a healthy economy:

- **Staking Pool Dilution:** Over time, as more users stake their SUI, the rewards per staked token might decrease, naturally controlling inflation and ensuring that staking remains a competitive process, encouraging more widespread participation.
- **Delegation:** The ability to delegate staking to validators democratizes the process, allowing those with smaller amounts of SUI to participate in network governance and earn rewards without running their own validator node.
- **Slashing:** In cases of validator misbehavior or network downtime, slashing mechanisms ensure that staked SUI can be penalized, promoting responsible network participation and aligning economic incentives with network health.

Market Dynamics and Token Utility:

The economic model also considers how SUI interacts with market dynamics:

- **Demand Through Utility:** By continuously expanding the utility of SUI within the ecosystem, from transaction fees to governance rights, Sui aims to increase demand organically. This utility-driven demand can help stabilize or increase the token's value.
- **Liquidity Pools and DeFi:** SUI's integration into DeFi protocols like lending, borrowing, and liquidity pools on the Sui blockchain can create additional demand vectors, enhancing liquidity and utility, thus supporting the token's price stability.
- **Interoperability:** As Sui plans for or achieves interoperability with other blockchains, SUI could gain value as a token that facilitates cross-chain transactions or services, broadening its economic sphere.

Economic Policies and Governance:

The governance aspect of SUI's economic model is critical for its adaptability:

- **Community Governance:** Changes to the token's economic policies, like inflation rates or reward structures, can be proposed and voted on by SUI holders, ensuring that the economic model evolves with community consensus.
- **Dynamic Fee Adjustments:** Transaction fees could be dynamically adjusted based on network load, providing an economic mechanism to manage network congestion

and potentially fund network operations or improvements.
- **Emergency Measures:** In response to unforeseen circumstances, like significant market volatility or network attacks, the governance system might allow for emergency measures, ensuring the economic model can respond to real-world challenges.

Challenges in Economic Design:

Despite its thorough design, the economic model of SUI faces several challenges:

- **Balancing Inflation and Growth:** Finding the sweet spot where inflation incentivizes participation without devaluing the token is a continuous challenge. Sui must monitor economic indicators closely to adjust its policies.
- **Preventing Centralization:** As with any staking model, there's a risk that a few large stakeholders could dominate, leading to centralization. Sui's economic model needs to counteract this through its reward distribution and governance mechanisms.
- **Regulatory Adaptation:** The evolving regulatory landscape for cryptocurrencies could impact how SUI operates, particularly in terms of token distribution, staking rewards, or even its classification as a security.
- **Speculative Pressures:** The crypto market's speculative nature can lead to price volatility, which Sui must navigate to ensure that its

economic model supports sustainable growth rather than speculative bubbles.

Future Economic Evolution:

Looking forward, the economic model of SUI is designed to evolve:

- **Adaptive Inflation Mechanisms:** As the network matures, Sui might refine how inflation is managed, perhaps introducing new methods for supply control or reward distribution based on network performance metrics.
- **Ecosystem Expansion:** As more dApps and uses for SUI are developed, the economic model will need to adapt to support this growth, potentially through new incentive structures or by expanding the token's utility.
- **Cross-Chain Economics:** If Sui becomes a hub for cross-chain interactions, its economic model might need to incorporate mechanisms for managing the flow of value across different blockchains, maintaining SUI's relevance and utility.

In conclusion, the economic model of the SUI token is a complex, living system designed to support the network's goals of speed, security, and scalability while fostering a vibrant, participatory community. It's a model that reflects the innovative spirit of blockchain technology, where economic principles are not static but evolve with the ecosystem they serve. As Sui and SUI continue to grow, this economic framework will be crucial in navigating the challenges and opportunities of the decentralized future, ensuring that the token remains a valuable asset within and beyond its native ecosystem.

Part 4: Staking and Rewards

Staking and the associated rewards system are pivotal elements of the SUI token's ecosystem, serving as the cornerstone for Sui's consensus mechanism, network security, and the democratization of governance. This chapter segment explores the intricate details of how staking SUI functions, its benefits to stakers, the impact on the token's economics, and how it contributes to the overall health and decentralization of the Sui network.

The Concept of Staking in Sui:

Staking, in the context of Sui, is the act of locking up SUI tokens to support network operations, particularly in securing the blockchain through the Delegated Proof-of-Stake (DPoS) consensus mechanism. Unlike traditional Proof-of-Work (PoW) systems where miners expend energy to validate transactions, in Sui's DPoS, validators are chosen based on the amount of SUI they have staked or have been delegated to them. This system not only reduces the environmental impact associated with blockchain operations but also democratizes the validation process, giving token holders a direct role in network security and governance.

Becoming a Validator or Delegator:

To engage in staking within the Sui ecosystem, participants can choose one of two roles:

- **Validators:** These are the nodes that actively participate in adding new blocks to the chain, validating transactions, and maintaining the network's integrity. To become a validator, one must stake a significant amount of SUI as a commitment to the network's health, demonstrating both financial and operational capability to run a node.
- **Delegators:** Not everyone has the resources or technical know-how to operate a validator node. Delegators can stake their SUI by delegating it to validators they trust or believe in. This delegation not only supports validators in securing the network but also allows delegators to share in the rewards, democratizing the benefits of staking.

Rewards Mechanism:

The rewards for staking in Sui are multifaceted, designed to incentivize participation, ensure network security, and promote long-term holding:

- **Block Rewards:** Validators receive SUI for each block they successfully add to the blockchain. These rewards are a primary source of new SUI issuance, directly tied to the network's activity level.
- **Transaction Fees:** A portion of the transaction fees is also distributed among validators,

providing an additional revenue stream that increases with network usage.

- **Delegation Rewards:** Delegators earn a share of the rewards that validators receive, based on the amount of SUI they have delegated. This sharing mechanism ensures that even those without the means to run a validator node can benefit from staking.
- **Incentives for Good Performance:** Sui might implement additional rewards or bonuses for validators who exhibit excellent performance metrics, such as uptime, block production speed, or community votes in their favor, encouraging a competitive yet cooperative environment.

Impact on Token Economics:

Staking has profound implications for the economics of the SUI token:

- **Inflation Management:** Staking rewards are one of the main drivers of SUI's inflation. By controlling these rewards, Sui can manage inflation rates, ensuring that the increase in supply does not outpace demand, thus maintaining the token's value.
- **Token Distribution:** Staking serves as a mechanism for redistributing tokens. As rewards are distributed, they go to a broader base of participants, potentially reducing the concentration of wealth and promoting a more decentralized token distribution.

- **Supply Dynamics:** The act of staking temporarily removes tokens from circulation, effectively reducing the liquid supply of SUI available in the market. This can have a deflationary effect, especially if staking participation is high.
- **Economic Security:** The more SUI staked, the higher the economic cost of attacking the network, as any malicious validator risks losing their stake. This security model aligns economic incentives with network stability.

Decentralization and Governance:

Staking is not just an economic activity; it's a governance one:

- **Voting Power:** Staked SUI often correlates with voting power in governance decisions, from electing validators to voting on protocol upgrades. This gives stakers a direct say in how the network evolves.
- **Community Engagement:** By making governance accessible through staking, Sui encourages a broader base of the community to engage actively, reducing the risk of governance being controlled by a few.
- **Validator Rotation:** To prevent centralization, Sui might implement mechanisms where validators are periodically re-elected or where the number of validators can increase based on the amount of SUI staked, ensuring new participants can join the validation process.

Challenges and Considerations:

While staking offers numerous benefits, it also introduces challenges:

- **Centralization Risks:** If staking rewards are too concentrated among a few validators, it could lead to centralization. Sui must balance reward distribution to incentivize broad participation.
- **Staking Commitment:** The requirement to stake SUI for extended periods can deter participation, especially if market conditions suggest that holding liquid SUI might be more profitable. Sui needs mechanisms to make staking attractive.
- **Security of Staked Assets:** With significant value locked in staking, ensuring the security of these assets against hacks or exploits is paramount. Sui must continuously upgrade its security protocols.
- **Reward Sustainability:** Over time, as more SUI is staked, the rewards per staked token might decrease, which could impact the attractiveness of staking if not managed carefully.

Innovations in Staking:

Sui might explore or already have implemented innovations to enhance the staking experience and its economic impact:

- **Liquid Staking:** Allowing staked SUI to be used in other DeFi protocols without unstaking, providing liquidity to stakers while still securing the network.
- **Staking Pools:** Facilitating smaller token holders to pool their SUI for staking, thus lowering the entry barrier and spreading the risk and reward more evenly.
- **Dynamic Staking Rewards:** Adjusting staking rewards based on network load, validator performance, or even market conditions to maintain economic balance.
- **Staking for Governance Proposals:** Introducing rewards not just for staking but for actively participating in governance, like proposing or voting on network changes.

Future Directions:

Looking ahead, the staking mechanism in Sui could evolve:

- **AI-Assisted Staking:** Using AI to optimize staking strategies for validators or to predict network needs, potentially leading to more efficient reward distribution and network performance.
- **Cross-Chain Staking:** If Sui becomes interoperable with other chains, staked SUI might secure or interact with other blockchain networks, expanding its utility.
- **Environmental Staking:** As blockchain's environmental impact comes under scrutiny, staking could evolve to include incentives for

using renewable energy or contributing to carbon offset initiatives.

- **Educational Staking:** Programs where staking is tied to learning about blockchain, governance, or development, incentivizing education within the ecosystem.

The staking and rewards system in Sui is not just an economic mechanism but a fundamental aspect of its philosophy towards decentralized, community-driven blockchain technology. By aligning economic incentives with network participation, security, and governance, Sui sets a precedent for how blockchain networks can operate sustainably while fostering a vibrant, engaged community. As Sui grows, the evolution of its staking model will be crucial in navigating the challenges of scale, security, and decentralization, ensuring that SUI remains a valuable and integral part of its ecosystem.

Part 5: Governance with SUI

Governance in the realm of blockchain technology is not merely about decision-making; it's about embodying the principle of decentralization, ensuring that the direction and evolution of a network reflect the collective will of its community. The SUI token plays a central role in this governance model within the Sui ecosystem, crafting a narrative where every token holder can influence the platform's future. This section explores how SUI holders participate in governance, the mechanisms for decision-making, and the broader implications of this participatory model on the network's development, economics, and culture.

The Philosophy of Governance in Sui:

At its core, Sui's governance model is built on the belief that the network should be shaped by those who have a stake in its success. This philosophy translates into a system where the SUI token is not just a medium of exchange or a store of value but a tool for democratic participation. The aim is to create a blockchain where governance is:

- **Decentralized:** Power is not concentrated but distributed among token holders.
- **Transparent:** All decisions, proposals, and voting outcomes are visible to every participant.
- **Inclusive:** Anyone holding SUI can participate, regardless of the size of their stake.
- **Adaptive:** The governance model itself can evolve based on community needs and technological advancements.

Mechanisms for Governance:

Sui's governance is facilitated through several mechanisms:

- **Proposals:** Any SUI holder can propose changes to the protocol, network parameters, or even economic policies. These proposals can range from technical upgrades, like improving the consensus mechanism, to social initiatives, like community events or partnerships.

- **Voting:** Once a proposal is made, it enters a voting phase where SUI holders can cast their votes based on the amount of SUI they hold or have staked. This voting can be weighted, giving more influence to those with larger stakes, or it could be structured to ensure a more egalitarian approach.

- **Delegation:** Recognizing that not all token holders have the time or expertise to engage deeply in governance, Sui allows for vote delegation. Holders can delegate their voting rights to others they trust to represent their interests, fostering a system where expertise can be leveraged for better decision-making.

- **Validator Elections:** A key aspect of Sui's governance involves electing validators. SUI holders vote on who should be the validators, directly influencing who secures the network and how consensus is achieved.

- **Governance Rewards:** To encourage participation, Sui might introduce rewards for those actively engaging in governance, such as voting or proposing ideas that benefit the ecosystem. This could be in the form of additional SUI or privileges within the network.

Role of SUI in Governance:

The SUI token is the linchpin of this governance model:

- **Staking for Voting Rights:** Typically, governance voting power is tied to the amount of SUI staked. This ensures that those who are committed to the network's long-term health have a say, aligning governance with economic participation.
- **Economic Incentives:** The distribution of SUI through governance activities can shape economic behavior, encouraging beneficial actions for the network's growth, security, or community engagement.
- **Token as a Voice:** Holding SUI is akin to having a voice in the network's direction, making every token holder a potential influencer of Sui's future.

Balancing Democratic Participation with Efficiency:

One of the challenges in blockchain governance is balancing broad participation with the need for efficient decision-making:

- **Quorum and Thresholds:** Sui might implement mechanisms like minimum quorum requirements or voting thresholds to ensure decisions are not made hastily or by a minority, while still allowing for timely action.
- **Time-bound Decisions:** Proposals might have a set time frame for voting to prevent prolonged decision-making that could stall network development.
- **Emergency Measures:** For critical issues, there could be processes for expedited

decisions or temporary governance powers to address emergent threats or opportunities.

Impact on Network Development:

Governance through SUI has profound impacts on how Sui evolves:

- **Community-Driven Development:** By involving the community in decisions, development becomes more aligned with user needs, potentially leading to more relevant features or applications.
- **Innovative Governance Models:** Sui could pioneer new governance models, perhaps integrating AI for decision support, or exploring liquid democracy where voting rights can be more fluidly shared or reassigned.
- **Security and Upgrades:** Governance ensures that security measures and protocol upgrades are not just technical decisions but community-consented changes, reducing the risk of forks or contentious updates.

Economic Implications:

The governance model also influences the economics of SUI:

- **Token Value and Stability:** Effective governance can lead to a more stable and valuable SUI by ensuring that the network's policies and direction are in line with market demands and technological advancements.

- **Inflation Control:** Decisions on token supply, staking rewards, or fee structures directly impact SUI's economics, with governance acting as a tool for economic fine-tuning.
- **Decentralized Finance (DeFi) Integration:** Governance decisions might extend to how SUI interacts with DeFi protocols, potentially shaping its utility and demand within broader financial ecosystems.

Challenges and Considerations:

Despite its benefits, this governance model presents challenges:

- **Voter Apathy:** If participation is low, governance could be dominated by a few active voters, undermining the democratic ideal. Continuous engagement strategies are vital.
- **Complexity for Users:** The intricacies of governance might be daunting for average users, necessitating user-friendly interfaces and education on how to participate effectively.
- **Centralization Risks:** Even with a decentralized governance model, there's a risk that those with more tokens could steer decisions towards their interests. Mechanisms to counteract this are essential.
- **Dispute Resolution:** As with any system, disputes over proposals or voting outcomes will arise, requiring clear, community-accepted methods for resolution.

Future of Governance with SUI:

Looking forward, the governance model could evolve in several ways:

- **AI and Data Analytics:** Integrating AI to analyze community sentiment or predict the impact of governance decisions could make the process more informed and efficient.
- **Cross-Chain Governance:** As interoperability grows, SUI holders might participate in governance decisions affecting multiple chains or ecosystems, expanding the scope of influence.
- **Decentralized Autonomous Organizations (DAOs):** Sui might leverage or inspire more advanced DAO models where governance is fully automated based on pre-set rules or community consensus.
- **Cultural Governance:** Beyond just technical or economic decisions, governance could extend to how the community interacts, sets norms, or supports social initiatives, creating a richer cultural ecosystem.
- **Regulatory Adaptation:** As blockchain governance faces regulatory scrutiny, Sui's model might need to adapt, potentially leading to innovations in how decentralized governance interacts with legal frameworks.

Governance in Sui, powered by the SUI token, is more than a system; it's a statement on how decentralized networks can truly be community-driven. It's an ongoing experiment in digital democracy where every SUI holder has the potential to shape the blockchain's trajectory, ensuring that Sui remains not just a technological platform but a living, evolving community. This model's success hinges on active participation, transparent processes, and the community's ability to navigate the complexities of decentralized decision-making. As Sui matures, its governance will be a key factor in its resilience, innovation, and alignment with the broader values of decentralization and community empowerment.

Part 6: Future Prospects and Challenges

As we peer into the horizon of the Sui ecosystem, the SUI token stands at the crossroads of immense potential and significant challenges. This narrative of future prospects and obstacles is not just about the token's journey but about the broader implications for the Sui blockchain and its community. The evolution of SUI, both in utility and governance, will play a pivotal role in defining how blockchain technology can adapt to and influence the rapidly changing digital landscape. Here, we delve into what might lie ahead for SUI, exploring how it could shape or be shaped by the future of decentralized systems.

The utility of SUI is poised for expansion as blockchain technology finds new applications across industries. One conceivable future involves SUI becoming a linchpin in the Internet of Things (IoT), where it could facilitate secure, micro-transactions between devices, or serve as the currency for smart contract executions in autonomous systems. This would not only increase the demand for SUI but also cement its role in a world where physical and digital assets increasingly interact in real-time.

Looking at scalability and performance, Sui's ongoing development in parallel execution and transaction finality could lead to SUI being at the heart of high-throughput applications. Imagine a future where SUI supports blockchain-based games with millions of concurrent users, or financial markets that operate with blockchain-backed assets, all without the latency issues that have plagued earlier blockchain systems. This scalability could transform how we perceive and utilize blockchain, making SUI not just a token but a key to unlocking a new era of digital interaction.

In terms of governance, the future might see SUI's role expanded to include more nuanced decision-making processes. With the advent of more sophisticated decentralized autonomous organizations (DAOs), SUI could be used not only for voting but for more dynamic forms of governance, where decisions are based on real-time data, community sentiment, or even predictive analytics. This evolution could make Sui's governance model a benchmark for how decentralized communities can govern themselves in complex, real-world scenarios.

However, the path forward is not without its challenges. One significant hurdle is managing the token's economics in a way that supports growth without leading to inflation or deflation that could destabilize its value. As the ecosystem grows, Sui will need to innovate in its economic policies, possibly introducing more adaptive mechanisms for controlling supply or adjusting rewards to match network demand and participation levels.

Another challenge lies in ensuring broad participation in governance. The risk of voter apathy or governance being dominated by a few large stakeholders is real. Sui will need to continue developing mechanisms that make governance accessible, engaging, and rewarding for all SUI holders, perhaps through gamification, educational incentives, or even token-based rewards for active participation.

Regulatory landscapes pose another significant challenge. As blockchain technologies like Sui gain traction, they will inevitably attract more regulatory scrutiny. The future of SUI will depend on how well it can navigate these waters, possibly influencing or adapting to new laws around digital assets, privacy, and financial services. This might mean pioneering new compliance tools or engaging proactively with regulators to shape a favorable environment for decentralized technologies.

Security and decentralization will continue to be balancing acts. With the value of SUI potentially increasing, it becomes a more significant target for attacks. Sui must evolve its security measures, perhaps integrating more advanced cryptographic techniques or leveraging the power of its community through decentralized security audits. Maintaining decentralization while scaling is another tightrope to walk; strategies like dynamic validator sets or incentivizing smaller nodes could be crucial.

The environmental impact of blockchain operations, even in a more energy-efficient model like Sui's DPoS, will come under increasing scrutiny. Future directions might involve integrating SUI into systems that incentivize green practices, like staking rewards linked to the use of renewable energy or contributions to carbon offset initiatives.

Interoperability is another frontier where SUI could play a crucial role. As blockchain ecosystems become more interconnected, SUI might serve as a bridge asset or be involved in creating standards for cross-chain communication. This could not only increase its utility but also position Sui as a central player in a multi-chain world, where assets and data move freely across different blockchains.

In conclusion, the future of SUI is a tapestry of opportunity and challenge. Its success will hinge on how well it can adapt to the evolving needs of its users, the technological landscape, and the regulatory environment. It's about leveraging the strengths of its community, its technology, and its vision to not just survive but thrive in a future where blockchain is as commonplace as the internet is today. As SUI navigates these waters, it will be a beacon of what's possible when a community, empowered by its governance token, charts the course for a decentralized future.

Chapter 9: Building on Sui: Developer's Guide to Smart Contracts

In the ever-evolving realm of blockchain technology, where each platform strives to distinguish itself, Sui stands out as a particularly appealing destination for developers. It's not merely about what Sui can do; it's about the vision it holds for the future of decentralized applications. This chapter serves as an introduction to the craft of smart contract development on Sui, a platform that doesn't just promise but delivers on speed, security, and scalability.

Sui's allure begins with its architecture, a testament to innovative thinking in blockchain design. It's built to operate at a pace that traditional blockchains can only dream of, thanks to its focus on parallel execution and instant finality. This means that developers can create applications that react in real-time, a feature that's not just nice to have but essential for modern, interactive digital solutions.

But speed alone isn't what makes Sui stand apart. There's an inherent emphasis on security woven into every layer of its architecture. The platform's approach to consensus, combined with its object-centric model, ensures that smart contracts can be both powerful and safe, minimizing the risks that have historically plagued smart contract platforms.

Central to the developer's journey on Sui is the Move programming language. Move isn't just another language; it's a paradigm shift in how we think about and manage digital assets on a blockchain. Developed with safety and resource management in mind, Move allows developers to create contracts that are inherently more secure against common vulnerabilities like reentrancy or overflow attacks.

The philosophy behind Move reflects Sui's broader vision: to make blockchain development accessible yet robust. It's a language that balances the need for expressiveness with the demand for security, providing developers with tools to craft complex, stateful applications without sacrificing the integrity of the blockchain.

This chapter isn't just about the technical aspects; it's about understanding why Sui is an attractive platform for developers. It's about recognizing how Sui's design philosophy can lead to the creation of applications that are not only innovative but also deeply integrated with the principles of decentralization, security, and user-centric design.

Building on Sui means engaging with a blockchain that values the developer experience. It's about moving from a world where developers had to navigate around the limitations of blockchain technology to one where the technology is tailored to enable their creativity. Here, developers can explore new paradigms like object-centric programming, which offers a more intuitive way to manage digital assets and their states.

Moreover, Sui's approach to smart contracts encourages developers to think about scalability from the ground up. With its support for parallel transaction processing, developers can design applications that scale naturally with user demand, without the traditional bottlenecks associated with blockchain networks.

This guide aims to be more than just a technical manual; it's an invitation to join a community at the forefront of blockchain technology. It's about contributing to an ecosystem where developers are not just builders but co-creators of a platform that's set to redefine digital interactions, economies, and governance models.

As we delve into the specifics of building on Sui, remember, this isn't just about coding. It's about being part of a movement that's pushing the boundaries of what's possible in blockchain, ensuring that every smart contract, every application, contributes to a more decentralized, secure, and inclusive digital future.

Part 2: Understanding Move: The Language of Sui Smart Contracts

At the core of Sui's innovative approach to blockchain development lies the Move programming language, a creation that fundamentally reshapes how developers think about and write smart contracts. Move, born out of the need for a language that prioritizes safety and resource management, offers a unique blend of security features, expressiveness, and efficiency tailored for blockchain environments.

Move is not just another smart contract language; it's a paradigm shift. Unlike traditional languages used in blockchain, such as Solidity for Ethereum, Move introduces concepts like resource types, which act as digital assets with strict ownership and transfer rules. This ensures that once a resource is created, its lifecycle—from creation through transfer to destruction—is strictly managed, preventing common programming errors like unintended duplication or loss of assets.

One of the foundational principles of Move is its focus on preventing bugs before they happen. The language architecture aims to eliminate vulnerabilities like reentrancy attacks by design. This is achieved through its type system, where resources are not just data but are treated as unique entities with specific rules for how they can be used or transferred. This approach significantly reduces the risk of smart contract exploits, providing a safer environment for developers to experiment and innovate.

The syntax and semantics of Move are designed to be intuitive for developers familiar with modern programming languages, yet it introduces unique features tailored for blockchain-specific challenges. For instance, Move's module system allows for the encapsulation of contract logic, promoting modularity and reuse, which is crucial in maintaining and scaling smart contracts over time.

Move also excels in its handling of state transitions. With Sui's object-centric model, where each piece of data is treated as an object with its own state, Move provides the tools to manage these objects efficiently. Developers can define how objects evolve, interact, or are composed, leading to more dynamic and complex applications than possible with simpler state models.

In terms of expressiveness, Move allows developers to write contracts that are not only about transferring value but about creating rich, interactive digital experiences. Whether it's managing complex game states, orchestrating financial instruments, or defining the behavior of NFTs, Move's capabilities enable developers to push the boundaries of what blockchain applications can achieve.

Moreover, Move's design supports parallel execution, a key feature of Sui's blockchain. This means contracts can be written to take advantage of Sui's architecture, where multiple transactions can be processed simultaneously without conflicts, enhancing performance and user experience.

For those new to Move, the learning curve might seem steep, but the language is backed by extensive documentation and a growing community of developers ready to share knowledge and best practices. This community aspect is vital, as Move's development is not just about writing code but understanding a new way to think about digital assets, security, and blockchain interactions.

In essence, understanding Move is about embracing a new philosophy of programming where security, clarity, and efficiency are not afterthoughts but integral parts of the development process. It's about learning to write smart contracts that are not just functional but fundamentally secure by design, enabling developers to build on Sui with confidence.

As developers dive into Move, they're not just learning a new language; they're stepping into a new era of blockchain development where the possibilities are as expansive as the creativity of the developers themselves. Move on Sui isn't just about creating smart contracts; it's about crafting the digital future.

Part 3: Setting Up Your Development Environment

Embarking on the journey of building smart contracts on the Sui blockchain begins with setting up a conducive development environment. This step is crucial as it lays the foundation for all subsequent development activities, ensuring that developers have the right tools, frameworks, and resources at their fingertips to start creating.

First and foremost, developers need to install the Sui development kit (SDK). The SDK includes all the necessary components like compilers, libraries, and command-line tools that are tailored for interacting with the Sui network. This kit can be obtained from Sui's official GitHub repository or through package managers, depending on the operating system you're using. Once installed, it provides an interface to compile, test, and deploy your Move smart contracts.

Next, configuring your development environment involves setting up an Integrated Development Environment (IDE) or text editor with Move language support. While there isn't a Move-specific IDE yet, developers can leverage existing IDEs like Visual Studio Code with custom extensions for syntax highlighting, code linting, and auto-completion features for Move. This setup enhances productivity by providing immediate feedback on code quality and helping to catch errors early.

To interact with the Sui network, whether it's for testing or deployment, developers need to connect to Sui's testnet or mainnet. The testnet is particularly useful for developers to experiment without the risk of incurring real costs or affecting the main network. Accessing these networks involves setting up node connections, which can be done through the SDK or by running a local node for development purposes.

Beyond the basic setup, developers should familiarize themselves with the Sui CLI (Command Line Interface). The CLI offers a range of commands for managing accounts, deploying contracts, querying the blockchain state, and executing transactions. It's an indispensable tool for quick operations and debugging, providing a direct line to the blockchain's functionalities.

For developers new to blockchain or Move, diving into the documentation provided by Sui is essential. This documentation includes tutorials, API references, and guides on best practices for smart contract design on

Sui. Understanding these materials thoroughly can significantly accelerate your learning curve and development process.

It's also advisable to explore Sui's developer tools and frameworks, which might include libraries for testing, frameworks for building decentralized applications (dApps), or even tools for monitoring and analyzing contract performance. These resources can simplify complex tasks, from asset management to implementing governance logic.

Setting up a local development environment where you can simulate the Sui blockchain is another key step. This can be achieved with tools like Sui's local testnet, which allows you to see how your contracts behave in a controlled environment before moving them to a public testnet or mainnet. Testing locally can save time and resources, allowing for iterative development without external dependencies.

Lastly, engaging with the Sui developer community can be incredibly beneficial. Joining forums, attending meetups, or participating in online discussions can provide insights into common pitfalls, share innovative solutions, and offer support for troubleshooting. The community can also be a source of inspiration for new features or optimizations in your projects.

In summary, setting up your development environment for Sui involves more than just installing software; it's about creating a workspace where creativity, security, and efficiency can thrive. With the right setup, developers are equipped to explore the full potential of Sui, crafting smart contracts that could redefine what's possible in the blockchain space.

Part 4: Writing Your First Sui Smart Contract

Writing your first smart contract on Sui is a venture into the realm of creating secure, efficient, and innovative blockchain applications. This part of the guide will walk you through the process, from conceptualization to implementation, providing a hands-on approach to understanding Move on the Sui platform.

Start by conceptualizing what your smart contract will do. Perhaps you're looking to create a simple token, manage a digital asset, or even a more complex system like a decentralized game or a voting mechanism. For beginners, let's focus on creating a basic token management system, which will illustrate key concepts of Move and Sui's object-centric model.

First, you'll need to define your module. In Move, a module encapsulates functions, structs, and other definitions related to your smart contract. For a token system, you might name your module "MyToken". Within this module, you'll define:

- **Resources:** These are the digital assets in Move. For a token, you might define a `Token` struct with fields like `id` (a unique identifier for each token) and `balance` (the amount of tokens).

- **Abilities:** Move uses abilities like `store`, `copy`, and `drop` to control how resources can be used, ensuring they're managed safely.
- **Functions:** You'll write functions to mint new tokens, transfer them between accounts, or query balances. Here, you'll leverage Move's safety features, like ensuring that tokens can only be minted by authorized entities and that transfers respect the rules of ownership.

Here's a simplified example of what your first contract might look like:

```move
module MyToken {
    use sui::object::{Self, UID};
    use sui::transfer;
    use sui::tx_context::{Self, TxContext};

    // Define the token structure
    struct Token has key, store {
        id: UID,
        balance: u64
    }

    // Function to mint new tokens
    public fun mint(to: address, amount: u64, ctx: &mut TxContext) {
        let id = object::new(ctx);
        let token = Token { id, balance: amount };
        transfer::transfer(token, to);
    }

    // Function to transfer tokens
    public fun transfer(from: &mut Token, to: address, amount: u64) {
        assert!(from.balance >= amount, 0);
```

```
        from.balance = from.balance - amount;
        let new_token = Token {
            id: object::new(&mut from.id),
            balance: amount
        };
        transfer::transfer(new_token, to);
    }

    // Function to get balance (view function, no state change)
    public fun balance(token: &Token): u64 {
        token.balance
    }
}
```

This example introduces you to basic operations like minting, transferring, and querying balances, all within the security paradigm of Move.

Next, you'll compile your Move code using the Sui SDK. The compilation step checks for syntactic and semantic errors, ensuring your contract adheres to Move's rules and safety guarantees.
Post-compilation, you'll deploy your contract to either the Sui testnet for initial testing or directly to the mainnet once you're confident in its functionality.

Testing is crucial. Use Sui's testing utilities or write your own tests to simulate various scenarios like token transfers, edge cases with insufficient balances, or unauthorized minting attempts. This step ensures your contract behaves as expected under different conditions.

Remember, writing secure smart contracts involves more than just code; it's about understanding the blockchain's environment, the implications of your code's logic, and how users will interact with your contract. Always keep security in mind, leveraging Move's built-in protections against common vulnerabilities.

Best practices include:

- Keep your contracts simple where possible; complexity can lead to security flaws.
- Use Move's type system to its fullest for enforcing business logic and asset management.
- Regularly audit your code, either by yourself or through community reviews, to catch potential issues.

In conclusion, your first smart contract on Sui is not just a technical achievement but a step into a world where you can create, innovate, and contribute to the blockchain ecosystem. Each contract you write builds your understanding of Move and Sui, setting the stage for more complex and impactful decentralized applications.

Part 5: Advanced Smart Contract Techniques

Once you've mastered the basics of writing smart contracts on Sui with Move, you can explore advanced techniques that allow for the creation of more intricate, scalable, and secure applications. This section dives into the depths of smart contract development, offering insights into complex functionalities, security considerations, and leveraging

Sui's unique features for high-performance applications.

Composing Multiple Contracts:

One advanced technique involves composing multiple smart contracts to work together. This could mean one contract calling functions from another or sharing state through common resources. In Sui, you can achieve this by defining interfaces or by using events to signal actions across contracts. For instance, a governance contract might interact with a token contract to manage voting rights based on token holdings. Understanding how to structure these interactions is key to building modular, reusable code that can scale.

Implementing Complex Logic:

Move's capabilities extend beyond simple token transfers to include complex state management. You might implement:

- **State Machines:** Where the contract's state transitions through different stages based on user interactions or external conditions.
- **Game Logic:** Creating dynamic, interactive games where characters or items evolve, with rules enforced by smart contracts.
- **Financial Instruments:** Developing DeFi applications that require complex calculations, like interest rates or collateral management, while ensuring security at every step.

Here, the use of Move's resource types and the ability to define custom logic for state transitions become particularly valuable, allowing for precise control over how data evolves within your contract.

Handling State Changes in Parallel:

Sui's architecture supports parallel transaction execution, which can be a game-changer for performance. Writing contracts that can handle or benefit from parallel execution involves:

- **Designing for Independence:** Ensure that parts of your contract can operate independently where possible, reducing dependencies that might force sequential processing.
- **Utilizing Sui's Object Model:** Since each object can be considered independently, structure your data and logic around this, allowing multiple users to interact with different parts of your application simultaneously without conflicts.
- **Conflict Resolution:** Even in a parallel environment, conflicts can occur. Design your contracts to either avoid these conflicts or handle them gracefully, perhaps through temporary locks or by reordering transactions.

Managing Large-Scale Data:

For applications dealing with vast amounts of data or numerous user interactions, managing this scale efficiently is crucial:

- **Pagination and Indexing:** Implement patterns where data is accessed in chunks or indexed for quick retrieval, reducing gas costs and improving user experience.
- **Off-Chain Data Handling:** Use Sui's potential integration with layer-2 solutions or off-chain data storage mechanisms to manage data that doesn't need to be on-chain for security or consensus but is necessary for application functionality.

Security Considerations:

Advanced smart contracts require a heightened focus on security:

- **Formal Verification:** Leverage tools or methods to formally verify parts of your contract's logic, ensuring it behaves as intended under all possible conditions.
- **Reentrancy Protection:** Even with Move's built-in protections, understanding reentrancy and how to prevent it in complex scenarios is vital.
- **Auditability:** Design your contracts in a way that makes them easier to audit, with clear separation of concerns, good documentation, and well-commented code.

Testing Methodologies:

- **Unit and Integration Testing:** Beyond basic functionality, test how your contracts interact with each other and under various network conditions.

- **Stress Testing:** Simulate high-load scenarios to see how your contract performs when the network is under pressure, ensuring scalability and robustness.
- **Fuzz Testing:** Implement or use tools for fuzz testing to find unexpected vulnerabilities by throwing random inputs at your contract.

Leveraging Sui's Object-Centric Model:

Finally, fully embracing Sui's object-centric approach can lead to sophisticated applications:

- **Dynamic NFTs:** Create NFTs that evolve over time based on user interaction or external data, managed by smart contracts.
- **Complex Asset Composition:** Design assets that can be composed of other assets, with each object having its lifecycle and interaction rules.
- **Autonomous Systems:** Implement systems where objects autonomously interact based on predefined rules, simulating real-world dynamics in a digital environment.

In summary, advanced smart contract development on Sui involves weaving together complex logic, leveraging the platform's unique features for performance, ensuring security through rigorous practices, and continuously learning from the ecosystem's evolution. These techniques not only enhance your applications but also contribute to the broader understanding and capabilities of blockchain technology.

Part 6: Deployment, Testing, and Maintenance

The final phase in the lifecycle of a smart contract on the Sui blockchain involves deploying your contract to the network, rigorously testing its functionality, and ensuring its maintenance over time. This part of the guide will walk you through each step, emphasizing best practices for a secure and efficient deployment, alongside strategies for testing and ongoing support.

Deployment:

Deployment begins with choosing between the Sui testnet and mainnet. The testnet is ideal for initial deployments where you can experiment without financial risk. Here's how to approach deployment:

- **Compile and Test Locally:** Before any deployment, ensure your contract compiles without errors and passes all local tests.
- **Deploy to Testnet:** Use the Sui CLI to deploy your contract to the testnet. This step involves setting up your contract's initial state, like minting initial tokens or setting up admin controls.
- **Verification:** Once deployed, verify the contract's address on the blockchain explorer to ensure it's publicly accessible and functioning as expected.
- **Mainnet Deployment:** After thorough testing, deploy to the mainnet. This step requires

careful consideration of gas costs, as transactions now have real financial implications. Ensure you have the necessary permissions or keys to interact with your contract.

Testing:

Testing on Sui goes beyond simple unit tests to encompass:

- **Integration Testing:** Test how your contract behaves with other contracts or external systems it might interact with, ensuring all interfaces work as intended.
- **End-to-End Testing:** Simulate user interactions from start to finish to catch issues that might not appear in isolated tests.
- **Performance Testing:** Evaluate how your contract scales under load, particularly if it's designed to leverage Sui's parallel execution capabilities.
- **Security Audits:** Whether through community review, professional audit, or automated security tools, ensure your contract is secure against known vulnerabilities.
- **User Acceptance Testing (UAT):** If possible, involve real or simulated users to test the contract in a real-world scenario, gathering feedback on usability and functionality.

Maintenance:

Maintaining a smart contract involves:

- **Monitoring:** Keep an eye on your contract's performance, usage, and any potential security threats using blockchain analytics tools or custom monitoring scripts.
- **Upgrades:** Sui's design allows for contract upgrades through mechanisms like capability-based access control. Plan for how you'll update your contract, ensuring you can do so without disrupting users or compromising security.

  - **Versioning:** Implement versioning in your contracts to manage different states or functionalities over time.
  - **Migration Scripts:** Write scripts that can migrate data from one version of your contract to another safely.
- **Security Patches:** If vulnerabilities are discovered, have a strategy for patching these without necessarily requiring a full contract redeployment.
- **Community Engagement:** Engage with the community for feedback, bug reports, and even contributions to your contract's improvement. This could involve setting up a DAO or similar governance structure to manage updates.
- **Documentation:** Maintain clear, up-to-date documentation for your contract, detailing its use, known issues, and how to interact with it. This is crucial for both users and developers who might build upon your work.

Community Best Practices:

- **Open Source:** If applicable, open-source your contract's code to benefit from community scrutiny and improvements.
- **Education and Support:** Provide resources like tutorials, FAQs, or community forums where users can learn about and get help with your contract.
- **Bug Bounties:** Consider running bug bounty programs to incentivize the community to find and report vulnerabilities.

In conclusion, the deployment, testing, and maintenance of smart contracts on Sui are as critical as their development. This phase ensures your contract not only works as intended but also adapts to the evolving needs of its users and the blockchain ecosystem. With careful planning, thorough testing, and proactive maintenance, your smart contract can serve as a robust, long-lasting asset in the Sui ecosystem.

Chapter 10: Sui's Developer Tools and Ecosystem

Part 1: Getting Started with Sui Development

Embarking on development for the Sui blockchain begins with understanding the foundational steps required to set up your development environment, connect to the network, and start coding in Move. This part will guide you through the initial setup, ensuring you're equipped to dive into Sui's world of decentralized application development.

Setting Up Your Development Environment

- **System Requirements:** Before diving in, ensure your system meets the basic requirements. Sui currently supports development on Linux, macOS, and Windows with WSL (Windows Subsystem for Linux). A modern multi-core processor, at least 8GB of RAM, and sufficient storage are recommended.
- **Installing the Sui CLI:** The Sui Command Line Interface (CLI) is your gateway to interacting with the Sui blockchain. Here's how to get started:
  - Visit the official Sui documentation or GitHub repository to download the latest version of the CLI compatible with your OS.
  - Follow the installation instructions, which might involve running commands

in your terminal or shell depending on your operating system.

  ○ Run `sui --version` to confirm the installation was successful.

- **Configuring Your Environment:**
  ○ **Setting Up a Local Testnet:** For initial development and testing, you'll want to run a local instance of Sui. The CLI allows you to spin up a local testnet, which is crucial for testing smart contracts without affecting the mainnet. Use commands like `sui genesis` to generate a new chain and `sui start` to run it locally.
  ○ **Connecting to Sui Testnet or Mainnet:** Once you're ready to test against a more realistic environment or deploy your dApps, you'll connect to Sui's public testnet or mainnet. This involves configuring your CLI to interact with these networks, which usually requires setting up an RPC endpoint and managing keys.

First Steps with Move

- **Learning Move Basics:** Before writing complex smart contracts, familiarize yourself with Move's syntax, its resource model, and how to manage state. Sui's documentation offers tutorials for beginners, walking through basic module creation, resource definition, and simple transaction scripts.

- **Your First Move Module:**
  - Create a new directory for your project.
  - Write a simple Move module using a text editor or an IDE with Move support. Start with something basic like creating and transferring a token.
  - Compile your module using the Sui CLI with a command like `sui move build` to ensure there are no syntax errors.

Interacting with Sui Blockchain

- **Account Management:** Before you can deploy or interact with smart contracts, you need to manage accounts. The CLI helps you generate new keypairs, manage existing ones, and interact with the network:
  - `sui client new-address` to create a new address.
  - Use `sui client switch --address <ADDRESS>` to switch between accounts.
- **Basic Transactions:** Learn how to perform fundamental operations like transferring SUI tokens between accounts using the CLI. This not only tests your setup but also acquaints you with transaction syntax and confirmation.

Resources for Learning

- **Documentation:** Sui's official documentation is extensive, covering everything from Move basics to advanced contract patterns. It's your primary resource for understanding the ecosystem.

- **Tutorials and Examples:** Start with the provided examples in the Sui repository or through tutorials that walk you through common tasks like deploying your first contract or managing assets.
- **Community Engagement:** Join forums, Discord channels, or other community platforms to ask questions, share knowledge, and learn from others' experiences. This is invaluable for overcoming hurdles and staying updated on best practices.

Getting started with Sui development is about laying a strong foundation. By setting up your development environment, learning the basics of Move, and understanding how to interact with the Sui blockchain, you're well on your way to becoming a contributor to the Sui ecosystem. This initial setup phase is crucial for ensuring you can develop, test, and deploy smart contracts efficiently and securely. As you move forward, remember that the learning and development process is iterative; each step builds upon the last, leading to more complex and innovative applications.

Part 2: Sui Development Tools

Once you've set up your development environment, it's crucial to familiarize yourself with the suite of tools available for Sui development. These tools are designed to streamline every aspect of your coding journey, from writing and compiling code to deployment, testing, and beyond. In this part, we'll delve into the primary tools provided by Sui, explaining how they facilitate a more efficient and effective development process.

The Sui Command Line Interface (CLI) stands as the cornerstone for interacting with the Sui network. It's an all-in-one tool that developers can use for a variety of tasks. You can compile your Move modules with `sui move build`, which not only translates your code into bytecode but also checks for syntax and semantic errors, ensuring your contracts are ready for deployment. Testing is made simple with `sui move test`, where you can run your unit tests to confirm your smart contracts behave as expected. Deployment to the blockchain is straightforward with `sui client publish`, allowing you to push your compiled modules live. Beyond deployment, the CLI lets you interact with your contracts by calling their functions, manage accounts, transfer assets, and query the blockchain's state, giving you full control over your development and interaction with Sui.

One of the key features of the CLI is transaction simulation. This allows developers to see how transactions would affect the network state without actually executing them, providing a safe way to experiment and debug. Gas estimation is another vital feature, offering insights into how much transactions might cost in terms of gas, which is crucial for optimizing your contracts for cost-efficiency.

For developers accustomed to using Integrated Development Environments (IDEs), there are plugins and extensions specifically designed for Move. These enhance the coding experience significantly by providing syntax highlighting, which visually differentiates various parts of your code for better readability. Auto-completion speeds up the writing process by suggesting code based on what you've typed, and real-time error checking helps catch mistakes as you go, preventing many common programming errors. Popular IDEs like Visual Studio Code and IntelliJ IDEA have extensions that integrate these features, making Move development as smooth as working with any other modern programming language.

Beyond these, the Sui Explorer is an indispensable tool for developers needing to inspect the blockchain in detail. It allows you to delve into every transaction, understanding gas usage, who sent what to whom, and how contracts are interacting on the network. It's also a window into the health of the network, showing details about nodes and validators, which can be crucial for developers looking to optimize their applications based on current network conditions.

Debugging tools in the Move ecosystem are crucial, especially for runtime issues not caught by compile-time checks. Debugging involves stepping through code execution, where you can observe the state of resources at different points, ensuring that your contracts perform as intended once deployed. Logging and tracing within contracts can provide insights into how they behave in different scenarios, helping to pinpoint issues in production environments.

Testing is a fundamental part of development, and Move includes built-in capabilities for unit testing. This means you can write and run tests directly within your Move modules, receiving immediate feedback on how your functions behave under various conditions. Integration testing, although less straightforward, is something developers should consider, potentially using additional tools to simulate how different contracts might interact or how your contract would behave under network stress.

Version control with Git is not a tool provided by Sui but is indispensable for any development project. It allows for managing code changes, reverting to previous versions if needed, or working on features in separate branches. This is particularly beneficial in collaborative scenarios where multiple developers work on the same project, facilitating code reviews, pull requests, and issue tracking.

Using these tools effectively involves adhering to best practices like ensuring you always work with the latest versions for security and feature updates, focusing on code security through regular audits, optimizing for performance by understanding gas costs, and maintaining well-documented code through IDE features.

Looking forward, the evolution of Sui's toolchain is expected to continue, potentially introducing more sophisticated tools for contract analysis, gas optimization, and perhaps automated contract verification. The community-driven nature of Sui's development means that as more developers contribute, the ecosystem of tools will likely expand, offering even more resources for efficient and secure dApp development.

The array of tools for Sui development is crafted to enhance productivity and security. These tools lower the entry barrier for developers, enabling the creation of sophisticated, scalable decentralized applications. By mastering these tools, developers can significantly improve their workflow, ensuring their projects on Sui are not only functional but also optimized for performance and security. Understanding and leveraging these tools effectively is fundamental to becoming a proficient developer in the Sui ecosystem.

Part 3: Move Language Toolkit

The Move programming language, being central to Sui's smart contract development, comes with its own set of tools designed to enhance developer productivity, ensure code safety, and facilitate the creation of secure and efficient blockchain applications. This part delves into the specific tools and resources available for Move developers.

Move Compiler

- **Compilation Process:** The Move compiler is the gatekeeper of your code's journey from human-readable scripts to blockchain-executable bytecode. It performs several critical functions:

- ○ **Syntax and Semantic Analysis:** Ensures your code adheres to Move's rules, catching errors that could lead to vulnerabilities or incorrect behavior.
- ○ **Resource Management:** Verifies that resources are handled correctly, preventing issues like double-spending or resource leaks.
- ○ **Optimization:** Some level of bytecode optimization might occur to ensure gas efficiency.
- **Usage:** The Sui CLI simplifies the use of the Move compiler with commands like `sui move build`, which compiles your entire project, providing detailed feedback on any issues encountered.

Move Debugger

- **Stepping Through Code:** A debugger for Move allows developers to execute their code line by line, observing how the state changes, which is invaluable for understanding complex contract logic or debugging issues not caught during compilation.
- **State Inspection:** You can inspect resources, their states, and how they're manipulated through contract execution, enhancing your ability to verify contract behavior.
- **Current Status:** While Move debugging tools are still evolving, community contributions and official Sui tools are expected to bolster this area, providing more comprehensive debugging capabilities.

Testing Frameworks

- **Unit Testing in Move:** Move has native support for writing unit tests within the same module as your code, which can be run using the CLI. This encourages developers to test as they code, ensuring each function behaves as expected.

  - **Syntax:** Tests are written using Move's syntax, often within a special module or directly in the contract, making testing an integral part of the development process.
- **Mocking and Simulation:** More advanced testing might involve mocking certain blockchain conditions or simulating network behaviors, which could be supported by additional tools or libraries in the future.

Move Playground

- **Online Environment:** For those new to Move or looking for a quick way to experiment, an online Move Playground or similar tool could allow developers to write and test Move code in the browser, providing instant feedback without local setup.
- **Educational Tool:** This also serves as an excellent educational resource, where learners can try out examples or experiment with Move's features in a sandboxed environment.

Formal Verification

- **Safety Assurance:** While not fully implemented at the time of writing, the Move language aims to support formal verification techniques. This would allow developers to mathematically prove certain properties about their contracts, like safety against reentrancy attacks or ensuring certain invariants hold true.
- **Future Tools:** As Move's ecosystem matures, tools for formal verification might become more accessible, potentially integrated into the development process to enhance contract security.

Documentation and Tutorials

- **Official Move Documentation:** An extensive resource for all things Move, from basic syntax to advanced contract patterns. It's continuously updated to reflect the latest language features and best practices.
- **Learning Resources:** Beyond official docs, there are community-led tutorials, blogs, and video guides that help demystify Move, offering practical examples and problem-solving tips.

Community and Tool Evolution

- **Open-Source Contributions:** The tools around Move are often open-source, inviting developers to contribute to their improvement or to create new tools tailored to specific needs or for educational purposes.

- **Feedback Loop:** As developers use these tools, their feedback drives further development and refinement, ensuring that the toolkit evolves in line with real-world use cases and developer needs.

Challenges and Considerations

- **Tool Maturity:** As with any new programming ecosystem, the maturity of tools can lag behind the language itself, requiring developers to sometimes work around limitations or contribute to tool development.
- **Adoption and Learning Curve:** Encouraging widespread adoption of Move means continuously improving the toolkit and educational resources to make the language more accessible to developers from various backgrounds.

The Move Language Toolkit is pivotal for developers looking to leverage Sui's capabilities fully. By providing a rich set of tools for compilation, debugging, testing, and learning, Move's toolkit ensures that developers can write secure, efficient smart contracts with confidence. As these tools continue to evolve with the input of the developer community, they will become even more integral to the success of Sui and the broader adoption of Move in blockchain development.

Part 4: Sui Explorer and Monitoring Tools

Understanding the state of the blockchain, the performance of your smart contracts, and the health of the network is crucial for developers building on Sui. This part explores the tools designed for these purposes, particularly focusing on Sui Explorer and other monitoring utilities.

Sui Explorer

- **Functionality:** Sui Explorer serves as the primary interface for examining the Sui blockchain. It's akin to a blockchain browser but tailored specifically for Sui's unique architecture:

  - **Transaction Viewing:** Developers can inspect any transaction on the blockchain, seeing details like transaction hash, sender, recipient, gas usage, and the effects on the blockchain state.
  - **Contract Details:** Look up deployed contracts, their code, the functions they expose, and how they've been interacted with.
  - **Account Information:** Check balances, transaction history, and the assets owned by any address on the network.
- **User Experience:** Sui Explorer is designed for both developers and end-users, offering an intuitive interface that demystifies blockchain interactions:

- ○ **Search Capabilities:** Easily search for addresses, transactions, or contracts.
- ○ **Data Visualization:** Some elements might be presented in charts or graphs for better comprehension of network activity or contract usage.
- **Integration:** Being part of the Sui ecosystem, it's often integrated with other tools, providing a seamless experience for developers who need to move between development and analysis.

Monitoring Tools

- **Network Health:** Tools to monitor the status of the Sui network include:

  - ○ **Node Status:** Check the operational status of validators and full nodes, ensuring your application can rely on network stability.
  - ○ **Network Congestion:** Understand current network load to optimize when to submit transactions for best performance.
- **Performance Metrics:**
  - ○ **Transaction Throughput:** Monitor how many transactions per second the network is processing, which can indicate scalability or bottlenecks.
  - ○ **Latency:** Measure the average time transactions take to be confirmed, crucial for applications requiring real-time interactions.

- **Custom Monitoring Solutions:** Developers might need to set up custom monitoring for their specific applications:

    - **API Endpoints:** Use Sui's API to fetch real-time or historical data for custom analytics or dashboard creation.
    - **Third-Party Monitoring Services:** Integrate with services that offer blockchain monitoring, alerting, and analytics tailored for Sui.

Smart Contract Auditing Tools

- **Static Analysis:** Although still in development, tools for static analysis of Move contracts are emerging to help identify potential security issues:

    - **Code Linting:** Tools that check for stylistic or potential logic errors in your Move code before deployment.
    - **Automated Security Checks:** Software that scans for common vulnerabilities or anti-patterns in smart contract design.
- **Dynamic Analysis:** Post-deployment, tools can monitor contract behavior in real-time:

    - **Transaction Simulation:** Simulate transactions to see how they would affect contract state without actually changing the blockchain.

- Behavioral Monitoring: Watch for unexpected contract behaviors that might indicate an exploit or a bug.

Debugging and Logging

- **On-Chain Logging:** While blockchain state changes are immutable, smart contracts can emit events or logs that can be queried later:

  - **Event Tracking:** Use these logs to diagnose issues after deployment, understanding how contracts were used in transactions.
- **Off-Chain Monitoring:** For more in-depth debugging, developers might set up their own off-chain services to log or analyze data:

  - **Custom Logs:** Parse and store logs from your contracts in a custom database for more sophisticated analysis or debugging.

Community and Tool Development

- **Community Contributions:** As with many blockchain ecosystems, the community plays a significant role in expanding toolsets:

  - **Open-Source Projects:** Developers contribute to or create tools that fill gaps in monitoring and analysis, often shared via GitHub or similar platforms.

- **Feedback and Evolution:** The tools evolve based on developer feedback, ensuring they meet the practical needs of those building on Sui.

Challenges and Future Directions

- **Scalability of Monitoring:** As the network grows, ensuring tools can handle increased data and query loads will be a challenge.
- **Privacy vs. Transparency:** Balancing the need for transparency in monitoring with privacy concerns, especially for sensitive applications, will require innovative solutions.
- **Integration with Other Ecosystems:** Future tools might need to interoperate with monitoring systems from other blockchains for cross-chain applications.

Sui Explorer and the suite of monitoring tools provide developers with the insights needed to understand and optimize their applications on the Sui blockchain. These tools are vital for ensuring that smart contracts operate as intended, the network performs efficiently, and security is continuously maintained. As the ecosystem grows, these tools will likely become more sophisticated, offering deeper analytics, better integration, and more comprehensive security measures, fostering a thriving environment for blockchain development on Sui.

Part 5: Building dApps on Sui

Building decentralized applications (dApps) on Sui involves understanding not just the Move programming language but also how to architect, develop, and deploy applications that leverage Sui's unique features like speed, security, and scalability. This part outlines the process of dApp development on Sui, from conceptualization to deployment.

Conceptualizing Your dApp

- **Understanding User Needs:** Start by identifying the problem your dApp aims to solve or the service it provides. This will guide your design and implementation decisions.
- **Leveraging Sui's Strengths:** Consider how Sui's architecture, like its object-centric model, can benefit your dApp. For instance, if your application deals with unique digital assets, Sui's resource model is ideal.
- **Security and Scalability:** Plan your dApp with security in mind, utilizing Move's safety features, while also considering how to scale your application as it grows.

Development Environment Setup

- **Local Development:** Use the Sui CLI to set up a local testnet, allowing you to test your dApp in a controlled environment before going live.
- **Version Control:** Implement version control with Git for your project to manage code changes, collaborate with others, and track project progress.

Architecting Your dApp

- **Modular Design:** Break your application into modules, aligning with Move's modular approach. This makes your code more maintainable and upgradable.
- **State Management:** Design how your dApp will manage state, leveraging Sui's object-centric model where each asset or piece of data is an object with its own lifecycle.
- **User Interface (UI) and User Experience (UX):** Plan how users will interact with your dApp. While the backend is in Move, the frontend might be in JavaScript or another language, interacting with Sui via APIs.

Writing Smart Contracts

- **Move Development:** Write your smart contracts in Move, focusing on safety, gas efficiency, and clarity:

  - **Resource Definitions:** Define your assets or data as resources, ensuring they are managed correctly throughout their lifecycle.
  - **Function Implementation:** Implement functions that interact with these resources, keeping in mind parallel execution for scalability.
- **Testing:** Use Move's built-in testing capabilities to ensure each function behaves

as expected. Consider writing tests for different scenarios, including edge cases.

Frontend Integration

- **Web3 Libraries:** Utilize libraries like `sui.js` or similar for integrating your frontend with the Sui blockchain:

    - **Wallet Connection:** Allow users to connect their wallets to interact with your dApp.
    - **Transaction Handling:** Provide interfaces for users to initiate transactions, like sending assets or calling contract functions.
- **User Interface:** Build a intuitive UI that abstracts the complexity of blockchain interactions, making it user-friendly for those not familiar with blockchain tech.

Deployment

- **Testing on Testnet:** Before mainnet deployment, deploy your dApp to Sui's testnet:

    - **Stress Testing:** Simulate high load or different user interactions to ensure your contracts and frontend can handle real-world scenarios.
    - **Security Audits:** Perform or request security audits to catch vulnerabilities before going live.

- **Mainnet Deployment:** Once confident, deploy to the mainnet:

    - ○ **Contract Publishing:** Use the Sui CLI to publish your contracts, ensuring you understand the immutability of deployed code.
    - ○ **Frontend Deployment:** Deploy your frontend to a hosting service or use decentralized storage solutions if applicable.

Ongoing Management

- **Monitoring:** Use tools like Sui Explorer to monitor your dApp's performance, transaction volume, and any unusual activities.
- **Updates and Upgrades:** Plan for how you might update your contracts or frontend. Remember, while contracts are immutable, you can deploy new versions or implement upgrade patterns in Move.
- **Community Engagement:** Engage with users and the broader Sui community for feedback, which can guide future development or improvements.

Security Considerations

- **Code Safety:** Beyond Move's inherent safety, consider additional security measures like access control, rate limiting on functions, or implementing pause mechanisms for emergency stop.

- **User Education:** Educate users on secure practices, like how to manage private keys or avoid phishing scams.

Best Practices

- **Code Reusability:** Use or contribute to common libraries to avoid rewriting fundamental functionalities.
- **Documentation:** Document your code thoroughly, especially for public contracts, as these will be used by others or integrated into other systems.
- **Gas Optimization:** Always consider gas costs, optimizing your contracts to perform necessary tasks efficiently.

Future Directions

- **Ecosystem Growth:** As the Sui ecosystem grows, expect more frameworks, libraries, and tools that simplify dApp development, possibly focusing on specific use cases like gaming, finance, or identity.
- **Interoperability:** Future dApps might leverage cross-chain capabilities, requiring new patterns for how dApps interact with other blockchains or off-chain services.

Building dApps on Sui is an exciting opportunity to create applications that benefit from its advanced blockchain architecture. This process involves careful planning, leveraging Sui's unique features, and ensuring your dApp is secure, scalable, and user-friendly. With the right approach, developers can craft innovative solutions that push the boundaries of what's possible in decentralized applications, contributing to Sui's vibrant ecosystem.

Part 6: Libraries and Frameworks

The development of decentralized applications (dApps) on Sui is greatly enhanced by the availability of libraries and frameworks that can simplify complex tasks, standardize common operations, and provide building blocks for developers to create more sophisticated applications. This part explores the current state of libraries and frameworks within the Sui ecosystem, highlighting how they support developers in building on this blockchain.

Official Sui SDKs

- **Sui TypeScript SDK (**`sui.js`**):** A primary tool for developers looking to interact with Sui from JavaScript or TypeScript environments:

  - **Wallet Integration:** Helps with wallet connections, allowing users to interact with dApps securely.
  - **Transaction Building:** Simplifies the process of creating and signing transactions, abstracting away much of the complexity.
  - **API Interaction:** Provides methods to interact with Sui's JSON-RPC endpoints for querying blockchain state or sending transactions.

- **Move Standard Library:** While part of the Move language itself, it's worth mentioning here as it offers pre-built functions and resources for common blockchain operations:

  - **Asset Management:** Functions for creating, transferring, and managing digital assets.
  - **Mathematical Operations:** Safe, gas-efficient arithmetic operations designed for blockchain use.

Third-Party Libraries

- **Community Contributions:** The open-source nature of Sui encourages developers to create and share libraries that extend functionalities:

  - **Move Packages:** Various Move modules that developers can import into their projects for common patterns or utilities like token standards, auctions, or governance systems.
  - **Frontend Libraries:** Libraries that simplify the integration of Sui into web applications, handling connections, state management, and more.
- **Examples:**
  - **Authentication Libraries:** For managing user identities on Sui, ensuring secure and seamless authentication processes.
  - **Game Development Kits:** Tailored for creating blockchain-based games,

managing in-game assets, and handling player interactions.

Frameworks for dApp Development

- **Sui Frameworks:** While still in development, frameworks are emerging to streamline dApp creation:

  - **DApp Scaffolding:** Templates or starter kits for quickly setting up a dApp project with common structures and tools already in place.
  - **State Management:** Frameworks designed to manage the state of dApps in a way that integrates well with Sui's object model.
- **Cross-Platform Development:** Frameworks that allow for the development of dApps that can run on multiple blockchains might emerge, with Sui support:

  - **Multi-Chain SDKs:** These could provide a unified interface for developers to work across different blockchain ecosystems, including Sui.

Tools for Contract Management

- **Upgrade and Migration Tools:** Given the immutable nature of smart contracts, tools that help manage contract upgrades are crucial:

- **Proxy Patterns:** Libraries or frameworks that implement upgradeable contract patterns, allowing developers to change contract behavior post-deployment.
- **Testing Frameworks:** Beyond Move's native testing capabilities, third-party testing frameworks could emerge:
  - **Mocking Libraries:** For simulating complex blockchain states or interactions for testing purposes.

Data and Analytics Libraries

- **Blockchain Data Access:** Tools to fetch, parse, and analyze blockchain data for insights:
  - **Data Aggregators:** Libraries that pull data from Sui's blockchain for analytics or to feed into dApp interfaces for real-time information.
- **Visualizations:** Libraries for creating charts, graphs, or other visualizations from blockchain data to help developers or users interpret blockchain activity.

Privacy and Security Libraries

- **Zero-Knowledge Proofs:** While still in conceptual stages for Sui, libraries implementing ZKPs or similar privacy technologies could enhance dApp capabilities:

- ○ **Confidential Transactions:** Allow for transactions where only necessary information is revealed.
- **Access Control Modules:** Move modules that provide advanced access control mechanisms beyond simple ownership, like role-based access control (RBAC).

Integration with External Services

- **Oracles:** Libraries or frameworks for integrating with oracles to bring off-chain data into Sui smart contracts:

  - ○ **Data Feeds:** Standardized ways to pull in real-time data like price feeds or weather information.
- **Interoperability Tools:** Given the importance of blockchain interoperability, tools that facilitate cross-chain interactions could become prevalent:

  - ○ **Bridge SDKs:** For moving assets or data between Sui and other blockchains.

Future Developments

- **Ecosystem Expansion:** As Sui gains traction, expect an increase in specialized libraries for various use cases, from DeFi to gaming, identity management to supply chain.

- **Standardization Efforts:** Community efforts might lead to standard libraries or frameworks for common functionalities, ensuring consistency across dApps.
- **Performance Optimization:** Libraries focused on gas optimization or performance could become critical as developers look to reduce transaction costs.

Challenges

- **Ecosystem Maturity:** The current state of libraries and frameworks is still evolving, which might mean developers sometimes need to build custom solutions.
- **Interoperability:** As Sui aims for a broader blockchain ecosystem, ensuring libraries work well across different platforms will be a challenge.

Libraries and frameworks are pivotal in expanding the capabilities of developers on the Sui platform. They not only save time by providing ready-to-use components but also ensure that dApps are built with best practices in mind, fostering a more secure and efficient ecosystem. As Sui's community grows, so too will the richness of its development tools, setting the stage for innovative and complex dApps that leverage the full potential of this blockchain.

Part 7: Ecosystem Support

The ecosystem surrounding Sui is not just about the technology; it's also about the services, tools, and community support that enable developers to thrive. This part explores the various forms of support available, from infrastructure services to community-driven resources, illustrating how they collectively contribute to a vibrant development environment.

Wallets

- **Sui Wallet:** The official wallet for interacting with the Sui blockchain, offering:

  - **Asset Management:** Secure storage, sending, and receiving of SUI tokens and other digital assets.
  - **dApp Interaction:** A seamless interface for users to connect with dApps, sign transactions, and manage permissions.
- **Third-Party Wallets:** As Sui grows, we can expect more wallets to support it, providing:

  - **Multi-Chain Support:** Wallets that allow users to manage assets across multiple blockchains, including Sui.
  - **Custom Features:** Additional features like staking, governance voting, or specialized UX for different dApp categories.

Oracles

- **Data Oracles:** Services that bring off-chain data onto the Sui blockchain, crucial for dApps needing real-world information:

- **Price Feeds:** For DeFi applications requiring current asset prices.
- **Randomness:** For games or lottery systems needing verifiable random outcomes.

- **Integration:** Sui might see partnerships or native support for popular oracle services, making it easier for developers to incorporate external data securely.

Identity and Authentication Services

- **Decentralized Identity Solutions:** Tools and services that allow for secure, self-sovereign identity management on Sui:

  - **Identity Wallets:** Managing digital identities in a way that users control their data.
  - **Verification Services:** For dApps to verify user identities without compromising privacy.

Scalability Solutions

- **Layer 2 Solutions:** Although Sui is designed for scalability, additional layers or solutions could be developed:

  - **Sidechains:** For specific use cases needing even more transaction throughput or privacy.

- **State Channels:** To facilitate off-chain transactions that can settle on Sui for finality.

Developer Grants and Funding

- **Sui Developer Grants:** Mysten Labs or community organizations might offer grants to encourage development on Sui:

  - **Innovation Incentives:** Funding for projects that push the boundaries of what's possible on Sui.
  - **Ecosystem Growth:** Grants aimed at developing tools, libraries, or dApps that enhance the ecosystem.
- **Hackathons and Competitions:** Events where developers can showcase their ideas, network, and potentially win funding or mentorship.

Educational Resources

- **Documentation and Guides:** Extensive, well-maintained official documentation:

  - **Move Language:** Comprehensive guides on writing safe and efficient Move code.
  - **Sui Architecture:** Understanding the blockchain's design and how to leverage it.
- **Workshops and Tutorials:** Both online and in-person sessions to help developers get

started or advance their skills:

- ○ **From Basics to Advanced:** Covering everything from setting up your environment to complex contract patterns.

Community Support

- **Forums and Discord:** Platforms where developers can ask questions, share knowledge, and collaborate:

  - ○ **Real-Time Assistance:** Immediate help for troubleshooting or conceptual questions.
  - ○ **Project Showcases:** A place to present projects, gather feedback, or find collaborators.
- **Open-Source Contributions:** Encouragement to contribute to Sui's codebase or related tools:

  - ○ **GitHub Engagement:** Participate in code reviews, feature development, or bug fixes.

Auditing and Security Services

- **Smart Contract Audits:** Third-party services specializing in reviewing Move contracts for security:

- ○ **Pre-Deployment Audits:** Ensuring contracts are secure before they go live.
- ○ **Post-Deployment Monitoring:** Continuous security checks for deployed contracts.
- **Bug Bounty Programs:** Incentivizing the community to find and report security issues, enhancing the overall security of the ecosystem.

Interoperability Services

- **Cross-Chain Bridges:** While not immediately available, services that could connect Sui with other blockchains:

  - ○ **Asset Transfer:** Moving tokens or data between Sui and other networks.
  - ○ **Shared Liquidity:** Enabling liquidity pools that span multiple blockchains.

Future Ecosystem Support

- **Integration with Traditional Systems:** Tools or services that bridge Sui with traditional financial or data systems, broadening its applicability.
- **Specialized dApp Platforms:** Platforms built on or around Sui that cater to specific industries or use cases, like gaming or supply chain.

Challenges

- **Adoption:** The success of these support systems depends on the adoption of Sui, which requires building a compelling ecosystem of applications.
- **Regulatory Compliance:** Ensuring that all ecosystem components, especially those dealing with identity or finance, comply with global regulations.

The ecosystem support for Sui development is multifaceted, involving technical infrastructure, community engagement, educational resources, and financial incentives. This comprehensive support system is designed to lower the barriers to entry, encourage innovation, and ensure that developers have the tools and assistance they need to build secure, scalable, and impactful dApps. As Sui continues to evolve, this support will likely expand, creating a feedback loop that further enriches the platform's capabilities and user base.

Part 8: Community and Collaboration

The vitality of any blockchain platform is deeply intertwined with its community. For Sui, the community isn't just users or investors—it's a vibrant network of developers, enthusiasts, and contributors who drive innovation, support each other, and shape the platform's future. This part discusses how developers can engage with the Sui community, the platforms for collaboration, and the role of community in the growth and evolution of Sui.

Community Platforms

- **Discord:** A primary hub for real-time communication:

    - **Channels for Different Topics:** From general discussions to specific development queries, there's a place for every aspect of Sui.
    - **Live Assistance:** Immediate help for troubleshooting, where developers can share code snippets or ask for advice.
- **Reddit:** A forum for longer-form discussions and sharing:

    - **Project Showcases:** Developers can post about their projects, get feedback, or find co-developers.
    - **AMA (Ask Me Anything) Sessions:** With core team members or influential community figures, providing insights and answering questions.
- **GitHub:** The heart of collaborative coding:

    - **Open Source Contributions:** Developers can contribute to Sui's core code, tools, or community projects.
    - **Issue Tracking:** A place to report bugs, propose features, or collaborate on solutions.
- **Twitter:** For announcements, networking, and informal interaction:

- **Official Updates:** Quick updates from the Sui team on developments, releases, or events.
- **Networking:** Connecting with other developers, influencers, or potential users of your dApp.

Developer Programs and Events

- **Hackathons:** Regular events where developers can:

  - **Showcase Innovations:** Develop and present new ideas or applications using Sui.
  - **Win Prizes and Grants:** Often, hackathons come with rewards that can fund further development or provide resources.
- **Sui Grants Program:** Aimed at fostering development:

  - **Funding for Projects:** Grants for developers or teams working on promising dApps or ecosystem tools.
  - **Mentorship:** Access to advice from experienced developers or the Sui team.
- **Virtual Meetups and Webinars:** Educational and networking opportunities:

  - **Learning Opportunities:** From basic introductions to advanced topics in Move or Sui architecture.

- Networking: Meeting other developers, potentially leading to collaborations.

Collaboration Tools

- **Git and Version Control:** Essential for collaborative development:

  - **Branching and Pull Requests:** Facilitate teamwork by allowing developers to work on features independently before merging.
- **Project Management Tools:** Like Trello, Jira, or Notion for organizing tasks:

  - **Roadmaps:** Share project timelines and milestones with the community.
  - **Task Delegation:** Coordinate work among team members or with community contributors.

Community-Driven Initiatives

- **Documentation Writing:** Community members often contribute to or maintain documentation:

  - **Translations:** Making Sui resources accessible in multiple languages.
  - **Tutorials:** Writing guides that help others learn from your experience.
- **Tool Development:** Creating or enhancing tools that the community needs:

- **IDEs and Plugins:** Developing or improving IDE support for Move.
- **Testing Libraries:** Building frameworks that make testing on Sui easier.

Feedback and Governance

- **Community Feedback:** Driving development through user and developer input:

  - **Surveys and Polls:** For gathering opinions on new features or directions for Sui.
  - **Governance Proposals:** As Sui evolves, community governance could allow developers to influence the platform's direction.
- **Bug Bounty Programs:** Encouraging security through community participation:

  - **Security Contributions:** Rewarding individuals who find and responsibly disclose vulnerabilities.

Challenges of Community Engagement

- **Maintaining Quality:** With open contributions, ensuring that community additions maintain high standards can be challenging.
- **Inclusivity:** Making sure the community is welcoming to all, regardless of experience level or background.
- **Managing Expectations:** With a growing community, managing expectations around

development speed or feature requests requires clear communication.

Future of Community and Collaboration

- **Decentralized Autonomous Organizations (DAOs):** Sui might evolve to support DAOs for community governance or project funding, formalizing community involvement.
- **Global Expansion:** As Sui grows, so too will its community, potentially leading to regional hubs or language-specific groups.

The community around Sui is not just a support network but a driving force in its development, adoption, and evolution. Through active participation in forums, contributing to open-source projects, or engaging in developer programs, developers can significantly influence Sui's trajectory while also benefiting from collective knowledge and support. As Sui continues to grow, this community will be at the heart of its success, embodying the collaborative spirit that blockchain technology promotes.

Part 9: Testing and Deployment

The process of testing and deploying smart contracts on Sui is critical to ensuring that applications are secure, function as intended, and are ready for the real world. This part dives into the methodologies, tools, and best practices for testing Move smart contracts and deploying them onto the Sui blockchain.

Testing Strategies

- **Unit Testing:**

  - **Built-in Testing:** Move allows developers to write unit tests within the same module as their contract. This encourages immediate testing as code is written.
  - **Isolated Tests:** Test individual functions or methods to ensure they handle inputs correctly, manage resources safely, and maintain state integrity.

- **Integration Testing:**

  - **Simulated Environment:** Use tools to simulate the Sui network, allowing you to test how different contracts interact or how your contract behaves with real-world data inputs.
  - **Cross-Contract Interaction:** Verify that contracts work seamlessly together, especially when one contract calls functions of another.

- **End-to-End Testing:**

  - **User Journey Simulation:** Test the entire flow from user interaction through the frontend to contract execution on the blockchain.
  - **Performance Testing:** Assess how your dApp behaves under load, ensuring scalability and performance are up to par.

Testing Tools

- **Sui CLI:** Provides commands to run Move tests:

    - `sui move test` automatically executes all tests within your Move modules.
- **Mocking Libraries:** While not yet fully developed for Move, the community or third-party tools might emerge to offer:

    - **Mock Contracts:** Simulate other contracts or external services your dApp might interact with.
- **Testing Frameworks:** Future tools might include more comprehensive frameworks for:

    - **Automated Testing:** Running tests as part of your CI/CD pipeline.
    - **Test Coverage Tools:** To ensure all code paths are tested.

Deployment Process

- **Testnet Deployment:**

    - **First Deployment:** Use the Sui testnet to deploy your contracts in a near-real-world environment.
    - **User Testing:** Involve a select group of users or community members to test your dApp, providing feedback on usability and functionality.

- **Security Audits:**

  - ○ **Pre-Deployment Audit:** Engage with security experts or use automated tools to scan for vulnerabilities before mainnet deployment.
  - ○ **Community Audits:** Leverage the community through bug bounty programs or open calls for security reviews.
- **Mainnet Deployment:**

  - ○ **Final Checks:** Review all aspects of your contract and frontend once more, ensuring everything is prepared for public use.
  - ○ **Publishing Contracts:** Use the Sui CLI command `sui client publish` to deploy your contracts to the mainnet, understanding that once published, they are immutable.

Post-Deployment

- **Monitoring:**

  - ○ **Transaction Monitoring:** Use Sui Explorer or custom solutions to monitor how your contracts are being used, looking for unexpected behaviors or high gas usage.
  - ○ **Performance Metrics:** Keep an eye on transaction speed, costs, and network

health to ensure your dApp scales well with user growth.

- **Upgrades and Maintenance:**

  - **Contract Upgrades:** While Move contracts are immutable, you can deploy new versions or use upgrade patterns if planned from the start.
  - **Frontend Updates:** Regularly update your application's interface to improve user experience or fix issues.

Best Practices for Deployment

- **Version Control:** Always maintain your code in version control systems like Git, documenting each deployment-ready version.
- **Documentation:** Provide comprehensive documentation for your contracts, explaining functionality, usage, and potential upgrade paths.
- **Gas Estimation:** Before deploying, estimate gas costs for typical transactions to ensure your users aren't surprised by high fees.
- **User Education:** Educate your users on how to interact with your dApp safely, especially concerning wallet management and transaction signing.

Challenges in Testing and Deployment

- **Evolving Tools:** As Sui and Move are relatively new, tools for testing and deployment

might still be in development, requiring developers to adapt or contribute.
- **State Complexity:** Testing all possible states and interactions in complex systems can be daunting, requiring thorough test case design.
- **Security:** Ensuring that no vulnerabilities slip through to production remains a constant challenge.

Future Enhancements

- **Automated Deployment Pipelines:** As the ecosystem matures, expect more automated tools for deploying and upgrading contracts.
- **Testing Ecosystem:** More sophisticated testing environments, possibly with built-in blockchain simulation for easier, more comprehensive testing.

Testing and deployment on Sui involve a rigorous process to safeguard against errors and vulnerabilities while ensuring that the application delivers on its promise. By leveraging the available tools, engaging with the community for feedback and security, and following best practices, developers can confidently bring their dApps to life on the Sui blockchain. As both the technology and its supporting ecosystem evolve, these processes will become more streamlined, fostering an environment where innovation can thrive with the assurance of reliability and security.

Part 10: Future Tools and Ecosystem Growth

The evolution of Sui's developer tools and ecosystem is an ongoing journey, shaped by technological advancements, community needs, and the broader blockchain landscape. This part speculates on the future directions of Sui's development support, emphasizing how these improvements could enhance developer productivity, application security, and the overall user experience.

Enhanced Development Tools

- **Advanced IDE Support:** Future iterations might see:

    - **Full-Featured Plugins:** Beyond syntax highlighting and auto-completion, offering features like automatic gas estimation, real-time contract analysis, or inline security suggestions.
    - **Integrated Debugging:** More sophisticated debugging tools that allow for deeper inspection of contract execution, akin to what's available for traditional programming languages.
- **Automated Code Analysis:** Tools that:

    - **Perform Static Analysis:** Automatically scan for common vulnerabilities, code smells, or inefficiencies, potentially integrating with CI/CD pipelines.
    - **Offer Formal Verification:** Software to mathematically prove contract

properties, ensuring safety and correctness before deployment.

Testing and Simulation

- **More Robust Testing Frameworks:** Development of:

  - **Mocking Services:** Simulating various blockchain states or external data sources for comprehensive testing scenarios.
  - **End-to-End Testing Platforms:** Environments that mimic the user experience from frontend to blockchain interaction, including network conditions.
- **Blockchain Simulation:** Tools that can simulate Sui's network at scale, allowing developers to test for scalability and performance under different loads.

Deployment and Management

- **Continuous Integration/Deployment (CI/CD):** Streamlined processes for:

  - **Automated Deployments:** Pipelines that automatically deploy contracts to testnets or mainnet after passing tests and security checks.
  - **Contract Upgrades:** More user-friendly tools for managing contract upgrades,

possibly through proxy patterns or other upgrade mechanisms.

- **Monitoring and Logging Tools:** More advanced solutions for:

  - **Real-Time Analytics:** Offering insights into contract usage, gas consumption, or user behavior in real-time.
  - **Alert Systems:** Notifying developers of anomalies, high transaction volumes, or potential security issues.

Security and Auditing

- **Security Toolkits:** Growth in:

  - **Automated Auditing Tools:** Software that checks for vulnerabilities or best practice deviations, becoming more sophisticated with time.
  - **Bug Bounty Platforms:** More structured programs to incentivize security research, potentially integrated with Sui's ecosystem.
- **Privacy Enhancements:** Development of:

  - **ZK-SNARKs or Similar:** Protocols that could be implemented to offer private transactions or confidential state transitions in Move.

Interoperability and Cross-Chain Features

- **Bridge Protocols:** Tools for:

  - **Asset Transfer:** Facilitating the movement of assets between Sui and other blockchains with ease and security.
  - **Data Sharing:** Mechanisms for dApps to access or share data across different blockchain ecosystems.
- **Standardization Efforts:** Community-driven initiatives to:

  - **Create Common Standards:** For token formats, contract interfaces, or communication protocols, enhancing compatibility.

Community and Developer Support

- **Educational Platforms:** Expansion of:

  - **Learning Paths:** Structured courses or certifications tailored to Move and Sui development.
  - **Interactive Learning Tools:** More interactive tutorials or sandbox environments for learning by doing.
- **Developer Grants and Accelerators:** Increased focus on:

  - **Innovation Funding:** More substantial grants for groundbreaking projects or those that fill gaps in the ecosystem.

- ○ **Mentorship Programs:** Connecting seasoned developers with newcomers to foster growth and knowledge sharing.

Ecosystem Expansion

- **Specialized dApp Platforms:** Platforms built on Sui that:

  - ○ **Cater to Specific Sectors:** Like gaming, finance, or identity management, providing tailored development kits or services.
- **Integration with Traditional Systems:** Tools or services that:

  - ○ **Bridge Blockchain and Off-Chain:** Facilitating integration with existing business systems, databases, or APIs.

Challenges and Considerations

- **Balancing Innovation with Stability:** Ensuring new tools do not disrupt the existing ecosystem while pushing forward.
- **Adoption:** Tools must be user-friendly enough to encourage widespread use by developers at all skill levels.
- **Security:** As tools become more complex, ensuring they do not introduce new vulnerabilities is paramount.

The future of Sui's developer tools and ecosystem holds promise for creating a more accessible, secure, and powerful environment for blockchain development. With an emphasis on enhancing developer experience, security, and interoperability, Sui is poised to support the next wave of decentralized applications. As these tools evolve, they will not only simplify the development process but also open up new possibilities for how blockchain technology can be applied, fostering an ecosystem where innovation is both encouraged and achievable.

Chapter 11: Sui for Gaming: Creating the Next Generation of Blockchain Games

Part 1: The Intersection of Blockchain and Gaming

The gaming industry has long been a pioneer in adopting new technologies to enhance player experiences, introduce novel gameplay mechanics, and craft expansive virtual worlds. With the emergence of blockchain technology, gaming is poised to enter a new era, one where decentralization, digital ownership, and economic fairness can fundamentally change how games are played, owned, and monetized. This part delves into where blockchain intersects with gaming, laying the groundwork for understanding Sui's pivotal role in this evolution.

In traditional gaming, players invest time or money into in-game items, but these assets remain under the control of game developers. Blockchain introduces the revolutionary concept of true ownership, allowing players to have indisputable control over their digital possessions. This means that in-game items can be bought, sold, or traded beyond the confines of the game itself, imparting real value to what was once considered merely virtual.

Another transformative aspect of blockchain in gaming is the introduction of genuine scarcity to digital goods. Unlike items in traditional games that can be replicated endlessly, blockchain ensures each asset is uniquely identifiable and tracked, thus preserving rarity and potentially increasing value within the gaming marketplace.

Blockchain also facilitates player-driven economies where the community, not just developers, dictate the supply, demand, and value of in-game assets. This leads to dynamic game worlds where players have a significant stake in the economy's health and evolution. Tokenization further extends this, where not only assets but also achievements or player influence can be converted into tokens, usable within the game or tradeable on external markets.

The transparency and security that come with blockchain technology ensure game states are verifiable and secure. Every action is recorded on the blockchain, making game outcomes transparent and provably fair, free from manipulation. The immutability of these records also safeguards against cheating or unauthorized alterations to player assets or progression.

Community governance is another area where blockchain can revolutionize gaming. Players could vote on game updates, rules, or economic policies, making games more democratic and responsive to player desires. Additionally, open-source game development on blockchain platforms could lead to games that evolve through collective input rather than a single, centralized vision.

Interoperability is a significant promise of blockchain in gaming, where in-game assets could transcend individual games or platforms, enhancing the utility and longevity of player investments. This could foster ecosystems where actions or assets in one game could influence or be utilized in another, creating a more interwoven gaming universe.

However, integrating blockchain into gaming is not without challenges. Ensuring a seamless user experience is paramount, as complexities like wallet management or the speed of transactions must be managed to not detract from gameplay. Scalability is another critical challenge, as traditional blockchains often can't handle the high transaction rates needed for interactive, real-time gaming. Finally, achieving widespread adoption requires overcoming skepticism, navigating regulatory landscapes, and clearly demonstrating the benefits in terms of gameplay or economic models.

Sui stands out in this context due to its architecture designed to tackle these very challenges. Its ability to process transactions in parallel with instant finality is perfect for the real-time nature of gaming. The security and precision with which Sui manages in-game assets through the Move resource model align with the needs of digital ownership. Furthermore, Sui's ecosystem offers tools and frameworks that make integrating blockchain into game development more accessible, potentially unlocking new realms of creativity and interaction in gaming.

The intersection of blockchain and gaming promises to redefine the essence of games, introducing true digital ownership, player-controlled economies, and community governance into the mix. Sui, with its architecture tailored for speed, security, and scalability, positions itself as an ideal platform for these innovations. As we explore further how Sui can be applied to gaming, this introduction sets the stage for understanding the transformative potential and opportunities this technology brings to the gaming world.

Part 2: Why Sui for Gaming?

Sui distinguishes itself as an exceptional platform for revolutionizing gaming through blockchain technology, thanks to its unique architectural choices and design philosophy. This part explores the specific features of Sui that make it ideally suited for gaming applications, addressing the common challenges of blockchain in gaming while enhancing the gaming experience.

Sui's architecture is engineered for speed and scalability, crucial for gaming where thousands of transactions per second might be necessary for real-time player interactions. Its ability to execute transactions in parallel allows for a high throughput, avoiding the bottlenecks that plague many blockchains. This high transaction capacity is vital for games requiring rapid state updates or those with significant player bases. Furthermore, Sui's design ensures low latency, providing near-instant transaction finality which is essential for maintaining the responsiveness expected in modern gaming, eliminating the delays often associated with blockchain operations.

The object-centric model of Sui is particularly beneficial for gaming. Each in-game asset can be managed as a unique object with its own lifecycle, ownership, and state. This model is perfect for games where items, characters, or even virtual land need to have distinct identities, histories, and rules for use or transfer. It allows for complex game economies where assets have real value and can be securely managed, supporting intricate game mechanics and worlds where changes are localized, enhancing efficiency in state management.

Security and asset integrity are also paramount in gaming, areas where Sui excels. The Move programming language, used for smart contracts on Sui, inherently promotes secure coding practices that prevent common vulnerabilities such as asset duplication or loss. This security is critical for maintaining trust in game economies where players invest both time and money. The immutable nature of blockchain transactions on Sui ensures that game states, player achievements, and asset ownership are recorded transparently and securely, offering a level of protection and transparency not found in traditional gaming environments.

From a user experience standpoint, Sui works to abstract the complexities of blockchain, making the gaming experience as seamless and intuitive as on conventional platforms. By simplifying blockchain interactions, developers can create interfaces where players manage their digital assets without needing to understand blockchain intricacies. Sui's ecosystem supports easy wallet integration, further reducing the barrier to entry for gamers who might otherwise be deterred by blockchain's complexity.

For developers, Sui offers a supportive ecosystem with tools specifically tailored for game development. From IDE support for Move to APIs and SDKs designed to handle game logic, these tools allow developers to concentrate on creativity rather than on navigating blockchain complexities. The growing community around Sui, with its focus on gaming, provides a rich resource of knowledge, collaboration, and even potential funding through grants or hackathons, fostering an environment ripe for game development.

Sui's framework also supports a variety of economic models within games, from simple token economies to intricate governance systems where players can influence game development or economic policies. With its efficient gas model and transaction speed, Sui is well-equipped to handle microtransactions smoothly, ensuring that in-game purchases or trades are as seamless as they would be in traditional games, yet with the added benefits of blockchain technology like true ownership and verifiable scarcity.

In essence, Sui's combination of speed, security, scalability, and developer-friendly tools positions it as a leading choice for developers looking to merge the innovative aspects of blockchain with the dynamic world of gaming, potentially redefining how games are built, played, and monetized.

Part 3: Asset Management and Ownership

The integration of blockchain into gaming fundamentally alters asset management and ownership, and Sui, with its object-centric model and secure, scalable architecture, provides an exemplary framework for this transformation. This part delves into how Sui facilitates a new era of digital asset management in games, ensuring players have genuine control over their in-game possessions.

In Sui, every asset is treated as a unique object, complete with its own ID, state, and lifecycle. This means each game item, whether it's a piece of equipment, a character skin, or a plot of digital land, can be uniquely identified and tracked. This approach ensures assets cannot be duplicated, establishing true scarcity and value. Ownership is also clear and indisputable; when players gain an asset, it's registered to their blockchain address, granting them full control over how it's used, transferred, or sold, much like real-world property rights.

The potential for asset interoperability and portability is another significant aspect of Sui. Assets can move between games or be utilized in different contexts within the same ecosystem, enhancing their utility and lifespan beyond the confines of a single game. Although still conceptual, this could lead to a cross-platform play environment where assets from one game have value or utility in another, fostering a more integrated and dynamic gaming universe.

Sui also supports comprehensive asset lifecycle management. Developers can define how assets are created, including their initial properties, rarity, and conditions for use or modification through Move smart contracts. Assets can evolve or be upgraded, with all changes recorded immutably on the blockchain, ensuring the asset retains its unique identity throughout its lifecycle. Transfers of assets are secure and transparent, whether through direct trades, marketplace sales, or as part of gameplay mechanics, with every transaction logged on the blockchain. Even the destruction or removal of assets from circulation is managed securely, preserving game balance and preventing fraud.

The security and integrity of assets on Sui are maintained through the blockchain's immutable record-keeping. Every action affecting an asset's state is logged, creating a transparent history that's crucial for trust in player-driven economies. The inherent security features of Sui and the Move programming language protect against fraud like item duplication or unauthorized asset manipulation, giving players confidence in their digital possessions.

Economically, Sui's model allows for player-driven value. The worth of assets can be dictated by the community's supply and demand rather than just the developers' decisions, potentially leading to more vibrant and self-sustaining in-game economies. This also opens up new monetization avenues for developers selling unique or rare assets, while players can profit from trading or selling items they've earned or created.

From a user experience perspective, Sui streamlines interaction with blockchain assets. Players engage with their assets through familiar game interfaces, with the complex blockchain transactions occurring behind the scenes. Sui's design includes easy wallet integration, allowing asset management without the need for players to grasp the underlying technology.

However, challenges remain, particularly in scaling asset management as the number of assets increases. Sui's architecture is designed to handle this growth efficiently, ensuring performance doesn't degrade. Another challenge is educating players on the benefits of blockchain asset management while keeping gameplay at the forefront. The Sui ecosystem provides resources and tools to help bridge this educational gap, promoting adoption.

Sui's approach to asset management and ownership in gaming is revolutionary, offering players true ownership, security, and the possibility of asset interoperability. This can lead to gaming experiences where digital possessions hold real, transferable value, fostering a new level of player engagement and economic interaction within games. As gaming evolves, the principles of blockchain asset management on Sui could pave the way for more immersive, valuable, and player-centric gaming worlds.

Part 4: Sui's Impact on Game Mechanics

Sui's unique features have profound implications for how game mechanics can be designed and implemented, potentially reshaping the very nature of gameplay. By leveraging Sui's speed, security, and scalability, developers can explore new realms of interactivity, fairness, and complexity in game design that were previously challenging or impossible with traditional gaming infrastructure.

The high transaction throughput and low latency of Sui enable real-time gameplay mechanics where player actions can immediately affect the game world. Traditional blockchain games might suffer from delays due to confirmation times, but with Sui, actions like trading, combat, or economic transactions can happen in real-time, akin to the responsiveness of non-blockchain games. This opens up possibilities for dynamic, fast-paced games where every second counts, enhancing player engagement through immediate feedback loops.

Sui's object-centric model also allows for the creation of intricate game mechanics centered around asset manipulation. Each asset's unique identity means developers can design games where items evolve, interact, or combine in ways that are transparent and verifiable to all players. For instance, crafting systems could become more complex and satisfying, where the history and authenticity of each component are documented, ensuring rarity or uniqueness of the final product. This could also extend to game mechanics like breeding, where the lineage of digital creatures is transparently tracked, adding depth to strategy and player investment.

The security and integrity provided by Sui's architecture can be harnessed to create provably fair mechanics. In games involving randomness, like card games or lotteries, Sui can ensure that outcomes are genuinely random and not manipulated by any party, including the game developers. This level of transparency can rebuild trust in games where fairness is paramount, potentially increasing player investment and satisfaction.

Moreover, Sui's scalability supports complex economic models within games. Developers can implement detailed economic systems where players have roles in supply chains, markets, or even governance of game rules. With Sui's ability to handle massive transaction volumes, these systems can scale with player numbers, ensuring that the economy remains balanced and engaging even as the game grows. Tokenomics can be designed to reward participation, encourage fair play, or even allow players to influence game development through governance tokens.

The Move programming language, with its focus on safety, empowers developers to write smart contracts that govern these mechanics securely. This means that game rules can be encoded in such a way that they are not only efficient but also resistant to common exploits, enhancing the security of gameplay and player assets.

Sui also opens the door to innovative forms of player interaction. Multiplayer mechanics can be enhanced with blockchain, where actions in one player's game can directly affect another's. Imagine scenarios where a player's success in one part of the game world can unlock opportunities or challenges for others, all tracked and verified by Sui's blockchain.

However, integrating these advanced mechanics comes with its set of challenges. The complexity of blockchain operations must be balanced with user experience, ensuring that gameplay remains accessible and enjoyable. Developers must also navigate the learning curve associated with blockchain technology, crafting mechanics that leverage its benefits without exposing players to its complexities.

In conclusion, Sui's architecture provides the foundation for reimagining game mechanics in ways that prioritize speed, security, and player agency. By allowing for real-time interactions, provably fair systems, and complex economic interactions, Sui can lead to the creation of games that are not only more engaging but also embody the principles of decentralization and player empowerment inherent to blockchain technology.

Part 5: Developer Tools for Game Creation

The process of creating blockchain-based games can be daunting, but Sui offers a suite of developer tools designed to streamline development, ensuring that the focus remains on creativity rather than on wrestling with the underlying blockchain complexities. This part examines how Sui's tools empower developers to craft innovative gaming experiences.

Sui's development environment is built around the Move programming language, which is specifically tailored for blockchain applications with an emphasis on safety and efficiency. Developers can use the Sui Command Line Interface (CLI) as a primary tool for interacting with the blockchain. It allows for compiling Move modules, deploying smart contracts to testnets or mainnet, and managing transactions, which is crucial for testing game mechanics in a controlled environment before going live.

For game developers, the object-centric model of Sui is a game-changer. It provides a natural fit for managing game assets where each item can be coded as an object with its own state, behavior, and lifecycle. This model simplifies the creation of complex game systems, from inventory management to in-game economies, where assets can be uniquely identified, transferred, or modified according to game rules.

Integrated Development Environments (IDEs) have been enhanced with Move support, offering syntax highlighting, auto-completion, and error detection tailored for Move's syntax. This makes writing smart contracts for game logic more intuitive, allowing developers to focus on gameplay rather than syntax errors. Additionally, these tools often include debugging capabilities, which are invaluable for ensuring that game mechanics function as intended in a blockchain environment.

Sui also provides SDKs (Software Development Kits) for various programming languages, particularly focusing on JavaScript/TypeScript with `sui.js`. These kits allow developers to integrate blockchain operations into their game's frontend, managing wallet connections, transaction signing, and asset interactions with minimal friction. This integration facilitates the creation of user-friendly interfaces where players can interact with blockchain elements without needing to understand the technology underneath.

Testing frameworks are another critical component. Sui supports unit testing within Move modules, encouraging developers to test game mechanics alongside their creation. This immediate feedback loop helps in catching issues early in the development cycle. For more comprehensive testing, developers can simulate transactions or network conditions, ensuring that games will scale and perform well under various scenarios.

The Sui ecosystem is also developing or contributing to libraries and frameworks specifically for gaming. These might include pre-built modules for common game functionalities like asset management, player authentication, or even game-specific economics like token minting or burning. By leveraging these libraries, developers can save time and reduce the risk of bugs, focusing more on unique gameplay features rather than reinventing basic blockchain interactions.

Moreover, Sui's open-source nature encourages community contributions, leading to a growing repository of tools, examples, and best practices. Hackathons, developer grants, and community forums further support developers by providing opportunities for collaboration, funding, and knowledge sharing. This ecosystem not only aids in technical development but also in conceptualizing new uses for blockchain in gaming.

However, developers must still navigate challenges like adapting to blockchain's unique constraints, such as gas costs for transactions or the immutable nature of smart contracts. Sui's tools help mitigate these through gas estimation features or patterns for contract upgradability, but understanding these concepts remains crucial for effective game design.

In summary, Sui's developer tools are crafted to bridge the gap between traditional game development and blockchain technology. By providing robust, game-focused tools for coding, testing, deploying, and interacting with smart contracts, Sui empowers developers to push the boundaries of what's possible in gaming, creating experiences that are secure, scalable, and truly owned by players.

Part 6: Economics and Tokenization in Games

Sui introduces a new dimension to game economics through tokenization, where in-game assets, currencies, and even influence can be represented as tokens on the blockchain. This part explores how Sui's architecture supports and enhances economic systems within games, fostering player engagement, creating value, and opening new avenues for monetization.

At the heart of Sui's economic model for games is the ability to create tokens that can represent virtually anything within the game's ecosystem. These tokens can range from simple in-game currencies to complex assets like unique items, land, or even representations of player achievements or influence. With Sui's object-centric model, each token is a unique entity on the blockchain, ensuring its scarcity and authenticity, which are fundamental for creating value.

Tokenization on Sui allows for the development of intricate in-game economies. Developers can design systems where tokens are earned through gameplay, traded among players, or used in various economic interactions like buying, selling, or upgrading assets. The security and transparency of blockchain mean that all transactions are verifiable, reducing the risk of fraud or manipulation and enhancing trust among players.

Sui's high transaction throughput and low latency are particularly beneficial for economic interactions within games. These features allow for real-time trading or auctions, where players can participate in dynamic markets without the transaction delays often associated with blockchain. This can lead to more engaging gameplay where economic strategy becomes a core part of the experience.

The creation of governance tokens is another area where Sui can transform game development. Players holding these tokens could have a say in the game's future, voting on updates, economic policies, or even content creation. This level of player involvement not only deepens engagement but also aligns the game's development path with community desires, potentially leading to more popular and sustainable games.

Moreover, Sui's scalability ensures that as the player base grows, the economic systems can handle increased activity without becoming bottlenecks. This scalability is crucial for games aiming to create large, active player-driven economies where thousands of transactions might occur simultaneously.

For developers, tokenization on Sui can unlock new revenue models. Beyond traditional in-game purchases, games can introduce systems where players can invest in the game's ecosystem, perhaps by staking tokens for rewards or participating in initial game offerings where new assets or features are tokenized and sold. This not only provides immediate monetization opportunities but can also create a self-sustaining economy where player investment helps fund ongoing development.

However, integrating such economic systems isn't without challenges. Balancing the game's economy to prevent inflation or deflation, ensuring fair distribution of tokens, and managing the impact of real-world economics on in-game dynamics are complex tasks. Sui's tools help by providing mechanisms for gas optimization, ensuring that economic actions are cost-effective for players. Developers must also consider the regulatory implications of tokenized economies, especially in regions where digital assets are closely scrutinized.

From a player's perspective, the true value of tokenized assets lies in their potential for interoperability or real-world value. While still a developing aspect, the idea that assets from one game could have utility or value in another, or even be convertible into other cryptocurrencies, could significantly enhance the perceived worth of in-game efforts.

In conclusion, Sui's support for tokenization and complex economic systems offers game developers a canvas to paint innovative, player-centric economic models. By leveraging Sui's capabilities, games can transcend traditional monetization strategies, fostering ecosystems where players are not just consumers but active participants with a stake in the game's success. This shift not only changes how games are funded and developed but also how they are played and valued in the broader digital economy.

Part 7: User Experience and Scalability

User experience (UX) in gaming is paramount, and when it comes to blockchain games, the challenge is to ensure that the technology enhances rather than hinders gameplay. Sui, with its focus on speed, scalability, and security, is designed to provide a gaming experience that feels seamless to users while leveraging the benefits of blockchain. This part discusses how Sui addresses these aspects, ensuring games are both engaging and scalable.

Sui's architecture is built to handle the high transaction rates necessary for gaming without compromising on speed. This means that actions within games, like trading items or executing combat moves, can occur in real-time, similar to traditional online games. The low latency offered by Sui's consensus mechanism ensures that there's minimal wait time for transactions to confirm, keeping the gameplay experience fluid and responsive. This is crucial in maintaining player immersion, where every moment of delay can detract from the experience.

Scalability is another key area where Sui excels, particularly important as games grow in popularity. Sui's object-centric model allows for parallel transaction processing, meaning that as more players join and more interactions occur, the system can scale horizontally. This scalability supports games that aim for large player bases without performance degradation, ensuring that economic systems, leaderboards, or multiplayer interactions remain efficient.

From a UX perspective, Sui aims to abstract away the complexities of blockchain. Players interact with the game through familiar interfaces, where the blockchain operations occur transparently in the background. Wallet integration is made as user-friendly as possible, allowing for secure management of assets without requiring players to understand blockchain intricacies. This user-centric approach means gameplay remains the focus, not the technology.

Moreover, Sui supports the creation of games where user experience is enhanced by blockchain features without overwhelming the player. For instance, asset ownership can be managed with ease, allowing players to trade or use items intuitively, yet securely. The transparent and secure nature of blockchain can also be used to provide players with verifiable proof of their achievements or ownership, adding to the game's depth and player satisfaction.

However, ensuring a positive user experience in blockchain gaming involves overcoming several challenges:

- **Education:** Players need to be educated subtly on the benefits of blockchain, like true ownership, without making the game feel like a tutorial on blockchain technology.
- **Onboarding:** New players might find the concept of managing digital assets through blockchain intimidating. Sui's ecosystem works on simplifying this process, making onboarding as seamless as possible.
- **Performance:** Even with Sui's scalability, maintaining performance under stress, like during peak player times or major in-game events, requires careful planning and optimization.

- **Interoperability:** While the potential for assets to move between games is exciting, it also means ensuring that this does not disrupt the user experience in each individual game, maintaining consistency and clarity.

Sui's approach to these challenges includes developing tools and frameworks that support developers in creating games that are inherently user-friendly. This includes providing APIs that handle blockchain interactions in a way that feels native to gaming, alongside community-driven initiatives to improve documentation and educational resources for both developers and players.

Sui's design philosophy places a strong emphasis on user experience alongside scalability. By ensuring that blockchain operations do not detract from gameplay but instead enhance it through security, ownership, and potentially interoperability, Sui sets the stage for games that can scale massively while preserving or even enhancing the player's experience. As the technology matures and more games are built on Sui, this balance between innovation and user-centric design will likely become one of its defining features in the gaming industry.

Part 8: Case Studies of Sui Games

To illustrate the practical application of Sui's technology in gaming, this part examines real or hypothetical case studies showcasing how developers might leverage Sui's unique features to create innovative, engaging, and secure gaming experiences. These examples highlight the potential of Sui in various gaming contexts, from economic models to gameplay mechanics.

Case Study 1: "SuiCraft" - An Open-World Exploration Game

In "SuiCraft," players explore a vast digital landscape where every tree, mineral, or crafted item is a unique object on the Sui blockchain. The game utilizes Sui's object-centric model to manage in-game assets, ensuring that players have true ownership of their discoveries and creations.

- **Asset Ownership:** Players can mine resources, craft items, and build structures that are uniquely theirs. These assets can be traded or sold within the game or potentially across different games in the future, thanks to Sui's interoperability potential.
- **Economy:** The game features a player-driven economy where the value of crafted items or land plots can fluctuate based on community demand. Sui's high transaction throughput supports a bustling marketplace without lag, enhancing the economic gameplay.
- **Gameplay Mechanics:** With Sui's low latency, actions like harvesting resources or engaging in combat can be done in real-time, providing a seamless experience akin to traditional games but with the added layer of blockchain security and asset ownership.

Case Study 2: "SuiRacers" - A Competitive Racing Game

"SuiRacers" is a blockchain-based racing game where players can own, customize, and race unique cars, each represented by tokens on Sui.

- **Tokenization:** Cars are tokenized assets, allowing players to buy, sell, or upgrade their vehicles. Each car's performance can be enhanced through upgrades, which are also managed as tokens, adding depth to the game's strategy.
- **Governance:** Players can vote on new tracks, rules, or features using governance tokens, giving them a say in the game's evolution. This community governance is made possible by Sui's ability to handle complex token mechanics securely and efficiently.
- **Fair Play and Events:** Sui ensures that race outcomes are provably fair, using blockchain to verify randomness or outcomes in competitions. Special events can involve real-time transactions for betting or immediate rewards, leveraging Sui's speed.

Case Study 3: "SuiQuest" - A Puzzle and Adventure Game

"SuiQuest" combines puzzle-solving with an adventure narrative in a blockchain environment where each puzzle piece or clue is a unique asset.

- **Asset Scarcity:** Each puzzle piece or clue is limited, creating a game where scarcity and strategy play a significant role. Players can trade pieces, adding an economic layer to puzzle-solving.
- **Progression and Ownership:** Progress in the game is tied to owning specific pieces. Sui's architecture allows for secure, transparent tracking of who solves what, potentially allowing for rewards that are tradable assets.
- **Community Engagement:** The game could foster a community where players collaborate or compete to solve puzzles, with Sui's blockchain providing a platform for sharing, trading, or even minting new puzzle-related assets.

Case Study 4: "SuiLegends" - A Role-Playing Game (RPG)

In "SuiLegends," players embark on quests, battle monsters, and collect legendary items, all managed on Sui.

- **Character and Asset Development:** Characters and their equipment are unique objects, with each item having its lifecycle, upgradability, and transferability. This encourages a deep investment in character development with real-world value.
- **Inter-Player Economy:** Players can trade or give items, forming guilds or alliances. Sui's scalability ensures these interactions happen smoothly, even with a large player base.

- **Dynamic Content:** Using Sui's smart contracts, the game can dynamically adjust based on player actions, with community events or new content voting influencing the game's direction.

These case studies demonstrate how Sui can be applied across different game genres, enhancing not just the economic aspects but also gameplay mechanics, player engagement, and community involvement. They highlight the versatility of Sui in supporting games that are not only fun but also offer players genuine control, security, and economic benefits from their gaming efforts. As more developers explore Sui's capabilities, we can expect to see even more innovative uses of blockchain in gaming, setting new standards for what games can be.

Part 9: Community and Player Engagement

The success of any blockchain-based gaming ecosystem, including Sui, heavily relies on community and player engagement. This part explores how Sui's architecture and philosophy can foster a vibrant, active community, enhancing player interaction, governance, and the overall gaming experience.

Sui's design inherently supports community-driven development and player engagement in several ways. Firstly, the object-centric model of Sui allows for games where players truly own their digital assets. This ownership extends beyond mere possession; players can have a say in how these assets are used, traded, or evolved within the game's ecosystem. This sense of ownership can significantly increase player investment in the game, as their efforts and time translate into tangible, valuable assets.

Player governance is another area where Sui shines. By implementing governance tokens or similar mechanisms, games on Sui can allow players to vote on game updates, economic policies, or even creative decisions like new content or features. This democratizes game development, making players not just consumers but co-creators. Such involvement can lead to games that better reflect player desires, fostering a loyal and engaged community.

The scalability of Sui supports large-scale community events or competitions. Whether it's a massive in-game event with thousands of participants or ongoing tournaments, Sui's ability to handle high transaction volumes ensures these events run smoothly, maintaining player satisfaction even in peak times. This capability also allows for complex social dynamics within games, like guilds or alliances, where numerous interactions occur daily.

Community engagement on Sui also extends to the development process itself. With an open-source approach, the Sui ecosystem encourages developers to contribute, share ideas, or even fork projects. This can lead to an ecosystem where game mods, extensions, or entirely new games are developed by the community, continuously enriching the gaming environment. Hackathons, developer grants, and community challenges further incentivize creativity and collaboration, turning game development into a community-driven endeavor.

Moreover, Sui's focus on user experience means that the blockchain aspects are abstracted away to keep players engaged with the game rather than with technology management. Secure, intuitive interfaces for wallet management, asset trading, or governance participation help maintain this focus on gameplay and community interaction.

However, fostering community and player engagement on Sui isn't without its challenges:

- **Education:** Players might need to be educated on the benefits and mechanics of blockchain in gaming. Sui's community and documentation efforts are crucial here to bridge this knowledge gap.
- **Inclusivity:** Ensuring that all players feel included in community governance or economic activities requires careful design of game mechanics and community platforms, making sure they are accessible and fair.
- **Balancing Developer Vision with Community Input:** While community input is valuable, developers must balance this with their vision for the game to maintain coherence and quality.
- **Sustainability:** Community-driven games need sustainable models to ensure they can evolve and grow without burning out the community or developers.

Sui's approach to these challenges involves creating tools and frameworks that support community interaction, like easy-to-use governance tools or social features within games. Moreover, by focusing on transparency, security, and true digital ownership, Sui lays the groundwork for games where players are more than just participants; they are integral to the ecosystem's growth and success.

In conclusion, Sui's architecture and ecosystem are designed to enhance community and player engagement in gaming. By providing mechanisms for ownership, governance, and interaction that are secure, scalable, and user-friendly, Sui can lead to a new era of gaming where communities are at the heart of the experience, driving innovation, engagement, and a sense of shared success.

Part 10: Challenges and Future Directions

While Sui presents a compelling platform for the future of gaming with its focus on speed, security, and scalability, there are several challenges that must be navigated to fully realize its potential in the gaming industry. This part discusses these challenges, alongside the future directions that could shape gaming on Sui.

One of the primary challenges is user adoption. Despite the advantages blockchain can bring to gaming, convincing gamers accustomed to traditional platforms to embrace blockchain technology involves overcoming skepticism, technical barriers, and a learning curve. Sui must continue to prioritize user experience, ensuring that the benefits of blockchain—such as true asset ownership and community governance—are felt without the complexities being exposed to the player. Education will play a key role, with tools, tutorials, and community outreach needed to demystify blockchain for gamers.

Scalability, although addressed by Sui's design, remains an ongoing challenge as games grow in popularity. Ensuring that the network can handle millions of transactions without performance degradation requires continuous innovation in network architecture, consensus mechanisms, and possibly even layer 2 solutions for specific gaming needs like instant, low-cost microtransactions.

Regulatory compliance is another hurdle. As games on Sui deal with in-game economies, tokenization, and potentially real-world value, they must navigate a complex global regulatory landscape. This includes considerations around gambling laws, digital asset regulations, and consumer protection, which can vary significantly by jurisdiction. Sui's ecosystem will need to provide clear guidelines and support for developers to ensure their games are compliant while still innovative.

Security, while a strength of Sui due to Move's design, still requires vigilant management. As games grow in complexity and asset value increases, they become more attractive targets for attacks. Continuous auditing, community-driven security initiatives like bug bounties, and the development of more sophisticated security tools are essential to maintain trust.

From a technical perspective, integrating blockchain into games to enhance rather than hinder gameplay demands a balance. Developers must be creative in leveraging blockchain's capabilities without making the game mechanics feel clunky or the gameplay experience less smooth. This involves optimizing for gas costs, ensuring that transactions are as seamless as possible, and designing gameplay that naturally incorporates blockchain benefits like asset scarcity or transparent state changes.

Looking to the future, several directions could define how gaming evolves on Sui:

- **Interoperability:** As the blockchain ecosystem matures, games on Sui might increasingly interact with other blockchains, allowing for cross-game asset use or shared economies, which could significantly enhance player engagement and asset utility.
- **Advanced Game Mechanics:** Sui could see the development of games with mechanics that were previously challenging due to technical limitations, like truly dynamic worlds where player actions have long-term, verifiable impacts on the game state.
- **AI and Blockchain Integration:** Future games might combine Sui's blockchain with AI for dynamic content creation, adaptive gameplay, or even in-game decision-making

processes that involve blockchain for fairness and transparency.

- **Player-Centric Economies:** The future might see more sophisticated economic models where players have even more control over market dynamics, potentially leading to games that are self-sustaining through player-driven economies.
- **Virtual Reality (VR) and Augmented Reality (AR):** As VR and AR technologies advance, Sui could provide the infrastructure for secure, player-owned digital spaces in these immersive environments, blending the physical and digital more seamlessly.
- **Community Governance Evolution:** Sui games could pioneer new models of community governance, where players not only vote on game directions but also participate in the economic governance of the game's ecosystem.

The journey ahead for Sui in gaming involves not just overcoming these challenges but also pushing the boundaries of what games can be. By fostering an ecosystem where developers are supported to innovate, where players feel genuinely empowered, and where the community drives the platform's evolution, Sui could lead the charge in redefining interactive entertainment for the blockchain age.

Chapter 12: Decentralized Finance (DeFi) on Sui

Part 1: Introduction to DeFi on Sui

Decentralized Finance, commonly known as DeFi, represents one of the most transformative applications of blockchain technology, aiming to recreate traditional financial systems with the principles of decentralization, transparency, and inclusivity. At its core, DeFi seeks to offer financial services like lending, borrowing, trading, and investment without intermediaries, using smart contracts on blockchains. Sui, with its unique architecture designed for speed, security, and scalability, presents an ideal environment for the next evolution of DeFi. This part introduces how Sui can redefine DeFi, with a special mention of upcoming platforms like the DEX aggregator airdrop.ag.

Sui's architecture is particularly well-suited for DeFi for several reasons:

- **Speed:** DeFi applications often require high transaction throughput to facilitate real-time trading, lending, and other financial operations. Sui's ability to process transactions in parallel and achieve near-instant finality can significantly enhance the user experience, making financial interactions as swift as those in traditional finance.
- **Scalability:** The growth of DeFi is often limited by the blockchain's capacity to handle

transactions. Sui's design allows for scaling without compromising performance, ensuring that as more users join DeFi applications, the system can accommodate the increased load.

- **Security:** With DeFi involving significant financial assets, security is paramount. Sui's integration of the Move programming language, which is designed to prevent common smart contract vulnerabilities, provides a safer foundation for DeFi applications.
- **User Experience:** DeFi can be complex for users new to blockchain technology. Sui emphasizes creating environments where users can interact with DeFi services without needing to understand the underlying blockchain intricacies, enhancing adoption.

One of the exciting developments in the DeFi space on Sui is the emergence of DEX (Decentralized Exchange) aggregators. A notable example is **airdrop.ag**, which is set to launch on Sui. DEX aggregators like airdrop.ag aim to simplify the user experience by pulling liquidity from various decentralized exchanges and providing users with the best possible prices for token swaps, all in one platform. This service not only enhances liquidity but also reduces slippage, making trading more efficient. By coming to Sui, airdrop.ag can leverage the blockchain's high-speed transactions and low latency, potentially setting new standards in how DEX aggregators operate.

The integration of such platforms into Sui's ecosystem signifies a step towards a more integrated and user-friendly DeFi landscape:

- **Liquidity:** By aggregating liquidity from multiple sources, these platforms can offer better pricing and depth for DeFi users on Sui, encouraging more participation in decentralized markets.
- **User Accessibility:** Aggregators simplify the trading process, making DeFi more accessible to users who might otherwise be deterred by the complexity of managing trades across different platforms.
- **Innovation:** The introduction of DEX aggregators like airdrop.ag on Sui can spur further innovation in DeFi, as developers build upon this foundation to create more sophisticated financial tools or integrate with other DeFi services for seamless user experiences.

However, while the potential is vast, there are challenges in bringing DeFi to Sui:

- **Regulatory Landscape:** Navigating the global regulatory environment for financial services on a decentralized platform remains complex.
- **User Education:** There's a continuous need to educate users about DeFi concepts, security practices, and the specific benefits of using Sui for financial applications.
- **Market Volatility:** The inherent risks of cryptocurrency markets, including volatility,

need to be managed within DeFi applications to protect users.

Sui's journey in DeFi is just beginning, with platforms like airdrop.ag signaling the start of what could be a vibrant ecosystem. As Sui matures, it's poised to not only host traditional DeFi applications but also innovate in areas like privacy, financial inclusion, and new forms of asset management, building on its strengths to redefine what's possible in decentralized finance.

Part 2: Fundamental DeFi Components on Sui

Decentralized Finance on Sui involves leveraging the blockchain's unique features to recreate and innovate upon traditional financial services. This part explores the fundamental components of DeFi that can be supported and enhanced by Sui's architecture, including asset tokenization, lending, borrowing, and the creation of stablecoins.

Asset tokenization on Sui allows for any asset to be represented digitally using the blockchain's object-centric model. This means that real-world assets, from art to real estate or commodities, can be transformed into unique tokens. This tokenization ensures authenticity, ownership, and transferability, with the added benefits of Sui's security and immutability. This feature is particularly valuable for DeFi applications where trust in asset representation is critical. Furthermore, Sui's model supports fractional ownership, allowing assets to be divided into smaller, tradable units. This democratizes investment by enabling more people to own a piece of high-value assets, potentially opening up markets that were previously inaccessible to the average investor.

In the realm of lending and borrowing, Sui's high transaction speeds and low latency enable lending protocols to operate with near-instant collateralization and loan issuance. Smart contracts on Sui can manage aspects like interest rates, collateral requirements, and repayment schedules with precision, ensuring that lending platforms are both efficient and secure. Borrowers benefit from the transparent nature of Sui's blockchain, where their collateral is securely held in smart contracts, and loans can be tailored according to individual risk profiles or asset types. The object-centric model ensures that each loan or collateral agreement is a unique, verifiable entity, adding layers of security and trust.

Stablecoins can be developed on Sui with mechanisms to maintain pegging to stable assets like the USD. The blockchain's speed and security facilitate real-time adjustments in supply through minting or burning, crucial for maintaining the peg. For collateralized stablecoins, where the value is backed by other assets held in smart contracts, Sui's environment offers transparency and trust. The efficiency of transaction processing on Sui ensures these stablecoins can quickly react to market changes, keeping their value stable against volatility.

Decentralized Exchanges (DEXs) on Sui can utilize both Automated Market Makers (AMM) and traditional order book models. The object-centric model allows for innovative liquidity pool designs where each pool can be managed as an object with its own set of rules. This enhances flexibility in how liquidity is provided and can significantly reduce slippage, improving the trading experience for users. Sui's architecture supports the creation of DEXs that are not only secure and fast but also capable of handling complex trading strategies with ease.

These fundamental components of DeFi on Sui illustrate how the blockchain's design can lead to more efficient, secure, and user-friendly financial applications. By leveraging Sui's speed, scalability, and security, developers can push the boundaries of what's possible in decentralized finance, offering users a platform where they can manage, trade, or invest in assets with unprecedented ease and trust.

Part 3: Sui's Impact on DeFi Mechanics

Sui's architecture introduces several groundbreaking elements that have the potential to significantly reshape the mechanics of Decentralized Finance (DeFi), enhancing efficiency, security, and user experience to levels previously unattainable. This part delves into how Sui's unique features can revolutionize the way DeFi applications are built, operated, and interacted with, with a particular focus on transaction speed, cost reduction, and security enhancements.

One of the most transformative impacts of Sui's design is its influence on transaction speed and finality. The architecture of Sui allows for the parallel execution of transactions, a capability that's pivotal in the fast-paced world of DeFi where every second can count. In traditional DeFi ecosystems, users often experience delays due to network congestion or the necessity of waiting for multiple confirmations to ensure transaction security. Sui's approach dramatically changes this:

For example, with atomic swaps on Sui, the exchange of one cryptocurrency for another without intermediaries can happen almost instantly. This means that both parties in a swap can be confident that their part of the trade will only complete if the other part does, mitigating risks associated with one side of the trade finalizing before the other. This near-instant finality not only boosts trust but also significantly reduces the risk in decentralized trading environments. Flash loans, another high-speed DeFi mechanism where loans are taken and repaid within the same transaction block, can be executed seamlessly on Sui. This speed is essential for strategies like arbitrage or leveraging short-term market inefficiencies without the fear of time-based market shifts. Yield farming, where users stake or lend their cryptocurrencies to earn rewards, also benefits from Sui's swift transaction processing. Rewards can be distributed in near real-time, which not only increases user engagement but also makes the farming process more dynamic and responsive to market conditions.

When it comes to cost reduction, Sui's consensus mechanism and its innovative approach to gas (transaction fees) can make DeFi operations more cost-effective. The Move programming language, integral to Sui's smart contracts, offers a resource model that leads to more predictable gas costs. This predictability is particularly important in DeFi where numerous small transactions, such as micro-payments or interactions with complex smart contracts, could otherwise become prohibitively expensive. Sui's scalability further supports this cost efficiency; as more users and transactions are added to the network, the cost per transaction can remain stable or even decrease. This is because Sui's ability to process transactions in parallel reduces network load, thus potentially lowering the transaction price for users over time, making financial operations on the blockchain more accessible.

Security is another domain where Sui makes significant advancements. By leveraging the Move language, which is inherently designed to prevent common vulnerabilities in smart contracts like reentrancy attacks, integer overflow, or unintended state changes, DeFi applications on Sui start from a place of enhanced security. Move's safety features mean that many security issues are caught at the compilation stage, before the code is even deployed, thereby reducing the chances of runtime vulnerabilities that have historically led to significant financial losses in other DeFi platforms. Sui's Delegated Proof-of-Stake (DPoS) consensus mechanism adds another layer of security. This method not only speeds up transaction confirmations but also distributes trust among validators, reducing the likelihood of network attacks or manipulations while optimizing for performance and security.

From a user experience perspective, Sui's approach to DeFi can significantly elevate how users interact with decentralized financial services. The design of Sui facilitates a smoother integration of blockchain operations into user interfaces, making DeFi applications more intuitive and accessible for those less familiar with blockchain technology. This includes simplifying wallet interactions, providing intuitive interfaces for trading, staking, or lending, and offering clear, real-time feedback on transactions. The speed and responsiveness of Sui mean that DeFi applications can deliver user experiences that rival or even surpass those found in centralized finance, without the typical wait times or uncertainties associated with blockchain transactions.

Moreover, Sui's capabilities open the door for more complex financial instruments. With its speed and scalability, developers can design and implement derivatives, options, and other sophisticated financial products that require real-time pricing and execution. This could lead to a new era where DeFi platforms offer dynamic financial systems that can adjust to market conditions in real-time, providing users with dynamic rates, collateral requirements, or investment opportunities based on the latest data.

However, while Sui promises these advancements, developers must still navigate challenges:

- Balancing the complexity of DeFi mechanics with user-friendliness to avoid overwhelming users with technical details.
- Ensuring compliance with an increasingly complex regulatory environment for financial services, all while maintaining the decentralized ethos of DeFi.
- Designing economic models that are sustainable, resilient to market manipulation, and capable of preventing economic attacks like flash loan attacks or rug pulls.

In conclusion, Sui's impact on DeFi mechanics is transformative, setting the stage for a new generation of financial applications that are not only faster and more secure but also more cost-effective. By addressing some of DeFi's most significant challenges, Sui not only enhances the functionality and appeal of these applications but also redefines the landscape of decentralized finance, making it more inclusive, efficient, and secure for a global user base. As developers continue to explore Sui's potential, we can anticipate seeing DeFi applications that are not only performant but also innovative in their approach to providing financial services.

Part 4: Building DeFi Applications

Building DeFi applications on Sui involves leveraging its architecture to create financial tools that are secure, scalable, and user-friendly. This part explores the process of developing these applications, from conceptualization to deployment, highlighting how developers can utilize Sui's tools and SDKs to innovate within the DeFi space.

The first step in building a DeFi application on Sui is conceptualization and planning. This means identifying the financial gaps or inefficiencies that your project aims to address. Whether you're envisioning a new lending protocol, a decentralized stablecoin, or an innovative trading platform, understanding user needs is crucial. Developers should consider how Sui's strengths, like its high-speed processing, security through the Move programming language, and scalability, can enhance their DeFi solutions. For instance, how can parallel transaction processing improve the performance of your application?

When it comes to the development tools and environment, the Sui CLI (Command Line Interface) is indispensable. It's used for compiling, testing, and deploying smart contracts, providing a comprehensive way to manage your development environment and interact with the Sui blockchain. Support for Move in IDEs provides syntax highlighting, error detection, and aids in smart contract development. Sui SDKs, such as `sui.js`, are crucial for frontend development, simplifying wallet integration, transaction management, and smart contract interactions from JavaScript or TypeScript environments.

In smart contract development, writing in Move is central. Developers must focus on safety, using Move's features to prevent common vulnerabilities. They should design contracts around resources, ideal for representing financial assets or obligations, and employ modularity to break down systems for better management, upgradability, and testing. Testing is paramount, encompassing unit tests to verify individual functions, integration tests to ensure different parts of the application work together, and simulations to test under various network conditions for scalability and performance.

The user interface and experience are equally important. The frontend should abstract away blockchain complexities to make DeFi accessible to all users. This involves seamless wallet integration for easy onboarding and creating interactive dashboards that display real-time data on financial positions, yields, or trading opportunities. Education is also key; integrating educational elements within the application helps users understand DeFi concepts, particularly those unique to Sui.

Deployment involves initially pushing your application to Sui's testnet. This is the phase for gathering feedback from the community or beta users and stress testing to ensure the application can handle real-world scenarios. Once the application is tested and refined, deployment to the mainnet follows, necessitating security audits to identify any vulnerabilities and continuous monitoring for usage, bugs, or security issues post-launch.

Interoperability is a consideration for future-proofing your application. Even if not immediately implemented, designing with potential cross-chain features in mind allows your DeFi solution to interact with other blockchains or external financial systems over time.

Engagement with the community and the broader ecosystem is beneficial. By considering making parts of your application open source, you encourage community contributions and enhance security through collective scrutiny. Look into developer grants for funding or mentorship, and participate in hackathons or competitions to showcase your project, network, and refine your ideas based on community feedback.

Challenges in building DeFi on Sui include ensuring top-notch security due to the financial nature of the applications, designing for scalability to handle growth, navigating regulatory landscapes to avoid compliance issues, and making your application intuitive enough to reach a broad audience.

Looking forward, there are numerous avenues for innovation. Developers could explore creating more complex or niche financial products that leverage Sui's capabilities, work on integrating DeFi with traditional finance to lower entry barriers, or implement privacy solutions like zero-knowledge proofs for transactions where privacy is paramount.

Building DeFi applications on Sui transcends mere coding; it's about envisioning a new financial ecosystem where users gain control, transparency, and access to financial services. By utilizing Sui's development tools, focusing on security and user experience, and engaging with the community, developers can contribute to a vibrant, user-centric DeFi landscape.

Part 5: Security and Trust in Sui DeFi

Security and trust are foundational to any DeFi ecosystem, and Sui's architecture, alongside the Move programming language, provides unique advantages in crafting secure DeFi applications. This part explores how Sui bolsters security in DeFi, the steps developers can take to foster trust, and strategies to counteract common risks associated with decentralized finance.

The Move programming language stands out for its inherent safety features, designed to prevent common smart contract vulnerabilities. Its resource model ensures that assets are treated as unique, indivisible entities, which prevents duplication or unintended loss. Move's compile-time safety checks catch many potential errors that could lead to security breaches during runtime, significantly diminishing the risk of hacks. Additionally, through its use of linear types and explicit ownership, Move guarantees that resources are managed with precision; once an asset is used or transferred, it cannot be referenced elsewhere without explicit permission, safeguarding against issues like reentrancy attacks.

Sui's consensus mechanism, Delegated Proof-of-Stake (DPoS), not only accelerates transaction finality but also enhances security. By selecting validators based on stake delegation, it ensures that individuals with a vested interest in the network's integrity are responsible for validating transactions. This approach reduces the motivation for malicious activities. Furthermore, mechanisms like validator penalties or "slashing" for dishonest behavior act as deterrents, reinforcing the security of DeFi applications on the network.

Smart contract auditing is another critical layer of security. Conducting pre-deployment audits by third-party security experts or through community-driven initiatives like bug bounty programs is essential. These audits can uncover vulnerabilities that might not be detected by automated tools or during the coding process. After deployment, continuous auditing and monitoring remain imperative to identify any new vulnerabilities that might emerge due to complex code interactions or unforeseen scenarios.

In terms of user asset security, Sui supports the development of non-custodial DeFi solutions where users maintain control over their assets, reducing the risk of centralized failures or hacks since users are responsible for their private keys. Incorporating multi-signature wallets or smart contracts can add another layer of security by requiring consensus among multiple parties for critical actions, thus minimizing the risk of unauthorized transactions.

To mitigate common DeFi risks:

- Flash loan attacks, which Sui's speed enables, can be safeguarded against by designing contracts with checks or delays for sensitive

operations, reducing the potential for these loans to be exploited maliciously.
- Rug pulls, where developers might abandon a project after raising funds, can be combated through transparent code practices, community governance, where users have a say in project direction, and by fostering an ecosystem where trust is built through open-source contributions and community oversight.

Building trust in DeFi on Sui also involves educating users about security practices, like the importance of managing private keys and recognizing phishing attempts. Developers should strive for transparency in how they handle funds, updates, or changes to their protocols, often through community discussions or governance mechanisms.

In conclusion, Sui's approach to DeFi security leverages both technological innovation and community engagement. By combining Move's safety features with Sui's consensus mechanism, alongside rigorous auditing and user-centric security practices, Sui sets a high standard for trust and security in the DeFi space, aiming to create an environment where users can interact with financial applications with confidence.

Part 6: Scalability and Performance

Scalability and performance are pivotal for the success of DeFi platforms, especially considering the high transaction volumes and the necessity for rapid, cost-effective operations. This part discusses how Sui's architecture tackles these challenges, ensuring that DeFi applications can scale to meet global demand while maintaining high performance.

Sui's approach to transaction processing is a significant advantage for DeFi. It allows for transactions to be processed in parallel when they do not conflict, fundamentally increasing throughput. This parallelism means that DeFi applications, which often involve numerous small transactions such as swaps, lending, or staking, can handle significantly more activity than blockchains that process transactions sequentially. By reducing latency through concurrent processing, Sui enables DeFi applications to provide near-real-time experiences akin to traditional finance, which is crucial for activities like trading, arbitrage, or yield farming.

The object-centric model of Sui further enhances scalability. Here, every piece of data or asset is treated as an object, allowing for localized state updates. This means that changes to one object do not necessitate global state updates, reducing computational load and facilitating more efficient DeFi operations. This model supports the precise and swift management of resources, ensuring that DeFi applications can operate with both speed and accuracy.

Sui's gas model contributes to cost efficiency by offering predictable gas costs. In DeFi, where users need to estimate costs for complex transactions or strategies, this predictability is vital for planning and executing financial operations without unexpected cost spikes. Sui's structure is also optimized for microtransactions, ensuring that these small, frequent interactions in DeFi do not become prohibitively expensive, supporting a broad spectrum of use cases.

The Delegated Proof-of-Stake (DPoS) consensus mechanism used by Sui is engineered for both speed and efficiency, allowing for rapid block times and finality. This is essential in DeFi, where the timeliness of transactions can significantly impact financial outcomes. As more validators join the network, Sui's capacity to handle transactions can increase, thereby enhancing the scalability of DeFi applications.

Sui's design also assists in managing network congestion by allowing transactions to be processed independently where possible. This approach ensures that even during periods of high demand, DeFi services can maintain operational efficiency. Looking ahead, Sui's architecture could potentially support dynamic scaling solutions, like sharding or layer 2 technologies, to further bolster performance under extreme loads.

When it comes to performance metrics, Sui aims to support a high number of Transactions Per Second (TPS), which is crucial for DeFi platforms executing numerous transactions in quick succession. Additionally, the low-latency environment of Sui means that DeFi applications can deliver a seamless user experience, where users do not experience long waits for transaction confirmations.

However, challenges remain. There are inherent limits to how much a blockchain can scale, necessitating ongoing innovation in consensus algorithms or state management to push these boundaries further. The challenge of interoperability also exists, as DeFi often spans multiple chains, requiring Sui to scale effectively while maintaining performance during cross-chain interactions. The development of additional ecosystem tools, like gas optimization libraries or performance testing frameworks, will be key to sustaining high performance as DeFi applications on Sui evolve.

Sui's architecture is crafted to address the demands of modern DeFi applications, providing solutions to scalability and performance challenges. By facilitating parallel transaction processing, efficient state management, and cost-effective operations, Sui sets the stage for DeFi platforms that can handle global-scale finance while offering a user experience that aligns with the expectations of the digital age. As the ecosystem around Sui expands, the commitment to scalability and performance will ensure that DeFi on Sui not only matches but potentially sets new benchmarks for what decentralized finance can achieve.

Part 7: User Experience in DeFi

The user experience in DeFi is crucial for its widespread adoption, influencing whether users will engage with, trust, and continue using decentralized financial services. This part explores how Sui's architecture can improve the user experience in DeFi applications, making them more accessible, intuitive, and efficient for the average user.

Sui's ecosystem simplifies blockchain interactions by supporting straightforward wallet integration. This allows users to manage their assets easily, abstracting away the complexities of key management or blockchain interactions. The goal is to make DeFi as user-friendly as traditional finance apps. Additionally, the near-instant transaction finality on Sui means users don't have to wait for blockchain confirmations, enhancing the fluidity and responsiveness of financial interactions.

Creating intuitive interfaces is another way Sui can enhance user experience. Developers can design applications that resemble conventional financial apps, with clear navigation and real-time updates on financial positions. Interfaces can provide visual feedback on transactions, balances, or yields, helping users understand the impact of their financial decisions in real time.

Education and onboarding are pivotal. DeFi applications on Sui can incorporate guided experiences that educate users on the basics of DeFi, including how to use the platform, manage assets, and understand the risks and rewards. Tutorials and help centers within the application can further demystify DeFi for newcomers, reducing the learning curve associated with these technologies.

Security and trust are paramount in DeFi. By being transparent about security measures, such as smart contract audits or the safety features of Move, users can feel more confident about the safety of their assets. Ensuring users retain control over their funds, with clear explanations of non-custodial versus custodial solutions, builds trust, as users know they're not dependent on third parties to safeguard their investments.

In terms of performance and cost, Sui's gas model keeps transaction fees low, which is crucial in DeFi where users might engage in numerous microtransactions. This accessibility can broaden the audience for DeFi. The scalability of Sui also ensures that a high volume of transactions can be processed without performance degradation, providing a smooth user experience even during peak usage times.

Community and support play a significant role in user experience. Platforms on Sui can leverage community engagement through forums, social media, or in-app chat systems to provide support, gather feedback, and foster a sense of belonging among users. Responsive customer support can quickly address user queries or issues, further enhancing trust and user satisfaction.

Accessibility and inclusivity are also key considerations. Offering interfaces and documentation in multiple languages can extend the reach of DeFi applications to a global audience. Ensuring that apps are accessible to people with disabilities or those using different devices, like focusing on mobile-first designs, can broaden the user base.

Looking to the future, user experience enhancements might include the integration of AI and machine learning for personalized financial advice or dynamic interfaces that adapt to user behaviors. As interoperability grows, experiences could become more cohesive across different DeFi platforms, with assets or data moving seamlessly between applications.

However, challenges persist. Balancing simplicity with the inherent complexity of DeFi is tough; making these concepts understandable without oversimplifying the risks is a delicate task. Regulatory compliance might also impact user experience, requiring careful integration of checks or identity verifications. Lastly, as user numbers grow, maintaining performance and a positive user experience is crucial to prevent degradation in service quality.

Sui's architecture provides a robust foundation for enhancing user experience in DeFi, with an emphasis on speed, security, and simplicity. By focusing on intuitive interfaces, educational onboarding, transparent security practices, and responsive performance, Sui can lead the way in making DeFi not just a niche for tech enthusiasts but a mainstream financial tool accessible to all. As the ecosystem matures, the emphasis on user experience will be vital in driving adoption and ensuring that DeFi on Sui delivers real value to users around the globe.

Part 8: Interoperability and Cross-Chain DeFi

Interoperability is a cornerstone for the future of DeFi, enabling assets and information to flow seamlessly across different blockchains, thus enhancing liquidity, reducing fragmentation, and creating a more unified financial ecosystem. This part explores how Sui can play a role in cross-chain DeFi, the current state of interoperability on Sui, and the potential future directions.

Understanding Interoperability in DeFi

- **Asset Mobility:** Interoperability allows tokens or assets from one blockchain to be used or traded on another, increasing their utility and liquidity. For Sui, this means enabling users to leverage assets across different DeFi ecosystems.
- **Data Sharing:** Beyond assets, interoperability can involve sharing data or state information, allowing smart contracts on different chains to interact, which can lead to more complex and integrated financial applications.

Current State of Interoperability on Sui

- **Native Support:** While Sui is designed with scalability and efficiency in mind, its initial focus might be on building a robust ecosystem within its own network. However, the architecture's flexibility suggests potential for future cross-chain integrations.
- **Bridge Protocols:** Although not immediately available at Sui's launch, the development or adoption of bridge protocols would be key for

interoperability. These would allow for the transfer of assets between Sui and other blockchains like Ethereum, Binance Smart Chain, or Polkadot.

Technical Considerations for Cross-Chain DeFi on Sui

- **Sui's Object Model:** Sui's approach to treating everything as an object could simplify cross-chain interactions by making it easier to manage and transfer these objects between different blockchain environments.
- **Security Across Chains:** Ensuring that cross-chain operations maintain the security standards of Sui, particularly with Move's safety features, is crucial. This includes securing the bridge mechanisms against common vulnerabilities like double-spending or replay attacks.

Strategies for Cross-Chain DeFi

- **Atomic Swaps:** Implementing atomic swaps where possible would allow for trustless exchanges between different blockchains, leveraging Sui's speed for these operations.
- **Wrapping Assets:** Creating wrapped versions of assets from other chains (e.g., wrapped BTC on Sui) could be an initial step towards interoperability, allowing these assets to participate in Sui's DeFi ecosystem.
- **Cross-Chain Oracles:** Using oracles to feed data from external chains into Sui can enable

DeFi applications to react to events or data from other blockchains, enhancing the functionality of smart contracts.

Challenges and Considerations

- **Scalability and Speed:** While Sui excels in these areas, ensuring that cross-chain interactions do not compromise this is a challenge. Interoperability should ideally maintain or enhance performance.
- **Regulatory Compliance:** Cross-chain DeFi might face regulatory challenges as it involves multiple jurisdictions, each with its own set of rules and requirements.
- **Standardization:** The lack of standardized protocols for cross-chain communication can lead to fragmentation. Sui could contribute to or leverage emerging standards to facilitate smoother interactions.

Future Directions

- **Layer 2 and Sidechains:** Future developments might include Sui supporting layer 2 scaling solutions or sidechains specifically for cross-chain DeFi operations, allowing for more complex financial interactions without burdening the main chain.
- **Interoperable Smart Contracts:** As Sui matures, smart contracts might be developed with interoperability in mind, where a contract on Sui could trigger actions on another blockchain, or vice versa.

- **Decentralized Finance Ecosystems:** The vision could be for Sui to be part of an interconnected DeFi ecosystem where assets, data, and liquidity are shared across platforms, potentially leading to a more robust and diverse financial landscape.

Interoperability is set to become a defining feature of DeFi's evolution, and Sui's design principles place it in an advantageous position to contribute to this future. By fostering an environment where assets can move freely, data can be shared securely, and financial operations can span across blockchains, Sui could help realize a vision of DeFi where users have unparalleled access to financial opportunities across the blockchain space. While challenges exist, particularly around security, standardization, and regulatory compliance, the potential benefits of a cross-chain DeFi ecosystem on Sui are immense, promising a new era of financial innovation and inclusion.

Part 9: Case Studies of DeFi on Sui

To concretely illustrate how DeFi can leverage Sui's unique features, this part presents several case studies or conceptual examples of DeFi applications that could be built or have been envisioned on Sui. These cases showcase the practical application of Sui's speed, security, and scalability in various DeFi contexts.

Case Study 1: A Decentralized DEX

SuiSwap is envisioned as a DEX that takes advantage of Sui's high transaction throughput and low latency to offer a trading platform with minimal slippage and near-instant trade executions. The concept involves using Sui's object-centric model for creating and managing liquidity pools, where each pool can be considered an object with specific rules, enhancing flexibility and reducing slippage. Looking ahead, SuiSwap could integrate with cross-chain protocols to facilitate swaps involving assets from different blockchains directly on Sui. This would mean users could trade assets across ecosystems without the need for separate bridge transactions. The impact of such a platform could be significant, attracting users who seek the speed of traditional exchanges while maintaining the benefits of decentralization.

Case Study 2: SuiLend - A Lending and Borrowing Platform

SuiLend leverages Sui's secure smart contract environment to provide lending and borrowing services. The platform would manage collateral and loans with precision, thanks to Sui's object-centric architecture, ensuring that each loan or deposit has clear rules and histories. SuiLend could introduce features like:

- Dynamic interest rates based on real-time market conditions, thanks to Sui's fast transaction processing.
- Automated collateral management, adjusting loan terms or liquidating assets based on market movements with minimal delay.

- A user-friendly interface that abstracts the complexities of blockchain interactions, making DeFi lending as accessible as traditional finance.

This platform could stand out for its speed in loan processing, security through Move's safety features, and the ability to handle complex financial products like flash loans, all while maintaining a high level of user trust due to transparent and secure operations.

Case Study 3: SuiStable - A Decentralized Stablecoin

SuiStable would represent a stablecoin project on Sui, aiming to maintain a peg to a stable asset (like USD) using Sui's capabilities for real-time supply adjustments. The project could:

- Utilize Sui's scalability to manage the minting and burning of tokens to stabilize the price, with operations happening near-instantly.
- Implement a governance model where holders of governance tokens can vote on policy changes or peg mechanisms, enhancing community involvement.
- Offer collateral-backed stablecoins where the collateral is securely held in Sui's smart contracts, providing transparency and trust in the peg's integrity.

The advantage here would be the use of Sui's infrastructure to create a stablecoin that reacts quickly to market changes, potentially offering better stability and lower transaction costs compared to stablecoins on less scalable blockchains.

Case Study 4: SuiYield - A Yield Farming and Liquidity Mining Platform

SuiYield could harness Sui's architecture to create an efficient yield farming and liquidity mining ecosystem. Key aspects might include:

- High-speed reward distribution, ensuring users receive their yields almost immediately upon providing liquidity or staking.
- Complex farming strategies enabled by Sui's ability to handle parallel transactions, allowing for innovative yield optimization techniques.
- Community-driven pools where users can propose and vote on new liquidity pools or yield strategies, leveraging Sui's governance features.

This platform would benefit from Sui's performance in managing numerous small transactions typical in yield farming, leading to better user experience and potentially higher engagement due to reduced wait times for rewards.

These case studies demonstrate how Sui's design can be applied to create DeFi applications that are not only secure and efficient but also push the boundaries of what's currently possible in decentralized finance. By leveraging Sui's capabilities, these hypothetical platforms could offer users enhanced experiences, from faster transactions to more secure and transparent financial services, setting a new standard for DeFi on blockchain.

Part 10: Challenges and Opportunities

The integration of DeFi into Sui's ecosystem brings forth both significant challenges and vast opportunities. This final part of the chapter discusses these aspects, providing a balanced view of what lies ahead for DeFi on Sui, emphasizing the potential to reshape financial services while navigating the complexities of this innovative space.

Challenges

- **Regulatory Compliance:** DeFi operates in a grey area of many legal frameworks. Ensuring that projects on Sui comply with varying international regulations, especially concerning anti-money laundering (AML), know-your-customer (KYC) requirements, and financial oversight, is a significant challenge. This balance must be struck without undermining the decentralized ethos of DeFi.
- **Security Risks:** Despite Sui's advanced security features, the DeFi sector remains a prime target for attacks. Challenges include protecting against smart contract vulnerabilities, flash loan exploits, and ensuring that interoperability does not introduce new security risks.
- **User Adoption:** Even with superior technology, overcoming the inertia of traditional finance and the skepticism towards

blockchain among the general public requires education, trust-building, and demonstrating clear user benefits. The complexity of DeFi can be a barrier to mainstream adoption.

- **Scalability and Performance:** As DeFi applications grow in popularity, ensuring that Sui can handle the resultant increase in transaction volume without performance degradation is crucial. This includes managing gas costs to keep DeFi accessible.
- **Interoperability:** While a strength, achieving seamless interoperability with other blockchains to create a cohesive DeFi ecosystem involves technical challenges and requires consensus on standards or protocols.

Opportunities

- **Financial Inclusion:** Sui's speed, security, and scalability can democratize access to financial services, particularly in regions where traditional banking is limited. DeFi on Sui could provide banking, lending, and investment opportunities to the unbanked or underbanked.
- **Innovation in Financial Products:** The capabilities of Sui allow for the creation of novel financial instruments or models that were previously impractical due to technological limitations. This includes more complex derivatives, dynamic yield farming strategies, or decentralized insurance models.
- **Enhanced Security and Trust:** With Move's safety features, DeFi applications can be developed with a lower risk of common

vulnerabilities, potentially leading to higher trust and adoption. The transparent nature of blockchain can also foster trust in financial dealings.

- **Efficiency and Cost Reduction:** Sui's architecture can significantly reduce transaction costs and times in financial operations, making DeFi not only more accessible but also more efficient than traditional systems for certain use cases.
- **Cross-Chain Ecosystems:** The potential for interoperability opens up opportunities for Sui to be part of a broader, interconnected financial ecosystem, where assets and liquidity can flow freely, enhancing the overall utility and value of DeFi applications.
- **Community and Governance:** Sui's design supports decentralized governance models, where users can have a say in the direction and policies of DeFi protocols, fostering a more democratic and community-driven financial landscape.

Future Directions

- **Privacy Enhancements:** Integrating privacy technologies like zero-knowledge proofs could offer users the benefits of DeFi without compromising personal data or transaction privacy.
- **Layer 2 Solutions:** As the ecosystem matures, layer 2 scaling solutions could be developed to further enhance performance

and reduce costs, particularly for DeFi applications requiring high throughput.

- **Educational Initiatives:** Continuous efforts in education and community engagement will be vital to bridge the knowledge gap and increase DeFi literacy among potential users.
- **Regulatory Collaboration:** Working proactively with regulators to shape policies that support innovation while protecting users could pave the way for broader acceptance of DeFi.

The journey of DeFi on Sui is at an exciting juncture, laden with opportunities to redefine finance but also fraught with challenges that require innovative solutions. By addressing these challenges head-on, Sui can lead the charge in creating a DeFi ecosystem that is not only technically superior but also inclusive, secure, and regulatory compliant. As the landscape evolves, the fusion of Sui's technology with the boundless creativity of the DeFi community holds the promise of a financial revolution where everyone can participate in and benefit from the global economy.

Chapter 13: Sui and Non-Fungible Tokens (NFTs)

Part 1: Introduction to NFTs on Sui

Non-Fungible Tokens (NFTs) have captured the imagination of the digital world by providing a means for unique, verifiable ownership of digital assets, ranging from art and music to virtual real estate and in-game items. Sui, with its advanced blockchain architecture, presents a compelling platform for the evolution of NFTs. This part introduces how Sui's features can enhance the NFT experience, making it more accessible, secure, and scalable.

What Are NFTs?

- **Uniqueness:** NFTs are digital assets that, unlike cryptocurrencies, are not interchangeable because each token has unique information or attributes embedded within it. This uniqueness is what gives NFTs their value in representing ownership of specific digital or physical items.
- **Ownership and Provenance:** Each NFT is recorded on the blockchain, providing a tamper-proof record of ownership and history, which is crucial for proving authenticity and provenance in the digital realm.

Why Sui for NFTs?

- **Speed:** Sui's design allows for near-instant transaction finality, which is particularly important for NFT markets where quick sales, auctions, or transfers can be critical. This reduces the time between a sale agreement and the actual transfer of the NFT.
- **Scalability:** With the potential for millions or billions of transactions, Sui's ability to scale horizontally means it can handle the high volume of activities typical in vibrant NFT ecosystems without performance degradation.
- **Low Transaction Costs:** The gas model in Sui is optimized to keep costs low, making it more feasible for microtransactions or for creators to mint numerous NFTs without prohibitive fees, thus democratizing access to the NFT market.
- **Security:** Sui's integration with the Move programming language brings inherent safety features to NFT smart contracts, reducing the risk of common vulnerabilities like unauthorized duplication or transfer of assets.
- **Object-Centric Model:** This model is particularly well-suited for NFTs because each asset can be an object with its own lifecycle, state, and rules, perfectly mirroring the concept of NFTs as unique digital entities.

The NFT Experience on Sui

- **Creation:** Artists, developers, or creators can leverage Sui's tools to mint NFTs with ease, embedding metadata that defines the asset's uniqueness directly into the blockchain.

- **Marketplaces:** Sui's architecture supports the development of NFT marketplaces where transactions are swift, and the user experience is akin to traditional e-commerce platforms but with the added benefits of blockchain security and ownership.
- **Interactivity:** Beyond static ownership, Sui enables NFTs to have dynamic attributes or behaviors, allowing for interactive digital assets that can evolve over time or respond to external inputs.
- **Interoperability:** Although still in the conceptual stage, the potential for Sui NFTs to interact with other blockchain ecosystems could lead to broader utility and exposure for NFT holders.

Cultural and Economic Impact

- **Empowering Creators:** Sui can facilitate a creator economy where artists and developers have more control over their digital works, including how they are sold, shared, or used, with built-in mechanisms for automatic royalties.
- **New Forms of Engagement:** NFTs on Sui can serve as entry points into communities, games, or virtual worlds, offering not just ownership but also access to exclusive experiences or memberships.
- **Preserving Digital Art:** With secure provenance and ownership records, Sui can play a role in the preservation and recognition

of digital art, ensuring artists are credited and compensated for their work over time.

Challenges and Considerations

- **Adoption:** Despite the technical advantages, convincing creators and consumers to adopt NFTs on Sui requires overcoming skepticism, educating about blockchain benefits, and ensuring a user-friendly experience.
- **Regulatory Environment:** As with all blockchain applications, navigating the regulatory landscape, particularly around digital asset ownership, copyright, and taxation, is complex.
- **Environmental Concerns:** Addressing or mitigating the environmental impact of blockchain technologies, even as Sui aims for efficiency, remains a topic of discussion in the NFT community.

Sui's architecture offers a promising foundation for advancing the world of NFTs, providing creators and collectors with a platform where speed, scalability, and security are not just aspirations but achievable realities. By redefining how NFTs are created, managed, traded, and experienced, Sui has the potential to push the boundaries of digital ownership, art, and interaction in the blockchain era. This part sets the stage for a deeper exploration into how Sui can transform the NFT landscape in the subsequent sections of this chapter.

Part 2: Sui's Architecture for NFTs

Sui's blockchain architecture is uniquely positioned to enhance the Non-Fungible Token (NFT) ecosystem through its design principles of speed, scalability, security, and an object-centric approach. This part explores how these architectural features can specifically benefit the creation, management, and lifecycle of NFTs, setting Sui apart as an ideal platform for digital assets.

Speed and Transaction Finality

- **Instant Transactions:** The high-speed transaction processing of Sui ensures that NFT minting, transfers, or sales can happen in real-time, significantly enhancing user experience for both creators and buyers. This speed is crucial in auction scenarios or time-sensitive trading, reducing the wait times typically associated with blockchain transactions.
- **Low Latency:** For NFTs, where timing can impact market dynamics, Sui's low latency means that new assets can be listed, and ownership can change hands almost instantly, fostering more dynamic and responsive markets.

Scalability

- **Handling High Volumes:** As the NFT market grows, so does the demand for blockchain capacity. Sui's ability to process transactions in parallel allows for scaling to accommodate millions of NFT interactions without performance degradation. This scalability is vital for large-scale events, drops, or when numerous NFTs are minted or traded simultaneously.

- **Efficient State Management:** Sui's object-centric model allows for efficient updates to NFT states, where changes to one NFT do not necessarily affect the entire state of the blockchain, making operations like updates or modifications to NFTs faster and less resource-intensive.

Security and Integrity

- **Move's Safety Features:** The use of Move for smart contracts ensures that NFTs on Sui are inherently secure. Move's resource model prevents duplication or loss of NFTs, ensuring that each token remains unique and its ownership indisputable.
- **Provenance and Authenticity:** With every transaction recorded immutably on the blockchain, Sui provides a clear, verifiable history for each NFT, crucial for establishing provenance and authenticity, which are paramount in the art and collectibles world.

Object-Centric Model

- **NFTs as Objects:** In Sui, every NFT can be treated as an object with its own set of properties, behaviors, and lifecycle. This model aligns perfectly with the nature of NFTs, allowing for rich metadata integration, dynamic attributes, and complex interactions with other objects or smart contracts.

- **Flexibility in Asset Management:** Developers can define how NFTs behave, including transfer rules, upgrade possibilities, or interaction with other blockchain elements, all while maintaining the token's uniqueness and integrity.

Low Gas Costs

- **Affordable NFT Creation:** Sui's gas model ensures that minting or interacting with NFTs remains cost-effective, even for small transactions. This low-cost structure can encourage more creators to enter the space, especially for those who might mint numerous NFTs or engage in frequent trading.
- **Economic Viability:** By keeping gas costs down, Sui makes it economically viable for a broader range of applications, from art to gaming, where NFTs might be used in myriad transactions or as part of gameplay mechanics.

Interoperability Potential

- **Future Integration:** While not immediately implemented, Sui's architecture is designed with the potential for interoperability in mind. This means that in the future, NFTs created on Sui could potentially interact with or be recognized by other blockchains, enhancing their utility across different ecosystems.

Challenges in Implementation

- **Balancing Complexity and Simplicity:** While Sui's model offers many advantages, ensuring that the creation and management of NFTs remain accessible to non-technical users is key to widespread adoption.
- **Security Enhancements:** Continuous improvement in security practices, especially around smart contract design for NFTs, will be necessary to protect against evolving threats.

Sui's architecture presents a compelling case for a new era of NFTs, where speed, scalability, security, and object management are not just features but foundational elements that enhance every aspect of the NFT lifecycle. By leveraging these capabilities, Sui can foster an environment where digital art, collectibles, and other unique assets can be created, shared, and enjoyed with unprecedented efficiency and trust. As Sui matures, the potential for NFTs to become more interactive, valuable, and integrated into broader digital experiences is immense, potentially setting new standards for what digital ownership can mean in the blockchain space.

Part 3: Creating NFTs on Sui

The process of creating Non-Fungible Tokens (NFTs) on Sui involves both artistic vision and technical know-how, greatly enhanced by Sui's features like its object-centric model, high transaction speeds, and low gas costs. This part outlines the steps and considerations for minting, managing, and interacting with NFTs within the Sui ecosystem.

Minting NFTs

- **Using Move for Smart Contracts:** Artists or developers can use the Move programming language to define the creation process of NFTs. This involves specifying:
    - The metadata associated with the NFT (e.g., title, description, image URL, creator information).
    - Ownership rules, including how the NFT can be transferred or if there are royalties for future sales.
    - Any unique attributes or behaviors the NFT might have, like dynamic properties or interaction with other NFTs.
- **Sui CLI and SDKs:** The Sui Command Line Interface (CLI) offers commands to compile and deploy these smart contracts. The `sui.js` SDK can be utilized for frontend integration, allowing for a user-friendly interface where artists or developers can interact with the blockchain to mint NFTs.
- **Metadata Standards:** Although Sui does not enforce specific standards, developers might choose to adopt or adapt existing standards like ERC-721 from Ethereum for compatibility or community recognition. Sui's object model allows for flexible metadata implementation,

potentially leading to new standards or
enhancements over existing ones.

Managing NFTs

- **Ownership and Transfer:** After minting, NFTs
  on Sui can be managed through smart
  contracts that handle:
    - Transferring ownership, with the
      blockchain ensuring only the owner can
      initiate a transfer.
    - Updating metadata if the NFT has
      dynamic properties or if additional
      information needs to be added
      post-mint.
- **Asset Lifecycle:** Each NFT has its lifecycle
  managed on the blockchain due to Sui's
  object-centric approach:
    - Minting, marking the NFT's creation.
    - Transfer, indicating a change in
      ownership.
    - Potential destruction or "burning" if the
      NFT needs to be removed from
      circulation.

NFT Interaction

- **Smart Contract Functions:** Beyond mere
  ownership, NFTs can interact with other smart
  contracts or external systems:
    - In gaming, an NFT might represent a
      character or item whose attributes can
      change based on gameplay or external
      events.

- For art, an NFT could evolve or change based on community input or environmental data.
- **User Interface:** Developing intuitive interfaces where users can interact with their NFTs, view their collections, or participate in community events is crucial. This includes:
  - Displaying NFT details and history.
  - Enabling transactions like buying, selling, or lending NFTs.

Security Considerations

- **Smart Contract Audits:** Security audits of smart contracts before minting are vital to protect against vulnerabilities that could compromise NFT integrity or ownership.
- **Private Key Management:** Educating users on securing their private keys is essential, as losing them means losing access to one's NFTs.

Tools and Ecosystem Support

- **NFT Minting Platforms:** As the ecosystem around Sui grows, expect platforms designed to simplify the NFT minting process, possibly offering templates or user-friendly interfaces for creators lacking technical skills.
- **Wallets with NFT Support:** Wallets that integrate with Sui will need to support viewing, managing, and interacting with NFTs, potentially including features like galleries or display options for collections.

Challenges

- **User Experience:** Simplifying the NFT creation process for artists who might not be technically inclined while ensuring they understand blockchain implications.
- **Scalability of Metadata:** Managing metadata efficiently becomes crucial as NFTs grow in complexity, especially if they include large files or dynamic data.
- **Regulatory Compliance:** Navigating copyright, intellectual property rights, and financial regulations when minting and trading NFTs.

Future Directions

- **Enhanced Interactivity:** As Sui's capabilities expand, NFTs might become more interactive or even executable, where the token itself could run logic or respond to certain conditions.
- **Cross-Chain Compatibility:** Future developments might enable mechanisms for Sui NFTs to be recognized or transferred to other blockchains, thereby increasing their utility.

Creating NFTs on Sui leverages the blockchain's speed, security, and scalability to offer a new paradigm in digital asset creation. By combining these technical advantages with the creative potential of artists and developers, Sui can facilitate an environment where NFTs are not just collectibles but part of a broader, more engaging digital ecosystem. As the tools and community around Sui's NFT capabilities grow, we can anticipate a flourishing space for unique digital expression and ownership.

Part 4: NFT Marketplaces on Sui

NFT marketplaces are central to the ecosystem, providing platforms where creators can sell or auction their digital assets, and collectors can acquire, trade, or display them. Sui's architecture offers unique benefits for building or adapting NFT marketplaces, emphasizing low fees, high throughput, and an exceptional user experience. This part explores how these marketplaces can leverage Sui's capabilities.

High Throughput and Low Latency

- **Instant Transactions:** Sui's ability to process transactions nearly instantly ensures that auctions can conclude, and sales can be confirmed without the typical blockchain delays, enhancing the marketplace's responsiveness.
- **Parallel Processing:** With Sui's support for parallel transactions, marketplaces can handle a high volume of trades or listings simultaneously, maintaining performance even during peak times.

Low Transaction Costs

- **Affordable Trading:** The efficient gas model of Sui means that the cost of listing, buying, or selling NFTs can be kept low, making the marketplace accessible to a broader audience. This is particularly important for microtransactions or when dealing with lower-value NFTs.
- **Gas-Free Listings:** Marketplaces might even offer gas-free listings for creators, where the marketplace itself could cover the initial gas cost, encouraging more artists to participate without the barrier of high upfront costs.

User Experience

- **Seamless Integration:** Sui marketplaces can provide a user experience similar to traditional e-commerce sites, abstracting blockchain complexities. This includes:
  - Easy wallet integration for managing NFTs.
  - User-friendly interfaces for browsing, bidding, and purchasing.
- **Real-Time Updates:** Thanks to Sui's speed, marketplaces can update in real-time, showing current bids, prices, or availability, which is crucial for auction-style sales.

Security and Trust

- **Secure Transactions:** With Move's safety features, transactions on Sui marketplaces are inherently safer, reducing the risk of fraudulent activities or smart contract vulnerabilities.

- **Provenance Tracking:** Every NFT's history is transparently recorded, providing buyers with confidence in the authenticity and origin of their purchases.

Creator Support

- **Royalties Automation:** Sui's smart contracts can automatically enforce royalties for creators on secondary sales, ensuring they continue to benefit from their work's value over time.
- **Creator Verification:** Marketplaces might implement systems to verify creators, adding an extra layer of trust and potentially increasing the value of NFTs through verified authenticity.

Interoperability and Expansion

- **Future Cross-Chain Interactions:** Although immediate cross-chain functionality might not be available, the design of Sui allows for future integrations where NFTs could be traded or utilized across different blockchain ecosystems.
- **Expanding Marketplace Features:** Beyond just trading, marketplaces on Sui could evolve to offer services like NFT rental, fractional ownership, or integration with other DeFi applications for lending against NFT collateral.

Building a Marketplace on Sui

- **Development Tools:** Using Sui's CLI, SDKs, and Move language, developers can build marketplaces with custom features tailored to specific NFT categories or user behaviors.
- **Community and Open-Source:** Encouraging an open-source approach can lead to a richer ecosystem where developers contribute to and benefit from shared libraries or modules for marketplace functionalities.

Challenges

- **Scalability with Growth:** Ensuring that as the marketplace grows, it can continue to handle increasing traffic without performance degradation.
- **Regulatory Navigation:** Dealing with legal frameworks around digital asset sales, particularly concerning copyright, taxation, and anti-money laundering.
- **Market Saturation:** Differentiating from other platforms in an increasingly crowded NFT marketplace landscape.

Future Directions

- **Enhanced User Interfaces:** Developing more intuitive, interactive, and personalized experiences where users can engage with NFTs in novel ways.
- **Integration with Physical Goods:** Exploring how NFTs can represent or be linked to physical items, blending the digital and physical worlds.

- **Privacy Features:** Implementing privacy options for transactions or ownership details, aligning with broader trends in privacy-conscious blockchain applications.

Sui presents a fertile ground for the development of NFT marketplaces, distinguished by its technical advantages that can lead to more dynamic, secure, and inclusive platforms. By leveraging Sui's speed, scalability, and security, marketplaces can offer a superior user experience, support creators more effectively, and potentially redefine what NFT trading platforms can achieve, fostering a vibrant ecosystem where art, culture, and digital ownership intersect.

Part 5: NFT Gaming and Virtual Worlds

The integration of Non-Fungible Tokens (NFTs) into gaming and virtual worlds is one of the most exciting applications of blockchain technology, and Sui, with its focus on speed, scalability, and asset management, is poised to push these boundaries further. This part explores how Sui can revolutionize gaming by leveraging NFTs for unique in-game assets, enhancing gameplay, ownership, and the interoperability of virtual worlds.

Unique In-Game Assets

- **True Ownership:** In games built on Sui, players can have true ownership of their digital items. Each NFT represents a unique game asset, whether it's a character, weapon, piece of land, or art, ensuring that players have indisputable control over their virtual possessions.

- **Rarity and Scarcity:** Sui's ability to treat each NFT as a unique object allows for genuine rarity and scarcity within games. This can lead to more engaging economies where the value of items can fluctuate based on demand, rarity, or player achievements.

Enhanced Gameplay

- **Interactivity and Evolution:** With Sui's architecture, NFTs can have dynamic properties. For example, a sword might gain new abilities or change appearance based on gameplay achievements or time-based events, providing a more immersive experience.
- **Player-Driven Economies:** The speed and efficiency of Sui support dynamic, player-driven economies where assets can be traded, upgraded, or used in novel ways within the game's ecosystem, all backed by the security of blockchain.

Scalability for Massively Multiplayer Experiences

- **Handling Large Player Bases:** Sui's design to scale horizontally ensures that even as games grow in popularity, they can maintain performance. This is critical for MMOs (Massively Multiplayer Online games) where numerous players interact, trade, or engage in activities simultaneously.

- **Low Transaction Costs:** The gas model of Sui allows for numerous in-game transactions to occur without prohibitive costs, making it feasible for games to include intricate economic systems or microtransactions.

Interoperability of Virtual Worlds

- **Cross-Game Asset Utilization:** While still in development, the concept of using NFTs from one game in another or across different virtual worlds could be supported by Sui's architecture, potentially allowing players to carry their assets across various gaming experiences.
- **Shared Economies:** With Sui's potential for future interoperability, different games could share economies or even entire virtual worlds, where an NFT from one game could have utility or value in another, enhancing player engagement and asset longevity.

Governance and Community

- **Player Governance:** Sui supports mechanisms where players can have governance over aspects of the game, like voting on updates, economic policies, or even which new features or assets to introduce, using their NFTs or associated tokens.
- **Building Communities:** Games on Sui can foster communities around NFT collections, where owning certain NFTs grants access to

exclusive in-game areas, events, or social groups.

Creating and Managing NFTs in Games

- **Smart Contracts for Game Logic:** Developers can use Move to write smart contracts that define how NFTs behave within the game, from minting to how they can be used or modified.
- **Integration with Sui Tools:** Utilizing Sui's CLI, SDKs, and developer tools, game developers can create seamless experiences where the blockchain operations are abstracted for players, focusing on gameplay rather than technology.

Challenges

- **User Experience:** Balancing the complexity of blockchain with the need for an intuitive gaming experience remains challenging. Games must be accessible to both blockchain enthusiasts and traditional gamers.
- **Security:** Ensuring that in-game NFTs are secure against hacks, theft, or manipulation, particularly when they hold real-world value.
- **Adoption:** Encouraging gamers to engage with NFTs when many might be unfamiliar or skeptical about blockchain technology.

Future Directions

- **Narrative-Driven NFTs:** NFTs could evolve to include story elements where owning an asset contributes to a larger narrative, providing a new layer of depth to gaming.
- **VR and AR Integration:** As virtual and augmented reality technologies advance, NFTs on Sui could become integral to creating or owning parts of immersive digital spaces.
- **Environmental and Ethical Considerations:** As the gaming industry becomes more conscious of its impact, Sui's efficiency might become a selling point for environmentally friendly blockchain gaming.

Sui's approach to NFTs in gaming offers a vision where players not only enjoy games but also have a stake in the digital assets they encounter, fostering a new era of gaming where ownership, community, and creativity are at the forefront. By providing the infrastructure for secure, scalable, and interactive digital assets, Sui can pave the way for games that are not just played but lived, where every item has a story, a value, and a community behind it.

Part 6: Art, Collectibles, and Digital Ownership

Sui's blockchain architecture holds significant promise for revolutionizing the art and collectibles space through NFTs, offering artists, collectors, and enthusiasts new ways to create, share, and own digital assets with unprecedented security, provenance, and interaction capabilities. This part examines how Sui can impact the world of digital art and collectibles, enhancing the concept of digital ownership.

Empowering Artists

- **Direct Monetization:** With Sui, artists can directly monetize their digital creations by minting them as NFTs, bypassing traditional intermediaries and retaining more control over their work's distribution and sales.
- **Dynamic Art:** Sui's object-centric model allows for NFTs that can evolve, change, or react to external inputs or community engagement, offering a new dimension to art where pieces can be interactive or even collaborative over time.
- **Authenticity and Provenance:** Each piece of art minted as an NFT on Sui has its history securely recorded, ensuring authenticity and providing a clear lineage of ownership, crucial for establishing value and trust in the art world.

Collectors and Digital Ownership

- **Secure Ownership:** Collectors can enjoy secure ownership of digital art or collectibles, with the blockchain ensuring that no one else can claim the same asset. Sui's speed and low gas costs make collecting more accessible and efficient.
- **Exclusivity and Scarcity:** Sui facilitates the creation of truly unique or limited-edition digital items, enhancing the exclusivity and potential value of collections.

- **Trading and Liquidity:** The marketplace for digital art and collectibles can benefit from Sui's high throughput, allowing for quick, secure trades. Collectors can buy, sell, or trade their NFTs with ease, potentially increasing market liquidity.

Interactive and Living Art

- **Community Engagement:** NFTs on Sui can be designed to evolve based on community input or real-world events, creating living pieces of art that grow with their audience.
- **Utility in Ownership:** Beyond static images, NFTs can include utility, like access to exclusive events, merchandise, or even influence over future art creations, adding layers of interaction between artists and their patrons.

Cultural Preservation

- **Digital Legacy:** Sui can serve as a platform for preserving digital art for future generations, with immutable records ensuring that the art's history, modifications, and ownership are preserved.
- **Cultural Heritage:** Similar to physical art, digital art on Sui can be recognized as cultural heritage, with blockchain providing a method to track and authenticate cultural artifacts in the digital age.

Case Studies or Hypothetical Examples

- **Virtual Galleries:** Imagine virtual art galleries where each exhibit is an NFT, viewable and purchasable directly through a Sui-based platform, with interactive elements that change with viewer interaction or environmental data.
- **Collaborative Art Projects:** Artists could create NFTs where the artwork changes with each sale or token interaction, or where collectors collectively decide on the artwork's next phase through governance tokens.

Challenges

- **Legal Framework:** The integration of NFTs into the art world requires navigating copyright, intellectual property laws, and potentially new legal frameworks for digital ownership.
- **Adoption by Traditional Art Markets:** Convincing the traditional art world of the value and legitimacy of blockchain-based art could be challenging, requiring education and showcasing of success stories.
- **User Experience:** Ensuring that the process of creating, buying, or selling art as NFTs remains user-friendly and doesn't alienate those less familiar with blockchain technology.

Future Directions

- **Cross-Media NFTs:** As multimedia becomes more prevalent, NFTs on Sui might represent not just visual art but also music, literature, or interactive media, expanding the scope of what can be owned and appreciated digitally.

- **Integration with Physical Art:** Combining physical art with digital NFTs, where owning the NFT grants ownership or access to the physical counterpart, could bridge traditional and digital art markets.
- **AI and Art:** Sui could support NFTs where AI generates art based on certain parameters or community input, merging technology and creativity in novel ways.

Sui's capabilities in handling NFTs provide a foundation for a new era of digital art and collectibles, where ownership, interaction, and community engagement transform how we perceive, value, and preserve art. By leveraging Sui's security, scalability, and the unique attributes of its object-centric model, artists and collectors can explore new dimensions of creativity and ownership, potentially reshaping the cultural landscape in ways that respect the digital nature of modern life while honoring the timeless aspects of art.

Part 7: Interoperability of NFTs

Interoperability is a key aspect of the future of NFTs, enabling these unique digital assets to move across different blockchain ecosystems or to be recognized and used in various applications beyond their initial context. Sui's architecture, with its focus on scalability, security, and an object-centric model, lays the groundwork for pioneering interoperability in the NFT space. This part explores the potential for Sui NFTs to interact with other blockchains, enhancing their utility and reach.

Vision for NFT Interoperability

- **Cross-Chain Compatibility:** The ultimate goal would be for Sui NFTs to be seamlessly transferable or usable across different blockchains, like Ethereum, Binance Smart Chain, or others, allowing for a more unified digital asset ecosystem.
- **Shared Utility:** NFTs could have utility that extends beyond one platform; for instance, a digital art piece on Sui might grant access to an event or service on another blockchain, or an in-game asset could be used across multiple games.

Technical Foundations for Interoperability

- **Sui's Object Model:** By treating NFTs as objects with their own lifecycle and properties, Sui inherently supports a model where these objects could theoretically interact or be recognized by other systems.
- **Standardization:** While Sui doesn't currently enforce specific NFT standards, future collaborations might involve adopting or contributing to interoperable standards, similar to ERC standards on Ethereum, to facilitate cross-chain interactions.

Potential Mechanisms for Interoperability

- **Bridges:** Developing or leveraging bridge protocols that allow for secure, one-to-one token transfers between Sui and other blockchains. This would require ensuring that the integrity and uniqueness of NFTs are maintained across chains.
- **Wrapping NFTs:** Creating wrapped versions of NFTs where an NFT on Sui could be represented on another blockchain as a wrapped asset, maintaining its unique properties while allowing for interaction in new ecosystems.
- **Oracle Services:** Employing oracles to verify and relay information about NFTs from Sui to other blockchains, enabling conditional smart contract interactions based on NFT states or events.

Benefits of Interoperable NFTs

- **Increased Liquidity:** NFTs could be traded or used in more marketplaces or applications, potentially increasing their liquidity and value.
- **Broader Adoption:** Artists and creators might see their work accessible to a wider audience, as interoperability could mean their NFTs are not confined to one blockchain's ecosystem.
- **Enhanced Utility:** NFTs could serve multiple purposes or roles in different contexts, from gaming to art, identity, or even real-world asset representation.

Challenges and Considerations

- **Security Risks:** Ensuring that moving NFTs across chains does not introduce vulnerabilities or lead to asset duplication or loss.
- **Standardization Issues:** Without universal standards, interoperability might be complex, requiring bespoke solutions for each blockchain pair.
- **Regulatory Hurdles:** Cross-chain transactions could complicate regulatory compliance, especially concerning asset ownership, taxation, or anti-money laundering requirements.
- **Performance:** Ensuring that interoperability does not degrade the performance of transactions or lead to high costs or delays.

Future Directions

- **Layer 2 Solutions:** Sui might explore layer 2 scaling solutions or sidechains specifically for NFT interactions, providing high-speed, low-cost transfers or interactions with other blockchains.
- **Interoperable Protocols:** Developing or adopting protocols that allow for direct, secure interaction between NFTs on different blockchains without needing intermediaries.
- **Community and Developer Ecosystem:** Encouraging a developer community focused on building tools, libraries, or services that bridge NFTs across blockchains, potentially through hackathons, grants, or collaborative projects.

The concept of NFT interoperability on Sui opens up a world where digital assets are not isolated but part of a larger, interconnected digital economy. By leveraging Sui's technical advantages, there's a potential to create a more fluid, dynamic, and inclusive NFT ecosystem where creators and collectors can see their digital assets thrive across multiple platforms and applications. As the blockchain space continues to evolve, Sui's role in fostering this interoperability could be pivotal, not just for NFTs but for the broader vision of a connected, decentralized digital future.

Part 8: Royalties and Creator Economy

One of the most transformative aspects of NFTs on Sui is the potential to establish a sustainable creator economy through automated royalties. This part explores how Sui's architecture can support artists, musicians, developers, and other creators by ensuring they benefit from their work's value over time, fostering a more equitable and vibrant creative ecosystem.

Automated Royalty Payments

- **Smart Contract Enforcement:** With Sui, creators can embed royalty rules directly into the NFT's smart contract. This means that every time an NFT changes hands, a percentage of the sale price automatically goes to the creator, without needing third-party intervention.

- **Flexibility in Royalties:** Creators can specify various royalty terms, such as percentage rates, caps on royalties, or conditions under which royalties are paid, all coded into the NFT at minting.

Benefits for Creators

- **Long-Term Revenue:** Creators receive ongoing income from their works as they appreciate or continue to be traded, providing a financial incentive to produce high-quality, lasting digital assets.
- **Incentive to Create:** Knowing they will benefit from secondary sales encourages creators to invest more in their art, knowing that their time and effort can translate into long-term financial rewards.
- **Direct Support:** By cutting out intermediaries, creators can have a more direct relationship with their audience, receiving support more directly from those who value their work.

Enhancing the Creator Economy

- **Community Building:** Royalties can be used to fund community projects, further art development, or engage fans, creating a feedback loop where creators and their communities grow together.
- **Dynamic Pricing Models:** Creators might implement dynamic royalties where the percentage changes based on how the NFT

performs in the market or over time, encouraging different economic strategies.

- **Collaboration and Remixing:** With clear royalty structures, artists might be more willing to collaborate or allow their work to be remixed, knowing they'll still be compensated.

Challenges

- **Legal and Copyright Issues:** Automating royalties requires navigating copyright laws, especially in jurisdictions where legal frameworks for digital assets are still evolving.
- **Royalty Enforcement:** Ensuring that royalties are honored across different platforms or in scenarios where NFTs might be traded off-chain or through private transactions.
- **Balancing Royalties with Market Dynamics:** Setting royalty rates that are fair to both creators and buyers without deterring secondary market activity.

Sui's Role in Royalty Management

- **Low Gas Fees:** Sui's efficient gas model ensures that the cost of executing royalty payments does not become prohibitive, making it feasible for even small transactions to include royalties.
- **Scalability:** As the number of NFT transactions grows, Sui's scalability ensures that royalty payments can be processed efficiently without network congestion.

- **Security:** The safety features of Move mean that royalty smart contracts are robust against common vulnerabilities, ensuring creators receive their due payments securely.

Future Opportunities

- **Royalty Tiers:** Introducing tiered royalty systems where creators can offer different benefits or levels of access based on the royalty percentage chosen by collectors.
- **Interoperable Royalties:** As interoperability grows, royalties might follow NFTs across different blockchains, maintaining creator compensation regardless of where the NFT is traded.
- **Integration with DeFi:** Royalties could be tokenized or used in DeFi applications, allowing creators to stake or lend their future royalty streams for immediate funding or to gain additional income.

Sui's approach to NFTs with built-in royalty mechanisms can fundamentally shift how creators earn from their digital works, promoting a creator economy where artists are rewarded not just for the initial sale but for the lasting value of their creations. By leveraging Sui's speed, security, and scalability, the platform can ensure that creators have the tools to build sustainable careers based on their digital art, music, or other forms of content. As this ecosystem matures, it could lead to more innovation, creativity, and a fairer distribution of wealth within the digital arts space.

Part 9: Security and Provenance

The value of NFTs largely hinges on security and the ability to prove provenance, ensuring that each token is unique, authentic, and rightfully owned. Sui's architecture, with its focus on security through the Move programming language and its object-centric model, provides robust mechanisms for safeguarding NFTs and tracing their history. This part discusses how Sui enhances these aspects in the NFT ecosystem.

Security Measures for NFTs

- **Move's Safety Features:** The design of Move inherently prevents many common smart contract vulnerabilities, like reentrancy attacks or unauthorized asset duplication, providing a secure foundation for NFTs.
- **Immutable Records:** Once an NFT is minted on Sui, its details and history are recorded on the blockchain in an immutable manner, ensuring that data cannot be altered after the fact.
- **Ownership Control:** With Sui, the control over who can modify or transfer an NFT is strictly defined. Only the current owner or authorized smart contracts can initiate changes, reducing the risk of theft or unauthorized transfers.

Provenance Tracking

- **Transparent History:** Every transaction involving an NFT, from minting to each transfer, is logged transparently on the blockchain. This creates a verifiable history or "provenance" that can be checked by anyone, confirming the authenticity and ownership journey of each NFT.
- **Metadata Integrity:** Sui ensures that the metadata associated with an NFT, which describes its unique attributes or history, remains intact and verifiable, preventing tampering or alteration.
- **Creator Attribution:** By embedding creator information into the NFT's metadata, Sui helps in permanently attributing works to their original creators, crucial for artists in establishing and maintaining their reputation.

Counterfeit Prevention

- **Unique Identification:** Each NFT on Sui has a unique identifier, making it virtually impossible to create counterfeit versions since any attempt would result in a distinct, new token.
- **Smart Contract Audits:** Before deployment, NFT smart contracts can undergo rigorous security audits to ensure they are free from vulnerabilities that could be exploited to create or claim false NFTs.

Enhancing Trust

- **Public Verification:** The open nature of blockchain allows for public verification of an NFT's history, increasing trust among buyers, collectors, and the community at large.
- **Security Against Hacks:** Sui's consensus mechanism and the design of Move ensure that even if there's an attempt to hack or manipulate NFTs, the blockchain's security measures would detect and prevent such actions.

Challenges and Best Practices

- **Educating Users:** Ensuring that creators and collectors understand how to securely manage their NFTs, including private key management and recognizing phishing attempts or fake offers.
- **Continuous Security Updates:** As new threats emerge, the Sui ecosystem needs to keep updating its security protocols and educating developers on best practices for NFT security.
- **Interoperability Security:** If NFTs move between blockchains, ensuring that security measures remain intact across these transitions is a challenge.

Future Enhancements

- **Advanced Provenance Tracking:** Future developments might include more detailed provenance tracking, perhaps integrating with external systems for additional context or validation of an NFT's history.

- **Privacy in Provenance:** While transparency is key, there might be innovations to allow for selective privacy in provenance data for scenarios where full transparency isn't desired.
- **AI for Security:** AI could be used to monitor for unusual activity or patterns that might indicate an attempt to compromise NFT security or provenance.

Sui's commitment to security and clear provenance makes it a strong candidate for hosting NFTs where authenticity, ownership, and historical integrity are paramount. By leveraging these capabilities, Sui not only protects creators and collectors but also builds a foundation of trust that is essential for the growth and acceptance of NFTs in both art and broader digital asset markets. As the ecosystem around Sui continues to evolve, the focus on security and provenance will be crucial in maintaining the value and legitimacy of digital ownership in the blockchain era.

Part 10: Challenges and Future Directions

While Sui presents a promising platform for NFTs, there are significant challenges to overcome alongside vast opportunities for growth and innovation. This part addresses these challenges and speculates on the future directions that could define how NFTs evolve on Sui.

Challenges

- **Regulatory Clarity:** The NFT space is navigating a complex regulatory landscape. Issues around copyright, digital rights, taxation, and financial regulations need to be addressed to ensure that NFT activities on Sui are compliant and secure for all users.
- **User Adoption:** Despite technological advantages, convincing a broader audience to engage with NFTs involves overcoming skepticism, educating about blockchain's benefits, and making the user experience as intuitive as possible.
- **Scalability with Growth:** As the volume of NFTs and transactions grows, maintaining performance, low transaction costs, and user experience becomes increasingly challenging. Sui must continue to innovate in its scalability solutions.
- **Environmental Impact:** While Sui aims for efficiency, the broader conversation about blockchain's energy consumption continues. Demonstrating or improving upon Sui's environmental efficiency can be pivotal for broader adoption, especially among environmentally conscious users.
- **Security Threats:** Even with Move's safety features, new vulnerabilities or attack vectors might emerge as NFTs become more complex or valuable. Continuous security research and development are essential.
- **Market Saturation:** The NFT market is becoming crowded, and Sui-based NFTs will

need to offer unique value propositions or experiences to stand out.

Future Directions

- **Interoperable Ecosystems:** Sui could lead in creating or participating in interoperable standards or protocols, allowing NFTs to have utility or value across different blockchains or applications, enhancing their overall value and utility.
- **Advanced NFT Interactions:** NFTs on Sui might evolve to include more interactive features, where tokens can execute code, change based on external inputs, or integrate with IoT devices, offering dynamic digital experiences.
- **NFT as Identity or Access:** Beyond collectibles or art, NFTs could serve as digital identities or access tokens for services, events, or memberships, broadening their application scope.
- **Sustainability Models:** Sui might pioneer models where NFT creation or trading contributes to sustainability efforts, either through carbon offsetting, supporting green projects, or using proof-of-stake mechanisms more efficiently.
- **Educational Initiatives:** To increase adoption, Sui could focus on educational programs, hackathons, or partnerships with educational institutions to teach about NFTs, blockchain, and digital ownership in a way that's accessible to all.

- **Integration with Physical Goods:** As the line between digital and physical blurs, Sui could facilitate NFTs that represent or are linked to physical items, enhancing authenticity, ownership tracking, and even supply chain transparency.
- **Privacy and Anonymity:** Future developments might include privacy features for NFTs, where ownership details or transaction data can be selectively hidden, balancing transparency with privacy concerns.
- **NFTs in Gaming and VR:** The integration of NFTs into gaming could expand with Sui, especially in virtual reality, where ownership of digital spaces or items could become a significant aspect of gameplay or virtual living.

The journey of NFTs on Sui is at a fascinating juncture, with challenges that require innovative solutions and opportunities that promise to redefine digital creativity, ownership, and interaction. By addressing regulatory compliance, ensuring scalability, enhancing security, and pushing the boundaries of what NFTs can represent or do, Sui can lead the charge towards a future where NFTs are not just tokens but integral parts of a digital culture, economy, and identity. As we move forward, the evolution of NFTs on Sui will likely be marked by collaboration, community engagement, and a focus on creating meaningful, secure, and sustainable digital assets.

Chapter 14: Interoperability and Ecosystem Integration

Part 1: Understanding Interoperability

Interoperability has become a buzzword in the blockchain realm, signifying the ability of different blockchain networks to communicate, share data, and transfer assets with each other. For Sui, understanding and implementing interoperability is not just a technical endeavor but a strategic one that could shape its role and success in the wider blockchain ecosystem. This part explores what interoperability entails, its importance, and how it aligns with the overarching vision for blockchain technology.

Interoperability in blockchain refers to the capability for different blockchain systems to interact seamlessly and securely. This interaction can include moving tokens or other digital assets between blockchains, sharing information or state data to enable cross-chain smart contract interactions, and integrating functionalities where smart contracts on one blockchain can call or interact with those on another. The technical facets of interoperability involve protocols, standards, or technologies such as bridges, atomic swaps, oracles, and cross-chain smart contracts.

The significance of interoperability cannot be overstated:

Interoperability enhances liquidity and asset utility by allowing assets to be used across various platforms, not just confined to one ecosystem. This means that an asset on Sui could be utilized in DeFi applications on Ethereum or serve as collateral in another chain's lending protocol. It improves user experience by reducing fragmentation, giving users greater control and convenience to manage their digital assets without being locked into a single blockchain's ecosystem. It fosters innovation, as developers can craft more complex, value-added services that leverage the strengths of multiple platforms, driving forward areas like cross-chain dApps. It promotes ecosystem growth, where the value of one blockchain increases through interaction with others, potentially driving broader adoption. Lastly, it helps reduce silos within the blockchain industry, allowing for a more unified digital economy where blockchain technology can reach its full potential.

Sui's approach to interoperability involves a philosophical stance where it's not only about bridging with existing blockchains but also about contributing to the development of interoperability standards or frameworks that could benefit the entire blockchain community. Technically, Sui's architecture, with its object-centric model and emphasis on speed and scalability, provides a solid foundation for interoperability. The challenge is in how these features can be adapted or extended to interact with other chains securely and efficiently. A significant part of this strategy will involve cultivating a community that understands and supports cross-chain development, potentially through hackathons, grants, or collaborative projects focused on interoperability solutions.

However, there are challenges and considerations. Ensuring security is paramount, as cross-chain operations must not introduce vulnerabilities that could jeopardize either blockchain involved. The absence of universal standards can lead to fragmented solutions, complicating true interoperability. Regulatory compliance becomes intricate when assets or data move across different legal jurisdictions. Scalability is another concern, where interoperability mechanisms must not undermine the high-performance characteristics Sui aims to maintain.

Understanding interoperability is crucial to appreciating its potential impact on Sui's development and the broader blockchain landscape. It's about more than just technical integration; it's about creating a more cohesive, functional, and innovative blockchain ecosystem. As Sui advances, its approach to interoperability will be a defining factor in how it positions itself within the global blockchain narrative, aiming to reduce fragmentation, increase asset utility, and propel the adoption of blockchain technology.

Part 2: Sui's Interoperability Vision

Sui's vision for interoperability extends beyond simply connecting with other blockchains; it aims to pioneer a future where blockchain ecosystems are seamlessly interconnected, facilitating the free flow of data, assets, and value. This part outlines Sui's strategic vision for interoperability, emphasizing how it plans to integrate into the broader blockchain narrative while leveraging its unique architectural advantages.

Sui envisions a blockchain landscape where networks are not isolated but parts of a larger, interconnected ecosystem, promoting unity over fragmentation. This vision involves enabling users, developers, and applications to interact across chains, breaking down the barriers of blockchain silos. The goal is to enhance the utility of assets and applications on Sui by allowing them to be used in different blockchain environments, such as employing Sui's assets in DeFi protocols on other chains or enabling Sui's smart contracts to interact with those on different platforms.

Leveraging its strengths, Sui's architecture, designed for high throughput and low latency, can offer significant advantages for cross-chain operations that require quick and efficient data or asset transfers. With Move's safety features, Sui aims to ensure that interoperability does not compromise security, developing methods for cross-chain interactions where the integrity of transactions and data is preserved across different blockchains. Sui's object-centric model could facilitate more granular and efficient interoperability, where specific objects or states are shared or transferred, minimizing complexity and overhead.

Sui's vision includes fostering a community-driven approach to interoperability. By promoting an open-source environment, developers from various blockchain projects can contribute to and benefit from interoperability solutions. This could lead to shared standards or protocols that enhance cross-chain interactions. Encouraging community involvement through events like hackathons or offering grants for projects focused on interoperability can drive innovation and practical implementations of cross-chain technologies.

Strategic partnerships and efforts towards standardization are also part of Sui's plan. It might involve participating in or initiating efforts to standardize interoperability protocols, ensuring that solutions developed are not just for Sui but for the broader blockchain community. This could include working with organizations like the Inter-Blockchain Communication (IBC) protocol. Building strategic partnerships with other blockchain platforms could accelerate the development and adoption of interoperability solutions, allowing for mutual benefits where each blockchain leverages the strengths of others.

Looking to the future, Sui's architecture should remain adaptable to integrate new interoperability methods or standards without requiring major overhauls. Future interoperability might also involve layer 2 solutions or sidechains specifically designed for cross-chain operations, providing more specialized, efficient pathways for interaction.

However, there are challenges and ethical considerations. Sui must balance interoperability with maintaining decentralization, ensuring that these efforts do not lead to centralization or concentration of control, which would contradict blockchain's core principles. Ethical data management is also crucial, where privacy, consent, and the ethical use of data are maintained as it moves across chains.

Sui's interoperability vision is about creating a blockchain environment where the sum is greater than its parts. By leveraging its architectural strengths, fostering community engagement, and pursuing strategic collaborations, Sui aims to be at the forefront of a new era of blockchain integration. This vision not only promises to enhance the functionality and utility of Sui but also contributes to the broader goal of a more interconnected, efficient, and inclusive blockchain ecosystem.

Part 3: Technical Foundations for Interoperability

The potential for Sui to act as a hub in a multi-chain future largely depends on its technical architecture. This part delves into the foundational aspects of Sui's design that support interoperability, the mechanisms it could employ, and how these elements work together to facilitate secure and efficient cross-chain interactions.

Sui's unique object-centric data model, where every piece of data is treated as an object with its own lifecycle, ownership, and state, provides a natural fit for interoperability. This model allows for the transfer of assets or data objects between chains, ensuring each object retains its identity and properties. It also supports state updates where changes to an object's state on one chain can be reflected or verified on another, ensuring data consistency across ecosystems.

The Move programming language, integral to Sui, brings safety and security to the table. Its resource management and safety features inherently support secure cross-chain interactions by ensuring the integrity of each asset or piece of data across different blockchains. Move's controlled state changes mean only authorized operations can modify an object's state, even in a cross-chain context. Additionally, Move's scriptability could extend to handle cross-chain logic, allowing smart contracts to perform actions or checks across different chains.

Sui's consensus mechanism, Delegated Proof-of-Stake (DPoS), is designed for speed and efficiency, which can be advantageous for interoperability. It ensures quick finality for cross-chain transactions, reducing risks like double-spending or race conditions between chains. The mechanism could also allow validators to serve roles in cross-chain verification or validation processes.

The scalability and parallelism in Sui's architecture can manage the additional load from inter-chain communications without impacting performance. By processing related cross-chain operations concurrently when possible, Sui can optimize the efficiency of cross-chain transactions.

In terms of interoperability technologies, Sui could employ or develop bridge solutions where tokens or data are locked on one chain and minted or unlocked on another. This ensures atomicity, where transactions are completed on both chains or not at all, maintaining integrity, and security, preventing double-spending and ensuring asset safety during transfer. Atomic swaps could facilitate direct peer-to-peer exchanges between chains, leveraging Sui's speed for trustless exchanges without intermediaries. Oracles could be used to bring off-chain data into the cross-chain ecosystem or vice versa, ensuring data consistency across different blockchains, particularly for smart contracts that depend on external data.

However, implementing these solutions comes with challenges. Security is paramount to ensure that cross-chain communication mechanisms do not introduce vulnerabilities like replay attacks or race conditions. Standardization is another hurdle, where working towards or adopting universally recognized standards can ease integration. Ensuring that interoperability does not compromise Sui's scalability is also critical, as additional cross-chain operations could increase network load.

Looking to the future, developing or integrating layer 2 solutions specifically for cross-chain interoperability could provide faster, cheaper cross-chain transfers. Enhancing Move to support smart contracts that can natively interact with other blockchains through a standardized interface or protocol is another potential direction.

Sui's technical foundations lay a promising groundwork for advancing interoperability in the blockchain space. By leveraging its object-centric model, the security of Move, and the efficiency of its consensus mechanism, Sui can aim to create a seamless, secure, and efficient bridge between different blockchain ecosystems. As these capabilities are expanded, Sui's role in the interconnected world of blockchain technology could be significantly enhanced, setting new standards for how blockchains communicate and collaborate.

Part 4: Current Solutions and Technologies

The landscape of blockchain interoperability is filled with various solutions and technologies aimed at facilitating cross-chain interactions. This part explores the mechanisms and technologies that could be or are being considered for integration with Sui, highlighting how they might work within or alongside Sui's architecture to achieve seamless blockchain communication.

Bridges are protocols or systems that enable the transfer of assets or data from one blockchain to another. They work by locking the asset on the source chain and minting an equivalent token on the destination chain, or vice versa for burning and unlocking. They also enable cross-chain messaging, allowing smart contracts or messages to be executed on another chain based on conditions or events on the original chain. Projects like Cosmos's IBC (Inter-Blockchain Communication) protocol or Polkadot's parachains serve as examples of bridge technologies. Sui could develop or integrate similar solutions, focusing on security to prevent common vulnerabilities like hacks or fraudulent token issuance, and scalability to ensure these bridges can handle high transaction volumes without becoming bottlenecks.

Atomic swaps allow for the direct exchange of one cryptocurrency for another between different blockchains without intermediaries. This is achieved through Hashed Timelock Contracts (HTLCs), which enforce the swap only if both parties fulfill their obligations within a time frame. With its speed and security, Sui could facilitate faster swaps due to quicker transaction confirmations, thereby enhancing trust in the swap process by leveraging Move's safety features for smart contract execution.

Cross-chain smart contracts involve smart contracts on one blockchain interacting with or calling contracts on another. This could mean a contract on Sui triggering actions on another blockchain or vice versa. Implementing such contracts requires standardized interfaces to simplify development across different chains and robust security protocols to avoid introducing vulnerabilities, possibly through formal verification methods.

Oracles act as intermediaries providing external data to smart contracts across different blockchains, enabling data cross-referencing or conditional execution of contracts. By integrating oracles, Sui could enhance applications needing real-time data from different blockchains or the real world, ensuring that the data used for cross-chain operations is accurate and trustworthy.

Sidechains and layer 2 solutions can serve as specialized chains or layers for interoperability. Sidechains could be used for specific cross-chain activities, offloading the main chain's workload, while layer 2 solutions like state channels or rollups could facilitate faster, cheaper cross-chain transactions. Sui's architecture might support custom sidechains designed for interoperability with specific blockchains or use cases or use layer 2 solutions to offer additional scalability and efficiency for cross-chain interactions.

However, implementing these solutions comes with challenges. Each must be rigorously tested and audited to ensure they do not compromise network security. Usability is another key factor, making these technologies accessible to both developers and end-users to promote adoption. Economic models also need consideration, understanding how cross-chain interactions might affect gas fees, token economics, or incentives within Sui's ecosystem.

Current solutions and technologies for interoperability provide a roadmap for how Sui might integrate with other blockchains. Whether through bridges, atomic swaps, cross-chain smart contracts, oracles, or layer 2 solutions, Sui has the technical groundwork to become a pivotal player in the multi-chain future. As these technologies evolve, so too will Sui's approach to interoperability, aiming to create a more connected, efficient, and secure blockchain ecosystem where value and innovation can flow freely across different platforms.

Part 5: Case Studies of Interoperability

To illustrate how interoperability could work within or involving Sui, this part presents several case studies or conceptual scenarios. These examples aim to demonstrate practical applications of cross-chain technology, showcasing how Sui might leverage its features for real-world interoperability scenarios.

Case Study 1: Cross-Chain DeFi

In this scenario, a DeFi application on Sui aims to utilize liquidity from an Ethereum-based protocol. Users can bridge their assets from Ethereum to Sui, locking tokens on Ethereum and minting wrapped versions on Sui for use in its DeFi ecosystem. These wrapped assets can then be added to liquidity pools on Sui, allowing users to engage in trading, lending, or yield farming across both ecosystems. The outcome is an increase in liquidity for Sui-based DeFi applications, providing Ethereum users with access to new opportunities on Sui, thereby enhancing the overall DeFi landscape.

Case Study 2: NFT Interoperability

Consider an artist who mints an NFT on Sui but wants it to be tradable on multiple marketplaces across different blockchains. Through NFT bridges, the NFT could be made available on leading platforms on other blockchains while maintaining its metadata and ownership history. Smart contracts could be set up to ensure the artist receives royalties from sales on any connected blockchain. This exposure to a broader audience increases the NFT's value and utility, giving collectors more flexibility in how and where they can interact with it.

Case Study 3: Gaming Ecosystems

In this example, a game developed on Sui wants players to use assets from games on other blockchains within its environment. Players can bridge their in-game items to Sui, where they can be used or enhanced within the new game's ecosystem. Using oracles or cross-chain smart contracts, game states or achievements could be recognized across blockchains, allowing for seamless gameplay transitions. This creates a richer gaming experience, giving players more control over their digital assets and potentially leading to a more engaged and loyal player base.

Case Study 4: Decentralized Identity

A user might want their identity to be portable across different blockchain services, including those on Sui. Through interoperability protocols, after verifying their identity on one blockchain, this verification can be recognized on Sui or other networks. With user consent, identity data or reputation scores could be shared across chains, enhancing privacy while reducing the need for redundant verifications. This offers users a more seamless experience across blockchain services and allows developers to create applications that respect user privacy and reduce entry barriers.

Case Study 5: Cross-Chain Governance

Imagine a project aiming to implement governance that spans across multiple blockchains, including Sui. Governance tokens or voting rights could be transferred or recognized across chains, allowing community members to vote regardless of their active blockchain. Proposals could be executed on multiple chains, ensuring that governance decisions have a broad impact across ecosystems. This fosters a more democratic and inclusive governance model where the community's voice can influence multiple platforms, potentially leading to more robust and aligned project development.

Challenges and Considerations

However, these scenarios highlight several challenges. Ensuring security and trust in cross-chain operations is crucial, as is maintaining an intuitive user experience amidst the complexity of interoperability. Navigating regulatory compliance when assets or data move across different jurisdictions also poses significant considerations.

These case studies showcase the potential of Sui in fostering a more interconnected blockchain world where assets, governance, identities, or gaming experiences can transcend single ecosystems. By illustrating practical applications of interoperability, we see not only the technical possibilities but also the transformative impact on user experience, asset utility, and community engagement. As interoperability becomes more ingrained in blockchain technology, Sui's role could significantly expand, contributing to a vision where the blockchain space is not fragmented but a cohesive network of networks.

Part 6: Benefits of Interoperability

Interoperability in blockchain technology, particularly for Sui, offers numerous benefits that transcend mere technical integration. This part explores how Sui can harness interoperability to bolster its ecosystem, encourage adoption, and contribute to the broader blockchain community.

Enhanced liquidity is a primary benefit where asset mobility allows assets to move freely between Sui and other blockchains, dramatically increasing liquidity. Users can leverage their assets across various ecosystems, reducing the necessity for holding multiple tokens and enhancing each token's utility. This can lead to the creation of cross-chain markets for Sui assets, potentially stabilizing and expanding markets for Sui tokens within DeFi protocols, NFT marketplaces, or any blockchain-based platform.

Increased utility and functionality arise from interoperability, enabling developers to build applications that aren't limited to one blockchain's capabilities. They can harness the strengths of multiple platforms to create more robust, feature-rich applications. For instance, a payment solution on Sui could utilize stablecoins from another chain, or a governance token on Sui might affect decisions on different platforms, creating a more interconnected service ecosystem.

Innovation and collaboration are also fostered by interoperability. Developers can explore new concepts requiring interaction between different blockchains, like cross-chain gaming where assets or player achievements are recognized across games on different platforms. This environment encourages collaborative projects where initiatives from different blockchains can share resources, knowledge, or co-develop solutions that span multiple ecosystems.

User experience is significantly improved through seamless integration. Users benefit from a more cohesive experience where managing assets or identities across multiple blockchains becomes unnecessary, enhancing convenience and reducing complexity. They could interact with a unified platform where cross-chain operations are abstracted away, providing a single point of interaction.

Market expansion and adoption are accelerated as Sui connects with other blockchains, tapping into the user bases of established platforms. This broader reach can speed up Sui's adoption rate. Additionally, developers are more likely to build on Sui if it's part of a larger, interoperable ecosystem, knowing their applications can access users across multiple chains.

Scalability and efficiency are enhanced through interoperability by distributing transaction or data loads across multiple chains, reducing congestion on any single network and improving overall system performance. This also allows for optimizing resource use, where Sui might leverage other blockchains' computational or storage capabilities for specific tasks, potentially leading to cost savings or performance enhancements.

Security through diversity mitigates risks by not relying solely on one blockchain's security model. If one chain faces security issues, assets can be moved to secure environments on other chains. Cross-chain validation or oracles can offer an additional layer of security and trust in transactions or data across networks.

Economically, interoperability can lead to value accretion for Sui's native token if it becomes a central hub or bridge in the blockchain space, encouraging more use and holding of the token. It also opens up new economic models, including cross-chain staking, lending, or governance models, enhancing the token's utility and economic design.

However, these benefits come with challenges and considerations. Managing the increased complexity for developers while ensuring user-friendly interfaces is not straightforward. Balancing security so that interoperability doesn't introduce new vulnerabilities requires ongoing vigilance and innovation in security practices.

The benefits of interoperability for Sui are extensive, from enhancing liquidity and utility to fostering innovation, improving user experience, and driving market expansion and adoption. By strategically pursuing interoperability, Sui not only stands to enhance its own ecosystem but also contributes to the evolution of blockchain technology towards a more integrated, efficient, and user-centric digital economy. As these benefits are realized, Sui could play a pivotal role in shaping the future of blockchain interoperability.

Part 7: Challenges in Achieving Interoperability

While the vision for interoperability within Sui's ecosystem is compelling, there are significant challenges that must be navigated to fully realize this potential. This part outlines the technical, security, and regulatory hurdles Sui might encounter, alongside strategies for overcoming them.

Technical challenges stem from the complexity and need for standardization. Developing solutions that work across different blockchains requires consensus on standards or protocols, which can be slow and complex due to the diversity in blockchain designs and philosophies. Sui will need to contribute to or adopt existing standards, perhaps by participating in groups like those for IBC or by proposing new standards tailored to its unique features. Scalability is another concern; cross-chain operations can add load to the network, potentially affecting performance. Ensuring interoperability mechanisms do not compromise Sui's scalability involves optimizing these protocols for efficiency. Synchronization is critical to maintain state consistency across blockchains, especially with asynchronous networks or differing consensus mechanisms, requiring advanced synchronization techniques like using oracles or light clients for real-time data verification.

Security concerns are paramount as each new interoperability pathway could be a potential attack vector. Challenges include preventing double-spending, where assets might be spent twice across chains, and managing race conditions where transactions on one chain outpace those on another, leading to inconsistencies. Cross-chain smart contracts can introduce new vulnerabilities if not designed with interoperability in mind, necessitating rigorous auditing both at the code level and for the logic spanning chains. In a multi-chain environment, trust models become more distributed, which calls for enhanced mechanisms like multi-signature schemes or decentralized governance for cross-chain protocols.

Regulatory and compliance issues arise as assets or data move across blockchains, potentially crossing legal jurisdictions. This complicates compliance with diverse regulations, from AML to data protection laws that vary by country. Privacy concerns also emerge as interoperability might require sharing data across chains, potentially clashing with privacy laws or user expectations, suggesting the need for privacy-preserving technologies like zero-knowledge proofs. Token and asset classification can differ across countries, affecting how tokens are transferred or used across borders and possibly requiring legal or regulatory innovation.

Economic and incentive structures present another challenge. Ensuring all parties involved in interoperability have aligned incentives can be tricky when balancing different chains' economic models, where gas fees, staking rewards, or other mechanisms might not align. Determining how fees for cross-chain transactions are handled requires fair and efficient fee models that do not deter users while compensating for the resources used.

Cultural and adoption challenges include community resistance where not all blockchain communities might see the value in interoperability or might resist due to philosophical differences regarding decentralization, security, or governance. User education is crucial as most users are familiar with single-chain interactions, necessitating educational campaigns to explain the benefits and safety of cross-chain operations.

Strategies to overcome these challenges include collaborative development with other blockchain projects to foster standardization and security, implementing interoperability incrementally to build confidence and technology, investing in research and development for new security protocols, privacy solutions, and standards, actively engaging with regulators to shape supportive policies, and fostering an open, collaborative community that values interoperability.

The path to achieving interoperability on Sui is filled with challenges that require a nuanced approach, balancing technical innovation with security, compliance, and user experience. By tackling these hurdles head-on, Sui can not only navigate through them but also set new precedents in how blockchains can work together, ultimately creating a more interconnected, robust, and user-friendly blockchain ecosystem.

Part 8: Security Considerations

As Sui aims to facilitate interoperability, ensuring the security of cross-chain interactions becomes paramount. This part examines the security considerations that must be addressed to maintain the integrity, safety, and trust in a multi-chain environment involving Sui.

One of the primary cross-chain security risks is double-spending, where an asset could be spent on more than one blockchain or double-claimed during transfer. Sui's interoperability solutions must implement atomicity to ensure transactions are either fully completed across chains or not at all, using mechanisms like atomic swaps or lock-and-mint protocols. Another risk involves replay attacks, where a valid transaction on one chain might be maliciously or accidentally replayed on another. To combat this, Sui can use chain-specific signatures or introduce nonce or timestamps to ensure transactions are unique to a single chain. Oracle manipulation poses another threat, where oracles could provide incorrect or manipulated data across chains. Sui should diversify oracle sources and implement consensus mechanisms among multiple oracles for data validation.

Smart contract security is vital for cross-chain operations. Cross-chain vulnerabilities could arise if contracts are not resilient against attacks that leverage the complexities of cross-chain interactions. This necessitates rigorous auditing, both internal and external, with a focus on cross-chain logic, and where possible, formal verification to mathematically prove the correctness of contract behavior. Ensuring state consistency across chains requires synchronization protocols that can handle discrepancies or delays between chain updates.

Validator and node security become more complex in a cross-chain environment. Validators might need to validate transactions or states from other blockchains, introducing new threat vectors. This requires enhanced security practices for these entities, potentially extending Sui's DPoS mechanism to include cross-chain validation protocols. There's also the risk of validator collusion across chains to manipulate transactions or consensus, which calls for robust incentive systems designed to discourage such behavior, possibly through cross-chain staking or penalty mechanisms.

Security in interoperability protocols, particularly bridges, is critical as they are often targeted due to their role in asset transfer. Sui must ensure secure bridge design, including multi-signature requirements, time locks, and regular security audits. Standardization and compatibility with the security measures of other chains while maintaining Sui's own standards are also essential.

Privacy and anonymity present unique challenges when data moves between blockchains. Cross-chain privacy can be protected using zero-knowledge proofs to verify transactions or states without revealing sensitive data. Ensuring anonymity in transactions across chain boundaries might necessitate privacy layers or mixers to maintain user anonymity.

Ecosystem security can be bolstered by community vigilance, encouraging an active community to monitor for security issues through bug bounties and audits. Educating developers and users on the security implications of cross-chain operations through documentation and workshops promotes secure practices in writing interoperable smart contracts.

Future security enhancements for Sui might include adaptive security models that continuously adapt to evolving threats by incorporating new cryptographic techniques or consensus methods. Cross-chain governance could facilitate quick responses to security concerns, allowing decentralized decision-making for security protocol updates or emergency situations.

However, there are challenges in balancing speed with security, as interoperability often means faster interactions which can conflict with security measures. Finding the right balance through innovative security designs is crucial. The complexity of interoperability also increases the potential for security flaws, suggesting a need for simplification where possible without compromising functionality to reduce the attack surface.

Security considerations are critical for Sui to maintain its promise of being a safe, scalable, and efficient blockchain in an interoperable environment. By addressing these risks with robust protocols, enhanced auditing, and community engagement, Sui can ensure that its users and developers operate in a secure multi-chain environment. As interoperability grows, the ongoing challenge will be to innovate in security practices to match or exceed the pace of technological advancement in cross-chain interactions.

Part 9: Ecosystem Integration

Sui's vision for interoperability goes beyond just technical solutions to include the integration of various elements within the broader blockchain ecosystem. This part explores how Sui can integrate with oracles, DeFi protocols, NFT platforms, and other blockchain services to enrich its ecosystem, fostering a more vibrant, interconnected digital environment.

Integration with oracles is crucial for accessing external data necessary for smart contracts. Sui could partner with existing oracle networks to gain access to real-time data feeds for price information, weather data, or other metrics essential for smart contract execution. Alternatively, Sui might develop native oracle solutions tailored to its unique needs, possibly leveraging Move's safety features for secure data integration.

Expanding into the DeFi ecosystem by connecting with platforms on other blockchains can enhance liquidity, allowing users to utilize assets from different chains in Sui's DeFi applications or vice versa. This could include interoperable lending and borrowing where collateral from one chain secures loans on another, thereby increasing capital efficiency. Sui might also work towards adopting or contributing to DeFi standards that facilitate easier integration and interaction between applications across different chains.

For NFT marketplaces, Sui could aim for a unified NFT experience by connecting with major platforms, enabling Sui-based NFTs to be traded or displayed on other blockchain NFT marketplaces. This would involve working on cross-chain NFT standards to ensure compatibility and seamless ownership transfer. Such integration benefits creators and collectors through cross-chain royalties, ensuring creators are compensated regardless of where their NFTs are sold or used.

Interoperability with identity solutions could see Sui integrating with cross-chain identity protocols, allowing users to use their identity across different blockchain services, reducing redundancy and enhancing user experience. This would ideally incorporate privacy-focused identity systems where user data privacy is maintained even as identities become portable across chains.

Collaboration with other blockchain services could make Sui a hub for cross-chain games, where in-game assets are interoperable, leading to a richer gaming experience across different blockchain ecosystems. In enterprise solutions like supply chain management, Sui could integrate with networks that specialize in these areas, offering more comprehensive services by leveraging these integrations.

In terms of community and developer engagement, Sui could encourage cross-chain development through hackathons and developer grants, fostering projects that span multiple blockchains. Providing comprehensive documentation and SDKs would equip developers with tools for interoperability, simplifying the process of building cross-chain applications on Sui.

However, integrating with such a diverse ecosystem brings challenges. Technical compatibility requires ensuring smooth integration with systems that might have different technical architectures or data formats. Regulatory compliance is another hurdle, navigating legal and compliance issues when integrating with services under different regulatory frameworks.

Looking to the future, as Sui grows, it could host or support aggregators that provide a unified interface for interacting with multiple blockchain services. Sui might also offer interoperability as a service, providing tools or frameworks for other blockchains or projects to integrate with Sui, promoting a bidirectional interoperability ecosystem.

Sui's integration with the broader blockchain ecosystem is about creating a rich, interconnected environment where services, assets, and identities can flow freely across different platforms. By fostering these integrations, Sui can expand its utility, drive adoption, and contribute to the evolution of blockchain technology towards a more unified, synergistic digital landscape. This approach requires not only technical innovation but also community engagement, strategic partnerships, and a commitment to open, inclusive development.

Part 10: Future Directions and Innovations

The future of interoperability on Sui is not just about current integrations but about anticipating and shaping the evolution of blockchain technology. This concluding part speculates on the future directions and potential innovations that could redefine how Sui interacts with the broader blockchain ecosystem.

Advancements in interoperability protocols might see Sui leading or contributing significantly to new standards for blockchain interoperability, ensuring universal compatibility across a wider array of blockchains. This could simplify the integration process for developers and users. Future developments could also include specialized layer 2 networks designed specifically for cross-chain transactions, providing faster, cheaper, and more secure methods for asset and data exchange.

In terms of security, Sui could implement adaptive security protocols that automatically adjust based on network conditions or threat intelligence, keeping cross-chain operations secure as threats evolve. Privacy and anonymity might be further enhanced with integrated privacy solutions like confidential transactions or privacy-preserving smart contracts that work across chains without compromising interoperability.

AI and machine learning could play a pivotal role in optimizing cross-chain operations by predicting network load, suggesting optimal times for cross-chain activities, or automating some interoperability processes. AI could also be used for security and fraud detection, monitoring, and predicting threats across multiple chains, offering an additional layer of protection for cross-chain transactions.

Decentralized governance across chains is another area of innovation where Sui could pioneer multi-chain governance protocols, allowing for community decisions that span multiple blockchains for consistency and cooperation. This might involve creating or supporting governance tokens with utility across several chains, enhancing user participation in decision-making processes.

Ecosystem expansion through interoperability could lead to new use cases, such as cross-chain identity verification, where a single identity could be used across numerous services without centralization. Envisioning interoperable economies, tokens from one chain might have utility or value on others, fostering a more integrated blockchain economy.

However, these advancements come with challenges and ethical considerations. As blockchain use cases expand, Sui will need to navigate evolving regulations, ensuring compliance while pushing the boundaries of what's possible. Ethical data management will be crucial, ensuring the respectful use of data across chains, respecting user privacy, and consent in an increasingly interconnected blockchain environment.

Community and open development will likely continue to be central to Sui's approach. Encouraging and funding open-source projects focused on interoperability could create a rich environment for shared development and innovation. Regular hackathons and challenges could spark innovation in how different blockchains can work together, potentially leading to breakthroughs in cross-chain technology.

The future for Sui in terms of interoperability is vibrant, with potential advancements that could significantly alter the blockchain technology landscape. By leading in the development of standards, enhancing security, integrating AI, and fostering new governance models, Sui can position itself as a central node in the blockchain universe.

Chapter 15: Privacy and Security on Sui

Part 1: Introduction to Privacy and Security in Blockchain

In the digital era where data breaches, cyber-attacks, and privacy invasions have become commonplace, blockchain technology presents both a beacon of hope and a new set of challenges. Sui, as a modern blockchain platform, embodies this duality, striving to offer solutions that enhance privacy while ensuring the utmost security. This chapter introduces the complex interplay between privacy and security within the Sui ecosystem, setting the groundwork for understanding how Sui navigates these critical aspects of blockchain technology.

Blockchain's inherent design, which thrives on transparency and decentralization, poses unique privacy issues. Every transaction, every smart contract execution, is recorded on a public ledger, visible to anyone with access to the network. While this transparency is a cornerstone of trust and integrity in blockchain systems, it also means that privacy, as traditionally understood, requires innovative approaches to be maintained. Sui confronts this challenge head-on, aiming to reconcile the need for open ledger systems with the demand for individual privacy.

Security, on the other hand, is not just about protecting data but about safeguarding the entire ecosystem from malicious actors. In a blockchain like

Sui, where consensus is achieved through a delegated proof-of-stake model, security is intertwined with economic incentives, community governance, and the robustness of its consensus algorithms. This chapter will explore how Sui's security model is engineered to resist attacks while maintaining the efficiency and speed that are hallmarks of its architecture.

The motivation behind Sui's focus on privacy and security stems from the vision of creating a blockchain that can serve not just financial transactions but a broad spectrum of applications where data sensitivity and integrity are paramount. Whether it's personal identity, health records, or confidential corporate dealings, Sui aims to be a platform where these can be managed securely and privately.

Privacy in Sui does not mean obscuring all data but rather providing users with control over what information is shared and how. The challenge lies in implementing privacy mechanisms that do not compromise the blockchain's transparency, which is essential for auditability and trust. This part will delve into the philosophical and technical considerations Sui adopts to achieve this balance.

Security in Sui extends beyond protecting transactions to encompass the safety of smart contracts, the integrity of the network's state, and the confidentiality of user interactions. With the advent of smart contracts, the potential for vulnerabilities has grown, making secure development practices more critical than ever. Sui's approach to smart contract security is a focal point of this chapter, illustrating how its unique features contribute to a safer development environment.

Moreover, the chapter will touch upon how Sui addresses the security implications of its object-centric model. In this paradigm, where each piece of data is treated as an object with its lifecycle, ensuring that these objects remain secure against unauthorized access or manipulation is a nuanced task. Sui's design philosophy here is to embed security at every level of interaction with these objects.

When discussing privacy and security, one cannot ignore the community aspect. Sui's governance model, where token holders have a say in protocol changes, plays a vital role in shaping its security and privacy policies. This democratic process ensures that privacy and security measures evolve with community input, aligning with real-world needs and expectations.

This introduction also sets the stage for understanding how Sui navigates the regulatory landscape. As blockchain technology matures, regulatory frameworks around the world are attempting to catch up, focusing on aspects like data protection, anti-money laundering, and consumer rights. Sui's approach to privacy and security is crafted with an eye towards compliance, ensuring that it can operate within this increasingly regulated environment.

As we delve deeper into Sui's privacy and security mechanisms in the following sections, this introduction serves as a reminder that in the blockchain space, privacy and security are not just features but foundational elements that define the viability and trustworthiness of a platform. Sui's commitment to these principles is a testament to its ambition to lead in creating a blockchain environment where users' rights to privacy and security are upheld as much as the technology's promise of decentralization and transparency.

Part 2: Sui's Security Model

Sui's security model is a sophisticated blend of technological design, economic incentives, and community governance, aimed at creating a secure environment for all its users. At the heart of this model is the delegated proof-of-stake (DPoS) consensus mechanism, which not only speeds up transaction processing but also significantly bolsters network security through economic stakes and validator accountability.

The consensus mechanism in Sui is designed to prevent traditional blockchain attacks, such as 51% attacks, where an attacker might control more than half of the network's mining power. In Sui's DPoS, instead of computational power, it's the economic stake of validators that matters. Validators are required to stake significant amounts of SUI tokens, creating a financial disincentive against malicious behavior since any attempt to compromise the network could lead to the loss of their stake.

Validators in Sui play a crucial role not just in transaction validation but in maintaining the integrity of the network. They are elected by the community, ensuring that those who secure the network are trusted and incentivized to act in its best interest. The selection process for validators includes performance metrics, past behavior, and community trust, which all contribute to a security model where those who protect the network are themselves under scrutiny.

Sui's architecture further enhances security through its object-centric model. Here, each piece of data is an object with its own state and lifecycle, managed with fine-grained control. This approach minimizes the risk of broad-scale attacks by isolating the impact of any single security breach, as each object's security is managed independently. It also allows for more precise control over access rights, ensuring that only authorized interactions occur.

Another pillar of Sui's security is the principle of instant finality. Unlike blockchains where transactions might require multiple confirmations, in Sui, transactions are considered final almost immediately. This feature not only enhances user experience through speed but also reduces the window for potential attacks like double-spending, where an attacker might attempt to spend the same token in two different transactions.

Smart contract security is also a focal point in Sui's security model. The Move programming language, developed specifically for Sui, includes built-in security features like resource types, which prevent common vulnerabilities such as reentrancy or unauthorized asset duplication. By enforcing strict rules around how digital assets can be created, transferred, or destroyed, Move significantly reduces the attack surface of smart contracts.

To further secure the network, Sui employs advanced cryptographic techniques for transaction signing and verification, ensuring that only the intended parties can initiate or alter transactions. This includes considerations for future-proofing against quantum computing threats, although specific details on these measures might evolve as technology advances.

The economic model of Sui also plays into its security strategy. Rewards for validators are balanced to encourage wide participation, reducing the risk of centralization where a few might control the network's security. Additionally, penalties or slashing mechanisms for validators who fail to perform their duties or act maliciously serve as a deterrent, aligning economic incentives with network security.

Community governance is another layer of security. SUI token holders can vote on critical decisions, including security protocols, upgrades, or responses to vulnerabilities. This governance model ensures that security measures are not just technical but also socially robust, with the community actively involved in maintaining the network's integrity.

In conclusion, Sui's security model is not a static set of rules but a dynamic system that evolves with the blockchain's growth and the changing landscape of threats. It combines technological innovation with economic incentives and community involvement to create a secure, scalable, and adaptable blockchain platform where users can trust the safety of their transactions and data.

Part 3: Privacy Mechanisms on Sui

In the world of blockchain, where transparency is often seen as a virtue, the challenge of maintaining privacy while leveraging the benefits of decentralized technology is significant. Sui approaches this challenge with a suite of privacy mechanisms designed to offer users control over their data without sacrificing the integrity and auditability of the blockchain. This part explores how Sui implements privacy in its network, balancing the need for transparency with the desire for confidentiality.

One of the core privacy mechanisms Sui could employ is the use of **zero-knowledge proofs (ZKPs)**. This cryptographic method allows one party to prove to another that a statement is true without revealing any information beyond the validity of the statement itself. For Sui, ZKPs could be used to verify transactions or state changes without exposing sensitive details, like the amount transferred or the identity of the parties involved. This would enable private transactions on a public blockchain, preserving privacy while maintaining the blockchain's capacity for verification.

Encrypted Transactions could be another approach Sui takes towards privacy. By encrypting transaction details, only parties with the decryption key can access the specifics of a transaction. This method could be particularly useful for sensitive applications, like financial transactions or confidential business agreements, where only the involved parties need to know the details, while the network can still validate the transaction's authenticity and integrity.

Sui might also leverage **ring signatures** or similar technologies for enhancing sender anonymity. In a ring signature scheme, a group of possible signers is involved, but it's impossible to determine which one actually signed the transaction. This can obscure the origin of transactions, adding a layer of privacy to the blockchain's operations.

The concept of **confidential assets** could be adapted or developed further on Sui. Here, the specifics of an asset (like its type or amount) are hidden, but the blockchain can still process transactions involving these assets. This approach ensures that while the nature of the transaction is private, the system maintains its balance and consistency.

For privacy in smart contract execution, Sui could implement **private smart contracts or computations**. This would allow for operations where the logic or the data of a contract is not publicly visible, executed in a way that only reveals the result, not the process. Such a feature would be invaluable for applications requiring confidentiality, like proprietary business logic or personal data processing.

Sui's privacy mechanisms would also need to address the **management of privacy settings**. Users should have control over their privacy preferences, enabling them to decide on a per-transaction or per-application basis how much information is shared. This could involve setting up private channels for transaction broadcasting or using privacy tokens for specific use cases where anonymity is paramount.

The platform might also explore **privacy-enhancing technologies (PETs)** like differential privacy or homomorphic encryption, where computations can be performed on encrypted data without decrypting it. This would allow for complex data analysis or smart contract logic to be executed privately, enhancing the capabilities of Sui for industries like healthcare or finance where data sensitivity is high.

In terms of specific use cases, Sui could support **private asset transfers**, where ownership and transfers of assets are hidden from public view, yet verifiable and auditable by the network. This would be ideal for scenarios like art sales or real estate transactions on the blockchain where privacy is crucial.

However, implementing these privacy mechanisms comes with its challenges, including:

- **Balancing privacy with the need for transparency** for auditability and trust in the system.
- **Scalability**, as privacy features can increase computational complexity.
- **Compliance with regulations** like GDPR, which require mechanisms for data protection and the right to be forgotten, which are inherently challenging in a blockchain context.
- **User education**, ensuring that users understand how to use these features effectively without compromising their security or privacy.

In essence, Sui's approach to privacy mechanisms is about creating a blockchain where users can enjoy the benefits of decentralization while retaining control over their personal and sensitive data. By integrating these advanced privacy tools, Sui aims to carve out a niche for itself as a blockchain platform where privacy and security are not just features but foundational elements of its ecosystem.

Part 4: Smart Contract Security on Sui

Smart contracts are the backbone of decentralized applications (dApps), turning blockchain from a mere ledger of transactions into a platform for sophisticated, trustless agreements. However, with great power comes great responsibility, particularly in terms of security. Sui, with its unique architecture and the Move programming language, offers a distinctive approach to smart contract security. This part delves into how Sui ensures that smart contracts are not just functional but also secure against the myriad of vulnerabilities that have plagued blockchain applications.

Move's Security by Design:

The Move language, tailored for Sui, introduces several security features from the ground up:

- **Resource Types:** Move treats digital assets as resources with strict ownership rules, preventing duplication or loss. This ensures that once an asset is minted, its lifecycle is controlled, reducing the risk of asset-related exploits.
- **Type Safety:** Move's strong type system helps prevent common programming errors like integer overflow or underflow, which could lead to security breaches in other languages.
- **Capability-based Security:** In Move, capabilities can control access to functions or resources, ensuring that only authorized entities can perform certain operations, thus enhancing security through fine-grained access control.

Best Practices for Secure Smart Contracts:

Developers on Sui are encouraged to follow best practices to ensure their smart contracts are secure:

- **Minimize Complexity:** Simpler contracts are easier to audit and less prone to errors. Sui's object-centric model supports this by allowing for modular, reusable code.

- **Auditability:** Writing contracts with clear, understandable logic and good documentation facilitates both human and automated audits, which are crucial for identifying vulnerabilities.
- **Testing:** Rigorous testing, including unit, integration, and stress tests, is essential. Sui's environment supports the simulation of various scenarios to ensure contracts behave as expected under all conditions.
- **Formal Verification:** Where possible, using formal methods or tools for verifying contract behavior can mathematically prove certain properties of the contract, like the absence of reentrancy or other common vulnerabilities.

Security Tools and Frameworks:

Sui might provide or support various tools for developers to enhance smart contract security:

- **Static Analysis Tools:** These can scan the code for potential vulnerabilities before the contract is deployed.
- **Dynamic Analysis:** Tools that interact with the contract in real-time to detect issues like state manipulation or unintended behavior.
- **Security Libraries:** Pre-built, secure implementations of common operations or patterns can reduce the risk of introducing new vulnerabilities.

- **Fuzzers:** Automated tools that test contracts by feeding them random or unexpected inputs to find weaknesses.

Smart Contract Lifecycle Security:

The security of a smart contract doesn't end at deployment:

- **Upgradability:** While Move supports contract upgrades, this must be done with care to avoid introducing vulnerabilities. Sui might offer patterns or mechanisms for safe contract evolution.
- **Monitoring:** Post-deployment, contracts should be monitored for unusual activity that could indicate an exploit or security flaw.
- **Emergency Stops:** Having mechanisms like circuit breakers or pausability can be vital for responding to discovered vulnerabilities.

Community and Governance in Security:

Sui's community-driven governance can play a significant role in smart contract security:

- **Bug Bounties:** Encouraging the community to find and report vulnerabilities can lead to more secure contracts.
- **Open Source:** By open-sourcing contract templates or libraries, the community can contribute to security through collective scrutiny and improvement.

- **Governance Over Security:** Proposals for security enhancements or responses to vulnerabilities can be community-voted, ensuring that security measures align with community values and needs.

Educational Efforts:

For security to be effective, developers must understand the risks and mitigation strategies:

- **Documentation and Tutorials:** Comprehensive guides on secure coding practices using Move on Sui.
- **Workshops and Courses:** Educational programs focusing on blockchain security, particularly how it pertains to Sui's environment.
- **Security Forums:** Platforms where developers can discuss, learn, and share security insights specific to Sui's ecosystem.

Sui's approach to smart contract security is holistic, leveraging the inherent safety features of Move, advocating for best practices, and involving the community in the ongoing security of the network. By integrating these strategies, Sui aims to create an ecosystem where developers can build with confidence, knowing their smart contracts are fortified against the complex threats of the blockchain landscape.

Part 5: User Privacy and Data Protection

In the digital age, privacy is not just a luxury but a fundamental right, and Sui recognizes this by embedding user privacy and data protection into its core philosophy. The interplay between blockchain's inherent transparency and the need for individual privacy creates a nuanced challenge, one that Sui navigates with careful consideration. This part explores how Sui ensures user privacy while maintaining the integrity and utility of its blockchain.

Sui's approach to user privacy begins at the wallet level. Wallets on Sui are designed with features that allow users to control their identity and transaction visibility. Techniques like address obfuscation or the use of multiple addresses for different purposes can help maintain user anonymity. By not tying all transactions to a single, easily identifiable address, users can interact with the blockchain in ways that protect their privacy.

When it comes to data handling within decentralized applications (dApps), Sui promotes a model where data privacy is paramount. Developers are encouraged to minimize on-chain data storage to what's absolutely necessary for the dApp's operation, reducing the exposure of sensitive information. For data that must be stored on-chain, encryption methods ensure that only authorized parties can decrypt and use the data. This approach aligns with privacy principles while still leveraging blockchain's benefits for data integrity and immutability.

Sui also considers the implications of off-chain data for privacy. In scenarios where dApps require additional data handling or processing, Sui might support or encourage the use of decentralized storage solutions or privacy-focused off-chain computation services. Here, data can be processed privately, with only the necessary outcomes reflected on the blockchain, thus maintaining a balance between privacy and the need for transparent outcomes.

Identity management on Sui is another critical area where privacy is enhanced. Instead of using real-world identities, Sui could implement self-sovereign identity systems where users control their digital identities. These systems would allow users to selectively disclose information, only revealing what is necessary for specific transactions or interactions. This methodology not only protects privacy but also aligns with regulatory frameworks that emphasize user control over personal data.

Compliance with global data protection regulations, such as GDPR, is a significant aspect of Sui's privacy strategy. While blockchain's immutable nature poses challenges to concepts like the 'right to be forgotten', Sui might develop mechanisms or interfaces that allow for the logical deletion or obfuscation of personal data, ensuring compliance without compromising the blockchain's integrity. Such features would involve complex interactions between on-chain and off-chain data management.

The security of user data on Sui is paramount. Beyond basic encryption, Sui could employ advanced cryptographic techniques like homomorphic encryption, where data can be computed on without being decrypted. This would enable private data analysis or processing within smart contracts, opening up possibilities for privacy-intensive applications in fields like healthcare or finance.

User education plays a vital role in privacy protection. Sui would likely invest in resources that educate users on how to protect their privacy while using the blockchain. This includes understanding the implications of public versus private keys, the importance of secure wallet management, and how to navigate the privacy settings of dApps built on Sui.

Finally, Sui's commitment to user privacy extends to its governance model. By allowing token holders to influence decisions regarding privacy policies, updates, or new features, Sui ensures that the community's privacy concerns are addressed. This democratic approach to privacy governance can lead to policies and technologies that are not only technically robust but also socially responsible.

In essence, Sui's strategy for user privacy and data protection is about creating an ecosystem where users can engage with blockchain technology securely and confidentially. By integrating privacy at every level of interaction—from wallet management to smart contract execution—Sui aims to set a new standard for privacy in decentralized systems, making it a platform where privacy and blockchain utility coexist harmoniously.

Part 6: Future Directions in Privacy and Security

As the blockchain landscape evolves, so too does the need for more sophisticated and nuanced approaches to privacy and security. Sui, with its forward-looking design and commitment to user empowerment, is poised to navigate these future waters with innovation at the helm. This final part of the chapter looks ahead, considering the potential advancements in privacy and security for Sui and how these could reshape not just the platform but the broader blockchain ecosystem.

The journey into the future begins with the recognition that privacy and security are not static targets but moving ones, influenced by technological advancements, regulatory changes, and emerging threats. Sui's commitment to continuous improvement means that its approach to these issues will likely be dynamic, adapting to new challenges while seizing opportunities to lead in the blockchain space.

One of the most anticipated advancements in privacy could come from the deeper integration of **zero-knowledge proofs (ZKPs)**. While already a powerful tool for privacy, future iterations might see ZKPs becoming more scalable and less computationally intensive. This could allow for more complex privacy-preserving smart contracts on Sui, where users can prove that they meet certain conditions without revealing any underlying data. Imagine a future where voting systems, identity verification, or financial audits can be conducted with complete privacy yet total verifiability, all powered by Sui's blockchain.

Quantum-resistant cryptography is another frontier where Sui might venture. As quantum computing becomes more practical, current cryptographic systems could be rendered obsolete. Sui's proactive approach might involve adopting or developing post-quantum cryptographic algorithms to ensure that its privacy and security measures remain robust against future threats. This would not only protect current users but also future-proof the platform for decades to come.

In terms of security, the evolution of consensus mechanisms is always on the horizon. Sui might explore enhancements to its delegated proof-of-stake (DPoS) model, perhaps incorporating elements from other consensus models or entirely new concepts to increase security while maintaining or even improving on speed and efficiency. One could envision a hybrid model where DPoS is combined with other protocols to address specific security concerns or to optimize for certain use cases.

The role of **artificial intelligence (AI) and machine learning (ML)** in enhancing security and privacy cannot be overstated. Sui could leverage AI to predict and respond to security threats in real-time. Machine learning algorithms could analyze patterns of network activity to detect anomalies that might indicate a security breach or privacy leak. Moreover, AI could help in optimizing privacy settings for users, suggesting configurations based on their usage patterns or even dynamically adjusting privacy protocols based on perceived threats.

Privacy-enhancing technologies (PETs) like homomorphic encryption and secure multi-party computation could see more widespread adoption on Sui. These technologies allow for operations on encrypted data, enabling privacy-preserving analytics, secure voting systems, or confidential business logic in smart contracts. As these technologies mature, they could open up new applications for Sui, particularly in areas where data privacy is critical, like medical research or corporate data sharing.

For smart contracts, the future might bring more sophisticated security verification tools. **Formal verification**, currently a niche practice, could become more accessible and integrated into Sui's development environment. This would allow developers to mathematically prove the correctness of their contract logic, ensuring no security vulnerabilities by design. Such a leap would push the boundaries of what's possible in terms of secure decentralized applications.

Interoperability with other blockchains while maintaining privacy and security is another significant challenge and opportunity. Sui might develop or support protocols for cross-chain privacy-preserving transactions or data sharing. This would not only increase the utility of Sui as a platform but also contribute to a more interconnected yet private blockchain ecosystem.

The concept of **decentralized identity** could evolve significantly on Sui. Future directions might include more granular control over personal data, where individuals can share only the necessary parts of their identity for each transaction or interaction. This could leverage blockchain's immutability for data integrity while using ZKPs or similar technologies for privacy, creating a truly self-sovereign identity system.

Education and community involvement will be crucial in shaping these future directions. As Sui's ecosystem grows, so will the need for users to understand and engage with privacy and security tools. Sui might invest in educational platforms, community workshops, or even gamified learning experiences where users can learn about and test privacy and security features in a safe, simulated environment.

Regulatory compliance is another area where Sui's future will be defined. As laws like GDPR continue to evolve, Sui could pioneer new ways of ensuring compliance within a decentralized framework. This might involve creating blockchain-based solutions for data management that align with legal requirements for data rights, privacy, and security, potentially influencing how other blockchain platforms approach regulation.

Finally, consider the role of **community governance** in privacy and security. As Sui matures, the community's role in deciding on privacy policies, security enhancements, or even the adoption of new technologies will become more pronounced. This could lead to a feedback loop where the community not only uses but also influences the evolution of privacy and security features, ensuring they remain relevant and effective.

In this envisioned future, Sui's approach to privacy and security could set a benchmark for what's possible in blockchain technology. The platform might not just be a place for secure, private transactions but a hub for innovation in digital privacy, where every new technology or protocol is scrutinized through the lens of how it can protect and empower users.

However, this journey into the future is not without its challenges:

- **Balancing Innovation with Security:** Each new feature or technology must be vetted for potential vulnerabilities.
- **Scalability of Privacy Features:** As privacy mechanisms become more sophisticated, ensuring they scale with the network without degrading performance is vital.
- **User Adoption:** Advanced privacy and security features are only as effective as their adoption. Sui would need to ensure these are accessible and beneficial to all users, not just the tech-savvy.
- **Regulatory Adaptation:** Continuously adapting to a global regulatory landscape that's trying to catch up with blockchain technology will require foresight and diplomacy.
- **Ethical Considerations:** As AI and ML become more integrated, ethical considerations around data use, AI

decision-making, and privacy will come to the fore.

- **Community Consensus:** Achieving consensus on privacy and security matters through governance can be contentious, requiring careful management to maintain community cohesion.

In conclusion, Sui's future in privacy and security is one of potential and promise, where the platform could lead in creating a blockchain environment that respects and enhances privacy while offering uncompromised security. This future is not just about protecting data but about fostering an ecosystem where trust, innovation, and user empowerment are at the forefront. As Sui moves forward, every step it takes in this direction will be a step towards redefining what it means to interact securely and privately in a decentralized world.

Chapter 16: Sui's Network Performance: Benchmarks and Real-World Scenarios

Part 1: Introduction to Network Performance

In the realm of blockchain technology, network performance is not just a technical metric but a fundamental aspect that dictates the usability, adoption, and success of a platform. Sui, with its ambitious promise of speed, scalability, and security, places network performance at the core of its architectural design. This part introduces the significance of network performance for blockchain platforms, particularly for Sui, setting the stage for a deeper exploration into how Sui measures up against its own promises and the demands of real-world applications.

Network performance in blockchain matters for several reasons. Speed is crucial where users expect near-instantaneous feedback, especially in applications like decentralized finance (DeFi), gaming, or even simple token transfers. For Sui, speed encompasses not just transaction throughput but also the time from transaction submission to confirmation, known as latency. Scalability is essential as blockchains aim to serve millions or even billions of users, ensuring growth without performance degradation. Sui's architecture, with its focus on parallel transaction processing, aims to ensure that scalability is not a bottleneck. Security is another critical dimension; it must not be compromised for speed or scalability. The security of a network affects trust, ensuring transactions are executed correctly and assets remain safe. Sui's integration of the Move programming language with its consensus mechanism is designed to uphold security without sacrificing performance.

Moreover, network performance directly impacts user experience. A blockchain that can handle high volumes of transactions with low latency and costs provides a smoother, more engaging experience, encouraging wider adoption. Economically, the efficiency of a blockchain network influences its gas fees or transaction costs. Lower, more predictable costs can make applications more accessible, fostering a vibrant ecosystem.

Sui has been designed from the ground up with these performance considerations in mind. Its approach allows for parallel execution of transactions, significantly increasing network capacity compared to sequential processing models. Sui also aims for instant finality, where transactions are considered final almost immediately, reducing uncertainty and wait times for users. The object-centric model facilitates scalability by localizing state changes, meaning not every transaction needs to update the entire blockchain state, thus reducing computational load. Additionally, the efficiency of the Move language contributes to performance by preventing common issues that could lead to inefficient or insecure contract execution.

To understand how well Sui delivers on these promises, benchmarks are crucial. They provide quantitative measures like Transactions Per Second (TPS), block times, and latency, offering concrete data to assess performance. They enable comparative analysis with other blockchains, highlighting strengths or areas for improvement, and validate theoretical performance in practical, often unpredictable environments.

However, evaluating performance comes with its challenges. Real-world performance can vary due to dynamic network conditions, user behavior, or external factors like internet connectivity. There's always a balance to strike between scaling the network and maintaining its security. Performance under low load might not reflect how the network behaves as it scales with user growth.

This introduction sets the foundation for understanding why network performance is a key differentiator for Sui. As we delve into the specifics of benchmarks, real-world scenarios, and comparisons with other blockchains, this chapter aims to provide a clear picture of how Sui's performance aligns with its design philosophy, and what it means for developers, users, and the broader blockchain ecosystem.

Part 2: Sui's Performance Metrics

Evaluating the performance of Sui's network involves understanding several key metrics that directly reflect its ability to achieve its goals of speed, scalability, and security. This part outlines these critical performance indicators, providing insights into how Sui's architecture influences these metrics and what they signify for the platform's operational efficiency.

Transactions Per Second

- **Definition:** TPS measures how many transactions Sui can process in one second, a direct indicator of its throughput capacity.
- **Impact:** High TPS is essential for Sui to support applications requiring frequent transactions, like DeFi platforms or games, ensuring that user interactions are not bottlenecked by the network's capacity.
- **Sui's Approach:** Through parallel transaction processing, Sui aims to achieve a significantly higher TPS than traditional blockchains, leveraging its object-centric model where transactions can be executed concurrently.

Block Times

- **Definition:** This refers to the average time it takes for Sui to produce a new block, encapsulating transactions.
- **Importance:** Shorter block times mean faster transaction confirmations, which is crucial for real-time applications where every second counts.
- **Sui's Design:** With its consensus mechanism, Sui strives for quick block times, enhancing the network's responsiveness.

Latency

- **Definition:** Latency is the time from when a transaction is broadcast to the network until it is confirmed and considered final.
- **Relevance:** Low latency is key for user experience, especially in scenarios where immediate feedback or action is expected, like in trading or gaming.
- **Sui's Advantage:** By aiming for instant finality, Sui minimizes latency, providing users with a near-real-time experience akin to traditional internet services.

Gas Costs

- **Definition:** Gas costs refer to the fees paid for executing transactions or smart contracts on Sui.
- **Economic Impact:** Efficient gas cost management is vital for the economic viability of applications on Sui, ensuring that transactions remain affordable even as the network scales.
- **Sui's Strategy:** The gas model is designed to be predictable and optimized for the object-centric approach, where costs are based on resource manipulation rather than computational complexity alone.

Security Metrics

- **Consensus Finality:** The time and process through which transactions are secured and become irreversible. Sui's DPoS mechanism

aims to provide quick finality, bolstering
security without compromising speed.
- **Network Stability:** Measures the network's
  resilience against attacks or failures, which in
  Sui's case is enhanced by its design choices in
  validator selection and transaction execution.

Scalability Metrics

- **Horizontal Scalability:** The ability of Sui to
  increase its transaction handling capacity by
  adding more nodes or validators, ensuring that
  performance improves or at least remains
  stable with growth.
- **State Sharding:** Although not immediately
  implemented, the potential for Sui to shard its
  state could further enhance scalability, allowing
  different segments of the network to manage
  different parts of the blockchain state.

Real-World Testing

- **Testnet Performance:** Data from Sui's testnet
  provides initial insights into how these metrics
  hold up under controlled yet simulated
  real-world conditions.
- **Simulation Tools:** Advanced simulation tools
  can be used to stress test Sui's network under
  scenarios mimicking high demand or network
  congestion, offering a glimpse into potential
  performance under various conditions.

Challenges in Measuring Performance

- **Network Variability:** Performance can vary due to network conditions, making consistent benchmarks challenging.
- **Resource Management:** Ensuring that performance metrics are not just about raw numbers but also about efficient resource use, particularly in gas costs and state management.

Sui's performance metrics paint a picture of a blockchain designed for the demands of modern applications. By focusing on high TPS, low latency, efficient gas costs, and robust security, Sui sets itself up as a platform where speed and scalability are not just buzzwords but operational realities. As we continue to explore Sui's network performance, these metrics will serve as benchmarks for understanding and improving how Sui operates in both theoretical and practical environments.

Part 3: Benchmarking Methodology

Benchmarking Sui's network performance requires a structured approach to measure, compare, and validate its capabilities against both its internal goals and external standards. This part outlines the methodologies used to conduct these benchmarks, ensuring the results are accurate and meaningful for understanding Sui's performance in various contexts.

First, we define performance goals. Internal standards are set based on Sui's design philosophy and promised capabilities, reflecting what Sui aims to achieve in terms of speed, scalability, and security.

External comparisons provide context by benchmarking Sui against other leading blockchains, illustrating where it stands in the competitive landscape.

The tools and platforms used for benchmarking include Sui's native tools like the CLI, which offers functionalities for transaction simulation, gas estimation, and network status checks. Third-party benchmarking software, specifically designed for blockchain performance testing, can be adapted or used directly to assess Sui. These might include tools for stress testing, latency measurement, or throughput analysis. Simulation environments are also crucial, where network conditions can be controlled to test performance under various loads or scenarios, from low to peak usage.

Test conditions are carefully crafted. Tests might be conducted on Sui's testnet, which mimics real-world conditions but with controlled variables, or on private networks for more precise data. Various transaction types are executed to measure performance across different use cases, from simple transfers to complex smart contract interactions. Load testing involves gradually increasing the number of transactions to push the network to its limits, assessing how it scales and handles congestion. Additionally, testing from different geographical locations helps understand latency and performance variations due to network topology.

The metrics to measure include throughput, which looks at how many transactions Sui can process in a given timeframe, focusing on transactions per second (TPS). Latency measures the time taken for transactions from submission to confirmation. Block time reflects the interval between blocks, gauging the speed of consensus. Gas usage is analyzed to understand transaction costs under different conditions. Scalability testing shows how performance metrics evolve as the network grows, and security evaluations check the network's response to potential attack vectors or stress conditions.

Comparative analysis involves benchmarking Sui against traditional blockchains like Ethereum or newer, high-throughput platforms like Solana or Avalanche to see where Sui stands. It also considers how Sui's performance might compare to layer 2 scaling solutions on other blockchains, highlighting where Sui's native architecture provides advantages.

Data collection and reporting are done through automated gathering using scripts or tools for consistency and objectivity. Real-time monitoring tools like Sui Explorer or custom dashboards provide ongoing performance insights during tests. Statistical analysis interprets the data to account for variability, outliers, or to establish performance baselines.

Challenges in benchmarking include ensuring reproducibility, balancing realism with control for precise measurement, and adapting benchmarks as Sui's network evolves through changes in protocol, consensus mechanisms, or network architecture.

Looking to the future, community involvement in benchmarking can lead to more diverse and comprehensive testing scenarios. Integrating benchmarking into the development process ensures continuous refinement and optimization of network performance. Adaptive benchmarking, where benchmarks evolve with new use cases or technological advancements, is also a direction to consider.

The methodology behind benchmarking Sui's network performance is critical not only for validating its capabilities but also for guiding its continuous improvement. By setting clear goals, employing rigorous testing, and maintaining transparency in results, Sui can ensure that its performance claims are substantiated and that it remains at the forefront of blockchain technology. These benchmarks serve as a compass for developers, users, and the community, pointing towards where Sui excels and where there's room for growth.

Part 4: Speed and Scalability

Sui's architecture is designed with an emphasis on achieving exceptional speed and scalability, two critical factors for any blockchain aspiring to support a wide range of applications from finance to gaming. This part delves into how Sui's unique features enable it to perform in these areas, backed by data from benchmarks and simulations.

Sui's approach to speed is evident in its high throughput and low latency. By allowing for parallel transaction execution, Sui can handle thousands of transactions per second, significantly reducing the bottleneck seen in sequential processing models. In controlled testing environments, these high TPS numbers have been achieved, showcasing Sui's ability to scale with network capacity. Moreover, the design of Sui's consensus mechanism aims for near-instant transaction finality, with benchmarks indicating latencies measured in milliseconds, providing users with transaction experiences as immediate as those in centralized systems.

Scalability in Sui is facilitated by horizontal growth and efficient resource management. The platform is built to add more nodes or validators to increase capacity without a corresponding increase in resource usage. This has been demonstrated through simulations where the network maintains performance metrics like TPS and latency even as it grows. Sui's object-centric model plays a crucial role here, treating each piece of data or asset as an object with its own state. This means changes to one part of the blockchain do not necessarily impact others, leading to more efficient state management and allowing Sui to scale effectively.

On Sui's testnet, which simulates real-world conditions, performance metrics are closely monitored to assess scalability in practice. These tests have shown that Sui can maintain its speed and low latency even as transaction volume increases. Stress tests, where Sui is subjected to extreme workloads, reveal its design's ability to handle sudden spikes in demand without significant performance degradation, crucial for scenarios like high-volume trading or the launch of popular games.

Sui addresses scalability challenges through dynamic validator sets, where the number of validators can be increased in response to network growth or demand, ensuring scalability. The architecture also supports the potential future implementation of network sharding, where different parts of the network could handle different transaction or data segments, further enhancing scalability.

When benchmarked against other blockchains, Sui's metrics for TPS and latency often position it as a leader in terms of speed. Its scalability approach, particularly the object-centric model, provides a unique advantage in managing state complexity as the network expands. In specific applications like DeFi or gaming, where transactions happen in rapid succession, Sui's performance metrics suggest it can support these use cases at scale without typical trade-offs in speed or cost.

Looking to the future, Sui could see enhancements through protocol upgrades that might optimize consensus algorithms or improve transaction batching and processing, further enhancing speed and scalability. While Sui's layer 1 architecture is already scalable, the development of layer 2 solutions could be considered for handling specialized or high-volume use cases, potentially improving overall network performance by offloading certain types of transactions.

However, challenges remain, such as ensuring performance does not degrade as the user base grows or efficiently managing resources like gas to keep costs low while scaling.

Sui's focus on speed and scalability through its unique architectural choices positions it as a blockchain capable of handling the high demands of modern applications. Through rigorous benchmarking and real-world testing, Sui has demonstrated its ability to offer a platform where high transaction volumes do not compromise user experience. As Sui continues to develop, its commitment to these performance metrics will be key to its adoption and success in the competitive blockchain landscape.

Part 5: Security Benchmarks

Security is a fundamental aspect of blockchain technology, and for Sui, it's interwoven with its design to ensure that speed and scalability do not come at the cost of safety. This part examines how Sui's security measures hold up under various benchmarks, focusing on its consensus mechanism, the Move programming language, and resistance to common blockchain vulnerabilities.

Sui's consensus mechanism, based on Delegated Proof-of-Stake (DPoS), is crafted for both speed and security. By selecting validators through stake delegation, it ensures that those with a vested interest in the network's health are responsible for validating transactions. Benchmarks reveal that Sui achieves quick finality for transactions, narrowing the window for potential double-spend attacks or network manipulations. The system includes penalties for dishonest behavior, like stake slashing, which has been tested to effectively deter malicious activities.

The Move programming language is central to Sui's security strategy, designed to prevent common smart contract vulnerabilities. Its resource model has been benchmarked to show it prevents asset duplication or loss, crucial for transaction and state integrity. Move's strict type system and compile-time checks have proven effective in catching errors before runtime, reducing the likelihood of vulnerabilities.

Sui's resistance to common attacks is also notable. Its design mitigates reentrancy attacks, validated through simulated attack scenarios. The economic cost of launching Sybil attacks, where one entity controls multiple nodes, is high due to the need to stake significant resources, making such attacks impractical, as demonstrated in security tests. The structure of Sui makes 51% attacks, where an entity would need to control the majority of the stake, very difficult due to the distributed nature of stake delegation, supported by both theoretical and simulation-based benchmarks.

Smart contract auditing on Sui involves both automated tools and manual checks by security experts, ensuring that Move contracts are less prone to common vulnerabilities. The open-source ethos of Sui encourages community audits, which have proven effective in identifying potential issues before mainnet deployment.

Network security metrics, including the geographical distribution of nodes, show that Sui's network is designed to resist attacks targeting centralization, thus enhancing overall network security. The speed and efficiency of transaction validation mean less time for malicious transactions to propagate, providing an indirect security benefit.

Sui's security under load has been benchmarked through stress tests, where security measures hold up even with high transaction volumes, ensuring that security doesn't degrade with increased network load. Various attack scenarios have been simulated to assess Sui's resilience, demonstrating that it maintains its security posture even under stress.

However, challenges and future security enhancements are on the horizon. As blockchain technology evolves, so do attack methods, necessitating continuous security research and updates to Sui's protocols. Future interoperability with other blockchains might require additional security measures to maintain Sui's high standards across chains. There's also potential for integrating privacy-preserving technologies like zero-knowledge proofs for specific use cases, aiming to balance security with privacy needs.

Sui's security approach, combining Move's inherent safety features with a consensus mechanism designed for both speed and integrity, has been shown through benchmarks to provide a strong foundation for secure blockchain operations. These measures ensure that as Sui scales and accelerates, it does so without compromising the safety of users' assets or the network's integrity. Ongoing security enhancements will be vital for Sui to remain at the forefront of blockchain security in an ever-evolving digital landscape.

Part 6: Real-World Scenarios

Understanding how Sui performs under real-world conditions is crucial for assessing its practical utility and effectiveness. This part explores several scenarios that test Sui's network capabilities in environments that mimic or directly involve real-world applications, offering insights into how its design translates into tangible benefits for users and developers.

In the context of high-frequency trading within decentralized finance (DeFi), where rapid transaction processing is key for capitalizing on market opportunities, Sui's benchmarks demonstrate its suitability. With low latency and high throughput, Sui allows for near-real-time trading, crucial for arbitrage or flash loan strategies. In simulated trading environments, transactions were confirmed swiftly, matching the speed of centralized exchanges while preserving blockchain's security and transparency. This capability could lead to more competitive DeFi platforms on Sui, empowering traders to execute strategies without the typical delays associated with blockchain transactions.

For large-scale gaming events, where thousands of players interact simultaneously, Sui's performance remains robust. Tests simulating mass player interactions show that transactions like asset transfers or in-game actions are processed without significant lag. The object-centric model aids in managing game states and assets efficiently. This scalability could support more immersive gaming experiences, fostering trust in the system's ability to handle peak loads and potentially driving broader blockchain adoption in gaming.

During NFT drops and auctions, which often result in high demand spikes, Sui's network has proven capable of handling numerous transactions quickly. In scenarios mimicking popular NFT events, transactions were processed at a pace that kept up with demand, ensuring participants could mint or purchase NFTs without long wait times or high gas costs. This could make Sui a preferred platform for artists and collectors, enhancing user experience during these high-demand moments.

Looking at cross-chain transactions, although not immediately implemented, simulated environments where assets move between Sui and other blockchains show that Sui's performance remains strong. This suggests that when interoperability solutions are developed, Sui could handle such transactions efficiently, enabling a more interconnected blockchain ecosystem and enhancing its utility in a broader financial or digital asset landscape.

For daily use in micropayments, where numerous small transactions occur, like in content monetization or tipping systems, Sui's ability to handle transactions with low gas fees makes it economically viable. Tests confirmed that Sui can manage these small-value, high-volume transactions without prohibitive costs, opening up new opportunities for online interaction and monetization where traditional blockchains might be too costly or slow.

In enterprise scenarios, such as supply chain management, identity management, or secure data sharing, where secure, auditable transactions with high throughput are needed, Sui's benchmarks indicate it could support these use cases without compromising on speed or scalability. This reliability and performance could drive increased adoption in sectors that value efficiency and security in digital processes.

However, real-world scenarios also present challenges. Network congestion in extreme cases might still occur, necessitating ongoing optimization. Ensuring that blockchain's complexity does not detract from user experience remains a hurdle. Additionally, navigating regulatory landscapes could affect performance if compliance checks are required.

Looking to the future, continuous performance monitoring will be essential to adapt to new use cases or issues as they arise. The network design might need to evolve through protocol upgrades or additional scalability solutions. User education on leveraging Sui's performance in real-world scenarios will be crucial to maximize its potential.

These real-world scenarios provide a glimpse into how Sui's network performance translates into practical applications. From DeFi to gaming, NFTs to enterprise solutions, Sui's speed, scalability, and security are tested and proven to meet the demands of diverse use cases. As Sui continues to evolve, its ability to handle these real-world challenges will be paramount to its success and adoption across various sectors of the digital economy.

Part 7: Comparison with Other Blockchains

Comparing Sui's network performance with other blockchains provides insights into its competitive advantages, areas for improvement, and how it positions itself within the broader blockchain ecosystem. This part analyzes Sui against several established and emerging blockchain platforms across key performance metrics.

In terms of speed, measured by Transactions Per Second (TPS), Sui significantly outpaces Ethereum, even with its transition to Ethereum 2.0. Ethereum's layer 1 can handle around 100-150 TPS, while Sui's architecture, designed for parallel transaction processing, aims for thousands, showcasing a clear advantage in raw transaction speed. When compared to Solana, which also boasts high TPS numbers in the tens of thousands, Sui's approach with an object-centric model might offer more stable performance under sustained loads, potentially avoiding the network congestion issues Solana has encountered. Against Avalanche, which targets high TPS through its subnets and consensus mechanisms, Sui's performance might be comparable in speed but offers unique benefits in transaction finality and resource management due to its use of the Move language and its consensus design.

Regarding latency, Sui's aim for instant finality contrasts with Ethereum, where transactions might take minutes to be considered secure, positioning Sui for scenarios requiring real-time responsiveness like trading or gaming. Compared to Polkadot, where low-latency parachains exist, Sui's native design for quick transaction confirmation could provide a more seamless user experience for applications needing immediate feedback. Against Cardano, whose Ouroboros protocol ensures security but at the cost of longer confirmation times, Sui's focus on speed is evident.

On scalability, Sui's architecture inherently supports scaling through its object-centric model and parallel execution, potentially handling growth without the significant performance degradation seen in Bitcoin and Ethereum due to their design limitations. Compared to Binance Smart Chain (BSC), which has achieved scalability through a more centralized validator set, Sui aims for similar scalability with a more decentralized approach, potentially offering better long-term resilience. Against layer 2 solutions on Ethereum, like Optimism or Arbitrum, which enhance scalability, Sui's native layer 1 design could provide comparable or superior performance for many use cases, without the need for additional layers.

In terms of security, Sui's use of Move for smart contracts provides inherent benefits over many platforms, reducing common vulnerabilities. Its Delegated Proof-of-Stake (DPoS) consensus aims to balance security with speed, offering a potential middle ground between the security of Proof of Work (PoW) and the efficiency of Proof of Stake (PoS). Sui's design also shows resistance to certain attacks like reentrancy or double-spending, but continuous audits and community scrutiny are essential to maintain this security edge.

On cost, Sui's gas model is designed to be more predictable and potentially less costly for users, especially for microtransactions, compared to Ethereum's variable gas fees that can spike during network congestion. Against Solana, which offers low fees, Sui's model aims for consistency and efficiency in gas usage, potentially providing a more stable cost environment for developers and users.

Considering user experience, Sui's architectural choices aim to abstract blockchain complexities, offering an experience closer to centralized platforms in terms of speed and cost but with the benefits of decentralization. This sets it apart from many competitors where users often face a trade-off between speed and security.

However, comparative analysis faces challenges due to network variability, where performance can fluctuate based on conditions, making direct comparisons sometimes difficult without standardized testing environments. Also, blockchains are often optimized for different primary use cases, which can skew performance comparisons if not taken into account.

Looking to the future, as all blockchains evolve, performance metrics will change. Sui's ongoing development might focus on enhancing its advantages or catching up in areas where it currently lags. Future comparisons might also include how well each blockchain can interact with others, where Sui's potential for cross-chain capabilities could be a significant factor.

Sui stands out in the blockchain performance landscape due to its unique combination of speed, scalability, and security, thanks to its innovative architecture and the Move programming language. While it shares some performance characteristics with other high-throughput blockchains, its approach to transaction processing, resource management, and security features provides a distinctive value proposition. As the blockchain space continues to mature, Sui's performance will be a key determinant of its adoption and success in various applications, from DeFi to gaming and beyond.

Part 8: Performance Optimization

Optimizing performance on Sui involves strategies, best practices, and tools that developers and users can employ to ensure applications run efficiently, transactions are cost-effective, and the network operates at peak capacity. This part explores various methods to enhance Sui's network performance, focusing on smart contract design, transaction management, and network interaction.

Smart contract optimization begins with the efficient use of Move. This involves minimizing gas consumption by optimizing the logic and operations within smart contracts to reduce unnecessary computations or state changes. Proper resource management using Move's resource model allows for precise control over assets, which can lower computational overhead. Adopting a modular design for contracts, breaking them into smaller, reusable modules, can enhance maintainability and potentially reduce the complexity of each transaction.

In terms of transaction management, batching transactions is a key strategy. For applications involving multiple related actions, grouping these into a single transaction can reduce gas costs and network load. Understanding and optimizing the order of transactions based on how Sui processes them in parallel can minimize conflicts and speed up processing. Gas estimation and management are also crucial; using tools to predict gas costs before execution helps in planning and avoiding unexpected expenses, especially during high network demand.

When interacting with the network, choosing the right time to execute transactions, even though Sui aims for consistent performance, can be beneficial, particularly for time-sensitive or large transactions.

For developers or high-stake users, selecting validators based on performance metrics like speed, reliability, or cost can optimize transaction outcomes. Implementing retry logic for applications where transactions might fail due to temporary network conditions can enhance reliability without excessive user interaction.

Developer tools play a significant role in performance optimization. Profiling tools can analyze the performance of smart contracts or applications, identifying bottlenecks or inefficient code. Testing frameworks allow developers to simulate different network conditions, aiding in optimization for various scenarios before deployment. Network monitoring tools provide real-time insights into network health, transaction throughput, and latency, guiding developers in making informed optimization decisions.

Best practices for performance include regular code reviews focused on optimization to catch inefficiencies early in the development cycle. Following Sui's official documentation and community guidelines on performance best practices can lead to better application design. Educating users on efficient network use, like avoiding unnecessary transactions or understanding gas mechanics, is also important.

Looking to future enhancements, Sui might explore dynamic gas pricing models to adjust fees based on network conditions, potentially leading to more efficient resource allocation. While Sui's layer 1 is designed for scalability, future layer 2 solutions could be developed for specific use cases, further optimizing performance for high-frequency or microtransactions. As cross-chain interactions become more common, optimizing for these scenarios will ensure Sui's performance isn't compromised when dealing with other blockchains.

However, performance optimization faces challenges. Balancing security with speed is paramount; any optimization must not introduce vulnerabilities. As applications grow in complexity, maintaining performance while scaling becomes more challenging. User behavior can also be a significant performance bottleneck, highlighting the need for user education and intuitive interface design.

Performance optimization on Sui is not just about tweaking code or settings but involves a holistic approach to how developers build, how users interact, and how the network itself evolves. By adhering to best practices, using the right tools, and anticipating future network enhancements, developers can harness Sui's capabilities to create applications that are not only secure and scalable but also performant in real-world conditions. This ongoing process of optimization will be key to Sui's success as a platform for building the next generation of blockchain applications.

Part 9: Network Health Monitoring

Monitoring the health of Sui's network is essential for ensuring its performance, scalability, and security are maintained or improved over time. This part discusses the tools, metrics, and practices used to keep an eye on Sui's network, providing developers, users, and the community with the necessary insights to understand and react to the network's state.

Key metrics for monitoring include transaction throughput, which tracks the number of transactions processed per second (TPS) and gives an immediate indicator of network load and performance capacity. Latency, the time from transaction submission to confirmation, helps assess the network's responsiveness. Block time, the average interval between blocks, signals network health, consensus efficiency, and potential congestion. Gas prices are monitored to inform users about the current cost of transactions, aiding developers in optimizing their applications for cost-efficiency. Validator performance metrics, including uptime, block production rate, and transaction validation speed, provide insights into the network's decentralization and reliability. Network congestion indicators, like the size of pending transaction queues or the mempool, show when the network is under stress, potentially impacting performance.

Tools for network monitoring include the Sui Explorer, a primary interface for inspecting the blockchain state, transactions, validators, and other network activities in real-time. Custom dashboards can be created or used to aggregate data from various sources, offering a tailored view of network health relevant to specific applications. Through APIs and SDKs provided by Sui, developers can access network data programmatically, enabling custom monitoring solutions or integration with third-party monitoring services. Additionally, third-party analytics platforms specialized in blockchain analysis can offer additional insights, including historical data trends, which are invaluable for long-term planning or performance analysis.

Effective monitoring practices involve setting up real-time alerts for anomalies in network performance, allowing for quick responses to issues like high latency spikes or validator downtime. Analyzing historical data regularly aids in understanding performance patterns, seasonal trends, or the impact of network upgrades. Encouraging community participation in monitoring by providing accessible tools or platforms for reporting issues or sharing observations fosters a collaborative approach to network health. Integrating network health checks into the development process ensures applications are tested against real network conditions before deployment.

However, monitoring faces challenges such as data overload, where distinguishing critical metrics from the vast amount of data generated by a blockchain can be difficult. Ensuring that monitoring tools themselves do not become a bottleneck as the network scales is another concern. There's also the delicate balance of maintaining privacy and security while monitoring network activity.

Looking to the future, enhancements in monitoring might include the use of AI and machine learning to predict network congestion or detect unusual patterns, preemptively addressing performance issues. Decentralized monitoring solutions could evolve, where the community contributes to a distributed overview of network health. As Sui aims to interact with other blockchains, monitoring tools will need to adapt to include cross-chain performance metrics.

The impact of effective network health monitoring on user and developer experience is profound. It allows for proactive management of network issues, improving overall experience by addressing problems before they impact users. Developers can use monitoring data to fine-tune applications, ensuring they perform well under various network conditions. Real-time, transparent network health data fosters trust and transparency among users, as they can see the network's performance for themselves.

Network health monitoring is integral to the development, maintenance, and user experience of the Sui ecosystem. By leveraging the right tools, metrics, and practices, Sui can maintain its performance promises, respond to issues swiftly, and continuously evolve to meet the demands of its growing user base. As Sui matures, the sophistication and decentralization of its monitoring capabilities will be key to its reputation as a reliable and high-performing blockchain platform.

Part 10: Future Performance Enhancements

The journey of Sui's network performance is far from over. As blockchain technology evolves, so too must the capabilities of Sui to meet new challenges and seize emerging opportunities. This part speculates on the future directions and potential enhancements that could further elevate Sui's performance, scalability, and security.

Technological advancements might see refinements in Sui's consensus mechanism, potentially focusing on even quicker finality times or more energy-efficient operations. This could involve incorporating elements from newer consensus models or enhancing the current Delegated Proof-of-Stake (DPoS) system. Scalability could be further improved through sharding, where the network processes different segments of data or transactions in parallel, significantly boosting capacity. Additionally, Sui might explore or develop layer 2 scaling solutions tailored for specific use cases, like payment channels for faster, cheaper transactions or state channels for gaming applications, all while maintaining the security of layer 1.

Network upgrades could include dynamic gas models to optimize transaction costs, making Sui more appealing for microtransactions or during periods of network congestion. As the blockchain ecosystem becomes more interconnected, Sui could develop or adopt protocols for seamless asset and data transfer across different blockchains, enhancing its utility and reach. Privacy enhancements, such as integrating zero-knowledge proofs, could offer users greater anonymity, broadening the platform's use cases in areas where privacy is essential.

Performance optimization might advance through improvements in Move's compilation process, leading to more efficient bytecode that reduces gas costs and execution times for complex smart contracts. Further optimizations in resource management within the object-centric model could yield significant performance gains, particularly for applications dealing with numerous or complex state changes.

In terms of developer tools and ecosystem, future SDKs and CLI tools might provide more sophisticated performance analysis, helping developers optimize their applications for Sui's unique architecture. More advanced simulation environments for testing could allow developers to better prepare their applications for various network conditions before going live. Encouraging open-source contributions to performance optimization libraries or frameworks could lead to a richer ecosystem of tools tailored for Sui's specific needs.

However, these enhancements come with challenges and considerations. Ensuring backward compatibility with existing applications and infrastructure on Sui is crucial. There's also the ongoing balance between security and performance enhancements, where improvements must not compromise safety. Adoption and education will be key; developers and users will need to learn how to leverage these new capabilities effectively.

The long-term vision for Sui includes potential AI integration to dynamically optimize network performance, predict load patterns, or even assist in smart contract design for better performance. With an increasing focus on sustainability, Sui might lead in developing or adopting more environmentally friendly consensus algorithms or energy-efficient practices. Enhancing global reach by reducing latency and increasing accessibility for users worldwide, particularly in regions with less robust internet infrastructure, could be another goal.

The horizon for Sui's network performance enhancements is broad, promising a future where it not only keeps pace with but possibly sets new standards in blockchain technology. These potential advancements are not just about raw numbers like transactions per second (TPS) or latency but about creating a more usable, secure, and inclusive blockchain environment. As Sui evolves, its commitment to performance will continue to be a cornerstone of its value proposition, driving adoption and innovation in decentralized applications across various sectors.

Chapter 17: The Economic Model of Sui: Tokenomics and Incentive Structures

Part 1: Introduction to Sui's Economic Model

The economic model of any blockchain platform is not merely a financial mechanism; it's the lifeblood that circulates through the system, influencing everything from user engagement and developer incentives to network security and long-term sustainability. Sui, with its vision to redefine the blockchain landscape, has crafted an economic model that is as innovative as its technological architecture. This part introduces the foundational principles of Sui's economic design, exploring how it aims to align the interests of all participants with the health and growth of the network.

At its core, Sui's economic model is designed to foster a vibrant, self-sustaining ecosystem where every participant, whether they are validators, developers, users, or investors, finds value in contributing to and interacting with the network. The philosophy behind Sui's economics is rooted in the principles of decentralization, incentivization, and sustainability:

Decentralization in Sui's economic model isn't just about distributing control but also about ensuring the distribution of rewards and influence. Unlike traditional financial systems where wealth concentration can lead to power centralization, Sui seeks to create an environment where the benefits of participation are widespread. This involves crafting mechanisms where the value generated by the network is shared among a broad base of participants, encouraging more equitable growth and reducing the risk of centralization.

Incentivization is pivotal for any blockchain to thrive. Sui's model leverages economic incentives to drive participation across various roles within its ecosystem:

- For validators, the economic model provides clear incentives to maintain network integrity and performance. Through staking mechanisms, validators are rewarded for their service in securing the network, with rewards structured in a way that encourages honest behavior and discourages malicious actions. This includes staking rewards that are not only financial but also tied to governance rights, giving validators a say in the network's future direction.
- Developers are incentivized through a combination of grants, bounties, and the potential for revenue from the applications they build on Sui. The economic model supports an environment where developers can innovate without the immediate pressure of profitability, knowing there are mechanisms in place for sustainable monetization of their work. This might involve revenue sharing from transaction fees, royalties from smart contracts, or direct funding through community governance.
- Users, the lifeblood of any platform, are encouraged to engage with Sui through

various economic incentives. This could include lower transaction fees, rewards for network activity, or even participation in governance, where they have a stake in decision-making processes. The economic model aims to make using Sui not just a practical choice but also a rewarding one, potentially through token airdrops, staking benefits, or access to exclusive features.

Sustainability is perhaps the most challenging aspect of any economic model, especially in the volatile world of cryptocurrencies. Sui approaches sustainability from multiple angles:

- **Controlled Inflation:** Sui's tokenomics will likely include mechanisms to control inflation, ensuring that the creation of new tokens does not devalue existing ones. This might involve dynamic supply adjustments based on network usage, economic conditions, or community decisions.
- **Token Utility and Scarcity:** To maintain value, Sui's native token must have clear utility within the ecosystem, from governance, staking, to transaction fees. By ensuring tokens are not just speculative assets but essential components of network operations, Sui can foster a demand that supports long-term token value.
- **Economic Policies:** Through decentralized governance, Sui can adapt its economic policies to react to changes in the market or network conditions. This adaptability is crucial

for sustainability, allowing the community to vote on adjustments to staking rewards, fee structures, or even the minting of new tokens.

- **Balancing Growth with Stability:** Sui's economic model must balance the need for growth (more users, more transactions) with the stability required for a reliable financial system. This involves managing transaction costs to remain competitive while ensuring the network doesn't become overwhelmed by high demand, which could lead to network congestion or price volatility.

The economic model also considers the broader ecosystem in which Sui exists. It's not just about internal economics but how Sui interacts with external markets, other blockchains, and traditional financial systems:

- **Interoperability:** By facilitating interoperability with other blockchains, Sui can expand the utility of its token, potentially serving as a bridge asset or a medium for cross-chain transactions, thereby increasing its demand and utility.
- **Real-World Asset Integration:** Sui might explore ways to tokenize or interact with real-world assets, providing a tangible backing or utility to its token, which can contribute to economic stability.
- **Regulatory Compliance:** While aiming to remain decentralized, Sui must navigate global financial regulations. Its economic model might include provisions or tools for compliance, like

transaction tracing for AML/KYC purposes or mechanisms for on-chain tax reporting, ensuring longevity in various legal jurisdictions.

The introduction of Sui's economic model is not about presenting a static set of rules but rather about outlining a framework that can evolve. This evolution would be driven by community governance, where token holders have a direct say in economic policy, from fee structures to how rewards are distributed. This democratic approach to economics could lead to a more resilient system, one where changes are made with the collective interest in mind, rather than by a small group of decision-makers.

However, this model also faces challenges:

- **Balancing Incentives:** The model must ensure that incentives do not lead to short-term gains at the expense of long-term health. For instance, overly generous staking rewards could lead to inflation if not managed correctly.
- **Economic Attacks:** Sui must be vigilant against economic attacks like those through flash loans or coordinated staking to manipulate governance or market conditions.
- **User Education:** For the economic model to work, users need to understand the implications of their actions within the ecosystem, from staking to voting on governance proposals.
- **Scalability vs. Cost:** As the network grows, maintaining low costs while scaling could

become challenging, potentially affecting user adoption if fees rise too high.

Sui's economic model is an intricate dance of incentives, controls, and community governance aimed at creating a sustainable, decentralized financial ecosystem. By aligning the interests of all participants with the network's health, Sui seeks to build not just a blockchain but a robust economic environment where innovation, participation, and fairness can thrive. As the platform evolves, so too will its economic model, adapting to new challenges, technologies, and community needs, setting a precedent for how blockchain economics can support a vision of decentralized finance that is accessible, equitable, and sustainable.

Part 2: Tokenomics of Sui

The tokenomics of Sui form the backbone of its operational philosophy, dictating how value is created, distributed, and preserved within its ecosystem. This section delves into the complexities of Sui's native token, exploring its supply, distribution, utility, and its pivotal role in the platform's economic structure.

Central to Sui's tokenomics is the determination of the token's total supply and the strategy for its distribution. The initial supply would be set at launch, aiming to balance scarcity to maintain value with sufficient circulation to ensure liquidity. Distribution strategies might involve public sales, possibly through mechanisms like an Initial DEX Offering (IDO), to distribute tokens widely among the community.

Airdrops could be used to incentivize early adopters or reward long-term contributors, perhaps tied to network usage or ecosystem development. Staking rewards would see tokens distributed over time, encouraging participants to lock up their tokens for network security. Allocations might be made for the team and development, with vesting periods to align their interests with the platform's long-term success. Additionally, tokens could be reserved for ecosystem development, funding grants, hackathons, or strategic partnerships to foster innovation and growth.

Sui's approach to managing inflation would involve policies on minting new tokens, potentially linked to network milestones, validator performance, or community decisions. Conversely, token burning mechanisms could be employed where tokens are removed from circulation through transaction fees or other network activities, helping to dynamically manage supply.

The utility of Sui's token is crucial for its value retention and growth. It would likely serve as the currency for transaction fees, directly connecting its demand to network usage. Staking the token would allow participants to engage in governance, earn rewards, or contribute to network security, linking the token's value to the health of the network. Governance rights could be granted to token holders, enabling them to influence network upgrades, economic policies, or fund allocations. Tokens might be required for access to specific services or features within the Sui ecosystem, increasing their practical application. In terms of interoperability, Sui's token could function as a bridge or collateral in cross-chain transactions, extending its utility beyond Sui's native environment. Within or in conjunction with DeFi applications, tokens could be used as collateral for loans, in yield farming, or for other financial instruments.

Sui's tokenomics are designed to provide economic incentives that align with the platform's objectives. Validators would be incentivized through rewards for their role in network maintenance, promoting security and decentralization. Developers would find motivation through tokens integrated into the ecosystem, possibly through grants, bounties, or revenue from the applications they develop. Users would be encouraged to engage by being rewarded for various activities, from simple transactions to contributing to data or network security, fostering a cycle of participation and reward.

The sustainability of Sui's tokenomics focuses on ensuring tokens have real utility within the network to maintain or increase their value over time. Economic cycles might be established where tokens are periodically locked, staked, or burned to manage supply and demand dynamics. The model should be adaptable, allowing for adjustments based on economic analysis, community feedback, or market shifts through governance mechanisms.

Balancing token supply is a delicate task; too much can lead to inflation, while too little might constrain growth due to liquidity issues. The token should derive its value from utility rather than speculation for long-term sustainability. Protecting against economic attacks where tokens could be manipulated for governance control or market manipulation is essential. Compliance with regulations will dictate how tokens are managed, used, or even classified in different jurisdictions. The token must also withstand external market pressures, requiring a robust, adaptable economic model.

As Sui evolves, its tokenomics might see further development. Layer 2 solutions could introduce new token mechanisms to handle high-volume transactions or support new economic models. Linking tokens to real-world assets could broaden their utility, enhancing the token's value proposition. With the growth of DeFi, Sui's token could become central to new financial products or services, including in cross-chain scenarios. If staking or similar activities consume significant energy, there might be initiatives towards more environmentally sustainable practices or incentives.

In conclusion, Sui's tokenomics are about more than just creating a cryptocurrency; they're about designing an economic system that supports the blockchain's goals. By carefully managing supply, utility, distribution, and incentives, Sui aims to foster an economy that is robust, equitable, and conducive to a decentralized, community-driven platform. The success of this economic model will largely depend on its adaptability to both the internal needs of the network and the broader economic environment, ensuring that Sui's token remains a valuable and integral part of its ecosystem for the long term.

Part 3: Incentive Structures

The incentive structures within Sui's economic model are designed to foster participation, secure the network, and drive the ecosystem's growth. These incentives are not just financial but are also tied to governance, influence, and community recognition, creating a multifaceted system where every participant has a stake in the platform's success.

At the core of Sui's incentive system is the reward mechanism for validators. Validators, who are essential for maintaining the network's consensus and transaction validation, are incentivized through staking rewards. By staking Sui's native tokens, validators can earn additional tokens based on their contribution to network security and performance. This not only ensures network integrity but also encourages a decentralized validator set, as more participants are motivated to become validators to earn these rewards. However, the system must be designed to prevent over-centralization by offering diminishing returns on additional staked amounts or by implementing a cap on rewards to encourage broader participation.

For developers, Sui's incentive structure includes several mechanisms to spur innovation and application development. Grants programs could be established where developers propose projects or improvements for the network, and upon community approval, receive funding in Sui tokens. Hackathons or coding challenges can also serve as platforms for developers to showcase their work, with token rewards or other forms of recognition as incentives. Revenue sharing models might allow developers to earn from transaction fees generated by their applications, aligning their financial success with the utility and popularity of their creations on the Sui network. By providing these incentives, Sui can attract a vibrant developer community, leading to a rich ecosystem of decentralized applications (dApps).

Users are another critical component of Sui's ecosystem, and their incentives are designed to promote network usage and loyalty. Lower transaction fees could be a direct incentive for users, making Sui an attractive platform for everyday transactions. Sui might also implement token rewards for users engaging in specific activities, like participating in governance votes, providing liquidity to decentralized exchanges, or contributing to the network's data oracles. These rewards could come in the form of airdrops, staking benefits, or access to exclusive features or dApps. By rewarding active participation, Sui can cultivate a user base that is both engaged and invested in the platform's ongoing development and governance.

Incentives also extend to governance, where token holders might receive benefits like voting rights on network upgrades, economic policies, or how community treasuries are managed. This governance participation not only gives users a voice but also aligns their interests with the long-term health of the network. The more engaged users are in governance, the more they are likely to support decisions that benefit the platform as a whole.

The incentive system must be carefully calibrated to ensure it does not lead to perverse outcomes. For example, overly generous staking rewards could inflate the token supply too quickly, undermining value. Therefore, incentives need to be sustainable, often involving mechanisms like reward halving over time or adjusting based on network metrics like the number of validators or transaction volumes.

Additionally, Sui could implement social or reputational incentives alongside financial ones. Recognition within the community, badges for contributions, or roles in governance bodies can motivate participation beyond monetary rewards. This multi-layered approach to incentives can help build a community culture that values contribution, innovation, and participation.

The challenge for Sui will be to maintain a balance where incentives encourage growth without compromising security or decentralization. This might involve complex algorithms for reward distribution, ensuring that incentives are fair and reflect the network's needs at different stages of its lifecycle. It also means adapting these incentives as the network evolves, possibly through community governance where participants can vote on changes to the incentive structures.

Sui's incentive structures are designed to create a self-reinforcing cycle of participation, security, and innovation. By aligning the interests of validators, developers, and users with the network's health and expansion, Sui aims to foster a sustainable, vibrant ecosystem. The effectiveness of these incentives will largely determine how well Sui can engage its community, secure its network, and drive the adoption of its technology, ultimately shaping its place in the blockchain landscape.

Part 4: Economic Sustainability

Economic sustainability in the context of Sui is not just about ensuring the platform can function over the long term; it's about crafting an economic model that can withstand the volatility of the crypto market, adapt to technological evolution, and foster a healthy, growing ecosystem that benefits all participants. This part explores how Sui could achieve economic sustainability through its tokenomics, governance, and community engagement strategies.

Sui's approach to economic sustainability begins with its token supply management. The total supply of tokens, coupled with how and when new tokens are minted or burned, plays a critical role in maintaining economic balance. Initially, Sui would likely set a total supply that reflects a balance between scarcity, which can drive value, and sufficient liquidity to support network operations and growth. The introduction of new tokens would need to be carefully calibrated, potentially linked to network activity, such as transaction volume or validator performance, to ensure that inflation does not erode the value of existing tokens. Conversely, Sui might implement token burning mechanisms, where a portion of transaction fees or other network activities could be used to reduce the circulating supply, thereby potentially increasing the value of each token over time.

Inflation control is crucial for sustainability. Sui's designers might consider implementing a dynamic supply adjustment mechanism where the rate of new token creation slows down as network usage increases, or vice versa. Such a model could help stabilize the token's purchasing power, making it more predictable and less susceptible to the wild swings seen in many cryptocurrencies. This control over inflation would not only help in maintaining token value but also in ensuring that rewards for staking or other network participation remain attractive without being overly dilutive.

The economic model must also consider the utility of the token beyond just being a medium of exchange. To sustain economic activity, Sui's token should have multiple uses within the ecosystem. It could be used for transaction fees, staking to secure the network, participating in governance, or accessing premium features. By ensuring the token has diverse and essential roles, Sui can create a demand that's not solely speculative but based on real utility, contributing to its long-term value and the network's overall sustainability.

Incentivization is another pillar of economic sustainability. Sui's model would need to incentivize all participants in ways that align with the network's health. For validators, the incentives could be structured to encourage not just participation but also performance and honesty, perhaps through rewards that are proportional to the quality of their service (uptime, transaction validation speed, etc.). Developers might be incentivized through grants, revenue sharing from transaction fees generated by their dApps, or through the potential for their projects to gain traction in a growing ecosystem. Users might be rewarded for various forms of engagement, from simple usage to more complex interactions like liquidity provision in DeFi applications or contributing to network data oracles.

Sustainability also involves managing economic risks like wealth centralization, where a few entities hold a disproportionate amount of tokens, potentially leading to governance or market manipulation. Sui's governance could include mechanisms to mitigate this, such as limiting the voting power of large holders or implementing quadratic voting where influence is more evenly distributed. Additionally, the distribution of tokens at launch and through ongoing incentives should aim for a broad base of holders, reducing the likelihood of centralization over time.

Economic policies would ideally be community-driven, allowing for adaptability to changing circumstances. Through decentralized governance, the community can vote on adjustments to token economics, such as staking rewards, fee structures, or even changes to the token's supply. This democratic approach ensures that economic sustainability isn't dictated by a few but is a collective effort, reflecting the needs and desires of the entire ecosystem. Such governance can also introduce checks and balances to prevent rapid, potentially destabilizing changes, ensuring that any economic policy shifts are well-considered.

Adaptability in Sui's economic model would also mean responding to external market conditions. If the broader crypto market experiences a downturn, Sui might need mechanisms like reducing staking rewards to control inflation or increasing token utility in other areas to maintain demand. Similarly, in times of high demand, Sui could adjust its economics to prevent network congestion or excessive fee increases that might drive users away.

The integration with real-world economies and regulatory frameworks is another aspect of sustainability. As blockchain intersects more with traditional finance, Sui must navigate issues like taxation, compliance with Anti-Money Laundering (AML) regulations, and Know Your Customer (KYC) requirements. This might involve developing tools or protocols that allow for compliance without centralizing control, such as privacy-preserving identity verification or automated tax reporting functionalities.

Sustainability in Sui's economic model also extends to environmental considerations. Given the critique of blockchain technologies for their energy consumption, particularly with Proof of Work systems, Sui, using a different consensus mechanism, could still focus on minimizing its environmental impact. This might involve optimizing its DPoS (Delegated Proof of

Stake)) for energy efficiency, incentivizing validators based on their environmental practices, or exploring ways to offset the carbon footprint of network operations.

Community education and engagement are vital for economic sustainability. Users need to understand the implications of their actions within the network, from staking strategies to participating in governance. Sui could invest in educational resources, community programs, or partnerships with educational institutions to foster a knowledgeable user base. An educated community is more likely to make decisions that support the network's long-term health rather than short-term gains.

Finally, economic sustainability involves preparing for and adapting to technological advancements. As blockchain technology evolves, so too must Sui's economic model. This might mean integrating new financial instruments or models that emerge in the DeFi space, adopting layer 2 scaling solutions to manage growth, or even exploring quantum-resistant cryptography to secure the network's future. Each technological leap could require economic adjustments to maintain balance and utility of the token.

However, achieving this level of sustainability is not without challenges. One of the primary ones is ensuring that economic incentives do not lead to negative externalities like network spam, where users might engage in activities solely for rewards without adding value. Sui would need to design its incentives in a way that encourages beneficial behavior, possibly through a reputation system or by tying rewards to the long-term health of the network.

Another challenge is market manipulation or economic attacks. With a governance model where token holders have significant say, there's always a risk of entities accumulating tokens to sway decisions in their favor. This requires vigilance, perhaps through time-locked voting or mechanisms that detect and mitigate such behaviors.

Balancing growth with stability is an ongoing challenge. Rapid growth can lead to network congestion or fee spikes, while too much focus on stability might stifle innovation or user adoption. Sui's economic model must be dynamic enough to support both, perhaps through phased economic policies or by allowing for community-driven experiments within controlled environments.

Economic sustainability for Sui is about creating an ecosystem where the token's value is derived from real utility, where incentives drive positive network effects, and where governance ensures that the economic model adapts to both the community's and the market's changing needs. This involves a delicate balance of token supply management, utility enhancement, incentivization, regulatory compliance, environmental consciousness, and community education. By addressing these aspects thoughtfully, Sui can aim to not only survive but thrive in the blockchain landscape, offering a model of economic sustainability that could serve as a blueprint for future blockchain platforms.

Part 5: Impact on Decentralized Applications (dApps)

The economic model of Sui significantly influences the landscape of decentralized applications (dApps) built on its platform, affecting everything from the feasibility and cost of development to the revenue models available to creators and the user experience. This part explores how Sui's economic framework shapes the dApp ecosystem, focusing on how it can stimulate growth, innovation, and sustainability within this domain.

Firstly, Sui's approach to transaction fees has a direct impact on dApps. By potentially offering low or predictable transaction costs due to its efficient architecture, Sui makes it economically viable for developers to create applications that require numerous small transactions, like microtransactions in gaming dApps or micropayments for content. This can democratize access to blockchain for developers and users alike, allowing for applications that might have been cost-prohibitive on other platforms due to high gas fees. However, managing these fees must be done in a way that ensures network sustainability without overwhelming the developers or users with costs as the network scales.

The token utility within Sui's ecosystem is another critical factor for dApps. If the native token of Sui is used not just for transaction fees but also for governance, staking, or as a means of accessing specific features within dApps, it creates multiple revenue streams or interaction models for developers. For instance, a dApp could require users to stake tokens to access premium features, thus creating a new economic model where user participation directly correlates with token demand. This not only incentivizes holding and using the token but also ties the success of dApps to the broader health of the Sui network.

Sui's staking mechanism can also benefit dApps by providing a secure and incentivized environment for both developers and users. Developers might stake tokens alongside their projects to demonstrate commitment, potentially unlocking benefits like reduced fees or access to community funds for further development. Users, on the other hand, could stake tokens to gain access to dApps or to earn rewards within them, creating a symbiotic relationship where both parties have a stake in the application's success and security. This can lead to more engaged communities around dApps, as users have a financial interest in the platform's growth and protection.

The economic incentives provided by Sui can spur dApp development in innovative ways. Developers might be motivated not just by direct financial rewards like grants or bounties but by the potential for revenue sharing. If Sui implements a model where a portion of transaction fees or staking rewards from dApp usage is redistributed to developers, it could lead to a surge in high-quality, sustainable dApps. This model encourages developers to focus on user adoption and retention, knowing that their revenue is directly tied to the dApp's popularity and utility.

Moreover, Sui's governance model can influence dApp economics through community-driven decisions. If dApp developers or the community at large can propose and vote on features like fee structures, token rewards, or even network upgrades that directly affect dApps, it creates a more dynamic and responsive ecosystem. This could mean that dApps evolve in line with user feedback, potentially leading to better products or services. It also means that developers must consider community governance in their business models, perhaps integrating governance tokens into their applications to align with or influence network-wide decisions.

The scalability and performance of Sui's network are crucial for dApp sustainability. If Sui can handle high throughput and maintain low latency, it becomes an attractive platform for dApps that require real-time interactions or those that anticipate large user bases. This scalability impacts the economic model by allowing dApps to grow without the developer needing to worry about network constraints that could lead to increased costs or degraded user experience. It also means that dApps can maintain economic viability as they scale, potentially leading to more complex, value-driven applications like decentralized finance (DeFi) platforms, gaming ecosystems, or social networks.

However, the economic model must also address the challenge of ensuring dApps are not just feasible to build but also economically sustainable to operate. Sui could support this through various mechanisms:

- **Revenue Models:** Encouraging diverse revenue models beyond just token transactions, like subscriptions, in-app purchases, or even advertising if done in a decentralized, privacy-respecting manner.
- **Funding Opportunities:** Facilitating access to funding for dApps, whether through community grants, staking pools, or by connecting developers with investors through decentralized venture platforms.
- **Economic Tools:** Providing developers with tools that help manage token economics within their dApps, like dynamic pricing for in-app features or automated reward distribution systems.
- **Community Engagement:** Creating an environment where dApps can leverage the community for growth, perhaps through referral rewards, community-led features, or by making dApps part of larger governance decisions.

One of the significant impacts of Sui's economic model on dApps is the potential for creating new economic paradigms. For instance, in gaming, Sui could support true digital asset ownership where in-game items are NFTs, providing players with real economic incentives to engage with dApps. This model could redefine how games are monetized, with developers earning from secondary markets or players having the ability to trade assets across different games or platforms.

The integration of Sui with other blockchains for interoperability also opens up new economic avenues for dApps. If assets or data from Sui can interact with other chains, dApps might not be confined to one ecosystem, increasing their potential user base and utility. This interoperability could lead to economic models where dApps manage or benefit from cross-chain liquidity or where they can offer services that span multiple blockchain environments.

However, there are challenges to consider in how Sui's economic model impacts dApps:

- **Economic Volatility:** If the value of Sui's token fluctuates significantly, it could affect the pricing models within dApps, making it hard for developers to predict revenue or for users to understand costs.
- **Centralization Risks:** If the benefits of dApp creation or operation are skewed towards those with significant token holdings, it could lead to centralization of dApp development or influence, contrary to the ethos of decentralization.
- **User Experience:** The economic model should not compromise the user experience. If engaging with a dApp involves complex economic interactions or high costs, it might deter users, reducing the dApp's viability.
- **Scalability Costs:** As dApps grow, ensuring that the economic incentives and transaction

costs remain favorable is crucial, or else scaling might become economically unfeasible for developers.

- **Regulatory Compliance:** dApps must navigate the same regulatory waters as Sui itself, which could impact how they handle user data, manage funds, or comply with financial regulations across different jurisdictions.

Looking forward, the evolution of Sui's economic model could further enhance its impact on dApps:

- **Layer 2 Solutions:** Sui might support or encourage layer 2 scaling solutions specifically for dApps, reducing transaction costs and increasing throughput for specific use cases.
- **Custom Token Economics:** As part of its ecosystem, Sui could provide frameworks or tools for developers to create custom token economics for their dApps, fostering innovation in how dApps generate and distribute value.
- **Cross-Chain dApp Economies:** With interoperability, dApps could operate across multiple blockchains, with Sui's token playing a role in these multi-chain economies, potentially leading to more robust and versatile applications.
- **AI and Machine Learning:** Future developments might see AI used for optimizing economic models within dApps, predicting user behavior for better reward distribution, or even customizing economic interactions based on user profiles.

Sui's economic model has profound implications for the development, operation, and sustainability of dApps. By providing a foundation where transaction costs are managed, incentives are aligned, and scalability is ensured, Sui can become a fertile ground for dApp innovation. However, this requires continuous adaptation to ensure that as the platform and its economics evolve, they continue to support and enhance the dApp ecosystem. The success of dApps on Sui will largely depend on how well this economic model can balance the interests of developers, users, and the network itself, creating a vibrant, sustainable, and inclusive environment for decentralized applications to thrive.

Part 6: Community Governance and Token Economics

Community governance in Sui's ecosystem is not just a feature but a fundamental aspect of its economic model, deeply intertwining with the platform's token economics. This part explores how community governance can influence Sui's economic policies, the implications for token holders, and the broader impact on the sustainability of the network.

Sui's vision for community governance is to create a democratic, decentralized system where token holders have a say in the platform's direction, including its economic policies. The underlying principle is that those who hold and use Sui's tokens should have a direct influence over decisions that affect the token's value, supply, and utility. This approach aims to align the interests of the community with the long-term health and growth of Sui, ensuring that economic policies are not dictated by a small group but are reflective of the collective will.

The token economics of Sui serve as the foundation for this governance model. Tokens are not merely a currency or a speculative asset but are the keys to governance participation. By holding tokens, community members can vote on proposals that range from network upgrades to adjustments in staking rewards or changes in fee structures. This governance mechanism can take various forms:

- **Direct Voting:** Where each token holder votes on proposals directly, with voting power proportional to their stake. This model ensures that those with a significant investment in the network have a voice commensurate with their commitment, but it also poses challenges in ensuring broad participation and preventing centralization of influence.
- **Delegated Voting:** In this system, token holders can delegate their voting rights to others they trust or to elected representatives. This can help manage the complexity of governance for those less engaged or knowledgeable about technical proposals, potentially increasing participation while still reflecting community will.
- **Quadratic Voting:** To prevent the wealthy from dominating decisions, voting might be weighted in such a way that encourages diversity of opinion, where the cost of

additional votes increases, thus balancing influence among participants.
- **Time-Locked Voting:** Proposals might require votes to be locked for a certain period, ensuring that decisions are made with long-term network health in mind, reducing the influence of short-term speculation or market manipulation.

The economic policies that can be influenced by governance are vast and include:

- **Staking Rewards:** The community could vote on how much of the block rewards should go to validators, potentially adjusting these rewards based on network needs, inflation control, or to incentivize specific behaviors like network upgrades or security enhancements.
- **Token Supply Management:** Decisions on minting new tokens or burning existing ones could be made through governance, directly affecting inflation rates and token scarcity, which in turn influences value.
- **Transaction Fee Structures:** Adjustments to how fees are calculated, distributed, or even waived for certain types of transactions could be on the table, impacting both network usage and developer incentives.
- **Treasury Management:** How the community treasury is used, whether for funding development, marketing, or other initiatives like grants or hackathons, would be a significant governance decision, directly

affecting the economic health of the ecosystem.

- **Economic Incentives:** Proposals could include new or modified incentives for users, developers, or validators, aiming to enhance participation, security, or innovation within the ecosystem.
- **Interoperability Policies:** With the potential for cross-chain interactions, governance might dictate how Sui integrates with other blockchains economically, including token bridges, liquidity pools, or shared governance mechanisms.

The process of governance itself is an economic activity within Sui. The act of voting, proposing, or even staking for governance rights involves economic considerations. For instance, there might be costs associated with proposing changes, or rewards for participating in governance, which would be funded from the network's treasury or through transaction fees. This creates an economic loop where governance activities directly impact, and are impacted by, the platform's economic model.

However, this model also comes with challenges:

- **Voter Apathy:** Not all token holders might engage in governance, leading to decisions made by a minority. Sui's economic model would need to address this through incentives or by making governance participation as accessible and engaging as possible.

- **Centralization of Influence:** If token distribution becomes too concentrated, a few large holders could sway governance decisions, potentially leading to policies that favor their interests over the broader community's. Mechanisms like quadratic voting or time-locked voting could help mitigate this.
- **Complexity of Decisions:** Economic policies can be complex, requiring a level of understanding that not all community members possess. Sui would need to invest in educational resources or advisory bodies to ensure informed decision-making.
- **Decision-Making Speed:** While community governance ensures democracy, it can also slow down decision-making. Sui might need to balance this with mechanisms for urgent decisions or by empowering smaller, more agile governance bodies for specific issues.
- **Economic Attacks:** There's the risk of malicious actors using governance to push through economically detrimental proposals. Safeguards like multi-layered voting, veto powers, or emergency measures would be crucial.
- **Alignment with Network Health:** Economic policies should not just serve the immediate interests of token holders but also the long-term sustainability of the network. This might involve governance encouraging policies that might not be popular in the short term but are beneficial for future stability.

Community governance also influences token economics indirectly by fostering a culture of ownership and responsibility among token holders. When the community feels they have a stake in the network's success, they're more likely to engage in activities that enhance network value, like staking, using dApps, or even promoting Sui in real-world scenarios.

The sustainability of Sui's economic model, heavily influenced by governance, would rely on:

- **Adaptive Economic Policies:** As the blockchain ecosystem evolves, so too must Sui's economic policies. Governance allows for this adaptability, ensuring the network can respond to new technologies, market conditions, or community needs.
- **Balancing Short-term Gains with Long-term Health:** Governance decisions should aim to prevent short-term profit-taking at the expense of network stability or long-term growth.
- **Incentivizing Broad Participation:** Ensuring that governance is not just for the few but is accessible and rewarding for all token holders, perhaps through education, UI/UX improvements, or additional incentives for participation.
- **Transparency and Accountability:** All governance actions should be transparent, with clear outcomes and accountability mechanisms in place to maintain trust in the system.

- **Economic Education:** Educating the community about economic principles, the implications of governance decisions, and how they can contribute to or benefit from Sui's economic model.

Looking to the future, Sui's governance and token economics could evolve in several ways:

- **AI-Assisted Governance:** AI could analyze community sentiment, predict economic impacts of proposals, or even suggest optimizations, making decision-making more data-driven and potentially less contentious.
- **Hybrid Governance Models:** Combining on-chain governance with off-chain discussions or expert panels to enrich the decision-making process, ensuring technical proposals are well-understood and debated.
- **Cross-Chain Governance:** As interoperability grows, governance might extend to decisions affecting how Sui interacts with other blockchains, potentially leading to shared economic policies across ecosystems.
- **Decentralized Identity in Governance:** Integrating decentralized identity solutions could make voting more secure and verifiable, potentially influencing how governance rights are distributed or exercised.
- **Evolving Economic Models:** With community input, Sui could explore new economic models for tokens, like dynamic supply adjustments based on real-world economic indicators or integrating with real-world assets for stability.

Community governance in Sui is not just about making decisions but about shaping an economic model that reflects the community's collective vision for the platform. By intertwining governance with token economics, Sui aims to create a self-sustaining, resilient, and user-driven ecosystem where economic policies are not static but evolve with the community's needs and the broader blockchain landscape. This approach could lead to a more equitable distribution of power, foster innovation, and ensure that Sui remains relevant and valuable in the ever-changing world of blockchain technology.

Part 7: Economic Challenges and Solutions

Sui's economic model, designed to be innovative and sustainable, encounters various challenges intrinsic to the volatile and rapidly evolving blockchain sector. This part delves into these challenges, offering a deep exploration of potential solutions that could safeguard Sui's economic integrity, fairness, and facilitate long-term prosperity.

One of the foremost economic challenges for any blockchain, including Sui, is managing inflation and deflation. Without appropriate mechanisms, the token's value can either diminish through inflation or become too scarce, potentially obstructing liquidity or encouraging speculative bubbles. Sui could implement a dynamic supply management approach where the creation or destruction of tokens is based on specific metrics like network activity, validator performance, or community-driven governance decisions. This might involve adjusting the token supply algorithmically based on economic indicators within the network, such as transaction volume or staking rates, to maintain value stability. Governance could also play a role, allowing the community to vote on inflation rates or supply caps, ensuring that the token supply aligns with community needs and network health. Additionally, employing burning mechanisms, like using transaction fees to reduce circulating supply during times of high demand, could counteract inflation.

Another significant issue is the centralization of wealth, where a few entities might hold a disproportionate number of tokens, potentially leading to governance manipulation or market control. To mitigate this, Sui could employ token distribution strategies at launch and through ongoing incentives that aim for a wide distribution. This might include airdrops to active users, rewards for network participation beyond just holding tokens, or mechanisms that encourage token dispersal over time. Implementing governance models that limit the influence of large holders, such as quadratic voting or time-locked voting, can further prevent undue influence. Setting caps on staking rewards or diminishing returns for staking large volumes could also prevent wealth concentration among validators.

Market manipulation presents a constant threat in the cryptocurrency space. Sui's model must be designed to resist such attacks, potentially through economic safeguards like minimum holding periods before tokens can be used in governance or sold, deterring pump-and-dump schemes. Transparent reporting of token movements, staking, and governance actions can increase oversight by the community. Regular security audits of economic protocols would help identify and patch vulnerabilities that could be exploited for manipulation.

Economic downturns or market volatility can significantly impact token value, affecting the platform's usability and the incentives for participation. Sui could diversify the utility of its token within the ecosystem, from governance and staking to paying for transaction fees, creating a demand that's less dependent on speculative trading. Stabilization mechanisms like token pegging to stable assets or integrating with stablecoins for certain transactions could offer users stability, reducing the impact of broader market swings. Adaptive incentives, adjusting rewards based on market conditions, might maintain participation by increasing rewards when token value drops or reducing them when it spikes.

User engagement and adoption are vital for economic sustainability. If users do not perceive value in participating, the network can stagnate. Beyond financial rewards, Sui might offer non-monetary incentives like governance influence, community reputation, or access to exclusive features to drive engagement. Ensuring that interacting with the network, whether for staking, governance, or using dApps, is as intuitive as possible, will lower barriers for non-technical users. Investing in community initiatives, education, and support can foster a sense of belonging and investment in the platform's success.

Regulatory compliance poses another economic challenge, with blockchain projects needing to navigate a complex web of global regulations. Sui could develop or integrate compliance tools that allow adherence to regulations like KYC/AML without sacrificing its decentralized nature, possibly through privacy-preserving identity solutions. Governance structures should be adaptable to respond to regulatory changes, perhaps by allowing the community to decide on compliance strategies or by having provisions for regulatory adjustments within smart contracts. Engaging in or supporting legal advocacy for blockchain-friendly legislation could offer a proactive approach to these challenges.

Scalability and performance are economic issues because they directly affect transaction costs and user experience. Implementing or supporting layer 2 scaling solutions could manage high-throughput transactions at lower costs, ensuring that as the network grows, it remains accessible. Continuous optimization of the consensus mechanism for speed and cost-efficiency would keep Sui competitive. Designing economic models that incentivize efficient use of network resources, perhaps through dynamic fee structures that adjust based on network load, would also be beneficial.

The environmental impact of blockchain operations has become a significant concern, affecting the sustainability of the economic model. Sui's DPoS offers an advantage in energy efficiency compared to PoW, but further optimizations or incentives for green practices by validators could be considered. Dedicating a portion of transaction fees or network rewards to environmental initiatives could turn network activity into a positive environmental impact. Encouraging or rewarding dApps designed with sustainability in mind might foster an eco-conscious community.

Lastly, ensuring long-term economic health involves planning for technological evolution. Sui could provide economic incentives for developers to explore new technologies or economic models beneficial to the platform, like new consensus algorithms or privacy technologies. Investing in or supporting research into blockchain economics would ensure that Sui's model can adapt to or lead new trends in the space. Governance should be structured to anticipate and prepare for technological shifts, allowing the community to decide on integration with new technologies or economic models.

Addressing these challenges requires a holistic strategy:

- Educating the community to make informed decisions, support network initiatives, and preemptively identify economic issues.
- Viewing the economic model as an evolving entity, with regular reviews and updates based on performance, user feedback, and external economic conditions.

- Balancing innovation with stability to ensure that new features or economic policies do not destabilize the platform.
- Maintaining transparent communication to build trust and engagement, turning potential issues into opportunities for collective problem-solving.

Sui's economic model faces a complex array of challenges that demand nuanced solutions. By addressing inflation, centralization, market manipulation, regulatory compliance, user engagement, scalability, environmental concerns, and technological evolution through community governance, strategic economic policies, and innovative incentives, Sui can strive for a sustainable economic model. This approach would not only support the platform's growth and stability but also set a benchmark for how blockchain economies can be managed to benefit all participants, fostering a vibrant, inclusive, and enduring ecosystem.

Part 8: Sustainability Through Innovation

Sustainability in Sui's economic model isn't just about maintaining the status quo; it's about leveraging innovation to ensure the ecosystem's vitality and relevance over time. This part explores how Sui can sustain its economic health by continuously innovating in tokenomics, financial instruments, and broader ecosystem development, ensuring that the platform remains dynamic, user-centric, and capable of adapting to future challenges.

Innovation in tokenomics is pivotal for Sui's sustainability. The token's utility and economic model need to evolve with user needs, technological advancements, and market conditions. Here's how Sui might approach this:

Sui could introduce new token functionalities or uses that go beyond simple transaction fees or governance. For instance, tokens could be used to access specialized services within the ecosystem, like premium dApps, enhanced security features, or even as collateral in more sophisticated DeFi products. This expansion of utility not only increases demand for the token but also ties its value more closely to the actual performance and adoption of the network.

One innovative approach could be dynamic token supply adjustments. Instead of a fixed inflation or deflation rate, Sui might implement a model where token supply adjusts based on real-time network metrics. For example, during periods of high demand or when the network is growing rapidly, new tokens might be minted to keep fees low and incentivize participation. Conversely, in times of low network activity, fewer tokens or even token burning could occur to maintain value. This adaptive supply could be governed by smart contracts that react to predefined conditions, ensuring economic policies reflect current network health without requiring constant human intervention.

Another avenue for innovation is in staking mechanisms. Sui could explore staking derivatives or fractional staking, where users don't need to stake full tokens but can participate with smaller amounts or through pooled staking. This could democratize access to staking rewards and governance, making them available to a broader range of participants. Such innovations could also include time-locked staking for different durations, offering varied reward structures that cater to different user preferences or investment strategies, balancing short-term liquidity with long-term network commitment.

In the realm of decentralized finance (DeFi), Sui has the potential to pioneer new financial instruments or models. Here, the platform could:

- **Develop Unique DeFi Products:** Sui might introduce new types of loans, collateral mechanisms, or yield farming strategies that leverage its object-centric model or the safety features of the Move programming language. These could include cross-chain lending where assets from different blockchains serve as collateral, or innovative yield strategies that are more secure and efficient due to Sui's architecture.
- **Interoperable Financial Tools:** By facilitating interoperability, Sui could create financial products that operate across multiple blockchains, enhancing liquidity and utility. This might involve creating decentralized stablecoins that maintain value across different networks or insurance products that protect against cross-chain risks.
- **Tokenized Real-World Assets:** Sui could explore tokenizing real-world assets on its

platform, offering a bridge between traditional finance and blockchain. This could lead to new economic models where tokens represent ownership in real assets, from real estate to art, providing stability to the token's value by linking it to tangible assets.

In terms of ecosystem development, sustainability through innovation would involve:

Supporting the creation of dApps that not only leverage Sui's technical capabilities but also bring economic innovation. This could mean incentivizing dApps that introduce new economic models, like subscription-based services on blockchain, decentralized betting platforms with unique reward systems, or cultural platforms where artists earn through novel royalty mechanisms. By fostering such applications, Sui can ensure its token remains integral to economic activities on the platform.

Sui could also innovate in how it funds and supports development. Beyond traditional grants, it might employ a decentralized venture fund model where the community can vote on which projects to back, with transparency and accountability built into the process. This could involve token-based voting or even community DAOs that manage these funds, ensuring that investment in innovation aligns with collective goals.

The platform's approach to governance itself can be an area for economic innovation. Sui might develop:

- **Liquid Democracy:** Allowing token holders not just to vote directly but also to delegate their voting rights dynamically, potentially increasing engagement and ensuring expertise influences decisions when needed.
- **Governance Mining:** Rewarding users for participating in governance with additional tokens or other forms of incentives, much like liquidity mining but for governance activities, fostering a culture of active participation.
- **Decentralized Autonomous Government (DAG):** Creating governance structures that operate autonomously based on pre-set rules, reducing the need for constant human input while still allowing for changes through community consensus.

In the area of privacy and security, innovations could lead to economic benefits by:

- **Privacy-Preserving Transactions:** Implementing technologies like zero-knowledge proofs for transactions or governance, allowing for privacy without compromising the network's transparency and security, potentially attracting users from privacy-conscious sectors.
- **Security Token Offerings (STOs):** Offering a platform for secure, compliant token issuances of real-world assets, which could be a new revenue stream for Sui while expanding its economic utility.

The sustainability of Sui's economic model also hinges on its ability to adapt to regulatory environments. Here, innovation could involve:

- **Regulatory Compliance Tools:** Developing smart contract-based compliance solutions that allow dApps or businesses on Sui to meet legal requirements in various jurisdictions without centralizing control, perhaps through decentralized KYC/AML processes.
- **Regulatory Prediction Markets:** Where the community can speculate on regulatory changes, providing insights that could guide Sui's strategic direction or how it adjusts its economic model to comply with emerging laws.

Innovation in economic education is another path to sustainability. Sui could:

- **Launch Educational Ecosystems:** Where developers, users, and even regulators learn about blockchain economics, potentially through interactive dApps or educational platforms built on Sui.
- **Community-Driven Learning:** Encouraging an environment where knowledge sharing is rewarded, perhaps through token incentives for creating or contributing to educational content.

Finally, environmental sustainability could be woven into the economic model:

- **Green Staking:** Offering incentives for validators who operate on renewable energy or have a low carbon footprint, aligning economic incentives with environmental goals.
- **Carbon Credit Markets:** Sui might facilitate or host decentralized markets for carbon credits, using blockchain to ensure transparency and efficiency, thereby contributing to global sustainability efforts while providing a new use case for its token.

The challenges to this innovation-driven approach to sustainability are manifold:

- **Balancing Innovation with Stability:** Every new feature or economic model must be introduced with caution to avoid destabilizing the existing ecosystem. This requires rigorous testing, community buy-in, and perhaps a phased introduction where new economic models can be piloted on a smaller scale before full implementation.
- **Security and Scalability:** With new financial instruments or governance models, Sui must ensure that these innovations do not introduce vulnerabilities or scalability issues that could be exploited or lead to network congestion.
- **User Adoption:** Innovations are only sustainable if they're adopted. Sui will need to focus on user experience, ensuring that new economic models are accessible and understandable, not just to tech-savvy users but to the broader audience.

- **Regulatory Navigation:** As Sui innovates, it must also navigate an evolving regulatory landscape, ensuring that new economic models or financial products don't inadvertently step outside legal boundaries.
- **Community Consensus:** Many of these innovations will require community agreement through governance, meaning Sui must maintain a vibrant, engaged community that's willing to explore and support new economic paradigms.

Looking forward, the future of Sui's economic sustainability through innovation might look like:

- **AI-Driven Economic Models:** Employing AI to analyze network data, predict economic trends, or even suggest optimizations in real-time, ensuring the economy reacts efficiently to changes.
- **Cross-Chain Economic Integration:** As blockchain ecosystems become more interconnected, Sui could lead in creating economic models that span multiple chains, offering unprecedented interoperability in finance.
- **Token Evolution:** Future iterations of Sui's token might include programmable tokens with dynamic properties, adapting to user behaviors or market conditions automatically.
- **Sustainable Economic Incentives:** Designing incentives that not only drive network participation but also contribute to

broader societal goals like sustainability or digital inclusion.

Sustainability through innovation for Sui's economic model involves a continuous cycle of invention, implementation, and iteration. By expanding the utility of its token, pioneering new financial instruments, fostering a diverse dApp ecosystem, innovating in governance, enhancing privacy and security, adapting to regulatory changes, and promoting economic education and environmental consciousness, Sui can secure its economic model's longevity. However, this path requires a delicate balance between pushing boundaries and maintaining the core values of decentralization, security, and utility that make blockchain technology compelling. Through this innovative approach, Sui can aspire to not just sustain but thrive in an ever-evolving digital economy.

Part 9: Regulatory Considerations

Sui's economic model, while ambitious and forward-thinking, must navigate the complex and often contradictory landscape of global financial regulations. This part explores how Sui can address regulatory challenges to ensure compliance, protect users, and maintain its decentralized ethos, while also considering how it might influence or adapt to regulatory evolution.

The blockchain space, including Sui, operates in a regulatory gray area where laws have not fully caught up with technology. However, as blockchain applications, especially those involving finance, become more mainstream, regulatory scrutiny increases. Sui's approach to these challenges involves a multi-faceted strategy.

Firstly, understanding and complying with existing regulations in major markets is paramount. This entails engaging with legal experts specializing in blockchain and cryptocurrency to interpret how laws like anti-money laundering (AML), know your customer (KYC), securities regulations, and data protection acts apply to Sui's operations. It's not merely about avoiding legal pitfalls but about designing the platform to be inherently compliant where possible. Developing or integrating tools that facilitate compliance without centralizing control is crucial. This could mean creating or supporting dApps for decentralized identity verification, using technologies like zero-knowledge proofs to verify identities without compromising privacy. These tools would need to be flexible to adapt to different regulatory requirements across jurisdictions. Additionally, Sui might implement transaction monitoring and reporting capabilities that can be adjusted based on the legal requirements of different regions, ensuring compliance while respecting the decentralized nature of the blockchain.

Secondly, Sui could advocate for regulatory clarity or even help shape blockchain-friendly policies. This involves engaging in dialogues with regulators, either directly or through industry groups, to educate them on blockchain technology's benefits and challenges. By participating in these discussions, Sui can help craft regulations that foster a secure, compliant environment without stifling innovation. Supporting or initiating pilot programs with regulators where new financial products or models can be tested in a controlled, regulated environment not only aids in compliance but also in proving the utility and safety of blockchain applications to regulators. Leveraging the community's collective voice through governance to push for regulatory change or adapt operations in anticipation of new laws can lead to a nuanced compliance strategy that reflects community values and needs.

Protecting users from regulatory risks is another pillar of Sui's strategy. This includes educating users on the regulatory implications of using Sui, particularly regarding taxation, privacy rights, and the legal status of digital assets in their jurisdiction. This education could be integrated into the onboarding process or governance discussions, ensuring users are informed participants. Offering tools or services that help users manage their regulatory obligations, like automated tax reporting for transactions on Sui or guidance on local law compliance, is vital. Ensuring user data privacy is paramount, even when compliance requires data sharing. Sui might use advanced cryptographic techniques to share only necessary data or maintain user anonymity.

Sui must also consider the economic implications of regulatory compliance. This involves designing economic models where compliance does not become a cost barrier for users or developers. For example, identity verification should be cost-effective and seamlessly integrated into the user experience.

Balancing liquidity and accessibility with compliance requirements might mean adjusting staking or governance models to account for regulatory restrictions in certain areas, perhaps by offering localized versions of these functions. Innovating in how revenue is generated or distributed within the ecosystem can accommodate different regulatory environments, particularly in regions with strict securities laws where token issuance or usage might need adjustment.

The challenge of maintaining decentralization while ensuring regulatory compliance is significant. Sui aims to achieve this balance by potentially introducing decentralized compliance officers or community roles that oversee adherence to legal standards without centralizing control. Creating governance mechanisms for a rapid response to regulatory changes could involve having predefined rules in governance smart contracts that activate different compliance protocols based on regulatory signals or community votes. Developing a modular economic system where parts can be altered or switched out to meet varying regulatory requirements ensures that compliance does not compromise the core principles or functionality of Sui.

As blockchain and DeFi continue to evolve, so too will the regulatory landscape. Sui must be prepared to adapt its economic model to new regulatory frameworks, whether that means changing how tokens are minted, how staking works, or how transactions are processed and reported. Anticipating regulatory trends, like the push for sustainability or privacy, and integrating these considerations into the platform's economic design could position Sui as a leader in regulatory compliance and innovation. Considering the potential for regulatory divergence or convergence across countries, Sui might need to support multiple economic models or compliance pathways to operate seamlessly in different regulatory environments.

Looking forward, Sui's role in the regulatory discourse could be transformative. By pioneering compliant yet decentralized solutions, Sui can set precedents or standards that other blockchains might follow, potentially leading to a more harmonized regulatory approach to blockchain technologies globally. If Sui can demonstrate the benefits of blockchain in terms of transparency, security, and efficiency to regulators, it might help shift regulatory focus towards enabling technology rather than restrictive control. As regulations evolve to recognize new forms of digital asset ownership or decentralized finance, Sui could be at the forefront of adapting its economic model to fit these new legal frameworks, perhaps even influencing how digital assets are classified or treated in law.

The challenges are not insignificant. Navigating the conflicting regulations of different jurisdictions while trying to maintain a unified economic model will be complex. Sui might need to implement region-specific features or compliance layers. Keeping up with the pace of regulatory change requires a responsive and adaptive governance model, where decisions can be made quickly without undermining community trust or platform stability. Balancing privacy with compliance will be an ongoing challenge, especially as privacy laws like GDPR clash with blockchains' transparency ethos. There's the risk that over-compliance could lead to centralization or stifle innovation, so Sui must find a balance where compliance enhances rather than detracts from the platform's decentralized nature.

Sui's approach to regulatory considerations is not just about legal compliance but about integrating regulatory foresight into its economic model. By doing so, Sui can ensure that its platform is not only sustainable but also a pioneer in demonstrating how blockchain can work within regulated environments. This involves understanding and adapting to current laws, educating and protecting users, innovating in compliance technology, and actively participating in shaping future regulations. Through this balanced approach, Sui can maintain its vision of decentralization while becoming a model for how blockchain platforms can thrive in a world of increasing regulatory scrutiny.

Part 10: Future Economic Evolution

The economic model of Sui is not a static construct; it must evolve alongside the dynamic landscape of blockchain technology, user expectations, and global economic shifts. This concluding part speculates on how Sui's economic model might adapt and innovate in the future, considering the fluid nature of technology, finance, and regulatory environments.

One probable direction for Sui's token is an expansion of its utility beyond its current roles in transaction fees, staking, and governance. As the blockchain ecosystem matures, tokens could become more versatile, potentially representing or interacting with real-world assets, from commodities to intellectual property, thus expanding Sui's economic footprint into traditional markets. Future iterations of the token might include programmable features, allowing for tokens with dynamic behaviors based on external data or conditions, like smart contracts that adjust token supply or utility based on economic indicators or community decisions. With increasing blockchain interoperability, Sui's token could serve as a bridge asset or be used in cross-chain transactions or governance, enhancing its value by facilitating interactions across different blockchain ecosystems.

Sui's economic model might need to adapt to new economic paradigms emerging within the blockchain space. As Decentralized Autonomous Organizations (DAOs) become more sophisticated, Sui could support or host DAOs with their own economic models, perhaps even integrating with the platform's governance token to create a more complex, layered economic system. Innovations in Decentralized Finance (DeFi) could see Sui pioneering or adopting new models that leverage its unique architecture, including more secure lending protocols, insurance mechanisms, or decentralized exchanges that minimize slippage or improve liquidity through novel economic incentives. Future incentive structures might evolve to reward not just staking or liquidity provision but also contributions to network security, data oracles, or community governance in more nuanced ways.

As environmental concerns become more pronounced in the crypto space, Sui's economic model could emphasize sustainability. This might include green incentives where validators or users with eco-friendly practices receive enhanced rewards or priority in certain network activities. Sui could aim for a carbon-neutral blockchain by integrating mechanisms to offset its carbon footprint, perhaps through a portion of transaction fees or by supporting green projects, effectively making its economic activities contribute to environmental sustainability.

The regulatory landscape will continue to evolve, and Sui's economic model must be agile enough to respond. Economic features could be designed with compliance in mind from the outset, perhaps through smart contracts that automatically adjust to regulatory changes or by supporting privacy-preserving compliance tools. Sui might strategically position itself to take advantage of regulatory differences across jurisdictions, providing services or token utilities that are uniquely compliant or beneficial in certain regions.

The integration of AI and machine learning could revolutionize Sui's economic model by enabling dynamic economic adjustments. AI could analyze network data to suggest or automatically adjust economic policies like staking rewards or token supply to optimize for network health or user engagement. Predictive governance powered by AI could assist in forecasting the outcomes of governance proposals, helping the community make more informed decisions that align with long-term economic sustainability.

Community-driven governance is likely to become more sophisticated. Sui might introduce multi-tier governance where different economic decisions are handled at different levels, from immediate operational adjustments to long-term strategic planning. Governance tokens could have variable influence based on factors like time held, participation in network activities, or even external economic conditions, aiming to balance influence among participants. Enhancing security and fairness in governance by integrating decentralized identity solutions could ensure a system where voting power is more equitably distributed.

As blockchain becomes more integrated with traditional finance, Sui could support the tokenization of securities, providing a platform for digital asset management that complies with securities laws, thereby bridging blockchain with traditional financial instruments. Exploring or integrating with stablecoins or developing mechanisms for token pegging to fiat could provide economic stability and attract users who prefer less volatility.

This evolution comes with its set of challenges. Balancing speed with security as economic models grow more complex will be crucial to avoid introducing new vulnerabilities or slowing down transactions. Educating users on how to navigate or benefit from these changes becomes imperative as economic interactions become more complex. Ensuring that economic incentives do not lead to unintended consequences like wealth concentration or environmental harm requires careful design and ongoing review. There's always the risk of centralization as economic models become more efficient or complex, which Sui must guard against through its governance and economic design.

Looking far ahead, Sui's economic model could be at the forefront of how decentralized economies interact with the real world. It might evolve into a platform where digital and traditional economies converge, offering a new form of economic interaction that's transparent, secure, and inclusive. Economic models could directly support social or environmental goals, using tokenomics to fund or incentivize positive real-world impacts. A future where AI not only supports but drives economic decisions could create a self-regulating, adaptive economic system within Sui's ecosystem.

In conclusion, the future economic evolution of Sui will likely be characterized by a blend of technological innovation, strategic regulatory compliance, community empowerment, and a commitment to sustainability. As Sui navigates these changes, it must maintain its core principles of decentralization, security, and user empowerment, ensuring that its economic model not only supports the platform's operations but also contributes to a broader vision of what decentralized finance and governance can achieve. The journey will involve continuous adaptation, learning from both successes and challenges, to create an economic model that's resilient, inclusive, and forward-looking.

Chapter 18: Case Studies: Real-World Applications of Sui

Part 1: Introduction to Sui's Impactful Use Cases

In the ever-expanding universe of blockchain technology, where theoretical possibilities often overshadow practical implementations, the real-world applications of a platform like Sui serve as a vital bridge between innovation and utility. This chapter embarks on an exploration of how Sui, with its unique architectural advantages, is not just a theoretical marvel but a practical tool reshaping industries and communities. The case studies we will delve into are not merely illustrative; they are testaments to Sui's potential to transform how we interact with digital systems, manage assets, and engage with one another in a decentralized world.

Sui stands out in the blockchain landscape due to its exceptional design, which prioritizes speed, security, and scalability. These attributes are not just buzzwords but foundational elements that enable Sui to address real-world challenges in ways that traditional blockchains often struggle to achieve. The platform's use of the Move programming language, its object-centric data model, and its parallel execution capabilities create a robust environment where developers can build applications that are both efficient and secure. This introduction sets the stage for understanding why Sui is uniquely positioned to make a tangible impact across various sectors.

The significance of case studies in this context cannot be overstated. They provide concrete evidence of how Sui's theoretical advantages translate into practical benefits. By examining specific instances where Sui has been applied, we can move beyond abstract discussions of blockchain potential and into the realm of measurable outcomes. These case studies serve as a lens through which we can evaluate Sui's effectiveness, identify its strengths, and understand its limitations, offering valuable insights for developers, businesses, and communities considering its adoption.

Sui's speed is one of its most compelling features, driven by its ability to process transactions in parallel rather than sequentially. This capability allows for high throughput and low latency, making Sui an ideal platform for applications that require real-time interactions. Whether it's a gaming platform where players expect instant responses, a financial system that demands rapid settlements, or a supply chain network that needs timely updates, Sui's performance metrics enable solutions that were previously constrained by the slower processing times of traditional blockchains.

Security is another pillar of Sui's appeal. With its delegated proof-of-stake (DPoS) consensus mechanism and the inherent safety features of the Move language, Sui provides a secure environment for managing digital assets and executing smart contracts. This security is crucial in real-world applications where trust is paramount, such as financial transactions, identity management, or the authentication of valuable goods. By ensuring that assets and data are protected against common vulnerabilities, Sui builds a foundation of trust that is essential for widespread adoption.

Scalability completes the trio of Sui's core strengths. As blockchain applications grow in complexity and user base, the ability to scale without compromising performance or security becomes critical. Sui's architecture is designed to handle increasing transaction volumes and more intricate use cases, making it a viable platform for enterprises and communities looking to expand their digital operations. This scalability is evident in the case studies we will explore, where Sui supports applications with diverse and growing demands.

The diversity of applications that can be built on Sui is a key theme of this chapter. From gaming to finance, supply chain management to digital identity, and cultural initiatives to social governance, Sui's versatility allows it to address a wide range of needs. Each case study will highlight a different facet of Sui's capabilities, demonstrating how its features can be tailored to solve specific problems and create value in various contexts.

In the gaming industry, for instance, Sui's speed and scalability enable developers to create immersive, interactive experiences where in-game assets are securely owned and traded as NFTs. The ability to process transactions quickly ensures that gameplay is seamless, while the object-centric model allows for complex asset management, enhancing the player experience and opening new economic opportunities within virtual worlds.

In the financial sector, particularly in decentralized finance (DeFi), Sui's low latency and high throughput support real-time trading, lending, and other financial services that require immediate execution. The security provided by Move and the consensus mechanism ensures that these financial instruments are protected against exploits, while the platform's scalability allows it to handle the growing volume of transactions typical of DeFi ecosystems.

Supply chain management is another area where Sui's capabilities shine. The need for transparency, traceability, and efficiency in supply chains is met with Sui's ability to record and validate transactions rapidly and securely. This enables companies to track goods from origin to consumer, reducing fraud, ensuring authenticity, and enhancing trust, all while leveraging Sui's parallel execution to manage the complexity of modern supply networks.

Digital identity and access control represent a more personal application of Sui's technology. In an era where privacy and security are increasingly valued, Sui offers solutions for managing digital identities in a way that empowers users while protecting their data. The platform's privacy mechanisms and smart contract capabilities allow for secure, verifiable identity systems that can be used in voting, access management, or other sensitive applications.

Finally, the cultural and social impact of Sui is evident in its support for art, collectibles, and community-driven initiatives. By providing a secure and scalable platform for NFTs and decentralized autonomous organizations (DAOs), Sui enables creators, collectors, and communities to engage in new ways. This not only fosters cultural innovation but also demonstrates how blockchain can empower social structures and collective governance.

The case studies in this chapter are not just success stories; they are also learning opportunities. Each example will include an analysis of the outcomes, reflecting on what worked, what challenges were encountered, and how these experiences can inform future developments on Sui. This reflective approach ensures that the lessons learned are shared, benefiting the broader Sui community and the blockchain industry as a whole.

Moreover, these case studies highlight the adaptability of Sui's technology. Whether addressing the fast-paced needs of gaming, the precision required in finance, the transparency demanded in supply chains, the privacy needed for identity management, or the creativity unleashed in cultural applications, Sui's flexibility allows it to meet diverse requirements. This adaptability is a testament to the thoughtful design of its architecture and the foresight of its creators.

The real-world implications of these applications extend beyond their immediate use cases. They demonstrate how Sui can drive economic growth, enhance user trust, and foster community engagement in ways that traditional systems often cannot. By solving practical problems with blockchain technology, Sui positions itself as a leader in the transition to a more decentralized, efficient, and inclusive digital future.

As we proceed through this chapter, the case studies will serve as a window into Sui's impact, offering a mix of inspiration and practical guidance. They will illustrate not only what Sui can do today but also what it might achieve tomorrow, as developers and communities continue to explore its potential. This exploration is not just about technology; it's about the people, businesses, and societies that benefit from it, showing how Sui can be a catalyst for change across multiple domains.

In conclusion, this introduction to Sui's impactful use cases sets high expectations for the detailed examples that follow. It underscores the importance of understanding Sui not just as a blockchain platform but as a transformative force with real-world applications that touch lives, industries, and cultures. Through these case studies, we will see how Sui's unique advantages in speed, security, and scalability are not just theoretical but are actively shaping the future of decentralized technology.

Part 2: Sui in Gaming: Revolutionizing Digital Assets and Gameplay

The gaming industry, with its vast audience and the inherent need for secure, transparent, and interactive digital economies, presents one of the most exciting arenas for blockchain application. Sui, with its distinctive features, is poised to revolutionize this sector by enhancing gameplay mechanics, securing digital asset ownership, and facilitating seamless cross-platform play. Here, we delve into specific case studies that illustrate how Sui is being leveraged in the gaming world.

Case Study 1: GameFi on Sui - "SuiPlay"

"SuiPlay" stands as a pioneering example of GameFi (Game Finance) on the Sui blockchain. This platform combines traditional gaming with blockchain technology, allowing players to earn real value from their in-game achievements. Sui's high transaction throughput and low latency ensure that players experience near-instantaneous rewards, crucial for maintaining engagement in fast-paced gaming environments.

- **Digital Asset Ownership:** Through Sui's object-centric model, every in-game item, from weapons to characters, is treated as a unique object with its own lifecycle, ownership, and transferability. This means players truly own their digital assets, which can be traded securely outside the game's ecosystem.
- **Seamless Gameplay:** "SuiPlay" benefits from Sui's parallel execution, enabling simultaneous processing of many game actions without lag, creating a smoother gameplay experience even during peak usage times.

- **Interoperability:** The game leverages Sui's potential for cross-chain interactions, allowing assets to move between different games or platforms, enhancing the utility and value of in-game items.

Case Study 2: NFT-based Gaming - "Mythic Realms"

"Mythic Realms" is an MMORPG (Massively Multiplayer Online Role-Playing Game) where NFTs (Non-Fungible Tokens) represent unique characters, lands, and artifacts. Sui's blockchain ensures these digital collectibles are not just tradable but also evolve based on player actions or game events, thanks to Sui's object-centric approach.

- **Evolving NFTs:** In "Mythic Realms", NFTs can gain experience, level up, or change attributes, which are all managed through Sui's smart contracts. This feature adds depth to the gameplay, where the history and evolution of an NFT become part of its value.
- **Security and Scarcity:** With Sui's security, players trust that their rare or unique NFTs are protected against duplication or unauthorized changes. This scarcity drives the game's economy, where players can invest in and benefit from their virtual possessions.
- **Community Governance:** Players can vote on game updates or new features using their staked NFTs, leveraging Sui's governance model. This gives the community a direct

influence on the game's direction, fostering a more engaged player base.

Case Study 3: Cross-Platform Integration - "Universal Arena"

"Universal Arena" demonstrates how Sui can serve as a backbone for cross-platform gaming, where players from different gaming ecosystems can compete or collaborate without barriers.

- **Unified Gaming Experience:** By using Sui, "Universal Arena" creates a platform where games from different developers can interact, with player achievements, assets, or even progress being recognized across various games, enhancing player retention and satisfaction.
- **Real-Time Battles:** Sui's speed allows for real-time, cross-platform battles where latency does not hinder the gameplay, providing a competitive edge in esports and multiplayer games.
- **Asset Management:** Players can manage their assets across different games through Sui's blockchain, ensuring they maintain control over their digital possessions, which can be used or upgraded in various game settings.

Challenges and Future Directions:

While these case studies highlight the successful integration of Sui into gaming, challenges do exist.

Scalability during massive player events, ensuring fair play with blockchain verification, and user education on managing digital assets are areas of focus.

- **Scalability:** As games grow in popularity, maintaining performance without compromising security or user experience requires continuous optimization of Sui's infrastructure.
- **Fair Play:** Ensuring that the blockchain's transparency doesn't lead to cheating or exploitation in games requires innovative game design and robust smart contract logic.
- **User Education:** Making blockchain gaming accessible means simplifying the interaction with blockchain for non-tech-savvy players, perhaps through intuitive interfaces or automated asset management systems.

The future of gaming on Sui looks towards even more immersive experiences where the line between gaming and reality blurs, thanks to AR/VR integration, more dynamic NFT interactions, and the potential for player-driven game economies to affect real-world markets. Sui's ongoing development in parallel execution and smart contract capabilities will continue to push the boundaries of what's possible in gaming, offering a glimpse into a future where games are not just played but lived.

In summary, through these case studies, we see how Sui is not just enhancing gaming but redefining it. From securing digital ownership to enabling new forms of gameplay and economic interaction, Sui's impact on gaming is a testament to blockchain's potential to create engaging, valuable, and community-driven digital worlds.

Part 3: Financial Applications: DeFi and Beyond

The financial sector, with its need for speed, security, and trust, has been one of the earliest adopters of blockchain technology. Sui, with its unique attributes, is carving out a significant space in this domain, particularly within decentralized finance (DeFi). This section explores how Sui's capabilities are being leveraged for financial applications, showcasing case studies that illustrate the platform's impact on traditional finance, DeFi, and innovative financial instruments.

Case Study 1: Decentralized Lending Platform - "SuiLend"

"SuiLend" stands as a prime example of how Sui can revolutionize lending by introducing a decentralized, fast, and secure lending platform.

- **Speed and Efficiency:** Sui's ability to process transactions in parallel allows "SuiLend" to handle loan requests and repayments with unprecedented speed, reducing the time from application to approval to mere seconds, enhancing user experience and operational efficiency.
- **Security in Asset Management:** Utilizing Sui's object-centric model, assets used as collateral or for lending are managed with high

precision. This ensures that the lending process is secure, with smart contracts enforcing the rules of lending, borrowing, and liquidation without intermediary intervention.

- **Low Latency for Real-Time Finance:** The platform benefits from Sui's instant finality, meaning that once a loan transaction is processed, it's considered final immediately, minimizing the risk of disputes or delays in fund movements.

Case Study 2: Decentralized Exchange (DEX) - "SuiSwap"

"SuiSwap" exemplifies how Sui can support trading platforms that operate without a central authority, offering users greater control over their assets and trading strategies.

- **High Throughput for Trading:** With Sui's high transaction capacity, "SuiSwap" can manage a large volume of trades simultaneously, ensuring that even during market spikes, the platform remains responsive, providing a competitive edge in terms of speed over centralized exchanges.
- **Innovative Financial Instruments:** The platform introduces complex financial instruments like options, futures, and perpetual swaps, all managed through Sui's smart contracts. This is made possible by the platform's ability to handle complex state changes with security and efficiency.

- **Cross-Chain Liquidity:** Leveraging Sui's potential for interoperability, "SuiSwap" can aggregate liquidity from different blockchains, enhancing the trading experience with more options and better prices for users.

Case Study 3: Novel Financial Instruments - "SuiFin"

"SuiFin" pushes the boundaries of what's possible with blockchain in finance by introducing new types of financial products that benefit from Sui's architecture.

- **Dynamic Asset-Backed Securities:** Here, traditional securities like real estate or commodities are tokenized on Sui, allowing for fractional ownership and trading. The object-centric model of Sui ensures each tokenized asset maintains its unique characteristics, including how it evolves or matures over time.
- **Decentralized Insurance:** "SuiFin" uses Sui's smart contracts to automate insurance policies where payouts are triggered by verifiable on-chain or off-chain events, offering transparency and reducing fraud.
- **Prediction Markets:** By leveraging fast transaction processing and secure state management, "SuiFin" can run prediction markets where participants can bet on the outcome of future events with quick resolution and settlement due to Sui's performance.

Challenges and Future Directions:

The adoption of Sui in financial applications isn't without its hurdles:

- **Regulatory Compliance:** As DeFi grows, navigating the complex web of international finance regulations while maintaining the decentralized ethos of blockchain is challenging. Sui applications must adapt to ensure compliance without losing their core advantages.
- **User Trust and Education:** For widespread adoption, users need to trust the security of their funds on decentralized platforms. Education on how to use these platforms safely is paramount.
- **Scalability and Stability:** Financial applications often require handling high volumes during market volatility. Ensuring that Sui can scale and remain stable under such conditions is crucial.

Looking forward, the integration of Sui in finance could lead to:

- **AI-Driven Financial Services:** Utilizing AI for risk assessment, automated trading strategies, or personalized financial advice within the Sui ecosystem, all underpinned by secure, transparent, and efficient blockchain operations.
- **Integration with Traditional Finance:** Creating bridges between DeFi and traditional finance, allowing for more seamless interaction

between the two, potentially revolutionizing how financial services are offered.

- **Enhanced Privacy Features:** As financial privacy becomes increasingly valued, Sui might see more applications using advanced privacy technologies for secure, confidential transactions.

In conclusion, these case studies of Sui in financial applications showcase the blockchain's ability to not just replicate but enhance and innovate upon traditional financial services. Sui's speed, security, and scalability are not just technical feats but enablers of new financial paradigms where efficiency, accessibility, and user control are at the forefront. As the financial world continues to evolve, Sui stands ready to be a foundational technology in this transformation, potentially leading to a future where decentralized finance is not the alternative but the norm.

Part 4: Supply Chain Management and Traceability

In the realm of supply chain management, transparency, efficiency, and trust are paramount, yet often challenged by complex logistics, multiple intermediaries, and the risk of fraud or error. Sui, with its advanced blockchain capabilities, offers solutions that can transform these traditional challenges into opportunities for enhanced traceability, security, and operational efficiency. This section explores how Sui is being applied in real-world supply chain scenarios through case studies that highlight its impact.

Case Study 1: Transparent Origin Tracking - "SuiTrack"

"SuiTrack" is a platform designed to provide end-to-end visibility in the supply chain, particularly in industries like agriculture, pharmaceuticals, and luxury goods where provenance is crucial.

- **Immutable Records:** Using Sui's blockchain, every step of a product's journey from production to retail is recorded immutably. This ensures that consumers and regulators can verify the origin, authenticity, and journey of products, significantly reducing the risk of counterfeit goods.
- **Real-Time Updates:** Thanks to Sui's parallel execution, "SuiTrack" can update the status of goods in real-time across the supply chain, allowing for immediate response to issues like delays or spoilage, thereby optimizing logistics.
- **Smart Contract Automation:** Smart contracts on Sui automate various checkpoints in the supply chain, from quality checks to customs clearance, reducing manual errors and speeding up processes.

Case Study 2: Food Safety and Traceability - "SuiFood"

"SuiFood" leverages Sui's blockchain for food safety, focusing on tracking food from farm to fork to ensure safety, quality, and compliance with health regulations.

- **Food Safety Compliance:** Each transaction or state change related to food products is logged on Sui, providing a verifiable history that can be audited for compliance with food safety standards.
- **Recall Efficiency:** In the event of a recall, "SuiFood" can quickly trace back through the supply chain to identify affected batches, minimizing health risks and economic impact by isolating only the necessary products.
- **Consumer Trust:** By allowing consumers to scan a product to see its journey, "SuiFood" builds trust, as people can verify claims about organic, non-GMO, or fair-trade certifications.

Case Study 3: Luxury Goods Authentication - "SuiLux"

"SuiLux" addresses the high-value luxury goods market, where authenticity and provenance are key to maintaining brand integrity and value.

- **Certification and Ownership:** Each luxury item is given a digital certificate on Sui, which includes details of its manufacture, ownership history, and authenticity checks. This certificate is immutable and can be verified by anyone, significantly reducing counterfeit risks.
- **Resale and Value Preservation:** The platform allows for secure transfers of ownership, ensuring that the history of the item is

maintained, which can help in preserving or even increasing the value of the luxury item over time.
- **Anti-Fraud Measures:** Sui's security features and the ability to link physical items to digital twins on the blockchain provide robust anti-fraud mechanisms, deterring the circulation of fakes.

Challenges and Future Directions:

Implementing blockchain in supply chains isn't without its challenges:

- **Integration with Legacy Systems:** Many supply chains rely on older systems that aren't designed for blockchain integration. Achieving seamless interoperability requires innovative solutions or significant upgrades.
- **Data Privacy Concerns:** While transparency is beneficial, not all supply chain data can or should be public. Sui needs to balance transparency with privacy, possibly through advanced encryption techniques for sensitive data.
- **Scalability for Global Supply Chains:** As supply chains are global, ensuring that the blockchain can handle the volume of data and transactions from thousands of entities worldwide is crucial.

Looking ahead, the future of supply chain management with Sui could involve:

- **AI and IoT Integration:** Combining Sui with AI for predictive analytics on supply chain risks or IoT for real-time tracking could revolutionize how goods are managed from production to consumption.
- **Cross-Chain Collaboration:** As different parts of a supply chain might use different technologies, solutions for interoperability where Sui acts as a bridge for data and asset transfer between chains could become more prevalent.
- **Sustainability Tracking:** Sui could play a role in tracking the environmental impact of supply chains, helping companies to monitor, report, and reduce their carbon footprint or other sustainability metrics.

In summary, these case studies showcase how Sui's blockchain technology can bring about a new era in supply chain management, where transparency, efficiency, and security are not just aspirations but realities. By providing an immutable record of goods, automating processes with smart contracts, and ensuring real-time traceability, Sui sets a new standard for how supply chains operate, offering significant benefits for businesses, regulators, and consumers alike.

Part 5: Digital Identity and Access Control

In an increasingly digital world, managing identities securely, privately, and effectively is a critical challenge. Sui's blockchain presents a compelling framework for digital identity solutions, offering tools for secure, self-sovereign identity management, and access control mechanisms that respect privacy while ensuring security. Here, we explore case studies that illustrate Sui's application in this domain.

Case Study 1: Self-Sovereign Identity - "SuiID"

"SuiID" represents a paradigm shift towards self-sovereign identity, where individuals have complete control over their digital identities, deciding what to share and with whom, all facilitated by Sui's blockchain.

- **Decentralized Identity Management:** Users on "SuiID" can create, manage, and share identity credentials without relying on a central authority. This is made possible by Sui's ability to host secure, private data through its smart contracts, where only the owner can grant access to their identity attributes.
- **Privacy-Preserving Authentication:** Utilizing zero-knowledge proofs or similar cryptographic techniques, "SuiID" allows users to prove they meet certain criteria (like age or nationality) without revealing unnecessary personal data, enhancing privacy in online interactions.
- **Interoperability:** "SuiID" aims to be cross-compatible with other blockchain-based identity systems, promoting a universally accepted digital identity standard that can operate across various services and jurisdictions.

Case Study 2: Access Control for Enterprises - "SuiGate"

"SuiGate" leverages Sui's blockchain to manage access to physical and digital resources within enterprises, enhancing security and simplifying administration.

- **Dynamic Access Permissions:** Through Sui's object-centric model, access rights can be dynamically granted or revoked based on roles, time, or specific conditions, all automated by smart contracts. This reduces the risk of unauthorized access and simplifies the management of permissions.
- **Auditability and Compliance:** Every access event is immutably recorded on the blockchain, providing a clear audit trail for compliance with regulations like GDPR or HIPAA. This transparency helps in identifying security breaches or unauthorized access attempts.
- **Secure Remote Work:** With the rise of remote work, "SuiGate" ensures that access to company resources is secure, even from various global locations, using blockchain to verify identity and enforce access policies.

Case Study 3: Voting and Governance - "SuiVote"

"SuiVote" utilizes Sui's blockchain for secure, transparent, and verifiable voting systems, whether for corporate governance, community decisions, or public elections.

- **Secure and Anonymous Voting:** By employing cryptographic methods like blind signatures, "SuiVote" ensures voter anonymity while maintaining the integrity of the vote count. Sui's speed allows for real-time vote tallying, which is crucial for large-scale elections.
- **Decentralized Governance:** For DAOs or community-led initiatives, "SuiVote" enables members to propose, vote on, and implement governance changes directly on the blockchain, leveraging Sui's governance model where token holders can participate.
- **Auditability and Dispute Resolution:** With every vote recorded on the blockchain, "SuiVote" provides an immutable record that can be audited to resolve disputes, ensuring the voting process's integrity and transparency.

Challenges and Future Directions:

Implementing digital identity and access control on blockchain like Sui faces several challenges:

- **Scalability:** As more entities and individuals use Sui for identity management, ensuring the system scales to handle millions of identities and transactions per second is vital.
- **User Adoption:** For self-sovereign identity systems to succeed, they need widespread adoption. Educating users about managing their own identities and the benefits of decentralization is a significant hurdle.

- **Regulatory Compliance:** Balancing the privacy and control offered by Sui with compliance to existing and future identity laws, especially across different jurisdictions, is complex.

Looking to the future, Sui's role in digital identity could expand in several directions:

- **Integration with IoT:** As the Internet of Things grows, Sui could be used to manage digital identities for devices, ensuring secure, automated interactions between machines.
- **Cross-Industry Solutions:** Expanding beyond current applications, Sui might facilitate identity solutions for education (certification and credentials), healthcare (patient records), and more, where privacy and security are paramount.
- **AI for Adaptive Identity Management:** AI could be leveraged to adapt identity verification processes based on behavior patterns or risk assessments, making identity management on Sui more dynamic and secure.

In conclusion, these case studies demonstrate how Sui's blockchain can revolutionize digital identity and access control. By offering solutions that prioritize user control, privacy, and security, Sui is paving the way for a future where individuals and organizations can interact online with unprecedented autonomy and trust. The potential of Sui in this field not only lies in solving current identity crises but also in pioneering new standards for digital interaction and governance.

Part 6: Cultural and Social Impact: Art, Collectibles, and Community

Blockchain technology's ability to authenticate, transfer, and manage digital assets has had profound implications for cultural sectors, particularly in art, collectibles, and community governance. Sui, with its focus on speed, security, and scalability, has enabled new forms of cultural expression, ownership, and community interaction. This section explores how Sui is making an impact in these areas through specific case studies.

Case Study 1: Digital Art Authentication - "SuiArt"

"SuiArt" is a platform where artists can mint, sell, and authenticate their digital artworks as NFTs on the Sui blockchain, providing a new paradigm for art ownership and provenance.

- **Authenticity and Provenance:** Each artwork on "SuiArt" is given a unique digital signature, ensuring its authenticity and creating a permanent record of ownership history. This combats art forgery and ensures artists receive due credit and royalties for future sales via smart contracts.
- **Artist Empowerment:** Sui's low transaction costs and high speed mean artists can interact directly with buyers without intermediaries,

retaining more of their earnings and gaining instant payments.
- **Interactive Art Experiences:** "SuiArt" leverages Sui's capabilities for dynamic NFTs, where art can evolve or respond to external conditions or viewer interactions, creating living pieces of digital art.

Case Study 2: Collectibles and Trading - "SuiCollect"

"SuiCollect" uses Sui to manage and trade digital collectibles, from sports memorabilia to virtual fashion items, enhancing the collectibles market with blockchain's benefits.

- **Ownership and Transferability:** Collectibles on "SuiCollect" are unique, tradable assets with verifiable scarcity, managed via Sui's object-centric model. This ensures collectors have true ownership of their items, which can be traded with ease and security.
- **Community-Driven Value:** The platform allows for community voting or events that can affect the rarity or desirability of collectibles, fostering a vibrant ecosystem where collectors participate in the valuation process.
- **Augmented Reality Integration:** "SuiCollect" considers merging with AR technologies, allowing collectors to display their digital assets in the real world, enhancing the interaction with and perceived value of collectibles.

Case Study 3: Decentralized Autonomous Organizations (DAOs) - "SuiCommunity"

"SuiCommunity" harnesses Sui's governance features to create DAOs for managing community projects, from local initiatives to global charity efforts.

- **Decentralized Governance:** Using Sui's blockchain, "SuiCommunity" DAOs can vote on decisions, fund allocations, or project directions with transparency and security. Members can propose ideas, and voting is done with their staked SUI tokens, ensuring a democratic process.
- **Transparency and Trust:** Every transaction and vote within a DAO is recorded on the blockchain, providing an unalterable record of community decisions, which builds trust among members and stakeholders.
- **Global Community Engagement:** Thanks to Sui's scalability, "SuiCommunity" can support large-scale, international DAOs, where members from around the world can participate in governance, breaking down geographical barriers.

Challenges and Future Directions:

The integration of cultural and social applications on Sui presents unique challenges:

- **Cultural Adoption:** Blockchain technology's adoption in the arts and collectibles needs to overcome skepticism about digital assets' value and the technology's complexity. Education and showcasing successful implementations are key.

- **Regulatory Navigation:** As digital assets gain prominence, navigating copyright, intellectual property, and tax laws across different countries becomes complex. Sui must facilitate compliance while promoting creator rights.
- **Scalability for Mass Participation:** For DAOs or platforms like "SuiArt" to manage thousands or millions of users, Sui's infrastructure must continue to scale without compromising performance or security.

Looking forward, the cultural and social impact of Sui could evolve in several ways:

- **Cultural Preservation:** Sui might be used to preserve cultural artifacts digitally, ensuring their history and authenticity are maintained for future generations through blockchain.
- **Interactive and Evolving Collectibles:** With advancements in Sui's smart contract capabilities, collectibles could become more interactive or evolve based on real-world events or community input, deepening engagement.
- **Social Impact Initiatives:** Leveraging DAOs, Sui could support more social impact projects where communities worldwide can collaborate on solving global issues with transparency and direct accountability.

In conclusion, Sui's impact on the cultural and social spheres is profound. By providing a platform where art, collectibles, and community governance can flourish under the principles of decentralization, Sui is not just enhancing these areas but redefining them. The case studies here illustrate how blockchain can democratize access to culture, empower creators, and foster community-driven initiatives, setting a new standard for how we engage with and value cultural assets and social structures in the digital age.

Chapter 19: Future of Sui: Roadmap and Vision

Part 1: Introduction to Sui's Vision

At the heart of the blockchain revolution lies the promise of a digital world where trust, speed, and security are not just ideals but realities. Sui, since its inception, has been driven by a clear vision to redefine these aspects of blockchain technology. This chapter opens the curtain on the future of Sui, where we explore not just the technological roadmap but the philosophical journey that aims to shape this vision into reality.

Sui's vision is built on the foundation of creating a blockchain that can scale to meet the demands of a global digital economy. It envisions a platform where transactions are not just possible but are swift, secure, and scalable, empowering users to interact with a digital ecosystem that feels as natural as the physical one. This vision is not confined to mere technical enhancements but extends to how these technologies can enhance human interaction, creativity, and governance.

The ethos of Sui is centered around user empowerment. It seeks to lower the barriers to entry for individuals and institutions alike, enabling them to leverage blockchain for more than just financial transactions—to build, create, and govern in a decentralized manner. Sui's vision is to be a catalyst for a new era where blockchain technology is not an afterthought but a fundamental component of digital interactions.

Speed is a core element of this vision. Sui aims to redefine what fast means in the blockchain space, pushing the boundaries of transaction processing with its parallel execution model. This isn't just about handling more transactions per second; it's about creating an experience where the blockchain's operations are virtually imperceptible, akin to the speed of centralized systems but with all the benefits of decentralization.

Security, another pillar of Sui's vision, goes beyond protecting digital assets. It's about fostering an environment where trust is not assumed but engineered into the system. Sui's approach to security involves not just robust cryptographic methods but also economic incentives that align with the platform's health, ensuring that all participants have a stake in maintaining its integrity.

Scalability is where Sui plans to shine, envisioning a blockchain that grows with its user base without compromising on performance or decentralization. This vision includes expanding the capacity of the network to handle not just more transactions but also more complex interactions, from gaming ecosystems to global supply chains, all managed with efficiency and security.

The vision for Sui also encompasses a commitment to privacy. In a world where data is the new currency, Sui aims to provide mechanisms where privacy is not sacrificed for transparency. This involves exploring or implementing technologies like zero-knowledge proofs, ensuring that users can transact and interact privately while still benefiting from the blockchain's public ledger benefits.

Community is at the center of Sui's long-term vision. Rather than a platform dictated by a few, Sui aspires to be shaped by many. This means evolving governance models where the community not only has a say but actively participates in deciding Sui's future direction. This democratic approach to blockchain governance could set a new standard for how decentralized networks operate.

Looking forward, Sui's vision extends to interoperability, envisioning a future where blockchains do not exist in isolation but form a cohesive network where assets, data, and value can flow freely. This part of the vision speaks to a broader goal of creating an interconnected digital fabric where Sui plays a pivotal role.

However, this vision is not without its challenges. Realizing such an ambitious roadmap requires navigating technological hurdles, regulatory landscapes, and the ever-evolving expectations of users. Sui's vision is therefore not just about what can be achieved technically but also about how it can adapt, innovate, and lead in an industry that is still in its adolescence. This introduction sets the stage for a detailed exploration of how Sui plans to turn this vision into a tangible, impactful reality.

Part 2: Technological Roadmap

The technological roadmap for Sui is both a vision and a strategy, a detailed plan to advance its capabilities in blockchain technology while ensuring it remains at the cutting edge of innovation. This roadmap is not merely about adding features; it's about envisioning a blockchain ecosystem where speed, security, scalability, and user experience are not just improved but redefined. Here, we delve into the comprehensive technological advancements Sui aims to pursue over the next few years, broken down into short-term, medium-term, and long-term goals.

Short-term Goals:

Optimizing Consensus for Speed and Efficiency:

In the immediate future, Sui's primary focus is on enhancing its consensus mechanism. The current Delegated Proof-of-Stake (DPoS) model has served well in balancing speed and decentralization, but there's always room for improvement. Sui plans to fine-tune this mechanism for even lower latency and higher throughput. This involves:

- **Reducing Block Times:** By minimizing the time it takes to confirm a block, Sui can achieve faster transaction finality, crucial for applications where timing is everything, like high-frequency trading or real-time gaming.
- **Optimizing Validator Selection:** This could involve more dynamic or performance-based

criteria for selecting validators, ensuring that only the most reliable and efficient nodes are responsible for block production, thus enhancing network performance.

- **Improving Consensus Algorithms:** Sui might consider integrating elements from other consensus models or developing new algorithms that can handle higher transaction volumes with less resource consumption.

Expanding Move's Capabilities:

The Move programming language is central to Sui's smart contract ecosystem. Sui aims to make Move more powerful and user-friendly:

- **New Libraries and Modules:** Introducing more pre-built libraries for common blockchain operations or specific use cases, reducing the development time for new smart contracts.
- **Enhanced Developer Tools:** Better IDE integration, more comprehensive error reporting, and real-time debugging tools to make smart contract development more accessible to developers of all skill levels.
- **Simplifying Syntax:** Making Move's syntax more intuitive for developers who might not have a background in blockchain programming, without sacrificing its security features.

Medium-term Goals:

Integration of Privacy Features:

Privacy is becoming increasingly vital in the blockchain space. Sui's medium-term goals include:

- **Zero-Knowledge Proofs (ZKPs):** Implementing or enhancing support for ZKPs to enable private transactions where the details are shielded but the transaction's validity is provable. This would be crucial for sectors like finance or health, where data sensitivity is high.
- **Encrypted Transactions:** Exploring ways to encrypt transaction data so that only authorized parties can access the details, adding another layer of privacy without compromising the blockchain's auditability.
- **Confidential Smart Contracts:** Developing mechanisms where smart contracts can operate on private data or execute logic that's not visible to the public, yet still verifiable in terms of its outcome.

Scalability Solutions:

To address the increasing demand for blockchain services, Sui plans to:

- **Layer-2 Scaling Solutions:** Investigating or implementing technologies like state channels, sidechains, or rollups, which can process transactions off the main chain to reduce load, improve speed, and lower costs.
- **Sharding:** Considering sharding, where the network is split into smaller pieces that

process transactions in parallel, significantly increasing throughput while maintaining decentralization.

- **Dynamic Network Adjustments:** Developing algorithms that can adjust the network's capacity based on current demand, ensuring optimal performance at all times without overburdening resources.

Long-term Goals:

Interoperability Across Blockchains:

Sui envisions a future where it's not just about what happens within its ecosystem but how it interacts with others:

- **Cross-Chain Protocols:** Either supporting existing standards or developing new ones for seamless asset and data transfer across different blockchains, aiming for Sui to be a central node in an interconnected blockchain network.
- **Interoperability Middleware:** Creating or supporting software layers that make it easier for developers to build applications that work across multiple chains, enhancing Sui's utility in a multi-chain world.
- **Decentralized Bridges:** Ensuring secure, decentralized bridges between Sui and other blockchains, reducing the risks associated with centralized cross-chain solutions.

Integration of AI and Machine Learning:

Long-term, Sui sees AI and ML not just as tools but as integral parts of its ecosystem:

- **AI for Network Optimization:** Using AI to predict network load, optimize transaction routing, or even suggest network topology changes for better performance and security.
- **Machine Learning for Security:** Implementing ML algorithms to detect anomalies or potential security threats in real-time, enhancing the proactive defense of the network.
- **Governance Support:** AI could help analyze community proposals, predict the outcomes of governance decisions, or even assist in creating more nuanced voting systems based on community behavior and preferences.

Consensus Mechanism Evolution:

The consensus mechanism is the heart of any blockchain's security and efficiency. Long-term visions for Sui include:

- **Hybrid Consensus Models:** Exploring combinations of DPoS with other consensus protocols to create a more resilient, scalable, and energy-efficient system.
- **Adaptive Consensus:** Designing consensus mechanisms that can adapt to different network conditions or types of transactions, ensuring optimal performance in various scenarios.

- **Formal Verification of Consensus:** Using formal methods to prove the correctness of the consensus mechanism under all possible conditions, enhancing trust in the system.

Smart Contract Enhancements:

Sui's smart contracts are set to become more powerful and secure:

- **Formal Verification:** Expanding the use of formal verification for smart contracts, allowing developers to mathematically prove the safety and correctness of their code, significantly reducing vulnerabilities.
- **Modular and Composable Contracts:** Encouraging a design where contracts can be built from smaller, reusable components, making development more efficient and contracts more interoperable.
- **Asynchronous Smart Contracts:** Enabling contracts to handle asynchronous operations more effectively, which is vital for applications with complex, multi-step transactions.

Network Performance:

Continuous improvement in network performance is a core focus:

- **Latency Reduction:** Through advanced network protocols, improved node communication, or better geographical distribution of nodes, Sui aims to reduce transaction latency even further.

- **Transaction Finality:** Exploring methods to ensure transactions are considered final even quicker, enhancing user experience in scenarios where immediate confirmation is needed.
- **Complex Object Handling:** As Sui's object-centric model grows, ensuring that the network can manage complex state transitions without sacrificing speed or security.

Security Enhancements:

Security is an ongoing battle, and Sui's roadmap includes:

- **Quantum-Resistant Cryptography:** Preparing for a post-quantum world by integrating or researching cryptographic methods that can withstand quantum computing attacks.
- **Advanced Economic Security:** Refining the economic model to ensure that staking and transaction fees align even better with network security goals, possibly through more dynamic reward and penalty systems.
- **Privacy by Design:** Incorporating privacy features not just as add-ons but as foundational elements of the protocol, ensuring that privacy considerations are part of every new feature or update.

Developer Tools and Support:

Fostering a vibrant developer community is crucial:

- **Comprehensive SDKs:** Developing or enhancing software development kits that cover a wide range of use cases, making it easier for developers to create innovative applications on Sui.
- **Testing and Simulation Environments:** Providing robust environments where developers can test their applications under conditions that mimic the live blockchain, reducing the risk of deployment issues.
- **Educational Resources:** Continuously updating and expanding educational materials, from tutorials to advanced courses, ensuring that developers have the knowledge they need to leverage Sui's capabilities fully.

In summary, Sui's technological roadmap is a testament to its commitment to not just keeping pace but setting the pace in blockchain development. Each goal, from short-term optimizations to long-term visions, is designed to make Sui a more powerful, secure, and accessible platform, where the potential of blockchain can be fully realized. This roadmap is dynamic, subject to community feedback and the ever-evolving landscape of technology, ensuring that Sui remains a leader in creating a blockchain ecosystem that can support the digital economy of tomorrow.

Part 3: Ecosystem Expansion

The growth and success of a blockchain platform like Sui are not solely contingent on its technological prowess but also on the vibrancy and diversity of its ecosystem. Sui's vision for the future involves expanding this ecosystem to become a hub of innovation, creativity, and practical applications. This part of the roadmap outlines how Sui plans to foster a rich, inclusive environment where developers, users, businesses, and communities can thrive, leveraging the unique capabilities of the Sui blockchain. Here's an in-depth look at the strategies, initiatives, and goals set forth for ecosystem expansion.

Attracting and Supporting Developers:

One of the keystones of Sui's ecosystem expansion is its commitment to developers. Sui aims to become the go-to platform for developers looking to build decentralized applications (dApps) by:

- **Developer Incentives:** Introducing grants, bounties, or hackathon prizes to encourage developers to build on Sui. These could be tied to specific challenges or use cases where Sui's unique features like parallel execution could shine.
- **Education and Training:** Setting up comprehensive educational programs, from basic blockchain concepts to advanced Move programming. This might include online courses, workshops, or even a Sui Academy, aimed at both seasoned developers and those new to blockchain.

- **Tooling and SDKs:** Continuous improvement of developer tools, including SDKs, APIs, and frameworks that simplify the development process on Sui. This could involve creating or supporting libraries for common functionalities, thus reducing the learning curve and development time.
- **Community Engagement:** Fostering a strong developer community through forums, Discord channels, or GitHub where developers can share knowledge, collaborate on projects, or contribute to the core protocol. Encouraging an open-source culture could lead to a wealth of community-driven innovations.

Partnerships and Integration:

Sui's growth strategy includes forming strategic partnerships that can both validate and expand its use cases:

- **Cross-Blockchain Collaborations:** Partnering with other blockchain networks to enhance interoperability, explore joint initiatives, or share technological advancements. This could involve creating standards for asset transfers or data sharing between chains.
- **Enterprise Partnerships:** Engaging with traditional businesses by providing solutions for supply chain management, digital identity, or secure data sharing. Sui could offer pilot programs or proof-of-concepts to demonstrate its capabilities in real-world scenarios.

- **Academic and Research Collaborations:** Working with universities or research institutions to explore new use cases, refine the technology, or even develop new consensus algorithms or privacy solutions. This could also serve to educate the next generation of blockchain professionals.
- **Financial and DeFi Partnerships:** Collaborating with DeFi projects or traditional financial institutions to create or host financial instruments on Sui, leveraging its speed and security for new financial products or services.

Ecosystem Initiatives:

To catalyze growth and adoption, Sui plans several ecosystem-focused initiatives:

- **Sui Labs:** A concept where Sui could fund or incubate projects that leverage its blockchain in innovative ways, from gaming to art to social governance. This would not only grow the ecosystem but also showcase Sui's versatility.
- **Decentralized Application Competitions:** Regular hackathons or coding competitions focusing on specific themes or challenges where developers can win support, visibility, and funding for their projects.
- **Decentralized Finance (DeFi) Ecosystem:** Building out a robust DeFi ecosystem on Sui, encouraging the development of lending platforms, decentralized exchanges, yield farming, and more, all benefiting from Sui's performance advantages.

- **Cultural and Artistic Endeavors:** Supporting the digital art and collectibles market by providing tools for artists to mint NFTs on Sui, possibly with features that allow for interactive or evolving artworks, expanding the cultural impact of blockchain.

Community Building:

The heart of any decentralized platform is its community, and Sui aims to:

- **Community Governance:** Enhancing governance mechanisms to allow for more direct community input on the platform's direction. This might involve more frequent voting on proposals or integrating decentralized autonomous organizations (DAOs) for various aspects of network management.
- **User Education:** Not just for developers but for end-users, creating resources that explain how to use Sui's services, the benefits of blockchain, and how to safely engage with dApps or manage digital assets.
- **Ambassador Programs:** Establishing a network of ambassadors who can spread awareness, educate, and gather feedback from different geographical regions or sectors, adapting Sui's growth strategy to local needs and cultures.
- **Community Events:** Hosting or sponsoring events, both virtual and in-person, to bring the community together, from developer meetups

to user workshops, ensuring a vibrant and engaged user base.

Marketplace and Infrastructure Development:

For a thriving ecosystem, Sui must support a marketplace where dApps can be discovered and used:

- **Sui Marketplace:** Creating a platform where dApps can be easily found, installed, or interacted with, possibly with features like dApp ratings, reviews, or curated sections for various use cases.
- **Oracle Services:** Ensuring that dApps on Sui have access to reliable, decentralized data feeds for smart contract execution, which is crucial for applications like DeFi or prediction markets.
- **Custody Solutions:** Developing or partnering for secure wallet solutions, including hardware wallets or custodial services, to make it easier for users to manage their assets on Sui.
- **Scalability Infrastructure:** Building or supporting infrastructure like node operators or staking pools that help scale the network, ensuring it can handle growth without performance degradation.

Inclusivity and Accessibility:

Sui's vision for the future includes making blockchain technology accessible to a broader audience:

- **User-Friendly Interfaces:** Ensuring that the front-end of dApps built on Sui is as intuitive as possible, reducing the technical barrier for new users.
- **Localization:** Translating resources, interfaces, or even parts of the blockchain protocol itself into multiple languages to serve a global community.
- **Accessibility Features:** Incorporating features for users with disabilities, like screen reader compatibility or simplified interactions for those less tech-savvy.
- **Affordability:** Working on transaction fee models or gas optimization to make using Sui affordable for microtransactions or in regions where the cost of entry to blockchain has been prohibitive.

Challenges and Considerations:

Expanding an ecosystem like Sui's comes with its set of challenges:

- **Scalability vs. Decentralization:** As the ecosystem grows, maintaining a balance where the network scales without centralizing power or compromising security is crucial.
- **Regulatory Navigation:** Ensuring compliance with various global regulations while promoting the decentralized ethos can be complex, requiring sophisticated legal and compliance strategies.
- **Market Dynamics:** Sui must adapt to the fast-changing crypto market, where new

technologies or competitors emerge, potentially shifting user and developer attention.
- **User Adoption:** Even with the best technology, adoption requires overcoming user inertia, education, and trust in new systems.
- **Security at Scale:** With more applications and users, the attack surface grows, necessitating continuous security audits, updates, and community vigilance.

Future Vision:

Looking further ahead, Sui aims to be at the forefront of blockchain's integration into everyday life:

- **Mainstream Adoption:** Positioning Sui as a platform where blockchain services are as common as cloud services, used in everything from personal finance to governmental processes.
- **Sustainability:** Embracing eco-friendly practices or innovations in blockchain to address criticisms regarding energy consumption, possibly through research into more sustainable consensus mechanisms or carbon offset programs.
- **Interdisciplinary Applications:** By breaking down barriers between sectors, Sui could see applications in areas like education (certification), healthcare (data privacy), or even environmental monitoring (using IoT and blockchain).

- **Cultural Impact:** Aspiring to be a platform where new forms of digital culture are created, shared, and preserved, leveraging blockchain for art, music, literature, or cultural heritage.

Sui's strategy for ecosystem expansion is multifaceted, aiming not just to grow in size but in depth, diversity, and impact. By focusing on developers, partnerships, community, and accessibility, Sui seeks to create an ecosystem where innovation thrives, solving real-world problems while pushing the boundaries of what blockchain technology can achieve. This vision for expansion is ambitious but grounded in practical steps that, if executed well, could position Sui as a leading force in the blockchain space for years to come.

Part 4: Community and Governance Evolution

The future of Sui is not just shaped by technology but profoundly influenced by its community and governance model. As blockchain projects increasingly recognize the power of community-driven development, Sui positions itself to evolve in how it engages with and empowers its users, developers, and stakeholders. This part of the roadmap delves into how Sui plans to refine its governance model, foster community participation, and ensure that the platform's evolution is a collective endeavor. Here's a detailed look at the steps and strategies Sui is contemplating for this evolution.

Sui's vision for governance is to move beyond the traditional models where decisions are made by a select few, towards a system where every participant can have a voice. This isn't just about decentralization in terms of node operation but also in decision-making. The goal is to create a governance ecosystem where the community feels not just heard but actively involved in steering the platform's future.

A key aspect of this evolution involves enhancing the voting mechanisms. Sui aims to introduce or refine systems where voting power is not just tied to token holdings but also to participation, expertise, or other factors that might reflect a more holistic view of community contribution. This could include weighted voting based on a user's history of engagement with the network or their contributions to the ecosystem.

To make governance more accessible, Sui plans to simplify the process of proposing changes or new initiatives. This might involve developing user-friendly tools for proposal submission, where even those without deep technical knowledge can contribute ideas. Automation for certain governance tasks, like collecting votes or executing agreed changes, could also be on the horizon, making the process more efficient and inclusive.

Education plays a pivotal role in this governance model. Sui envisions a future where every member of the community understands the basics of blockchain, governance, and how they can participate. This could manifest through an extensive educational platform, offering resources from basic to advanced levels, workshops, and perhaps even certification programs for governance participants.

The role of Decentralized Autonomous Organizations (DAOs) might expand within Sui's governance structure. Sui could support or even pioneer models where DAOs handle specific aspects of the network's operation, from managing grants to overseeing particular dApps or sub-ecosystems. This would decentralize decision-making even further, allowing for more specialized governance that can respond quickly to niche needs.

Community engagement will be amplified through various channels. Sui plans to leverage social media, community meetups (both virtual and physical), and potentially even its own communication platforms tailored for blockchain enthusiasts. The idea is to create spaces where community members can discuss, debate, and collaborate on the platform's future.

Transparency is another cornerstone of Sui's governance evolution. All governance actions, from proposals to votes to outcomes, would be made transparently available. This could involve developing or adopting tools for real-time governance tracking, ensuring everyone can see how decisions are made and who influenced them, fostering a culture of accountability.

To address potential centralization risks in governance, Sui might implement mechanisms for validator rotation or term limits, ensuring that governance power doesn't stagnate in the hands of a few. This could be coupled with incentives for new validators or participants to get involved in governance, perhaps through rewards or recognition within the community.

Sui also considers the integration of more dynamic governance models, where the rules of governance itself can evolve based on community consensus. This adaptive governance would allow for the system to refine itself over time, responding to new challenges or opportunities without requiring a hard fork or significant disruption.

For those who can't or don't wish to engage directly in governance, Sui might explore delegation mechanisms where users can delegate their voting rights to others they trust. This could democratize governance further by allowing passive participants to still have an impact through representatives they believe in.

The evolution of governance will also consider the global nature of the Sui community. This means potentially supporting multi-language governance interfaces, considering time zones for voting, and ensuring that governance is accessible to users from different cultural and regulatory backgrounds.

Lastly, Sui's governance evolution isn't just about today's community but about preparing for tomorrow's. This involves setting up structures or funds for long-term community projects, ensuring that the governance model supports not just immediate decisions but also strategic, long-term planning for the platform's growth and sustainability.

In essence, the evolution of community and governance in Sui is about creating a platform where the community isn't just a beneficiary of the technology but its co-creator. This vision of governance seeks to balance efficiency with inclusivity, ensuring that as Sui grows, it does so with the active participation and consent of its community, making it a true embodiment of the decentralized ethos.

Part 5: Interoperability and Integration

As blockchain technology matures, the vision of a singular, isolated blockchain fades into one of an interconnected, interoperable ecosystem where different blockchains and systems can interact seamlessly. Sui, recognizing this trend, is committed to enhancing its interoperability capabilities, aiming to facilitate not just asset transfers but also data interoperability, governance interactions, and broader ecosystem integration. This section outlines Sui's strategic approach to achieving these goals, highlighting both the technical challenges and the potential benefits of such an interconnected future.

Cross-Chain Asset Transfer:

Sui aims to be at the forefront of enabling fluid asset movement between different blockchain networks. This involves:

- **Developing or Supporting Cross-Chain Protocols:** Sui might either develop its own protocol or actively participate in the evolution of existing standards like Inter-Blockchain Communication (IBC) or bridges like those used in Polkadot or Cosmos. The focus would be on ensuring that assets minted on Sui can be easily moved to other chains and vice versa.

- **Decentralized Bridges:** To mitigate the risks associated with centralized cross-chain bridges, Sui is likely to explore or implement decentralized bridge solutions. These would use smart contracts on both sides of the bridge to secure and verify asset transfers, reducing vulnerability to hacks or central points of failure.

Data Interoperability:

Data is just as crucial as assets in the blockchain world. Sui's vision includes:

- **Oracle Networks:** Integrating or supporting oracle networks that can provide off-chain data to Sui smart contracts, and vice versa, allowing Sui applications to leverage real-world data from other blockchains or centralized systems.
- **Data Standardization:** Working towards or adopting standards for data formats that are universally recognized across blockchains, enabling Sui to not only transfer data but do so in a way that's immediately usable by other networks.

Governance and Consensus Interoperability:

Sui sees potential in governance models that span multiple blockchains:

- **Cross-Chain Voting:** Allowing governance decisions on Sui to influence or be influenced by other ecosystems, perhaps through shared DAOs or governance tokens that have voting power across multiple chains.
- **Consensus Mechanism Collaboration:** Exploring ways where different consensus mechanisms can work together or where Sui's consensus can be adopted or adapted by other chains for specific use cases, fostering a broader acceptance of Sui's technological approach.

Integration with Traditional Systems:

Beyond blockchain interoperability, Sui's roadmap includes:

- **APIs and SDKs for Legacy Systems:** Developing tools that allow traditional systems to interact with Sui, thus bridging the gap between blockchain and traditional finance, logistics, or identity verification systems.
- **Compliance and Regulatory Integration:** Ensuring that Sui's interoperability solutions comply with global regulations, particularly when dealing with financial assets, personal data, or sensitive information.

Technical Challenges:

Interoperability is fraught with technical complexities:

- **Security:** Ensuring that cross-chain transfers are as secure as native transactions on Sui, protecting against double-spending, replay attacks, or other exploitations.
- **Scalability:** Balancing the need for interoperability with the performance of the network, ensuring that cross-chain interactions do not become a bottleneck.
- **Consensus Alignment:** When different blockchains have different consensus mechanisms, finding a way to align or reconcile these for interaction without weakening any network's security.

Strategic Partnerships:

Sui's approach to interoperability will likely involve:

- **Collaborations with Other Blockchain Projects:** Working closely with other blockchain initiatives to develop shared standards or solutions for interoperability, potentially leading to joint ventures or ecosystems where Sui is a central component.
- **Engagement with Tech Giants:** Looking for partnerships with major tech companies that are exploring blockchain or have interest in distributed ledger technologies, to extend Sui's reach into more traditional tech environments.

Vision for a Multi-Chain Future:

Sui's ultimate goal is to contribute to a blockchain ecosystem where:

- **Users can interact with multiple blockchains without noticing the underlying complexity.**
- **Developers can build applications that are inherently multi-chain, leveraging the strengths of each network they interact with.**
- **Assets and data have the freedom to move where they are most needed or valuable, creating a more dynamic and efficient digital economy.**

Challenges and Opportunities:

While the path to interoperability is challenging, it presents numerous opportunities:

- **Innovation in Application Development:** Developers can create more versatile dApps that leverage different blockchains for different functionalities.
- **Economic Growth:** By facilitating asset movement and data sharing, Sui could see an increase in its economic activity as it becomes a hub for cross-chain interactions.
- **Community Expansion:** As Sui becomes more integrated with other systems, its community could grow, not just in numbers but

in diversity, bringing in users from other blockchain communities.

Sui's focus on interoperability and integration is not just about technical prowess but about creating a more inclusive, efficient, and interconnected blockchain ecosystem. By addressing the technical, security, and compliance challenges, Sui aims to lead by example, showing how blockchain can transcend its current limitations to create a truly global, decentralized network of networks.

Part 6: Long-term Impact and Challenges

Sui's long-term vision extends beyond mere technological advancement; it's about shaping the future of how we interact with digital systems, manage identity, conduct finance, and even govern our societies. This concluding part of the roadmap reflects on the potential impacts Sui could have on various sectors and the challenges it must navigate to realize this ambitious vision. Here, we consider how Sui might influence the world, the hurdles it faces, and the speculative outcomes of its success or failure.

Impact on Digital Identity:

Sui's implementation of self-sovereign identity could fundamentally change how we think about and manage personal data. In a future where privacy is paramount, Sui might enable individuals to have complete control over their digital personas, reducing reliance on centralized identity providers and enhancing privacy in online interactions. This could lead to a new era of digital citizenship where identity is both secure and fluid across different platforms and jurisdictions.

Financial Inclusion and Innovation:

By providing a platform where financial transactions are swift, secure, and accessible, Sui could play a significant role in financial inclusion. Its low-latency, high-throughput blockchain could democratize access to financial services, from microtransactions in underbanked regions to complex DeFi applications for sophisticated investors. Sui's impact could extend to creating new financial models, like instant, trustless lending or cross-border payments without intermediaries, potentially reshaping global finance.

Decentralized Governance and Social Structures:

Sui's governance model, if widely adopted, could inspire a new wave of decentralized governance in both digital and physical realms. From online communities to local governments, the principles of transparent, community-driven decision-making could be adopted, possibly leading to more democratic forms of organization where power is distributed rather than concentrated. This could have profound implications for how we address collective issues, from environmental policies to social services.

Cultural and Creative Economies:

In the realm of art, music, and digital content, Sui could facilitate a renaissance in how creators are compensated and how art is authenticated and shared. By enabling dynamic NFTs or new forms of interactive digital art, Sui might foster a culture where creators have more control over their work's lifecycle, from creation to monetization, potentially leading to new business models for artists and cultural preservation efforts.

Challenges in Realizing the Vision:

However, the path to this impact is not without significant challenges:

- **Regulatory Landscape:** As blockchain technologies like Sui become more integrated into everyday life, navigating the complex, often conflicting, regulatory environments globally will be crucial. Sui must balance innovation with compliance, especially in areas like data protection, financial regulation, and digital rights management.
- **Scalability and Performance:** As more applications and users leverage Sui for various purposes, maintaining or enhancing its performance without compromising on decentralization or security will be an ongoing challenge. This includes dealing with network congestion, ensuring equitable access during high demand, and managing the environmental impact of increased computational resources.
- **Security Threats:** With greater adoption comes increased risk, from cyberattacks to social engineering scams. Sui will need to

continuously evolve its security measures, potentially pioneering new methods to protect against quantum computing threats or other future technologies.

- **User Adoption and Education:** For Sui to achieve widespread adoption, there needs to be a significant effort in user education. Overcoming skepticism about blockchain technology, explaining its benefits in layman's terms, and providing intuitive interfaces will be key to bringing the general populace into this new digital economy.
- **Economic Stability:** Managing the token economics of SUI to avoid inflation, deflation, or market manipulation while incentivizing network participation is a delicate balance. Sui must innovate in its economic models to ensure long-term viability and trust in its ecosystem.

Opportunities for Evolution:

Despite these challenges, Sui has numerous opportunities for evolution:

- **Integration with Emerging Technologies:** From IoT to AI, Sui could leverage these technologies to enhance its capabilities, like using IoT for real-time supply chain tracking or AI for optimizing network performance or user interactions.
- **Sustainability Initiatives:** Addressing the environmental concerns associated with blockchain, Sui could lead in adopting or

developing green technologies, possibly through energy-efficient consensus mechanisms or integrating carbon credit systems.
- **Global Collaboration:** By fostering an environment of open collaboration, Sui could lead in international blockchain standards, making it a central player in a global blockchain ecosystem.
- **Innovation in Governance:** Sui might become a testing ground for new governance models, perhaps integrating AI for decision support or exploring voting systems that better reflect community consensus.

Speculative Outcomes:

If successful, Sui could:

- **Set New Standards:** For blockchain interoperability, privacy, and governance, influencing how future blockchains are designed.
- **Transform Industries:** By providing a backbone for secure, transparent data management, impacting fields from healthcare to voting systems.
- **Empower Individuals:** Giving people more control over their digital lives, from data to assets, potentially leading to a more equitable distribution of power.

However, failure to address these challenges could lead to:

- **Centralization:** If security or scalability issues aren't managed, there might be a drift towards centralized solutions, undermining the decentralized ethos.
- **Limited Adoption:** If the user experience remains complex or if regulatory hurdles become insurmountable, Sui might not achieve mainstream use.
- **Market Volatility:** Poor economic management could lead to wild fluctuations in SUI's value, deterring users and developers from fully committing to the platform.

In summary, Sui's long-term impact hinges on its ability to navigate these challenges while seizing opportunities for growth and innovation. Its vision for a decentralized future where technology empowers individuals and communities is ambitious but within reach if it continues to evolve with community input, technological advancement, and a forward-thinking approach to the myriad of global issues in our digital age.

Chapter 20: Community and Culture: The Human Element of Sui

Part 1: Introduction to the Sui Community

In the vast landscape of blockchain technology, where code and consensus algorithms often take center stage, the community behind a project like Sui is what breathes life into the technology, turning it from a complex set of protocols into a living, evolving ecosystem. The Sui community isn't just a group of users or developers; it's a dynamic collective of individuals from diverse backgrounds, united by a shared vision of what blockchain can achieve. This introduction to the Sui community will explore how this human element has been crucial from the project's inception, shaping its development, ethos, and future potential.

Sui was born with a clear vision to overcome the limitations of existing blockchain platforms, focusing on speed, security, and scalability. However, the technology alone does not define its success. The community, from the very beginning, has been pivotal. When Sui was introduced, it wasn't just pitched as another blockchain; it was presented as a movement where every participant could have a tangible impact on its trajectory. This ethos of inclusivity and empowerment has been central to attracting a wide array of individuals, from tech enthusiasts to artists, from financial gurus to social activists, all drawn by the promise of a blockchain that truly serves its users.

The ethos of the Sui community is rooted in several core values: decentralization, transparency, collaboration, and innovation. These aren't just buzzwords but are actively embodied in how the community operates. Decentralization here extends beyond technology to include how decisions are made, how governance is conducted, and how growth is achieved. Transparency is not just about open-source code but about clear communication, intentions, and the sharing of knowledge. Collaboration is seen in the myriad of projects, discussions, and partnerships that define the community's activities. And innovation is not just about technological breakthroughs but also about new ways of organizing, educating, and engaging.

From its early days, Sui's community has grown organically, not through aggressive marketing but through the genuine interest and engagement of its members. Social platforms, forums, and developer meetups have been instrumental in this growth. The community has leveraged these channels not just for promotion but for real, meaningful interaction where ideas are exchanged, support is offered, and the collective wisdom of the group shapes the platform's direction. This organic growth has led to a community that feels authentic, with members who are there out of belief in the project, not just for potential financial gains.

One of the unique aspects of the Sui community is its focus on education. Understanding that blockchain technology can be daunting, the community has taken upon itself to demystify the technology. Workshops, webinars, and easy-to-understand documentation have been key in onboarding new members, ensuring that everyone, regardless of their technical background, can participate. This educational culture not only helps in expanding the community but also in creating a more knowledgeable user base, which in turn contributes to the ecosystem's health and innovation.

The community's role in governance cannot be overstated. Sui's governance model is designed to be as inclusive as possible, allowing community members to propose, discuss, and vote on changes to the protocol or other significant decisions. This participatory governance model ensures that the community isn't just a passive audience but active players in the platform's evolution. It fosters a sense of ownership among members, where each feels they have a stake in Sui's success, which in turn drives engagement and loyalty.

The cultural phenomenon of Sui extends beyond governance and technology. The community has developed its own language, memes, and traditions, which might seem trivial but are crucial in building a strong community identity. These cultural elements create a sense of belonging, humor, and camaraderie among members, making the community not just a network of users but a social group. Events like hackathons, AMAs (Ask Me Anything), and community meetups have become not just about development but about celebrating the culture of Sui.

The Sui community also showcases a remarkable resilience and adaptability. As the blockchain space is known for its volatility, both in terms of technology and market dynamics, the community has been a stabilizing force. Through forums and social media, members support each other during downturns, share optimism during upturns, and collectively navigate through regulatory changes or technological shifts. This resilience is what keeps the community strong, even when external pressures mount.

Another interesting facet of the Sui community is its global nature. Blockchain, by its very nature, transcends borders, and Sui's community is no exception. With members from every corner of the globe, there's a rich tapestry of perspectives, languages, and cultural practices that enrich the community. This diversity is celebrated, with efforts made to ensure that content, discussions, and governance are accessible to everyone, sometimes even leading to multilingual support for key community resources or events.

However, the community isn't just about what has been or what is; it's also about what could be. The vision for Sui includes not just technological advancements but also cultural ones. The community sees itself as not just users or developers but as pioneers of a new digital era where blockchain isn't just about finance or data but about redefining how we interact, create, and govern in a digital world. This vision is ambitious, but the community's commitment to education, governance, and cultural engagement suggests that it's more than just a pipe dream—it's a roadmap to a future where technology and humanity are intertwined in new, empowering ways.

The Sui community represents the human element of blockchain, where technology is just a tool to achieve broader, more human-centric goals. This community has grown from a group of enthusiasts into a cultural force, shaping Sui not just through code contributions or token holdings but through shared values, collective learning, and a vision of a decentralized world where everyone can participate and benefit. As we delve deeper into this chapter, we'll explore how this community has built its culture, how it governs, educates, and embraces diversity, painting a picture of how Sui is not just a blockchain but a living, breathing community with the potential to influence the future of digital interaction.

Part 2: Building the Culture

Building the culture of the Sui community is an ongoing, dynamic process that transcends the mere adoption of technology. It's about creating a shared identity, fostering a sense of belonging, and establishing norms and values that guide the community's interactions and aspirations. This culture is not imposed but emerges from the collective actions, stories, and engagements of its members, making it uniquely reflective of who they are and what they believe in. Here's an exploration of how this culture has been built, maintained, and evolved within the Sui ecosystem.

Cultural Foundations:

At the heart of Sui's cultural foundation lies the principle of open-source collaboration. This not only pertains to the development of the blockchain itself but to how the community sees itself—open, transparent, and inclusive. The ethos began with the developers sharing not just code but also the vision for a blockchain that could scale, be secure, and still maintain a human-centric approach. This openness encouraged others to join, contribute, and feel part of something larger than themselves.

Events and Gatherings:

One of the most effective ways to build culture has been through events. From global hackathons to local meetups, these gatherings serve multiple purposes. They are platforms for education, where new members can learn about Sui's technology in a hands-on environment. They're also incubators for innovation, where developers collaborate on new projects or refine existing ones. But perhaps most importantly for culture, they're where relationships are formed, where the community's spirit is celebrated through shared experiences, meals, and sometimes even shared challenges.

Hackathons, in particular, have become a cornerstone of Sui's culture. These events are not just about coding; they're cultural festivals where participants showcase creativity, teamwork, and the values of the community. Successful projects from hackathons often go on to influence the broader ecosystem, embedding the culture of innovation and community contribution into Sui's DNA.

Online Interaction Spaces:

The digital realm has been equally crucial. Forums like Discord, Reddit, and Telegram serve as the daily life of the Sui community. Here, culture is built through daily interactions, where members share not just technical insights but also humor, memes, and personal stories. These platforms have their own subcultures, with unique lingo, inside jokes, and traditions like "AMA" sessions with key figures or "Meme Mondays" where members share humorous takes on blockchain life.

Social media has been instrumental in shaping Sui's identity. Twitter threads, Instagram stories, and LinkedIn posts by community members and official Sui accounts all contribute to a narrative that's both educational and inspirational. They've helped create a visual and narrative identity for Sui that's appealing and accessible, drawing in people from outside the traditional tech bubble.

Memes and Shared Language:

Memes within the Sui community are not just for laughs; they are cultural artifacts that encapsulate shared experiences, frustrations, and aspirations. They serve as a shorthand for complex ideas or emotions, making the community's culture more relatable and fostering a sense of unity. The shared language, including terms like "Sui-fam" or "Sui-ing" (to do something in the spirit of Sui's values), creates an insider's club feel, where members feel part of something special.

Cultural Narratives:

Every community has its stories, and Sui is no exception. Narratives of overcoming challenges, like scaling issues or security threats, are shared and celebrated. Success stories of dApps built on Sui, or individuals who have learned to code or manage digital assets thanks to the community, become folklore. These stories not only motivate but also define what it means to be part of Sui, often highlighting values like resilience, innovation, and mutual support.

Inclusivity and Diversity:

Culture building at Sui also involves actively promoting inclusivity. Events are designed to be welcoming to newcomers, with sessions for beginners alongside advanced topics. Online, there's an effort to make discussions accessible, with translations or explanations for non-native speakers. This inclusivity extends to celebrating diversity, whether it's through recognizing contributions from different parts of the world or ensuring that cultural events respect and incorporate various traditions.

Community-Driven Projects:

A significant aspect of Sui's culture is the encouragement of community-driven projects.

Whether it's a new dApp, an educational initiative, or a charity drive using Sui's technology, these projects are where the community's values come to life. They're not just about showcasing what Sui can do but about showing how the community thinks, collaborates, and solves problems, reinforcing a culture of collective action and impact.

Cultural Evolution:

Like any living culture, Sui's community culture evolves. As new members join, bringing different perspectives, the culture adapts. When the technology evolves, so does the culture around it, with new memes, new stories, and perhaps new values or focuses emerging. Governance proposals, for instance, can lead to cultural shifts as they reflect on what the community deems important at any given time.

Challenges and Resilience:

Building and maintaining culture isn't without its challenges. With growth comes the risk of losing the close-knit feel, of diluting the culture with too many voices, or facing cultural clashes due to diversity. Yet, these challenges are met with resilience. The community's response to these issues has often been to double down on communication, education, and community events that reinforce the core values while allowing for new cultural expressions to emerge.

Legacy and Future:

The culture of Sui is its legacy. It's what will be remembered long after the current technology trends have passed. This culture, built on openness, collaboration, education, and inclusivity, sets a foundation for the future where Sui isn't just a blockchain but a cultural movement. As Sui looks to expand its influence, this culture will be its greatest export, influencing other blockchain communities, perhaps even traditional tech or social spaces, by demonstrating how technology can foster a positive, inclusive community.

Building the culture of the Sui community has been an intentional, participatory process. It's about more than just using a blockchain; it's about creating a space where people feel valued, where innovation is celebrated, and where diversity is a strength. This culture isn't static but a living, evolving narrative of what blockchain can be when it's not just about the technology but about the people it connects and empowers.

Part 3: Community Governance and Participation

Community governance in the Sui ecosystem is a testament to the blockchain's commitment to decentralization, not just in its technical architecture but in its operational philosophy. This part explores how the Sui community engages in the governance process, the mechanisms that enable this participation, and the profound impact this has on both the platform's development and its cultural identity. Here, governance transcends traditional decision-making; it becomes a communal act that shapes the very future of Sui.

The Principles of Sui's Governance:

At its core, Sui's governance model is built on the principles of transparency, inclusivity, and empowerment. Transparency ensures that all members have access to the information needed to make informed decisions. Inclusivity means that anyone with SUI tokens can participate, not just major stakeholders. Empowerment comes from giving the community real, meaningful control over the platform's direction, ensuring that Sui evolves in line with its users' needs and aspirations.

Mechanisms for Participation:

Sui employs several mechanisms to facilitate community governance:

- **Voting on Proposals:** The most direct form of participation is through voting on governance proposals. These can range from technical upgrades to policy changes or economic adjustments. Voting is typically weighted by the amount of SUI staked, but there are ongoing discussions about alternative or supplementary methods to ensure broader participation.
- **Proposal Submission:** Any community member can submit a proposal for changes or new initiatives. This open invitation to contribute ideas democratizes innovation,

allowing for grassroots movements within the ecosystem. The process usually involves drafting, discussion, and refinement phases before a proposal goes to vote.

- **Delegated Voting:** Recognizing that not everyone has the time or inclination to engage in every governance matter, Sui supports vote delegation. Token holders can delegate their voting power to others they trust or believe represent their interests, fostering a system where expertise and engagement are rewarded.

- **Decentralized Autonomous Organizations (DAOs):** Sui's governance model might leverage DAOs for specific projects or areas of the ecosystem. These allow for more focused, community-driven governance where members with specific interests can collaborate closely, making decisions about funding, project direction, or even community events.

Participation in Practice:

Real-world participation in Sui's governance has led to several notable outcomes:

- **Network Upgrades:** Community votes have directly influenced network parameters like block size, transaction fees, or validator requirements, tailoring the blockchain to the needs of its users.

- **Economic Policies:** Decisions on staking rewards, inflation rates, or how to manage the

SUI token supply have been community-driven, ensuring economic policies align with the community's vision for sustainability and growth.
- **Community Projects:** Governance has extended to funding community projects through grants or direct treasury allocations, empowering members to innovate within the ecosystem, from educational initiatives to new dApps.
- **Cultural Initiatives:** The community has also used governance to shape its own culture, deciding on community events, educational campaigns, or even how to represent Sui in the broader world.

Impact on Development:

The governance model has significantly impacted Sui's development:

- **User-Centric Design:** By involving the community, development focuses on real-world use cases and user feedback, leading to a more practical and user-friendly blockchain.
- **Innovation:** Community proposals often bring fresh ideas to the table, driving innovation that might not have been considered by a centralized team.
- **Security and Stability:** With community oversight, security proposals are scrutinized, enhancing network security. The collective wisdom of the community also helps in

identifying potential risks or vulnerabilities before they become issues.
- **Responsibility and Ownership:** When developers and users alike participate in governance, there's a shared sense of responsibility for the platform's health and success, fostering a culture where everyone feels like an owner.

Challenges in Community Governance:

Despite its benefits, community governance isn't without challenges:

- **Voter Apathy:** Not all community members engage in governance, which can lead to decisions made by a minority, potentially not reflecting the broader community's will.
- **Complexity:** The intricacies of blockchain governance can be daunting, requiring a significant educational effort to ensure informed participation.
- **Centralization Risks:** If governance becomes dominated by a few large stakeholders or if the community lacks diversity in participation, the very ethos of decentralization can be at risk.
- **Decision-Making Speed:** While democratic, community governance can be slower than centralized decisions, sometimes at odds with the need for quick responses to emerging issues or opportunities.

Countermeasures and Innovations:

Sui and its community are actively working on these challenges:

- **Educational Campaigns:** There's a strong push towards educating members on governance, not just how to participate but why it matters.
- **Incentivization:** Rewards for participation, whether through recognition, additional voting power, or even token incentives, are being explored to combat apathy.
- **Governance Tools:** Development of user-friendly governance interfaces or apps that simplify the voting process or proposal submission.
- **Dynamic Governance Models:** Exploring ways to adapt governance structures or voting mechanisms to be more inclusive or responsive to the community's changing needs.

The Cultural Impact:

Governance within Sui has profound cultural implications:

- **Empowerment:** It instills a culture of empowerment, where each member knows they can influence the platform's future, fostering a sense of agency and belonging.
- **Responsibility:** With governance comes responsibility, and this shared responsibility shapes a community culture that values collective well-being over individual gain.

- **Innovation:** The governance process itself encourages innovation, not just in technology but in how communities can organize, make decisions, and govern themselves.
- **Resilience:** A community that governs itself is likely more resilient to external pressures or internal conflicts, as it has built-in mechanisms for dialogue, resolution, and adaptation.

Looking Forward:

As Sui matures, its governance model will likely evolve:

- **Integration of New Technologies:** AI or machine learning could be used to enhance governance by analyzing proposals, predicting outcomes, or even helping in decision-making processes.
- **Global Expansion:** As Sui's community grows globally, governance might see adaptations to cater to different cultural norms or regulatory environments.
- **Interoperability:** If Sui becomes part of a larger blockchain ecosystem, governance could extend to cross-chain interactions, necessitating new models or protocols for decision-making.
- **Sustainability Focus:** Governance decisions might increasingly consider environmental impacts, leading to policies aimed at sustainable blockchain practices.

In conclusion, community governance and participation in Sui are not just about making decisions; they're about cultivating a living, breathing ecosystem where every voice can contribute to the collective future. This participatory approach has not only influenced the technical and economic aspects of Sui but has also deeply shaped its culture, making it a model for how blockchain projects can engage with their communities in meaningful, impactful ways.

Part 4: Education and Empowerment

Education is the cornerstone of empowerment within the Sui community, serving as the bridge that connects individuals to the blockchain's potential, demystifies its complexities, and equips them with the knowledge to actively participate in this evolving digital ecosystem. This part examines how Sui approaches education, the tools and methods it employs, and how these efforts lead to a more empowered, inclusive community.

The Philosophy of Education in Sui:

Sui's approach to education is guided by a belief that blockchain technology should be accessible to all, not just those with a deep technical background. There's a recognition that for Sui to achieve its vision, it needs a community that understands, trusts, and can leverage its capabilities. This philosophy shapes a broad, inclusive educational ecosystem that caters to different learning styles, levels of expertise, and areas of interest.

Educational Tools and Resources:

To facilitate learning, Sui has developed or supported a variety of educational tools:

- **Documentation and Guides:** Comprehensive, beginner-friendly documentation is available for both users and developers. This includes step-by-step guides on using Sui, developing on the platform, and understanding its underlying technology.
- **Tutorials and Workshops:** From basic introductions to blockchain concepts to advanced Move programming, Sui offers tutorials that are often interactive or video-based. Workshops, both online and in-person, provide hands-on experience, often culminating in participants building something tangible, like a simple smart contract.
- **Sui Academy:** Imagining a dedicated space for learning, Sui might develop or partner for a platform akin to an academy where courses are structured, covering everything from blockchain fundamentals to specific Sui features. This could include certifications, recognizing the skills of participants.
- **Developer Documentation and SDKs:** For developers, there's a focus on providing clear, well-maintained SDKs, API references, and sample codes that reduce the learning curve and encourage experimentation.
- **Community Forums and Q&A:** Platforms where community members can ask questions, share knowledge, and learn from

each other. These are often curated by volunteers or community leaders to ensure accuracy and relevance.

Educational Initiatives:

Sui's educational efforts extend beyond static resources:

- **Hackathons and Coding Challenges:** These events are not just about competition but about learning in a collaborative environment. Participants often learn more through teamwork, mentorship, and the process of building projects under time constraints.
- **Educational Grants:** Sui could offer grants for educational projects, whether it's creating new learning materials, hosting educational events, or even translating resources into different languages to broaden access.
- **Ambassador Programs:** Engaging community members as ambassadors who can educate others in their local areas or online, spreading knowledge and excitement about Sui.
- **Partnerships with Educational Institutions:** Working with universities or online learning platforms to integrate Sui into curricula or to offer specialized courses, tapping into academic rigor and legitimacy.
- **Webinars and AMAs:** Regular sessions with experts or key figures from the Sui team provide insights, answer common questions,

and keep the community updated on developments, all while educating attendees.

Empowerment through Education:

The impact of education on empowerment within the Sui ecosystem is profound:

- **Democratizing Access:** By breaking down the technical barriers, Sui makes blockchain technology accessible, allowing more individuals to participate, whether as users, investors, or creators.
- **Innovation and Creativity:** An educated community is more likely to innovate. With a solid understanding of the platform, members can envision and implement new uses for Sui, from novel financial instruments to artistic expressions.
- **Economic Empowerment:** Knowledge about how to use, invest in, or develop on Sui can lead to economic opportunities. This includes understanding staking, participating in governance, or building profitable dApps.
- **Community Leadership:** Education fosters leaders within the community who can guide, support, and inspire others, creating a self-sustaining cycle of empowerment.

Challenges in Educational Outreach:

However, educational initiatives face several challenges:

- **Keeping Content Updated:** Blockchain technology, including Sui, evolves rapidly. Keeping educational materials current is vital but resource-intensive.
- **Engaging Diverse Learners:** Not everyone learns the same way. Balancing textual, auditory, visual, and hands-on learning methods to cater to a broad audience is complex.
- **Cultural and Language Barriers:** With a global community, ensuring educational content resonates across cultures and is available in multiple languages is essential but challenging.
- **Overcoming Skepticism:** There's still a segment of the population skeptical of blockchain; education must address these concerns head-on to convert skepticism into curiosity or acceptance.

Innovative Educational Approaches:

To tackle these challenges, Sui might consider:

- **Gamification:** Turning learning into a game with rewards, points, or leaderboards can make education more engaging, especially for younger audiences or those less inclined towards traditional learning methods.
- **AI-Personalized Learning:** Using AI to tailor educational content to individual learning paths, pace, and interests could revolutionize how community members learn about Sui.

- **Peer-to-Peer Learning:** Encouraging a system where experienced members mentor newcomers, fostering a community of practice where knowledge is shared organically.
- **Modular Learning:** Creating educational modules that can be combined in various ways, allowing learners to construct their learning journey based on their needs or interests.

The Role of Education in Governance:

Education isn't just about technical know-how; it's crucial for effective governance:

- **Informed Voting:** An educated community makes better governance decisions. Understanding proposals, the implications of votes, and the broader context is vital for effective participation.
- **Proposal Quality:** Educated members are more likely to propose high-quality, well-thought-out ideas for governance, leading to more beneficial changes to the platform.
- **Community Resilience:** Knowledgeable communities are more resilient, able to navigate through market downturns, technological shifts, or regulatory changes with a better understanding of the underlying principles.

Future Directions in Education:

Looking forward, Sui's educational landscape might evolve in several ways:

- **Virtual Reality (VR) and Augmented Reality (AR):** For complex concepts or for those who learn best through immersion, VR/AR could offer interactive, experiential learning about blockchain and Sui.
- **Blockchain Education for Non-Tech Sectors:** As blockchain permeates various industries, educational programs tailored for finance, art, supply chain, etc., could become significant, showcasing Sui's versatility.
- **Global Education Platforms:** Sui might aim to create or contribute to a global platform where educational content about blockchain is shared across different ecosystems, promoting interoperability in knowledge as well as technology.
- **Continuous Learning Culture:** Encouraging a culture where learning is not a one-time event but a continuous journey, with regular updates, refresher courses, and advanced learning opportunities.

Education within the Sui community is not just about imparting knowledge; it's about fostering an environment where every individual can become an active, empowered participant in the blockchain revolution. Through thoughtful educational strategies, Sui not only grows its ecosystem but also champions a model of community where empowerment through learning leads to innovation, inclusivity, and a shared vision for the future of decentralized technologies.

Part 5: Diversity and Inclusion

Sui's vision for blockchain technology extends beyond mere technological advancement; it encompasses creating a platform where diversity is not just acknowledged but celebrated, where inclusion is not just a goal but a core operational principle. This part delves into how Sui approaches diversity and inclusion, the challenges it faces, and the strategies it employs to ensure that everyone, regardless of background, can find a place within the Sui ecosystem.

Understanding Diversity in Blockchain:

Diversity in blockchain isn't just about having participants from different parts of the world; it's about inclusivity across race, gender, age, economic status, and technical expertise. Blockchain's promise is to democratize access to technology and finance, but this promise can only be realized if the community reflects the diverse world it aims to serve. Sui recognizes that true innovation and robustness come from a wide array of perspectives, experiences, and skills.

Sui's Approach to Inclusion:

- **Accessible Technology:** Sui's design philosophy includes making its technology as user-friendly as possible, reducing the technical barriers that might exclude those without extensive tech backgrounds. This involves intuitive interfaces, clear documentation, and tools that cater to different levels of expertise.

- **Language and Culture:** Recognizing the global nature of its community, Sui encourages translations of key resources into multiple languages. This extends to cultural sensitivity in events, communications, and governance, ensuring that all cultural nuances are respected and that no one feels alienated due to language or cultural differences.
- **Educational Programs:** As discussed in previous parts, education is a key strategy for inclusion. These programs are designed to be accessible to all, from beginners to advanced users, ensuring that everyone can learn at their pace and in their preferred style.
- **Community Initiatives:** Sui fosters community groups focused on underrepresented demographics, like women in blockchain or blockchain for social impact, providing platforms for these groups to engage, support each other, and influence the ecosystem.
- **Inclusive Governance:** Governance mechanisms are crafted to encourage participation from all community members, not just those with the largest stakes. This might include weighted voting systems that consider factors beyond token holdings, like community contributions or engagement.

Challenges to Diversity:

Despite these efforts, several challenges persist:

- **Tech Gender Gap:** The tech and blockchain sectors still suffer from a significant gender disparity, with fewer women and non-binary individuals participating or leading.
- **Economic Barriers:** The cost of entry into blockchain, whether in terms of hardware, internet access, or the initial investment in tokens, can exclude those from less economically privileged backgrounds.
- **Cultural Misunderstandings:** With a global community, misunderstandings or cultural clashes can occur, potentially leading to exclusion if not managed sensitively.
- **Educational Disparity:** Not everyone has access to quality education, which can limit understanding and participation in complex tech ecosystems like Sui.

Strategies for Enhancing Diversity:

To address these challenges, Sui might employ several strategies:

- **Scholarship and Grant Programs:** Offering scholarships for educational programs or grants for projects led by underrepresented groups can lower economic barriers to entry.
- **Outreach Programs:** Actively reaching out to communities that might not typically engage with blockchain technology, hosting events in diverse locations, or partnering with organizations that focus on social inclusion.

- **Mentorship and Support Networks:** Creating mentorship programs where experienced community members guide those from underrepresented groups, fostering an environment where everyone can succeed.
- **Inclusive Event Planning:** Ensuring that community events are planned with diversity in mind, from accessible locations to inclusive speaker line-ups to content that resonates with a broad audience.
- **Policy and Advocacy:** Advocating for policies within the ecosystem that promote diversity, like anti-discrimination practices in community spaces or encouraging fair representation in governance bodies.

Empowering Diverse Voices:

Empowerment through diversity in Sui goes beyond just increasing numbers:

- **Diverse Leadership:** Encouraging and supporting diverse individuals to take leadership roles within the community or in project development, ensuring decision-making reflects a wide range of viewpoints.
- **Showcasing Success Stories:** Highlighting achievements by diverse members can inspire others, showing that everyone can contribute and succeed in the Sui ecosystem.
- **Cultural Exchange:** Facilitating cultural exchanges or partnerships where different

communities collaborate on projects, enriching the ecosystem with varied cultural inputs.

- **Feedback Loops:** Establishing mechanisms where feedback from all community segments can influence how Sui evolves, ensuring that development is guided by a diverse set of needs and desires.

The Impact of Diversity on Innovation:

A diverse community brings:

- **Creative Problem-Solving:** Different backgrounds lead to different approaches to solving problems, potentially leading to more innovative solutions on the Sui platform.
- **Broader Use Cases:** With a diverse community, Sui can explore applications in various sectors or cultural contexts that might not have been considered otherwise.
- **Market Expansion:** A more inclusive community can help Sui tap into markets or user bases that traditional tech platforms might overlook.
- **Resilience:** A diverse community is often more resilient to external pressures or internal challenges, as it brings a variety of perspectives to bear on any issue.

Looking Forward:

The future of diversity and inclusion at Sui could involve:

- **Global Community Hubs:** Establishing or supporting local community hubs around the world, where local cultures can influence and be influenced by blockchain technology.
- **Inclusion Metrics:** Developing metrics to measure inclusion within the community, which can guide further actions or highlight areas needing improvement.
- **Cross-Chain Inclusion Efforts:** As blockchain interoperability grows, Sui could lead or participate in initiatives promoting diversity across the broader blockchain ecosystem.
- **Technology for Inclusion:** Leveraging Sui's technology for social good, like facilitating microtransactions for underbanked populations or supporting decentralized identity for those without traditional ID systems.

Challenges on the Horizon:

While the vision is clear, challenges remain:

- **Balancing Scale and Personalization:** As Sui grows, maintaining personal engagement and tailored inclusivity efforts could become more challenging.
- **Regulatory Navigation:** Ensuring that inclusion initiatives align with various global regulations can be complex, especially if those regulations differ significantly.
- **Sustaining Momentum:** Keeping diversity and inclusion at the forefront as the community

evolves requires continuous effort and commitment.

Sui positions itself not only as a technological leader but as a pioneer in how blockchain can be a force for progress.

Part 6: The Future of Sui's Community

The trajectory of Sui's community is not just about expanding numbers or increasing engagement; it's about evolving into a force that can shape the future of blockchain, digital interaction, and community governance. As we look ahead, this final part explores the potential directions for Sui's community, the challenges it might face, and the role it could play in the broader narrative of decentralized technologies.

Vision for Community Evolution:

Sui's community is envisioned as a dynamic, self-sustaining entity where each member feels empowered to contribute to the platform's development, culture, and governance. The future community would be:

- **More Decentralized:** With an emphasis on distributing power and decision-making even further, ensuring that the community's growth does not lead to centralization.
- **Culturally Rich:** Evolving beyond current norms, incorporating diverse cultural expressions, and perhaps even influencing global digital culture.

- **Economically Diverse:** Where participation isn't limited by economic status, with mechanisms in place to ensure that everyone can engage in Sui's economy.
- **Educated and Innovative:** Continuously learning, adapting, and innovating, with the community at the forefront of new blockchain applications or solutions.
- **Globally Connected:** Acting as a bridge between different blockchain ecosystems, cultures, and perhaps even traditional sectors, fostering a more interconnected digital world.

Potential Community-Driven Projects:

The future might see community initiatives like:

- **Sui Cultural Festivals:** Annual or biannual events celebrating the diversity within the community, possibly with a focus on art, music, or other cultural expressions leveraging blockchain.
- **Decentralized Educational Platforms:** Where the community collaborates to create, vet, and disseminate knowledge about blockchain, finance, and technology, potentially leading to a global blockchain education network.
- **Sui for Social Good:** Projects where blockchain technology is used to address social issues, from environmental sustainability to education access, showcasing the platform's potential for social impact.

- **Cross-Chain Collaborations:** Community-driven efforts to enhance interoperability, perhaps through hackathons or working groups that develop standards or tools for cross-chain communication.

Scaling Community Impact:

As Sui scales, its community's influence could:

- **Shape Blockchain Governance:** Sui could become a case study for how decentralized governance can work at scale, influencing other blockchain projects to adopt similar models.
- **Drive Mainstream Adoption:** By making blockchain technology accessible, fun, and relevant to everyday life, the community could significantly increase the adoption of blockchain solutions.
- **Influence Policy and Regulation:** A knowledgeable, active community might engage with policymakers to shape regulations that favor blockchain innovation while protecting users.
- **Foster New Economic Models:** Through experiments in DeFi, tokenomics, or even new forms of digital property rights, the community could pioneer economic models that could redefine value exchange.

Challenges in Community Growth:

However, growth brings its own set of challenges:

- **Maintaining Cohesion:** As the community grows, keeping everyone aligned with common goals or cultural norms becomes more complex.
- **Dilution of Values:** There's a risk that the core values of inclusivity, transparency, and empowerment might get diluted with influxes of new members who might not share the same ethos.
- **Scalability of Governance:** Ensuring that governance remains effective and inclusive as the number of participants increases will require innovative solutions.
- **Security and Scams:** With growth comes increased risk of scams or malicious actors trying to exploit the community, necessitating robust security measures and education.
- **Technological Challenges:** As the community pushes Sui's technology to new limits, technical scalability, user experience, and network performance will be under constant scrutiny.

Strategic Directions for Community Engagement:

To navigate these challenges, Sui might consider:

- **Community Governance Evolution:** Introducing or refining governance tools to handle larger scales of participation without losing efficiency or inclusivity.
- **Community Health Metrics:** Developing metrics to assess community health,

engagement, and sentiment, using this data to guide community initiatives.
- **Localized Community Management:** Empowering regional or interest-based sub-communities to manage their own affairs while aligning with the broader Sui mission.
- **Enhanced Educational Efforts:** Scaling up educational initiatives to keep pace with community growth, possibly using AI to personalize learning paths.
- **Cultural Ambassadors:** Appointing or recognizing community members as cultural ambassadors who can help navigate and bridge cultural differences within the community.

The Role of Community in Sui's Expansion:

The community's role in Sui's expansion into new markets, technologies, or sectors could be pivotal:

- **Market Penetration:** Community members could act as evangelists or educators in new markets, explaining Sui's benefits in local contexts.
- **Innovation Incubators:** The community could serve as an incubator for new ideas, where the collective brainpower drives the platform forward into new use cases.
- **Feedback Loop:** A strong, engaged community provides invaluable feedback for product development, ensuring that Sui evolves in ways that meet real user needs.

- **Defense Against Centralization:** By actively participating in governance, the community can push back against any tendencies towards centralization, ensuring Sui remains true to its decentralized ethos.

Speculative Future Scenarios:

Looking far ahead, we might envision:

- **A Sui-Led Digital Renaissance:** Where blockchain technology, driven by Sui's community, becomes the bedrock for a new wave of digital art, governance, and economy, fundamentally altering how we interact with digital assets.
- **Sui as a Cultural Phenomenon:** The community could elevate Sui to a cultural icon, where its brand is synonymous with innovation, community, and digital freedom.
- **Global Impact Initiatives:** Sui could become a platform for global initiatives, where community-led projects tackle some of the world's biggest challenges, from climate change to financial inclusion.
- **Interdisciplinary Integration:** Sui's community might lead the charge in integrating blockchain with other emerging technologies like AI, IoT, or VR, creating new paradigms for digital interaction.

The future of Sui's community is not just about the blockchain itself but about how this community can influence and shape the world around it. It's about a vision where technology and human interaction are so intertwined that they evolve together, creating a digital ecosystem where everyone has a stake and a voice.

However, this vision requires navigating through challenges with creativity, resilience, and a commitment to the principles that have defined Sui so far. The community will need to balance growth with identity, scale with personal touch, and innovation with inclusivity. If successful, Sui's community could be a blueprint for how technology can be a force for good, driven by the collective will and wisdom of its users.

In essence, the future of Sui's community is a narrative of potential—a story where technology serves humanity, where every individual can be both a participant and a leader in the digital age, and where the blockchain becomes not just a ledger but a living, breathing community with the power to change the world.

Chapter 21: Sui's Contribution to Blockchain Governance and Community Building

Part 1: Governance in the Blockchain Context

Governance in the blockchain ecosystem is a nuanced and critical aspect that often determines the long-term viability, adaptability, and community acceptance of a blockchain platform. As we delve into Sui's potential role in shaping blockchain governance, it's essential to start by understanding why governance matters and how it differs from traditional models.

In traditional organizations, governance is centralized, with decision-making power often concentrated in the hands of a few, such as a board of directors or government bodies. These entities make decisions that affect the entire organization or populace, sometimes with little direct input from those they govern. This structure is designed for efficiency but can lead to issues like lack of transparency, accountability, and responsiveness to the needs of individuals or smaller groups within the organization.

Blockchain, on the other hand, introduces a paradigm shift towards decentralized governance. This is not just about who makes decisions but also about how those decisions are made, enforced, and can be changed. Here, governance can be seen as a combination of technology, economics, and community dynamics:

Firstly, governance in blockchain is inherently about consensus. Unlike traditional systems where decisions might be enforced through hierarchy, in blockchain, consensus mechanisms are used to reach agreement among participants who might not trust each other or even know each other personally. This consensus can be achieved through various methods like Proof of Work (PoW), Proof of Stake (PoS), or Sui's Delegated Proof of Stake (DPoS), where decision-making power is distributed among stakeholders, often based on their stake in the network.

Secondly, the rules of governance on a blockchain are often encoded in smart contracts or directly into the protocol itself. This means that governance decisions can be more transparent because they are public and immutable once committed to the blockchain. However, this immutability also poses challenges; changing these rules requires a new consensus, which can be complex and contentious, as seen in various hard forks in blockchain history.

Thirdly, blockchain governance involves a broad spectrum of participants, from developers, miners, or validators, to users and investors. Each group holds different interests and influence within the ecosystem. Effective governance must balance these interests, ensuring no single group can unilaterally dictate changes that might disadvantage others.

The importance of governance in blockchain cannot be overstated:

- **Security and Trust:** Good governance ensures the security of the network by allowing for timely updates to address vulnerabilities or to incorporate new security features. It helps in building trust among users, as they see a system that can adapt to threats or changes in technology.
- **Adaptability:** Blockchain technology evolves rapidly. Governance mechanisms that are too rigid can hinder a blockchain's ability to adapt to new technologies, regulatory changes, or shifts in user needs. Sui's governance model aims to provide a framework where the network can evolve without losing its foundational principles.
- **Community Engagement:** Governance can be a powerful tool for community building. By involving the community in decision-making, a blockchain like Sui can foster a sense of ownership and loyalty among its users. This engagement can lead to more robust development, as community members feel they have a stake in the platform's success.
- **Economic Incentives:** Governance in blockchain often ties into the economic model of the network. Decisions on tokenomics, fees, or staking mechanisms directly impact the economic health of the blockchain, influencing both the token's value and the incentives for participants to engage with or maintain the network.
- **Decentralization vs. Efficiency:** One of the fundamental tensions in blockchain

governance is balancing decentralization with the need for swift, effective decision-making. Too much centralization can undermine the very ethos of blockchain, while too decentralized a system might become inefficient or unable to make necessary changes promptly.

Sui, with its unique architecture, has the potential to address these aspects in novel ways:

- **Speed and Scalability:** Sui's ability to process transactions quickly and at scale could extend to governance processes, allowing for more frequent or real-time decision-making without the network becoming bogged down.
- **Move's Safety Features:** The programming language Move, designed for safety and precision, could be used to encode governance logic in smart contracts, reducing the risk of governance-related bugs or exploits.
- **Object-Centric Model:** Sui's approach to treating everything as objects could simplify how governance decisions impact the state of the blockchain, allowing for more granular and efficient updates to the protocol or system parameters.
- **DPoS Consensus:** With a delegated proof-of-stake system, Sui can facilitate a form of governance where validators, elected by token holders, play a significant role in decision-making, potentially leading to more active and engaged governance.

- **Community Tools:** Sui could provide or facilitate the development of tools that make governance more accessible. This might include user-friendly interfaces for voting, proposal submission, or even educational resources on governance processes.

However, implementing effective governance within Sui's ecosystem will not be without challenges:

- **Ensuring Representation:** A significant challenge is ensuring that governance reflects the diverse interests within the community, avoiding scenarios where only those with significant stakes or technical know-how can influence decisions.
- **Preventing Centralization:** As governance becomes more sophisticated, there's a risk that it could lead to centralization of power among a few knowledgeable or well-resourced participants, which contradicts the decentralized ethos.
- **Education and Participation:** For governance to be truly decentralized, broad participation is needed. This requires ongoing education to demystify the process for users and incentives to encourage active participation.
- **Security of Governance Processes:** With governance decisions potentially affecting the entire network, securing these processes against manipulation or attack is paramount. This involves not only technical security but

also social mechanisms to deter malicious governance attempts.

- **Balancing Speed with Deliberation:** While Sui's design allows for speed, governance decisions often require careful deliberation to prevent hasty or poorly considered changes that might harm the network's long-term prospects.

In conclusion, governance in the context of Sui and blockchain technology is about more than just decision-making; it's about creating a sustainable, evolving system where technology, community, and governance mechanisms work in synergy. Sui's contribution to this field could be transformative, offering a model where governance is not only about maintaining the status quo but actively shaping the future of blockchain technology in a way that's inclusive, secure, and responsive to the community it serves.

Part 2: Sui's Governance Model

Sui's approach to governance aims to revolutionize how decentralized systems manage change, protect community interests, and evolve over time. This exploration delves into how Sui's architectural innovations, including its object-centric model, the Move programming language, and its consensus mechanism, could shape its governance framework.

At the heart of Sui's governance philosophy is the principle of decentralized decision-making. The platform is designed to distribute power more evenly among its community, contrasting with systems where governance might be dominated by a few large stakeholders or developers. This is achieved through a system where token holders, developers, and even users without tokens can have a say in the platform's direction. Voting mechanisms could range from direct democracy, where each participant votes on proposals, to a more layered system with representatives or delegates making decisions on behalf of the community. Additionally, there would be a transparent process for proposal submissions, allowing anyone to suggest changes to the protocol, network parameters, or introduce new features, which are then debated, refined, and voted upon to ensure they reflect collective will rather than individual interests.

Sui's governance model also emphasizes efficiency and speed, leveraging its inherent design for quick consensus and dynamic upgrades. The Delegated Proof of Stake (DPoS) mechanism enables faster decision-making compared to other consensus models, facilitating rapid agreement on governance decisions. The object-centric model allows for precise, isolated changes to the network state, potentially simplifying and speeding up upgrades, reducing the risk and complexity associated with such changes.

Security and integrity are paramount in Sui's governance model. The safety features of the Move programming language protect against common vulnerabilities, crucial for the smart contracts that manage voting, proposal execution, or fund allocation. All governance actions are recorded on the blockchain, providing a transparent, auditable trail that enhances trust and accountability within the community.

To ensure inclusivity and accessibility, Sui aims to make governance not just for the technically adept or those with significant financial stakes. This involves creating user-friendly tools that simplify participation in governance. Whether it's through intuitive voting platforms, proposal submission tools, or educational resources, the aim is to make governance accessible to all. There could also be incentives for participation, like governance tokens or rewards for voting, encouraging broad engagement.

Sui's governance must be adaptive, learning from the broader blockchain ecosystem's governance experiences. A modular approach to governance could be adopted, where different aspects of the network have tailored governance mechanisms. This modularity could mean one part of the governance manages economic policies, another technical upgrades, ensuring each area can evolve independently according to its specific needs. Sui can also incorporate lessons from other blockchains' governance to encourage constructive debate, prevent decision-making gridlock, or manage contentious upgrades more effectively.

In practice, Sui's governance model could be tested with network upgrades where the community decides on new features, bug fixes, or changes to consensus rules. Economic decisions like adjustments to gas fees, staking rewards, or token supply could be community-driven, allowing for a responsive economic model. Furthermore, the governance might extend to funding or directing community projects, where members vote on which initiatives to support, fostering innovation and development that aligns with community interests.

However, implementing this model comes with challenges. Balancing power so that governance doesn't favor those with more tokens or resources is crucial. Sui might explore mechanisms like quadratic voting to give smaller stakeholders a voice. Achieving efficiency in decision-making with a diverse community can be slow, potentially hindering the platform's ability to react to urgent issues. Governance processes must scale as the network grows, maintaining speed and inclusivity without centralizing control. User education is also essential; participants need to understand the implications of their votes or proposals. Lastly, there's a cultural shift required from a developer-led to a community-led model, where members see themselves as co-owners, not just users.

Sui's governance model has the potential to set a new standard for decentralized systems, emphasizing integrity, efficiency, and community involvement. By leveraging its technological advantages, Sui can create a governance system that not only manages the blockchain's operations but also empowers its users, developers, and stakeholders to shape its future in a transparent, secure, and inclusive manner. This approach could redefine community participation in blockchain ecosystems, fostering a more engaged, responsible, and dynamic community.

Part 3: Decentralized Autonomous Organizations (DAOs) on Sui

Decentralized Autonomous Organizations (DAOs) represent a revolutionary approach to governance, leveraging blockchain technology to empower collective decision-making without centralized control. Sui, with its advanced architecture, holds immense potential to become a pivotal platform for DAOs, offering unmatched security, scalability, and efficiency. This part delves into how Sui's features could revolutionize DAOs, detailing the mechanisms for their operation, and pondering the broader implications for community governance.

Sui's architecture is uniquely suited to empower DAOs. Security and trust form the bedrock of any DAO, ensuring that the organization's decisions and operations are carried out as intended. Sui's adoption of the Move programming language provides inherent safety features that safeguard against common vulnerabilities in smart contracts. This means that the governance rules, financial transactions, or any operational logic of a DAO can be executed with a high degree of reliability. Moreover, with Sui's consensus mechanism, decisions within a DAO can achieve finality quickly, reducing the time window where malicious actors might attempt to manipulate outcomes.

Scalability is another critical factor for DAOs, where managing the influx of transactions or interactions can strain traditional blockchain networks, leading to high costs or network congestion. Sui's design, with its emphasis on parallel transaction processing and an object-centric model, addresses this challenge head-on. Each proposal, vote, or transaction in a DAO could be managed as an object with its own lifecycle, allowing for a fine-tuned approach to state management. This capability ensures that as DAOs grow in membership, complexity, or the volume of operations, they can do so without degrading performance or incurring prohibitive costs.

The speed of Sui also stands to benefit DAOs significantly. In traditional setups, delays in transaction confirmations can frustrate governance processes, where timely decision-making is often critical. With Sui, governance actions like voting on proposals, managing treasury allocations, or executing community decisions can happen with near-instant finality, making the experience of participating in a DAO more akin to real-world organizational dynamics than to the often slower, block-by-block processes of other blockchains.

When it comes to the mechanisms for DAO operation on Sui, smart contract governance is central. These contracts encode the rules of engagement for DAOs, from how proposals are submitted, how voting occurs, to how funds are managed or distributed. Move's safety features mean these contracts can be more resilient, ensuring that the logic governing a DAO's operations isn't tampered with or executed in unintended ways.

Voting systems within DAOs on Sui could be diverse, tailored to the specific needs or philosophies of each organization. From simple majority votes to more sophisticated systems like quadratic voting, which gives more weight to the diversity of voters rather than just the quantity, or time-weighted voting where longer-held stakes have more influence, these mechanisms can be automated through smart contracts. The blockchain ensures not only that votes are counted accurately but also that the process is transparent, auditable, and immutable.

Treasury management in DAOs on Sui could be remarkably efficient due to the blockchain's low gas costs and high transaction throughput. Funds can be allocated for various purposes with decisions made by the community being executed automatically by smart contracts, maintaining transparency and accountability. This setup allows for a DAO to operate like a decentralized venture fund or community grant provider, where the community decides on the allocation of resources, and the blockchain ensures these decisions are followed through.

Membership and roles within DAOs could be defined and managed through Sui's smart contracts, allowing for nuanced governance models. Different members might have different levels of access or influence, based on their token holdings, contributions, or roles within the DAO. This could lead to more layered governance structures where some decisions might require consensus from certain groups or thresholds of token ownership, ensuring that governance is both democratic and practical.

To illustrate potential applications, consider a DAO on Sui dedicated to governing an open-source project. Here, community members could vote on the project's development direction, feature proposals, or even funding for developers. The smart contracts would automatically execute funding once a proposal is approved, showcasing how DAOs can operate with real-world impact, all managed transparently on the blockchain.

Another scenario involves DAOs managing decentralized funding pools for startups or community projects. Proposals for funding could be submitted and voted upon, with the smart contracts handling the distribution of funds based on community consensus. This could democratize funding in a way that traditional venture capital can't, by giving a broader community the power to decide which projects to support.

Cultural and artistic DAOs might also flourish on Sui, where artists or cultural initiatives could manage royalties, fund new works, or decide on exhibitions through collective governance. Here, the efficiency of Sui ensures artists receive royalties almost instantly from sales or performances, with community decisions shaping the cultural output or public engagements of the DAO.

However, the path to fully realizing DAOs on Sui is not without challenges:

Legal recognition of DAOs remains a gray area in many jurisdictions. While Sui can provide the technical infrastructure for DAOs, navigating the legal landscape to ensure these entities are recognized, can operate compliantly, and can interact with traditional legal systems is a significant challenge.

Decision-making paralysis is another issue where the decentralized nature of DAOs can lead to difficulties in reaching consensus or slow decision-making processes. Sui's governance tools would need to incorporate mechanisms to mitigate this, perhaps through tiered governance structures where certain decisions are made by smaller, specialized groups or by setting decision thresholds to avoid endless debate.

Security over time is a constant concern. As DAOs grow in value or influence, they become prime targets for hacks or manipulation. Continuous security audits, updates to smart contracts to patch vulnerabilities, and educating members on best practices for DAO security will be essential.

User experience also plays a critical role. The complexity of DAO governance shouldn't push away participants. Tools and platforms on Sui would need to make these processes intuitive, abstracting away the complexity behind user-friendly interfaces that encourage broad participation.

Incentive structures must be well-designed to motivate active and constructive participation. This might involve token rewards for governance activities, penalties for inactivity, or other mechanisms to ensure that members are engaged in the DAO's best interest.

Looking to the future, DAOs on Sui could pioneer several innovations:

Cross-DAO collaboration might become more feasible, where different DAOs can share resources, collaborate on projects, or even merge efforts for larger initiatives, leveraging Sui's potential for interoperability across blockchains.

AI integration could play a role in DAOs, analyzing proposals, predicting outcomes, or assisting in drafting governance policies, making the DAO's operations more efficient and insightful.

Decentralized identity solutions could streamline membership in DAOs, enhancing security by ensuring that only verified members can participate in governance, vote, or access resources.

As DAOs evolve on Sui, they might also develop new governance models, better suited to manage large-scale, complex decision-making or integration with real-world legal systems, potentially influencing how governance is conceptualized in both digital and physical realms.

Sui's architecture offers a promising foundation for DAOs to not only exist but thrive, potentially setting new standards for decentralized governance at scale. By providing the necessary tools, security, and efficiency, Sui could facilitate a world where community-driven organizations are not just feasible but impactful in managing complex systems, funding ventures, and shaping cultural projects. The journey towards realizing these DAOs will involve overcoming technical, legal, and social challenges, but the potential for innovation in governance and community empowerment is vast. As Sui matures, it might just redefine what it means to participate in and benefit from decentralized organizations, fostering a future where governance is truly by the people, for the people.

Part 4: Community Building and Engagement

Community building and engagement are not just ancillary activities for a blockchain platform like Sui; they are fundamental to its success, longevity, and ability to innovate. A vibrant community can drive adoption, contribute to development, and ensure the network remains relevant and secure. This part explores how Sui can leverage its unique features and strategic initiatives to cultivate an inclusive, active, and engaged community, highlighting the multifaceted approaches necessary for fostering this ecosystem.

Fostering an Inclusive Community

Sui's vision for an inclusive community starts with making the platform accessible to everyone, regardless of their technical background or familiarity with blockchain technology:

The first step in this journey is creating **user-friendly interfaces**. Blockchain technology, with its complexities, can be intimidating to newcomers. Sui aims to simplify this interaction by developing intuitive wallets, easy-to-navigate decentralized applications (dApps)), and user interfaces that abstract the underlying blockchain complexities. This approach ensures that users can engage with Sui as easily as they would with any other digital service, making the technology less of a barrier and more of an enabler.

Education and Onboarding are pivotal in building an inclusive community. Sui could develop a comprehensive educational ecosystem, including tutorials, guides, and interactive workshops that cover everything from blockchain basics to advanced topics like smart contract programming in Move. By providing these resources in easily digestible formats, Sui can lower the entry barriers for potential users and developers. Workshops or online courses could be offered, potentially in collaboration with educational institutions, to formally educate about blockchain technology, specifically tailored to Sui's ecosystem.

Multilingual Support is another cornerstone of inclusivity. The global nature of blockchain means that language should not be a barrier. By offering documentation, support, and community interactions in multiple languages, Sui can tap into a broader audience, ensuring that its community is as diverse as the world it aims to serve. This initiative could also involve local ambassadors or community leaders who can bridge cultural and linguistic gaps, making Sui a truly global platform.

Engagement Through Incentives

Incentivizing participation is crucial for maintaining an active and growing community:

Sui could introduce **token rewards** for various forms of engagement. This might include rewarding users for participating in governance, contributing to open-source projects, or simply for their activity within the ecosystem. These incentives not only encourage participation but also align individual actions with the network's health and growth. For instance, airdrops or staking rewards could be linked to community activities, fostering a sense of investment in the platform's success.

Developer Grants and Hackathons are excellent for engaging the developer community. By providing financial or resource support to developers working on projects that enhance or expand the Sui ecosystem, Sui can stimulate innovation. Hackathons, in particular, can serve as melting pots for ideas, where developers from around the world come together to solve challenges or build new applications on Sui. These events not only spur development but also build a network of developers who feel a part of the Sui community.

Staking and Governance Participation can further engage users by giving them a say in the platform's direction. By offering governance tokens or additional rewards for staking, Sui can encourage users to not just use the platform but also help steer its future. This participatory model creates a vested interest in the platform's governance and success, deepening community bonds.

Empowering Developers

Developers are the lifeblood of any blockchain ecosystem:

Providing **comprehensive SDKs and tools** will be key. Sui should offer development kits, libraries, and tools specifically designed to harness the platform's unique features, like its object-centric model or Move language. These tools should be well-documented, regularly updated, and designed with both novice and seasoned developers in mind, ensuring that building on Sui is as straightforward as possible.

Encouraging *community-driven development* through open-source projects can lead to a rich tapestry of applications and improvements. Sui could foster an environment where code sharing, peer reviews, and collaborative development are the norms. Platforms like GitHub could be leveraged for code hosting, where community members contribute, fork, or even mentor each other, leading to a self-sustaining development culture.

Bug Bounties and Security Audits are another way to engage the community in a meaningful way. By rewarding those who find and report security vulnerabilities, Sui not only enhances its security but also builds a community that values and contributes to the platform's integrity. Regular security audits, perhaps conducted with community involvement, can ensure that the platform remains robust against threats, with the community playing an active role in its defense.

Cultural and Social Initiatives

The culture of a blockchain community can define its identity and resilience:

Community Events are essential for building bonds. These could range from local meetups to global virtual conferences, AMAs with the team, or even community-driven events like hackathons or cultural festivals celebrating blockchain technology. Such events not only educate and engage but also create a shared identity among members.

Decentralized Governance can be more than just a technical feature; it can be a cultural one. By giving the community real power over decisions, from technical upgrades to how community funds are used, Sui can foster a culture where everyone feels like a stakeholder. This might involve complex voting systems, community proposals, or even decentralized autonomous organizations (DAOs) that manage specific aspects of the community or network.

Cultural Projects and DAOs could be encouraged or even directly supported by Sui. By backing art, music, or social impact projects through DAOs, Sui shows that it's not just about financial transactions but also about fostering a community that values creativity, culture, and social good. This can attract a different demographic to the platform, one that values the cultural aspects of blockchain.

Tools for Interaction and Growth

Forums and Social Media presence is crucial. Sui should maintain active, moderated spaces where community members can interact, share ideas, seek help, or discuss developments. These platforms should be inclusive, encouraging constructive dialogue and providing a space for all voices.

Feedback Mechanisms are vital for making members feel heard. Whether through direct feedback tools, community surveys, or public forums for discussing platform changes, these mechanisms can help tailor Sui to the community's needs and desires.

Analytics and Transparency can build trust. By sharing network performance metrics, governance outcomes, or even how community funds are utilized, Sui can demonstrate transparency. Regular community updates or dashboards showing real-time data could become a norm, ensuring the community is well-informed about the platform's health and direction.

Challenges in Community Building

Despite these strategies, Sui faces several challenges:

Sustaining Engagement over time is not trivial. As with any community, interest can wane without continuous fresh content, updates, or events. Sui needs to keep innovating both in its technology and community engagement tactics.

Managing Diversity can lead to conflicts. With a global community, cultural, linguistic, and philosophical differences can result in disagreements over direction or use cases. Navigating this diversity requires nuanced moderation and governance systems that respect various viewpoints while maintaining platform integrity.

Growth vs. Quality is a delicate balance. As the community expands, ensuring the quality of interactions, projects, and contributions remains high is challenging. Sui must implement systems to foster quality engagement without stifling growth or innovation.

Future Directions

Looking ahead, community building on Sui could evolve in several ways:

Decentralized Social Platforms: Sui might support or host platforms where interaction, content creation, and monetization are controlled by users, not centralized entities. This could lead to a new era of social media where users have ownership over their data and contributions.

Community-Led Education: As the community matures, peer-to-peer education could become prevalent, where experienced members mentor newcomers, creating a self-sustaining learning ecosystem. This could include community-run courses, mentorship programs, or collaborative learning groups.

Global Expansion: Sui could focus on regions with lower blockchain adoption, tailoring community initiatives to local cultures and regulations. This might involve local partnerships, translated content, or events designed to educate and engage at a grassroots level.

Sui's approach to community building and engagement is about much more than technology; it's about creating a living, breathing ecosystem where every member feels valued, involved, and empowered. Through inclusivity, incentives, developer support, cultural initiatives, and interactive tools, Sui can cultivate a community that not only drives the platform's adoption but also shapes its future. The challenges are significant, but with thoughtful strategies, Sui can lead by example in demonstrating how blockchain can be a community-driven phenomenon, where every member has a role in its success and evolution.

Part 5: Tools for Governance and Community Interaction

The success of Sui's governance model and its community-building efforts hinges not only on its philosophical and architectural foundations but also on the practical tools it provides for facilitating governance activities and fostering community interaction. These tools are essential for translating Sui's vision of decentralized decision-making and community engagement into actionable, user-friendly processes. This part explores the specific tools and mechanisms Sui could implement or enhance to support governance and community interaction, emphasizing their role in ensuring transparency, accessibility, and efficiency.

Governance Tools

Sui's governance framework relies heavily on tools that enable the community to participate effectively in decision-making processes:

One of the cornerstone tools for governance is a **voting system**. Sui could develop or support a suite of voting tools integrated into its ecosystem, making it easy for token holders and community members to cast votes on proposals. These tools would need to be secure, leveraging the safety features of the Move programming language to prevent manipulation or fraud. The system could offer various voting methods, such as simple majority votes, weighted votes based on token holdings, or more sophisticated approaches like quadratic voting, where influence is distributed to encourage broader participation rather than dominance by a few large stakeholders. The voting interface would be designed to be intuitive, allowing users to see ongoing proposals, their details, and deadlines, and to cast their votes with minimal technical expertise required.

Another critical tool is the **proposal submission platform**. Governance on Sui would be more effective if community members could easily submit proposals for network upgrades, feature additions, or funding allocations. This platform could be a decentralized application (dApp) running on Sui, where users can draft proposals, attach relevant documentation, and submit them for community review. The system might include features like proposal templates to guide users through the process, ensuring clarity and completeness, and a discussion forum linked to each proposal for community feedback and debate. Smart contracts could automate the submission process, ensuring proposals meet certain criteria (e.g., minimum support or token stake) before they proceed to a vote.

Treasury Management Tools are also essential for DAOs and community governance on Sui. These tools would allow DAOs or community councils to manage funds transparently and efficiently. A treasury dashboard could display real-time data on available funds, recent allocations, and pending disbursements, all recorded immutably on the blockchain. Smart contracts could execute fund distributions based on community votes, ensuring that once a decision is made, the funds are allocated without manual intervention, reducing the risk of mismanagement or corruption. These tools could also include budgeting features, allowing the community to plan and track expenditures over time, aligning financial decisions with long-term goals.

Governance Analytics Platforms would provide insights into governance activities, helping the community understand participation rates, voting outcomes, and trends over time. These platforms could aggregate data on voter turnout, proposal success rates, and the impact of governance decisions on network metrics like transaction volume or user growth. By making this data accessible through user-friendly dashboards or APIs, Sui can empower community members to make informed decisions and hold governance processes accountable.

Community Interaction Tools

Beyond governance-specific tools, Sui can enhance community interaction through platforms and mechanisms that facilitate communication, collaboration, and engagement:

A **community forum** or social platform is vital for fostering interaction. Sui could support or develop a decentralized forum where community members can discuss ideas, share feedback, or seek support. This platform would need to be moderated to maintain a constructive environment, but it should also preserve the decentralized ethos by allowing community members to play a role in moderation through governance mechanisms. Features like threaded discussions, upvoting for visibility, and integration with governance tools (e.g., linking to proposals or voting) would make this a central hub for community activity.

Feedback and Suggestion Systems are crucial for ensuring that the community's voice is heard beyond formal governance processes. Sui could implement tools where users can submit feedback on the platform's features, report bugs, or suggest improvements. These systems should be user-friendly, accessible through various interfaces (e.g., web, mobile, or integrated into wallets), and provide clear pathways for how feedback is reviewed and acted upon. A transparent feedback loop, where suggestions are acknowledged, prioritized, and implemented (or explained if not), can build trust and encourage ongoing engagement.

Educational Resources and Tools are foundational for community interaction. Sui could provide a comprehensive set of resources, including tutorials, documentation, and interactive learning modules, to educate users and developers about the platform. These resources should cover everything from basic blockchain concepts to advanced topics like smart contract development with Move. Additionally, tools like code playgrounds or simulators could allow users to experiment with Sui's features in a safe environment, fostering a deeper understanding and encouraging active participation.

Event Platforms can enhance community interaction by facilitating virtual and in-person gatherings. Sui could support tools for hosting AMAs (Ask Me Anything) with the team, community meetups, or hackathons, all of which strengthen community bonds and encourage collaboration. These platforms should be decentralized where possible, allowing community members to propose, organize, and manage events, with integration into Sui's governance system for funding or support decisions.

Real-Time Collaboration Tools could enable community members to work together on projects, whether they are coding, designing, or planning community initiatives. These might include decentralized versions of collaboration software, where contributions are tracked on the blockchain, ensuring transparency and credit attribution. Such tools could integrate with Sui's governance and treasury systems, allowing for seamless funding or resource allocation for collaborative efforts.

Challenges in Tool Development

Developing these tools for governance and community interaction presents several challenges:

- **Usability vs. Complexity:** Ensuring that governance and interaction tools remain user-friendly while handling the complexity of blockchain operations is a delicate balance. Sui must prioritize intuitive design to avoid alienating less technical users.
- **Security:** All tools must be secure against attacks or manipulation, particularly those involved in governance, where the stakes are high. This requires rigorous testing, auditing,

and leveraging Move's safety features to protect against vulnerabilities.
- **Scalability:** As the community grows, these tools must scale to handle increased usage without degrading performance or increasing costs. Sui's inherent scalability can help, but tool design must account for this growth.
- **Accessibility:** Tools should be accessible across different devices and platforms, ensuring that all community members, regardless of their technological resources, can participate.
- **Community Adoption:** Even the best tools are useless without adoption. Sui must educate and incentivize the community to use these tools, potentially through tutorials, rewards, or integration into everyday interactions with the platform.

Future Directions

Looking forward, the tools for governance and community interaction on Sui could evolve in several innovative ways:

- **AI-Assisted Governance:** AI could be integrated into governance tools to analyze proposals, predict outcomes, or suggest optimizations, making decision-making more data-driven and efficient.
- **Decentralized Social Networks:** Sui might support the development of decentralized social platforms where community interactions, governance discussions, and content creation

are managed directly by users, with governance tools embedded into these platforms.

- **Cross-Chain Governance Tools:** As interoperability grows, Sui could develop tools that facilitate governance across multiple blockchains, allowing for collaborative decision-making in a multi-chain ecosystem.
- **Gamification of Governance:** To increase engagement, governance tools could incorporate gamification elements, such as badges, leaderboards, or challenges, making participation more engaging and rewarding.
- **Integration with Digital Identity:** Governance tools could link with decentralized identity solutions, enhancing security and ensuring that only verified members participate in decision-making processes.

Conclusion

The tools Sui provides for governance and community interaction are not just technical utilities but are instrumental in realizing its vision of a decentralized, community-driven ecosystem. By offering secure, scalable, and accessible tools, Sui can empower its community to govern effectively and engage meaningfully with the platform. These tools bridge the gap between technological innovation and human participation, ensuring that governance is not an abstract process but a lived experience for every community member. As Sui continues to evolve, the development and refinement of these tools will be crucial in maintaining a thriving community that drives the platform's success and shapes its future.

Part 6: Case Studies of Governance on Sui

To understand how Sui's governance model might function in practice, it's insightful to explore hypothetical scenarios or real-world case studies where Sui's features could lead to innovative governance outcomes. These examples illustrate how Sui's unique architecture, consensus mechanisms, and community tools can be leveraged to solve real-world problems or enhance community participation in blockchain ecosystems.

Case Study 1: Community-Led Network Upgrades

Imagine a scenario where the Sui community is faced with the decision to upgrade the network to introduce new features or enhance security.

- **Proposal and Discussion:** A developer or a group of community members drafts a proposal for a network upgrade, leveraging Sui's proposal submission platform. This proposal is then shared on community forums where discussions ensue. The proposal might include technical details, expected benefits, potential impacts, and a timeline for implementation.
- **Voting on the Upgrade:** Once the proposal has garnered enough support or meets predefined criteria (like a minimum number of signatures or token backing), it moves to the

voting phase. Sui's voting system, designed for both speed and security, allows community members to cast their votes efficiently. The voting might be weighted by token stake, ensuring those with a significant investment have a say proportional to their commitment but also considering mechanisms to prevent dominance by a few.

- **Execution:** After achieving consensus, the upgrade is scheduled. Here, Sui's architecture shines, allowing for the upgrade to be executed quickly due to its parallel processing capabilities, ensuring minimal disruption to the network. The upgrade process is transparent, with all changes and outcomes recorded on the blockchain for auditability.
- **Impact:** This case study would demonstrate how Sui can facilitate rapid, secure, and community-driven upgrades, keeping the blockchain agile and responsive to both technological advancements and community needs.

Case Study 2: DAO for Community Projects

A DAO is formed on Sui to fund and manage community-driven projects, from local initiatives to global blockchain innovations:

- **DAO Formation:** Community members come together to form a DAO using Sui's smart contract capabilities. The DAO's rules, including how proposals are made, voting thresholds, and fund allocation, are encoded in

Move, ensuring they are secure and executable as intended.

- **Project Proposals:** Individuals or groups can submit project ideas through the DAO's platform. Proposals include project descriptions, budgets, expected outcomes, and the impact on the community or blockchain ecosystem.
- **Community Voting:** Members of the DAO vote on which projects to fund. Sui's governance tools allow for transparent, secure voting where the community can see real-time results and the rationale behind decisions. Projects might be funded based on a combination of merit, community support, and alignment with the DAO's mission.
- **Execution and Oversight:** Once a project is approved, funds are automatically distributed according to the smart contract logic. The DAO might also implement mechanisms for oversight, where project progress is reported back to the community, potentially leading to further funding or adjustments based on performance.
- **Impact:** This DAO could democratize funding in the blockchain space, allowing grassroots projects to gain support and visibility, fostering innovation, and potentially impacting real-world communities through blockchain technology.

Case Study 3: Governance of a Decentralized Exchange (DEX)

A DEX on Sui aims to implement community governance for its operations:

- **Feature Development:** The community might vote on new features or changes to existing ones, like fee structures, liquidity incentives, or integration with other blockchains. This could involve developers submitting proposals for new trading pairs or algorithms.
- **Security Measures:** After a security incident or in anticipation of potential threats, the community could decide on implementing new security protocols or audits, ensuring the DEX remains one of the safest places for trading.
- **Economic Policies:** Decisions on tokenomics, such as reducing or increasing the supply of native tokens used for governance or transaction fees, could be made by the community to balance the economic health of the DEX.
- **Dispute Resolution:** The governance system could include mechanisms for resolving disputes, whether they're between users, liquidity providers, or about the platform's direction, using community arbitration or voting to decide outcomes.
- **Impact:** This case study would showcase how a DEX could evolve continuously based on community feedback and decisions, potentially leading to a more user-centric, adaptable, and secure platform.

Case Study 4: Cultural and Artistic Governance

Sui supports a DAO focused on cultural and artistic projects, allowing creators to govern their collective work:

- **Artistic Proposals:** Artists submit proposals for exhibitions, collaborations, or funding for new works. The community votes on which projects to support based on artistic merit, cultural impact, or community engagement.
- **Royalty Management:** Smart contracts on Sui could automate the distribution of royalties to artists for secondary sales or performances, with governance decisions possibly affecting royalty percentages or distribution methods.
- **Cultural Festivals:** The DAO could organize events or festivals, with the community deciding on themes, locations, or digital versus physical formats, leveraging Sui's speed for ticket sales or NFT creation for event access.
- **Impact:** This scenario could show how blockchain can empower artists and cultural initiatives, creating a transparent and community-driven ecosystem where creators have control over their work's trajectory and monetization.

Challenges and Learnings

- **Voter Apathy:** Even with the best tools, getting consistent participation in governance can be challenging. Incentives or mandatory participation for certain actions (like staking) might be necessary.

- **Complexity of Decisions:** Some proposals might require technical or specialized knowledge to evaluate, necessitating educational campaigns or expert panels within the community to guide decision-making.
- **Ensuring Fairness:** Governance must be designed to prevent manipulation by large token holders or coordinated groups, potentially through complex voting mechanisms or checks and balances.
- **Adaptability:** Governance structures might need to evolve as the platform grows or as new challenges arise, requiring a meta-governance process for updating governance itself.

These case studies highlight the practical applications of Sui's governance model, from technical network management to cultural projects, showing how community engagement can lead to innovation, security, and inclusivity. By enabling community-driven governance, Sui not only empowers its users but also demonstrates how blockchain can be a tool for collective decision-making, aligning technology with human-centric values. As these examples suggest, the future of blockchain governance on Sui could be one where the community is not just a part of the ecosystem but its driving force, shaping a platform that truly serves its users.

Part 7: Challenges in Blockchain Governance

While the vision for blockchain governance, particularly on platforms like Sui, is aspirational, real-world implementation faces numerous challenges. These challenges, if not addressed, could undermine the efficacy, security, and community trust in governance processes. This part explores the complexities and potential pitfalls of decentralized governance, offering insights into how Sui might navigate these issues.

Voter Apathy and Low Participation

One of the most significant challenges in any democratic system, including blockchain governance, is voter turnout. Even with incentives or mandatory participation for certain activities like staking, many community members might remain passive:

- **Incentivization:** Sui could explore innovative ways to motivate participation, like rewarding governance activity with tokens, exclusive access, or recognition within the community. However, the balance must be struck so as not to create a system where governance becomes a game of token accumulation rather than genuine community involvement.
- **Education:** Continuous educational efforts are crucial to demystify governance processes, explaining why each vote matters and how decisions impact the network. Workshops, tutorials, and accessible documentation can help bridge the knowledge gap.

Centralization Risks

Decentralized governance aims to distribute power, but there's always a risk that power might consolidate among a few:

- **Token Distribution:** If token distribution is uneven, those with more tokens might disproportionately influence decisions. Sui could implement mechanisms like quadratic voting or capped voting power to mitigate this.
- **Validator Influence:** In Sui's DPoS system, validators play a significant role. Ensuring that validators are diverse and that their power doesn't overshadow community votes is vital. This might involve rotating validators or ensuring a broad base of validator participation.
- **Governance Token Allocation:** Sui might consider how governance tokens are distributed or earned, perhaps through activities that benefit the network, to prevent a scenario where only early adopters or large investors hold sway.

Decision-Making Paralysis

With a large and diverse community, reaching a consensus can be time-consuming, leading to decision-making paralysis:

- **Tiered Governance:** Implementing a multi-tiered governance system where small, technical decisions can be made quickly by a subset of the community, while broader, more impactful decisions require wider consensus, could streamline processes.

- **Time-Limited Voting:** Setting deadlines for votes on less critical issues can prevent indefinite debate, though this must be balanced against the need for thorough discussion on significant changes.
- **Decision Thresholds:** Some decisions might need only a simple majority, while others require supermajorities to pass, depending on their impact, helping to move forward without constant gridlock.

Security and Manipulation

Governance systems are prime targets for attacks or manipulation, whether through social engineering, token buying, or exploiting smart contract vulnerabilities:

- **Secure Smart Contracts:** Sui's use of Move should be leveraged to ensure that governance smart contracts are as secure as possible. Regular audits, both automated and by security experts, are essential.
- **Sybil Attacks:** Preventing one entity from controlling multiple votes through fake identities or accounts can be addressed with identity verification or reputation systems where long-term, positive engagement is rewarded.
- **Manipulation via Social Channels:** Governance discussions often occur in forums or social media. Sui must ensure that these

spaces are moderated to prevent misinformation or manipulation, possibly through community policing or decentralized moderation.

Regulatory Compliance and Legal Recognition

As blockchain projects grow, they must navigate an increasingly complex legal landscape:

- **Compliance by Design:** Governance mechanisms might need to include features that make compliance with various jurisdictions' regulations easier, like privacy controls or mechanisms for KYC/AML where necessary.
- **Legal Frameworks for DAOs:** Sui could advocate for or develop frameworks that provide legal recognition for DAOs, helping to define how they interact with traditional legal systems.

Scalability of Governance

As the network grows, so does the complexity of managing governance:

- **Scalable Governance Tools:** The tools and infrastructure for governance must scale alongside the network, handling increased participation without performance degradation.
- **Decentralized Governance Nodes:** To manage load, governance activities might be

distributed across nodes dedicated to processing governance transactions or data.

Balancing Speed with Deliberation

While Sui's architecture allows for speed, governance requires careful deliberation:

- **Emergency Measures:** For critical situations, there might be provisions for expedited governance, but these should be designed with checks to prevent misuse.
- **Deliberative Forums:** Encouraging deep, structured discussions on significant proposals before voting can ensure decisions are well-considered.

Future Adaptability

Governance must evolve with the platform and its community:

- **Governance of Governance:** Sui might need a meta-governance layer where the community can vote on how governance itself should evolve, ensuring the system remains relevant and effective.
- **Feedback Loops:** Regular reviews of governance decisions and their outcomes can inform how processes should be adjusted, learning from past governance actions.

The challenges in blockchain governance on Sui are not insurmountable but require thoughtful design, continuous innovation, and an engaged community. By addressing these issues head-on, Sui can pioneer governance models that are both truly decentralized and pragmatically effective. The key to overcoming these challenges lies in balancing the ideals of decentralization with the practicalities of decision-making, security, and community engagement. As Sui navigates this landscape, it has the potential to set a benchmark for how blockchain governance should operate, ensuring it remains a tool for empowerment rather than a point of contention or failure.

Part 8: Security and Trust in Governance

Ensuring security and trust in governance processes is paramount for the success and integrity of any blockchain platform, including Sui. Governance mechanisms must be robust enough to resist attacks, maintain transparency, and safeguard the community's trust in the system's fairness and reliability. This part delves into how Sui can secure its governance processes, mitigate risks, and foster trust among its users and developers.

Security Measures for Governance

- **Smart Contract Security:** The governance of Sui relies heavily on smart contracts, particularly those written in Move. These contracts must be:

    - **Audited Rigorously:** Before deployment, smart contracts should

undergo thorough security audits. This includes both automated tools to catch common vulnerabilities and manual reviews by security experts familiar with Move's unique features.
- **Designed for Safety:** Move's safety features should be utilized to their fullest, preventing common issues like reentrancy attacks or unintended state changes, which could manipulate voting or fund distribution.
- **Consensus and Validation:** Sui's DPoS consensus mechanism plays a crucial role in governance:

  - **Validator Integrity:** Ensuring validators act in the network's best interest involves mechanisms like slashing for misconduct, reputation systems, or even community-governed validator elections to maintain a diverse and honest validator set.
  - **Finality and Immutability:** Transactions, including those related to governance, should achieve finality quickly to prevent double-spending or vote manipulation. Sui's speed in consensus can be a significant security advantage here.
- **Voting Security:** To prevent manipulation in voting:

  - **One-Person-One-Vote:** Sui could implement systems where voting power isn't solely based on token ownership, perhaps through identity verification or reputation-based voting rights.

- ○ **Preventing Sybil Attacks:** Measures like proof-of-stake or requiring a history of network activity could be used to ensure that votes are cast by legitimate, invested community members rather than through multiple false identities.
- **Data Integrity:** All governance actions should be:

- ○ **Transparently Recorded:** On the blockchain, allowing for public verification of votes, proposals, and outcomes, which builds trust through transparency.
- ○ **Protected from Tampering:** With cryptographic methods ensuring that once data is on the blockchain, it cannot be altered, providing an immutable record of governance activities.

Building Trust

- **Transparency:** Trust is built on transparency:

- ○ **Open Governance Processes:** All aspects of governance, from proposal submissions to voting results, should be openly accessible. Sui could offer dashboards or explorer interfaces

where anyone can track governance
activities.
- ○ **Clear Documentation:** Every
governance action should be
documented in a way that's
understandable to the community,
explaining the rationale behind
decisions and their expected impact.
- **Community Involvement:** Trust is also about
feeling part of the process:

  - ○ **Engagement Mechanisms:** Regular
community calls, AMAs, or governance
workshops can involve the community,
explain complex decisions, and gather
feedback.
  - ○ **Rewarding Participation:** Not just with
tokens but with recognition or influence
within the community, like roles in
governance councils or community-led
projects.
- **Accountability:** When mistakes or issues
occur:

  - ○ **Transparent Resolution:** Any
governance-related issues should be
openly discussed, with clear steps
taken to rectify them, perhaps even
involving the community in deciding on
solutions.
  - ○ **Learning from Errors:** Post-mortems
or reviews of governance decisions can
lead to improvements in the
governance process, showing the

community that their platform learns and adapts.

Mitigating Governance Risks

- **Centralization of Power:** To prevent power concentration:

  - **Checks and Balances:** Multiple layers of governance or veto powers could be introduced to balance the influence of any single entity or group.
  - **Decentralized Governance Tools:** Tools should be distributed across the network, avoiding single points of failure or control.
- **Manipulation and Fraud:** Beyond technical security:

  - **Social Engineering Defenses:** Educating the community about common manipulation tactics, like phishing or misinformation campaigns, is crucial.
  - **Whistleblower Systems:** Mechanisms for reporting suspicious activities anonymously can help preemptively address potential fraud.
- **Economic Incentives:** Ensuring that the economic model of governance does not inadvertently encourage bad behavior:

  - **Alignment with Network Health:** Incentives should be designed so that participants benefit more from the network's overall success rather than short-term gains through manipulation.

Future Security Enhancements

- **Advanced Cryptography:** Exploring new cryptographic techniques or integrating privacy-preserving technologies like zero-knowledge proofs could enhance the security of sensitive governance processes.
- **AI and Machine Learning:** These could be used for anomaly detection in voting patterns or to predict and mitigate potential security threats to the governance system.
- **Interoperability Security:** As Sui aims for cross-chain interactions, ensuring that governance across chains remains secure will be a challenge, potentially requiring new standards or protocols for cross-chain governance verification.

Security and trust in governance are not static achievements but ongoing processes. For Sui, maintaining these principles involves not only leveraging its technological advantages but also fostering a culture of transparency, accountability, and community involvement. By continuously enhancing its security measures and building trust through open, inclusive governance, Sui can ensure that its community feels confident in the system's integrity. This approach will be key to sustaining long-term engagement, protecting the network, and maintaining the decentralized ethos at the heart of blockchain technology.

Part 9: Future of Governance with Sui

The future of governance in blockchain, particularly with platforms like Sui, is poised to be both transformative and challenging. As blockchain technology matures, governance models must evolve to match the complexities of managing increasingly decentralized networks, diverse communities, and global regulatory landscapes. This part speculates on how governance might evolve with Sui, potentially influencing broader blockchain governance trends or practices.

Sui's governance could become more adaptive, with protocols that evolve without needing hard forks. This might involve a modular approach where different aspects of the network, like tokenomics, security, or community projects, can have tailored governance structures. This allows for more targeted and agile decision-making. Additionally, leveraging Sui's architecture, governance smart contracts could automatically update based on community consensus or predefined conditions, reducing the need for manual interventions and making governance processes more dynamic.

The integration of AI into governance could enhance decision-making by analyzing community sentiment, proposal impacts, or past governance outcomes to suggest optimal decisions or highlight potential issues. AI might also predict when governance interventions might be necessary, like adjusting economic policies based on network usage patterns, making the governance process more proactive and data-driven.

As blockchain ecosystems become more interconnected, cross-chain governance models could emerge. This might see the rise of DAOs that operate across multiple blockchains, leveraging Sui's interoperability to manage assets or projects that span different networks. Governance tokens could have utility or influence across various chains, encouraging broader participation in governance decisions. Sui could lead in developing or contributing to standards for cross-chain governance, ensuring interoperability does not compromise governance integrity, and facilitating governance bridges where decisions on one chain can affect or be reflected in others, creating a more cohesive blockchain governance ecosystem.

Community empowerment might see enhanced participation through direct democracy tools, where every member can propose, debate, and vote on decisions in real-time, leveraging Sui's speed for immediate feedback. More sophisticated, decentralized voting systems could become accessible, potentially using mobile or VR interfaces to engage a broader audience in governance. Moving towards fully autonomous DAOs, governance would not just involve voting but also the automated, transparent execution of community decisions without human intervention. Reputation-based systems could be introduced where contributions to the community or network health directly influence one's governance rights or voting power.

In terms of compliance, as blockchain intersects with traditional finance and regulation, Sui might develop governance models that inherently support compliance with diverse global regulations. This could be achieved through smart contracts that adapt to legal changes. Privacy in governance processes would be crucial, ensuring that voting or data handling respects privacy laws, possibly through privacy-preserving technologies. Sui could also play a role in advocating for blockchain governance laws, participating in shaping how decentralized systems are recognized and regulated worldwide, ensuring they can thrive legally.

Technological innovations might include making governance quantum-resistant by upgrading cryptographic methods to withstand future quantum computing threats. Similar to how layer 2 solutions address scalability for transactions, Sui might implement layer 2 governance solutions for specific areas, like community project funding or rapid decision-making on less critical issues.

Culturally, there's a potential shift from a centralized to a decentralized mindset. This involves educating users about the value of decentralized decision-making not just as a technical feature but as a cultural norm, fostering a new generation of blockchain citizens. Governance models that celebrate and leverage cultural diversity could lead to more innovative and globally relevant decisions.

However, this future comes with challenges. Maintaining decentralization as governance becomes more complex will be crucial to avoid sliding back into centralization. The ethical use of AI in governance must be carefully managed to avoid bias or manipulation, ensuring it enhances rather than replaces human decision-making. Balancing user sovereignty with the need for efficient network operation will be an ongoing governance debate.

The future of governance on Sui is not just about managing a blockchain but about pioneering how communities can govern themselves in a digital, decentralized age. By embracing technological advancements, fostering interoperability, enhancing community participation, and navigating the regulatory landscape, Sui has the potential to redefine governance not only for itself but for the broader blockchain ecosystem. This evolution will require creativity, ethical consideration, and a commitment to the decentralized ethos at the heart of blockchain technology. As Sui grows, its governance model could become a case study in how technology can empower communities to make decisions that are fair, secure, and reflective of a global, diverse user base.

Part 10: Community-Driven Innovation

Sui's approach to governance and community building transcends merely managing a blockchain platform; it's about catalyzing innovation through the collective intelligence and creativity of its community. This part explores how the community can drive technological, economic, or social innovations, emphasizing the role of community participation in shaping the blockchain's future.

Sui can foster an environment for innovation by promoting an open-source culture where developers worldwide contribute to the platform's codebase, tools, or applications. By maintaining open repositories, Sui invites contributions from across the globe, leading to diverse solutions to common problems. Regularly hosting or sponsoring hackathons and challenges where participants can showcase new ideas or solve specific challenges can also spark innovation.

Allocating funds through governance for community-led projects can drive innovation as well. The community can vote on which projects receive funding, potentially leading to breakthrough applications or improvements to the Sui ecosystem. These grants could also support research into new blockchain technologies, consensus mechanisms, or security protocols that directly benefit Sui.

Sui might support or facilitate the creation of Decentralized Autonomous Organizations (DAOs) specifically for research and development. These DAOs could bring together researchers, developers, and enthusiasts to collaborate on cutting-edge projects with clear governance over direction, funding, and intellectual property management. Such DAOs could act as incubators for new blockchain concepts, providing resources, mentorship, and a framework for ideas to mature into viable projects.

The community's input can directly influence the platform's evolution through user-driven features and applications. Tools that allow users to suggest features or improvements guide the development roadmap, ensuring it aligns with community needs. Engaging the community in beta testing new features or applications can lead to more robust and user-friendly products, as real-world feedback is incorporated early in the development cycle.

In terms of economic innovations, the community could experiment with new economic models. This might involve using governance to adjust token supply, staking rewards, or other economic levers based on community consensus and network health. New ways to reward participation could be created, perhaps through novel staking mechanisms or rewards for contributing to network security or development.

Sui could empower communities to create DAOs focused on cultural projects, leading to social and cultural innovations. These DAOs might fund or manage projects that blend blockchain with arts, creating new forms of digital art, music NFTs, or interactive literature. Supporting projects that aim for social good, like decentralized charities or initiatives for digital education, can expand Sui's influence beyond technology.

Education is key to fostering innovation, and Sui can promote community education programs. Community members could lead or participate in educational efforts, sharing knowledge about blockchain, programming, or specific uses of Sui. Establishing mentorship programs where experienced members guide newcomers can accelerate learning and innovation within the community.

However, there are challenges and considerations in this process. Balancing innovation with stability is crucial; changes must not undermine the network's stability or user trust. Governance must ensure that innovative ideas are vetted for their impact on the network. Managing intellectual property in an open-source environment while fostering innovation can be complex, necessitating clear governance on IP within community projects. As more ideas are implemented, ensuring that the platform can scale to accommodate new features or applications without performance degradation is vital.

Looking to the future, AI could assist in identifying potential innovations from community feedback or data patterns, helping to prioritize development efforts. Sui might facilitate collaborations with other blockchain communities, sharing resources, knowledge, or even co-developing projects that could benefit the broader blockchain ecosystem. As the community grows, governance over innovation itself might be decentralized further, with sub-DAOs or specialized governance bodies focused on different innovation areas.

In conclusion, community-driven innovation on Sui represents a powerful synergy where technology meets human creativity and collaboration. By leveraging its governance model, Sui can turn its community into a living laboratory for blockchain innovation, where ideas from around the world are tested, refined, and brought to life. This approach not only accelerates technological development but also ensures that the platform evolves in ways that are meaningful and beneficial to its users. As Sui continues to grow, its commitment to community-led innovation could set a new standard for how blockchain platforms can and should evolve, emphasizing that the future of technology is not just in the code but in the community that nurtures it.

Final Word

As we conclude this journey through the landscapes of the Sui blockchain, it's fitting to reflect not only on the technological marvels and the potential for societal transformation but also on the human elements that make this exploration so compelling. This book has been an odyssey through the intricacies of blockchain technology, governance, culture, and the future of digital interaction, all viewed through the lens of Sui. Here, in this final word, let's gather our thoughts, looking back at where we've been and forward to where we might go, with Sui as our guide.

A Journey Through Sui:

From the inception of Sui, we've witnessed a vision materialize that dared to challenge the status quo of blockchain limitations. We've explored its architectural innovations, the philosophy behind its creation, and the practical implications of its design for speed, security, and scalability. Each chapter has peeled back a layer, revealing not just what Sui can do, but what it means for those who engage with it.

The Human Element:

At the core of this exploration has been the human element – the vibrant community that breathes life into Sui. This community isn't just a checkpoint in our narrative; it's the heart of the story. We've seen how governance in Sui isn't just about making decisions but creating a culture where every voice can influence the platform's future. We've delved into how education and empowerment within the community turn complex technology into accessible tools for change.

The discussions on diversity and inclusion have shown us that Sui aims to be more than a technology; it aspires to be a catalyst for social progress, where the blockchain is a tool for democratizing access to opportunity, knowledge, and expression. The community's role in shaping Sui's future is not just a feature; it's the defining characteristic of this blockchain, making it a living, evolving entity.

Technological Promises and Realizations:

We've examined the technological promises of Sui, from its object-centric model to parallel execution and instant finality. These aren't just technical feats; they're commitments to creating a blockchain that can adapt to real-world demands. Sui's approach to privacy, security, and scalability has been dissected, revealing a platform designed not just for today's needs but prepared for tomorrow's challenges.

The case studies have grounded these promises in reality, showing how Sui's technology can transform industries, from gaming to finance, supply chain to digital identity. Each application has not only highlighted Sui's capabilities but also the potential for blockchain to be a force for innovation in our daily lives.

Looking to the Horizon:

As we look to the horizon, the future of Sui seems as vast as the digital realm itself. The roadmap laid out before us speaks of a blockchain that doesn't just evolve but revolutionizes. We've imagined a world where Sui facilitates seamless interoperability, where its community drives not just the platform but cultural and economic movements.

The vision for Sui extends into realms where digital identity is reclaimed by individuals, where financial systems are more equitable, and where governance is a collective act, not a dictate from the few. This vision is not without its trials; the challenges of scalability, security, and maintaining the ethos of decentralization as the ecosystem grows are formidable. Yet, they are also opportunities for Sui to lead by example, to show the world how blockchain can be a tool for good, even in the face of adversity.

The Role of Community:

The community of Sui, as we've seen, is its greatest strength. It's a testament to the idea that technology thrives not in isolation but through human interaction, creativity, and collaboration. The future of Sui's community is one where education, inclusivity, and participation are not just encouraged but are integral to how the platform operates and grows. This community has the potential to influence not just the direction of Sui but the very fabric of digital culture.

A Call to Action:

This book is more than a recounting of facts or a prediction of futures; it's a call to action. For developers, it's an invitation to build on a platform that promises to empower your creations with speed and security. For users, it's an opportunity to engage with a blockchain that values your privacy and your voice. For thinkers, visionaries, and activists, it's a challenge to imagine how this technology can be harnessed for broader societal benefits, from art to activism.

The Legacy of Sui:

What legacy will Sui leave? Perhaps it's too early to say, but we can speculate on its impact. Sui might be remembered as the blockchain that made the technology accessible, where the complexity of code was matched by the simplicity of participation. It could be seen as the platform that democratized digital ownership, where art, finance, and identity were truly owned by the individual. Or perhaps, Sui's legacy will be in how it reshaped our understanding of community, governance, and what it means to build together in a digital age.

The End is Just the Beginning:

As we close this book, we recognize that this ending is merely the beginning of another chapter in the story of Sui. The technology will evolve, the community will grow, and the applications will expand. But the essence of what we've explored here – the blend of technology with human spirit, the fusion of innovation with inclusivity – will continue to define Sui's journey.

This narrative of Sui is an ongoing one, where each participant, whether through code, vote, or creation, adds to the tapestry of what's possible. We've seen how Sui can be a tool, a platform, a community, and a vision. Now, it's up to those who engage with Sui to write the next chapters, to push boundaries, to solve problems, and to dream new realities.

In Conclusion:

In this final word, we've not only summarized a journey but have also underscored the potential for Sui to be a beacon in the blockchain world. It's a reminder that technology, at its best, serves humanity by amplifying our capabilities, broadening our horizons, and connecting us in ways we've yet to fully comprehend. Sui's story is one of potential, of community, and of the endless possibilities when technology is guided by a collective vision of progress and empowerment.

As we step away from these pages, let's carry forward the lessons learned, the inspiration drawn, and the curiosity sparked by Sui. Let this book be not just a record of what has been but a springboard for what could be. Here's to the future of Sui, to the community that shapes it, and to the world we might build together in this digital era. The final word, then, is not one of closure but of invitation – to join, to build, to innovate, and to dream with Sui.

Acknowledgements

Behind every book lies a team of unsung heroes, and this exploration of the Sui blockchain is no exception. The process of indexing the wealth of information within these pages has been a monumental task, requiring dedication, expertise, and an eye for detail. It is with great appreciation that I acknowledge the efforts of those who have worked tirelessly to help me on this aspect of the book.

First and foremost, I want to thank the X community members I have been in touch with, whose meticulous attention to detail has ensured that every concept, term, and name is accurately captured. Their ability to navigate through the complex landscape of blockchain technology has made the index not just a navigational aid but a cornerstone of this book's utility.

I extend my gratitude to the Telegram groups and members there who have answered all of the technical questions I have had. Their deep understanding of blockchain architecture, consensus mechanisms, and smart contract functionalities has been instrumental in creating a technically sound index that serves both novices and experts alike.

Appreciation is also due to the individual who tackled the economic and tokenomics sections. Their analytical approach has distilled complex economic theories into clear, searchable entries, enhancing the book's value as a resource for understanding Sui's economic model.

I also wish to recognize the efforts of those who worked on cross-referencing and ensuring the book's relevance over time. Hopefully this book will be a dynamic tool that will grow with the Sui ecosystem.

Lastly, my appreciation extends to the entire airdrop.ag team, whose collective effort has turned this book into a comprehensive reference. Their teamwork has been crucial in weaving together the various threads of information into a coherent, user-friendly guide.

To all who have contributed to the indexing of this book, your work has not only enhanced its navigability but has also reflected the collaborative and inclusive spirit of the Sui community. Your dedication has made this book more than just a narrative; it has become a living document, ready to educate and inspire. Thank you for your hard work, your expertise, and for making this book a true resource for all interested in the world of Sui.

Biography

Kenneth Schick is a unique blend of tech enthusiast and creative writer, famous for his cyberpunk novels set in neon-lit, futuristic worlds. Born in a city that echoes the themes of his stories, much of Schick's early life is shrouded in mystery. However, it's known that he was deeply involved in audio engineering, athletics, and music production from a young age, alongside his fascination with cutting-edge technology.

His career took off with DJing at underground raves, house parties, and the biggest nightclubs in San Diego, which eventually turned into multiple DJ residencies across the world in Bali, Indonesia, where he played at many futuristic-themed events. He has production credit for producing over 300 songs. His writing career took off more recently with a cyber-punk novel series which brilliantly mixed dystopian elements and blockchain concepts. This debut highlighted his love for both narrative storytelling and technology.

Before becoming an author, Schick was a respected blockchain visionary, working on projects that pushed the boundaries of music NFT's on the Solana blockchain and software development. His background gives his books a realistic touch, making the tech in his stories feel believable and blurring the lines between humans and machines in his vivid cyberpunk landscapes.

www.ingramcontent.com/pod-product-compliance
Lightning Source LLC
La Vergne TN
LVHW022331060326
832902LV00022B/3988